EMPOWERMENT FOR SUSTAINABLE TOURISM DEVELOPMENT

TOURISM SOCIAL SCIENCE SERIES

Series Editor: Jafar Jafari

Department of Hospitality and Tourism, University of Wisconsin-Stout, Menomonie WI 54751, USA.

E-mail: jafari@uwstout.edu

Associate Editor (this volume): David H. Harrison

London Metropolitan University, UK

The books in this Tourism Social Science Series (TSSSeries) are intended to systematically and cumulatively contribute to the formation, embodiment, and advancement of knowledge in the field of tourism.

The TSSSeries' multidisciplinary framework and treatment of tourism includes application of theoretical, methodological, and substantive contributions from such fields as anthropology, business administration, ecology, economics, geography, history, hospitality, leisure, planning, political science, psychology, recreation, religion, sociology, transportation, etc., but it significantly favors state-of-the-art presentations, works featuring new directions, and especially the cross-fertilization of perspectives beyond each of these singular fields. While the development and production of this book series is fashioned after the successful model of *Annals of Tourism Research*, the TSSSeries further aspires to assure each theme a comprehensiveness possible only in book-length academic treatment. Each volume in the series is intended to deal with a particular aspect of this increasingly important subject, thus to play a definitive role in the enlarging and strengthening of the foundation of knowledge in the field of tourism, and consequently to expand its frontiers into the new research and scholarship horizons ahead.

Published and forthcoming TSSSeries titles include:

JÓZSEF BÖRÖCZ (Rutgers University, USA)
Leisure Migration: A Sociological Study on Tourism

MICHAEL CLANCY (University of Hartford, USA)
Exporting Paradise: Tourism and Development in Mexico

ERIK COHEN (The Hebrew University of Jerusalem, Israel)
Contemporary Tourism: Diversity and Change Collected Articles

DENNISON NASH (University of Connecticut, USA)
Anthropology of Tourism

DENNISON NASH (University of Connecticut, USA)
Beginnings of an Anthropology of Tourism: A Study of Intellectual History

PHILIP L. PEARCE, GIANNA MOSCARDO & GLENN F. ROSS
(James Cook University of North Queensland, Australia)
Tourism Community Relationships

BORIS VUKONIĆ (University of Zagreb, Croatia)
Tourism and Religion

NING WANG (Zhongshan University, China)
Tourism and Modernity: A Sociological Analysis

Related Elsevier journals

Annals of Tourism Research
Cornell Hotel and Restaurant Administration Quarterly
International Journal of Hospitality Management
International Journal of Intercultural Relations
Tourism Management
World Development

EMPOWERMENT FOR SUSTAINABLE TOURISM DEVELOPMENT

TREVOR H.B. SOFIELD

University of Tasmania, Australia

COLEG SIR GAR	
Cypher	23.02.04
338.4791	£85.00

2003

Pergamon
An imprint of Elsevier Science

Amsterdam – Boston – London – New York – Oxford – Paris
San Diego – San Francisco – Singapore – Sydney – Tokyo

ELSEVIER SCIENCE Ltd
The Boulevard, Langford Lane
Kidlington, Oxford OX5 1GB, UK

First edition 2003

Library of Congress Cataloging in Publication Data
A catalog record from the Library of Congress has been applied for.

British Library Cataloguing in Publication Data
A catalogue record from the British Library has been applied for.

ISBN 0-08-043946-2

∞ The paper used in this publication meets the requirements of ANSI/NISO Z39.48-1992 (Permanence of Paper).
Printed in The Netherlands.

Contents

Illustrations

Figures

Tables

Acknowledgments

In the course of writing a book such as this, the many journeys which have been undertaken to bring it to fruition have necessarily resulted in assistance from very many people along the way. All must be thanked, though it is impossible to mention each and every one of them by name.

The journey of scholastic endeavor, delving into conceptual and theoretical constructs, has a strong foundation in the author's association with David King, an old South Pacific hand who is now at James Cook University in Queensland, who guided this work through a crucial period in its formative stages. Dick Butler, Valene Smith, David Harrison, and Margaret Byrne Swain commented most constructively on the manuscript. A special debt is also owed to Alastair Birtles, Philip Pearce, and other former colleagues in the Tourism Department at James Cook University; with former colleagues from the Hong Kong Polytechnic University, especially John Ap; and with the many scholars of tourism who "lent their ears" at a wide range of international conferences from Strathclyde in the United Kingdom to Bali in Indonesia, from Montreal in Canada to Auckland in New Zealand, from Suva in Fiji to Buenos Aires in Argentina. Their comments, criticisms, and suggestions were invariably stimulating and contributed more to the final outcome than perhaps they realize. Former colleagues from the South Pacific Forum Secretariat in Suva, who included nationals from ten Island countries, enriched understanding of their worlds immeasurably.

The journeys of discovery to Fiji, Solomon Islands, and Vanuatu would have been impossible without the advice, assistance, and support from many people in those countries. Special thanks are due to Adrian Sofield (brother) and his wife Carol, resident in Fiji, and to a friend of more than 20 years, Brendan O'Shea, in Solomon Islands, for providing a "home away from home" on more than one occasion. To the 30 South Pacific Islands students who enrolled in tourism studies at James Cook University, who volunteered so many insights about their islands, their problems, their aspirations and the issues of tourism development, and who opened their homes and their families in extended fieldtrips throughout the region: "vinaka vakalevu", "malei-lei", "tangkyiu tumas", thank you. Often the author was the pupil and they were the teachers.

There are three other people without whom this book would not have been written. They are Myalee, Merryn, and Nicholas (two daughters and one son), who put up with the author's peripatetic schedule over the years and oft-times accompanied him around the Pacific. They were constant sources of support and encouragement.

To Sarah (the author's wife) are reserved the greatest thanks. A fellow tourism academic, she was able to keep the intellectual fires burning, to raise spirits when they were flagging, to turn a mundane explanation into a more stimulating analysis through her acute questioning, and to counsel patience when the author's had evaporated. Her enthusiasm for this book and her thorough proof reading of the many drafts steered this canoe through the sometimes less than tranquil waters of the Ocean of Writing which was not always "pacific". One can only say, simply but profoundly, Thank you.

Chapter 1

Introduction

An examination of issues of tourism development has the potential to take the explorer down many different roads but in this instance a lesser traveled path points the compass towards the concept of "empowerment" and the involvement of communities in a small and remote part of the world, the South Pacific region. The issues of economic growth, of social equity, and improved living standards, of sustainable development, of community empowerment are large and dominate much of the debate about development globally. By contrast, most of the South Pacific countries are insignificant in global terms, just tiny specks of land on a map of the world separated by vast areas of ocean swept by the trade winds.

The beauty of their palm-fringed lagoons, coral reefs and rainforest peaks, and the friendliness of their peoples have been romanticized for centuries by writers such as Robert Louis Stevenson and artists such as Paul Gauguin, so that in the lexicon of tourism they conjure up images of "paradise". They are an inherent part of Urry's "tourist gaze" (1991), Selwyn's tourism myths (1996), van den Berghe's "quest for the other" (1994), and Dann's "socio-linguistic register" of tourism (1996). While such images are intrinsic components of the "socially constructed boundaries of a network of attractions referred to as 'destination'" (Hall 1998:140), the reality in the South Pacific is often different, and the general lack of natural resources by most of these countries has impelled them, sometimes reluctantly, towards tourism and forms of development at odds with their traditional value systems and lifestyles.

Tradition as a concept is here construed as the opposite of "modern" or "Western", and includes beliefs, value systems and behavior derived from pre-contact times. In accepting this notion, however, the idea of tradition as static and unchanging is contested. Each generation redefines its traditional heritage in response to new understandings, new experiences, and new inputs from an ever-increasing range of sources, both internal and external. Interpretation of the past may change to suit or satisfy particular needs because tradition, its ownership and its presentation will involve considerations of changing values, power structures, and politics. Tradition is thus not an object, static in time, but through continuous interpretation and re-interpretation may be viewed as a process.

The political and social significance of tradition lies in its association with identity. It is fundamental in helping individuals, communities, and nations define who they are, both to themselves and to outsiders. It may provide a sense of belonging in a cultural sense and in terms of place. In this context, ownership of tradition is linked to ideology and its symbolism takes on strong political overtones (Keesing and Strathern 1998). In many parts of the South Pacific, "appeals to 'tradition' as a political legitimator have been common for some considerable time" and may be seen as an attempt to ameliorate the prior dominant values and views of their former colonial mentors (Lawson 1991:1). In the triadic context of development, tourism and empowerment this theme will emerge in a number of the chapters that follow.

This study encompasses a certain focus on the traditions of indigenous peoples who, following Butler and Hinch (1996), are defined as:

> races of people who are endemic or native to a destination region. As such this group may represent either the majority or a minority group in the destination. The term is inclusive and global in its application (1996:9).

This definition is consistent with that adopted by the United Nations for its International Year for the Indigenous Peoples of the World, 1993.

The concept of sustainable development is readily accepted by the governments of most of the South Pacific countries, since their traditional cultures espoused many of its principles and values. But as populations have burgeoned, placing enormous strains on scarce resources, and as new forms and structures for society have changed traditional patterns, sustainability of biophysical and sociocultural assets becomes more difficult.

Tourism development can contribute to or adversely impact upon their resources. Policies may be contradictory, poorly implemented and focused on the short term rather than the longer term. Externalities may impinge and impede national objectives. Tourism development in these countries especially by communities raises many of the issues of development confronting many larger, more powerful countries and economies; and empowerment of, by and for such communities constitutes the kernel of this book. The series of accompanying case studies in particular seeks to understand not only how communities in several South Pacific countries have responded to tourism within their social and geopolitical space, but whether the environment governing the power relationship between community and agents of tourism development is an enabling or disabling one, whether it is empowering or disempowering.

In this context the study goes beyond a focus on the impacts of tourism to explore the relevance of a body of political, economic, and sociological theory in terms of its application to tourism development. The treatise synthesizes aspects of development theory, including the concept of sustainable development, with an enlarged concept of empowerment focused on community, politics and policy formulation, and insights from social anthropology, to provide a useful standpoint from which to consider the community/tourism development relationship.

The approach that has been adopted also attempts to combine the emic paradigm with the etic, that is one in which analysis relies upon "the actors' interpretations and local inside knowledge of the meaning of the behavior under study" (Pearce 1988:91) as well as upon externally constructed models by "outsider" researchers to describe the social situation under discussion. Social representations theory in examining conflict situations alludes to this as "interaction between the consensual universe (everyday knowledge) and the reified (technical, scientific) universe" (Moscovici 1984; Pearce, Moscardo, and Ross 1996:209).

Proceeding further down this line of thought, the study moves beyond tourism impacts to look at how communities react and adapt to the presence of tourism within their social space. They are not passive sponges simply absorbing it or more brittle polities being dented and degraded by its forces, but rather are dynamic and capable of responding in complex ways. This is consistent with an emerging literature reframing tourism impacts as a two-way process (Lanfant, Allcock, and Brunner 1995; Picard 1993; Picard and Wood 1997; Wood 1993) and the case study presented in Chapter 9 in particular explores this phenomenon in some detail.

Theoretical and Conceptual Considerations

Development Theory

In the five decades since the end of World War Two, the international order has changed dramatically, with colonial empires being dismantled and more than 90 former dependent territories gaining their independence. In the 1950s and 1960s the economic disparities and standards of living between the "old" countries and the newly emergent states initiated a vigorous examination of the latter's needs, and "development" became the globally desired objective. Countries were arranged somewhat simplistically by economic rationalists on a continuum from "developed, First World" countries to "undeveloped, Third World" nations.

Development plans at the national, regional and local levels were actively promoted. In 1975, the United Nations recorded no less than 323 existing national development plans with which its technical agencies were involved, all prepared since 1951 (Mehmet 1978). The early emphasis was on industrialization, increased commodity output, and export-led growth to generate foreign exchange and improve the balance of trade, rather than on the people involved in this production (United Nations Development Program Annual Reports 1950 to 1960; Rostow 1960; Goulet 1968; Seers 1969). "Development" was equated to economic growth aligned to capitalist models, modernization was seen as the necessary transformation from rurally-based subsistence economies to industrialized Western models, and questions of equity were put to one side.

Modernization was then subjected to vigorous criticism by some writers in the late 1960s and 1970s (Bauer 1972) who considered that modernization theory was simply a way of disguising the adverse impacts of colonial rule and dependency. In the view of these critics the capitalist system was responsible for the chronic "underdevelopment" of Third World countries and they advocated a counter-revolution in development that tended to be based on the application of Marxist principles (Toye 1987). Amarshi, Good, and Mortimer (1979) writing specifically about Papua New Guinea, argued similarly. Dependency theory, with the metropolitan powers perceived as the center engaged in a global capitalist conspiracy to control the periphery as perpetually underdeveloped and/or underdeveloping states, became the dominant theme in development analysis.

One result from this new approach was the addition of a social dimension: development was interpreted as part of the much wider process of social change. Education and health were seen as important and redistribution of economic benefits was integrated into development as social justice (Mehmet, for example, incorporated the phrase in the title of his 1978 book, *Economic Planning and Social Justice in Developing Countries*). Seers (1969, 1977) suggested that it would be "strange" to label a doubling of per capita income as development if there had been no commensurate reduction in poverty, unemployment, and inequality. By the late 1980s equity principles were firmly entrenched in concepts of development, although their implementation has continued to prove problematic in many countries.

Subsequently dependency theory was, like modernization, attacked for being too sweeping in its generalizations and unable to explain the diversity of non-typical manifestations of development in different states and regions. A post-modernist framework that borrowed some of the concepts from both modernization and dependency theories began to focus more narrowly on the particular in attempts to analyze development (Apter 1987; Harkin 1995).

Sustainable Development

A paradigm shift in the development debate occurred about 15 years ago with the advent of the concept of sustainable development. It has since come to dominate the debate. In its broadest sense, sustainable development encompasses both biophysical and sociocultural spheres, following a meeting of the World Commission on the Environment and Development (WCED) in 1987 that issued the so-called Brundtland Report, *Our Common Future*. This enunciated a set of principles, the major one of which is the notion of inter-generational equity, meaning development that "meets the needs of the present generation without compromising the ability of future generations to meet their own needs" (WCED 1987:43). Its second major principle is the conservation of biological diversity and ecological integrity that may entail constraint on certain kinds of economic activity. The non-evolutionary loss of species and genetic diversity needs to be halted and the future of evolutionary processes assured.

Sustainable development is problematical in a variety of ways and it is difficult to operationalize. Who, for example, is to measure current consumption of a resource and make judgments about what is the appropriate level of exploitation to ensure that the needs of future generations are met? How is that level of consumption to be determined? How are any proposed restrictions to be enforced? Who is to determine just what is of value that needs to be preserved, protected, and conserved? By whose value system are such pronouncements to be made? Given undoubted continuing technological innovation who can determine what finite level of resources is in fact necessary to be preserved today to ensure future generations have the same level of access as currently enjoyed? These questions are by no means exhaustive: they are simply indicative of the challenge of defining and refining the concept of sustainable development.

In an attempt to deal with such issues, a key element of sustainable development is the adoption of an anticipatory and precautionary policy approach. This is designed to ensure that policy decisions err on the side of caution where scientific evidence of the impacts of development is lacking or where uncertainty exists. In this context, environmental and social impact assessments have become a common tool for guiding policy decisions and development. Since social equity is regarded as a key principle in a sustainable society, consultations with affected communities have also become a feature of some of those states that have adopted the principles of sustainable development. Often, however, these consultations are reactive (that is, communities are asked to respond to development plans formulated outside their community), rather than being genuinely empowering.

The paradigm of sustainable development presents a major challenge to conventional ones of development because it questions *inter alia* the positions of countries in the developmental hierarchy as determined by modernization, dependency, and neo-Listian development theories. Its values for measurement of "development" are radically different; it gives primacy to ecological (environmental and cultural) values over others. It also challenges the claims of universalism of other development theories since it espouses specific models that may be distinct to a country or region because of its own unique ecology and culture. At the same time it advances the notion of globalization in the context of countries accepting responsibility that actions undertaken locally may extend across political boundaries with adverse environmental impacts for another country, another region, or globally.

Tourism Development

The tourism sector has been a relative late-comer to the development debate and to its responsibilities and role in advancing sustainable development. In the immediate post-World War Two rush to develop, tourism was initially ignored in the national development plans of most Third World countries. For example, tourism as a sector worthy of its own discussion and strategy did not appear until the eighth Five Year Development Plan for Fiji (Fiji Government 1985), despite the fact that the industry had overtaken sugar in terms of foreign exchange earnings and had more paid employment than the entire agricultural sector. In other parts of the Third World, such as the Caribbean, the importance of tourism had been recognized earlier and led to such descriptions by economic advocates as "tourism, passport to development" (challenged by de Kadt in his 1979 book of that name).

In the past two decades tourism has begun to find general recognition as an economic sector that can make a contribution to "development". Virtually all countries around the globe have now embraced tourism, with greater or lesser enthusiasm, and this phenomenon has attracted an increasing number of serious researchers drawn from a range of disciplines.

Tourism research has been characterized by four "platforms" (Jafari 1990) in which a lively debate has moved from advocacy of tourism through somewhat simplistic assertions about the adverse impacts (both economic and socio-cultural) of tourism to a more balanced view of those impacts and more recently to a postmodern view in which the normative cost-benefit frameworks of earlier assessments about tourism development and its impacts have been challenged as naive (Archer 1996; Butler 1990, 1992; Cohen 1987; Wood 1993).

Given the widely divergent views of researchers and the rapidity with which tourism as a sector has expanded, it is perhaps not surprising that in many instances governments have not fully understood the extent of the growth of this industry. Consequently there tends to be a mismatch between the rhetoric of policy and actual resources devoted to this economic sector *vis-à-vis* others.

The *nature* of tourism has also not been fully understood and development theory is deficient in providing a framework by which some of the issues may be resolved. Of particular interest to this study is that in some countries indigenous communities tend to have been marginalized from the process of development and participation in tourism ventures and this is often despite government policies designed specifically to draw them in.

Empowerment

Having discussed the strengths and deficiencies of development theory, it is proposed to add another element to the focus on socioeconomic factors and distributive justice, and that is empowerment of communities. It will be argued that without empowerment, sustainable tourism development by communities is difficult to attain (Sofield 2001). Like sustainable development, it is a term that has been abused and mis-used. Empowerment is also a major component, *inter alia*, of the debate about community development. Because communities in many countries are left outside the decision-making process, policies and decisions are made *for* them not *by* them. One result is often an inability by governments, planners, and developers to implement policy and/or to maintain the sustainability of an initiative. This is a situation that should be addressed by community empowerment.

Planning has in recent years attempted to deal with this situation by paying greater attention to the impacts of tourism on host communities and exploring ways to incorporate their views into the planning process (D'Amore 1983; McIntosh and Goeldner 1986). Murphy (1985), in particular, advocated an ecological approach to tourism planning that emphasized that control over the development process should reside in the local community. However, substantial problems remain in implementing the laudable sentiments expressed about the process of community involvement (Haywood 1988).

Despite concerns about the need for community involvement in planning, empowerment in any conceptual detail has to date tended to remain outside considerations of tourism development. It has been more strongly explored in education literature; indigenous issues related to discrimination and justice; nursing science where the professional health worker/patient relationship has been subjected to very detailed scrutiny in terms of empowerment; some aspects of sociology such as social exchange theory; political science; and management practices. Empowerment for individual self-growth also has a varied literature, but is basically outside the terms of reference for this study where the emphasis is on community empowerment.

In discussing empowerment the relationship between politics and tourism must also be canvassed, because politics, reduced to its fundamentals, is about power. Power is about who gets what, where, how, and why and the politics of development are also about who gets what, where, how and why. While the relationship between this industry and politics is of course concerned with political parties, elections, and government influence on tourism policy, the primary impact is one of power (Hall 1994). One aim of this study is to ensure that the politics of tourism development in the South Pacific are fully integrated into the analyses of a range of situations. Only through an understanding of the politics of a situation can the concept of empowerment be meaningfully broached.

As used in this book, the concept of empowerment by and of communities is at once both a process and an outcome. It is an amalgamation of several different emphases, although two key components are the role of the state (government) without which legality of action and behavior may be challenged and sustainability of tourism developments difficult to achieve, and the decision-making model that moves beyond consultations to encompass application or implementation of decisions (Sofield 2001). This concept is derived in part also from the social exchange theory literature, especially power/dependence relations (Blau 1964, 1977, 1987; Emerson 1962, 1972, 1987; and Molm 1981, 1986, 1987a, 1987b, 1988). In this context, empowerment of communities, societal groups, or organizations may be considered a strictly social phenomenon. Similarly the concept of empowerment may be considered an outcome of the social processes of social exchange where those processes result in a change of the power balance between the actors.

Propositions

This study constitutes a synthesis of the concepts of empowerment, tourism development (especially involving indigenous communities), and sustainable development to take account of the political and socioeconomic environments. It postulates five propositions:

- That without the element of empowerment tourism development at the level of community will have difficulty achieving sustainability.
- That the exercise of traditional or legitimate empowerment by traditionally oriented communities will of itself be an ineffectual mechanism for attempting sustainable tourism development.
- That such traditional empowerment must be transformed into legal empowerment if sustainable tourism development is to be achieved.
- That empowerment for such communities will usually require environmental or institutional change to allow a genuine reallocation of power to ensure appropriate changes in the asymmetrical relationship of the community to the wider society.
- That, conversely, empowerment of indigenous communities cannot be "taken" by the communities concerned drawing only upon their own traditional resources, but will require support and sanction by the state, if it is to avoid being short-lived.

Context of the Analysis

To move the discussion from the theoretical and conceptual to the real world, these propositions are examined in the context of tourism development regionally, nationally and locally with reference to the South Pacific. First, the region as a whole is considered. Some of the constraints and also the mismatch of resources between traditional sectors of the island economies and the new — and in many cases, largest — sector, tourism, are explored.

Next, the move by the micro-states of the South Pacific to cooperate on a region-wide basis for tourism development and marketing through the agency of an intergovernmental organization, the Tourism Council of the South Pacific (TCSP), re-named the South Pacific Tourism Organisation (SPTO) in 1999, is subjected to analysis in the context of empowerment. The TCSP/SPTO is critiqued against a backdrop of former colonial domination and subsequent attempts by the South Pacific island states to establish not only political but economic independence. Sovereignty, dependency theory, and core–periphery relations are key concepts that are examined in the context of the role and operational status of the TCSP/SPTO.

Having set the scene regionally a range of tourism case studies from Solomon Islands, Vanuatu, and Fiji is drawn upon to illustrate various manifestations of the author's expanded interpretation of the role of empowerment in tourism development as an agent of change at the national and local community levels. The first two case studies dissect empowerment failure in Solomon Islands, looking at policy deficiencies at the national level first and then reducing the broad perspective to the particular by focusing on a specific community's involvement with a resort on Anuha Island. After more than ten years of attempting to assume a non-dependent relationship with the foreign-owned resort of Anuha, in which the local village was little more than a source of unskilled labor, the community took dramatic protest action that destroyed the resort.

A case of successful community empowerment in Vanuatu where several traditionally oriented villages have been supported by government agencies to maintain control over their "culture as tourism", is then analyzed. Traditional ownership of the *ghol* ceremony is regarded as essential to its authenticity. Thus, authenticity and heritage as a process rather than a static object are also considered.

The third community case study scrutinizes a complex situation of empowerment and disempowerment surrounding a resort development, Mana Island, in Fiji. In this instance a new community has arisen to challenge the primacy of control exercised by the traditional chiefly elite of the landowning community from which the resort owners have leased Mana Island.

Study Structure

Following this introductory chapter which sets out the research approaches and applications utilized to undertake the study, Chapters 2 and 3 explore development theory and the concept of empowerment respectively. A key purpose of Chapter 2 is to examine "development" in the broad sense as it has been pursued, thrust upon, or acquiesced in by Third World countries in general and by the small Island states of the South Pacific specifically. Chapter 3, in exploring empowerment, identifies shortcomings in current definitions and applications of the concept and sets out the discussion leading to an expansion of the concept in the context of tourism development by communities in the South Pacific and the formulation of the five propositions to be examined.

Chapter 4 provides an overview of tourism development in the South Pacific region, identifying constraints arising from smallness and isolation. Then Chapter 5 focuses on the dynamics of regional cooperation as the micro-states have attempted to establish control over their tourism industries by setting up a multilateral tourism agency. Chapter 6 probes the national tourism development policies of Solomon Islands and advances the concept of "pioneer space" to empower communities. Chapters 7, 8, and 9 compare and contrast empowerment, development and tourism in the lives of three communities in Solomon Islands (Anuha Island Resort), Vanuatu (the Pentecost "land divers") and Fiji (Mana Island Resort), respectively. The final chapter summarizes the various issues of development, empowerment, and sustainability with reference to community involvement in tourism and relates them to the five propositions outlined above.

Research Approaches and Applications

A multidimensional approach has been adopted in pursuing the strands of this study. A comprehensive library search of the existing body of literature covered such areas as the study of development and development theory; a review of some of the literature on the nature of states and the power that they exercise; the role of tourism in the development processes of states and national strategies; the literature on other areas relevant to development such as dependency theory, social exchange theory, and social representations theory; development problems and issues in the South Pacific and the role of tourism in that process; colonialism, plantation economies, and dependency theory; tourism planning and the phenomena of indigenous peoples; and the concept of empowerment.

Case Studies

A major part of this treatise proceeds by case studies. The cases provide details of socioeconomic and political data relating to a particular situation or sequence of events from which theoretical inferences about empowerment and tourism development are drawn. The case studies are distinguished from more general ones by the detail and particularity of each account. Each case is thus a survey of a specific configuration of events or material in which a distinctive set of actors or institutions have been involved in a defined situation at either a particular point in time or over a period of time. A major aim is to impart a sense of the concrete to an abstract concept, and an important characteristic of the case studies is synchronic analysis of the interrelation of institutions within the existing socio-political whole. The researcher is then strategically placed to appreciate the theoretical significance of these interconnections in the context of the general principles of empowerment and development.

To examine the propositions on empowerment outlined above, a range of situations has been selected from South Pacific countries, based on three main categories: scale; their location on a traditional/modern continuum; and their sustainability (or lack thereof).

Figure 1.1 illustrates the integration of these three categories in a schematic representation.

Scale

Four different levels of involvement in tourism development have been selected for scrutiny, that is, international, regional, national and community.

International: Constraints of tourism development are examined in a region-wide context, drawing upon the development experience in some 20 South Pacific Island countries.

Regional: A number of the South Pacific Island Countries formed a regional authority originally called the Tourism Council of the South Pacific (TCSP) to assist them in the development and promotion of their tourism industries. The issues of over-dependence upon a single major aid donor (the European Community) and neocolonialism are examined in the context of the capacity of the TCSP to determine and serve the interests of its members.

National: At this level, Solomon Islands was selected because of the time and effort expended by the government in formulating a national tourism policy and strategy. Despite policies designed to facilitate community-based tourism ventures, it has been ineffective.

Community: At this local level, three different communities were selected, one each from Fiji, Solomon Islands, and Vanuatu, which have been involved in tourism development.

Traditional/Modernizing Communities

With reference to scale at the community level, each of the three communities occupies a different position on a continuum ranging from highly traditionally oriented to strongly adaptive modernizing. Each has responded very differently to the pressures for change arising from the contact situation generally and the impacts arising directly from tourism *per se*.

Pentecost Island, Vanuatu: The Sa village communities presented in this case study occupy one of the extreme poles having strongly resisted modernization.

They have rejected Christianity and formal education among other Western influences, and have retained a high measure of traditional beliefs and practices. Very few speak English, some speak Bislama (Vanuatu pidgin), and most converse in their *kastom* (traditional customary) language. They have established a successful tourism venture based on their culture.

Anuha Island, Solomon Islands: The Rera village community which is on Nggela and owns nearby Anuha Island, is devoutly Christian. It has a primary school and espouses a wide range of Western values. All members are fluent in pidgin, and some are reasonably fluent in English, although their most commonly used language is the traditional one. But the community's geographical isolation has resulted in a visible degree of traditional orientation and its land tenure system is wholly *kastom* (traditional). It occupies a somewhat central position on the traditional/modern continuum. The community was involved in leasing customary land for a four-star resort owned by foreign investors.

Mana Island, Fiji: There are now two separate communities, Yaro village and Yaro Levu (or New Yaro) associated with this resort development where previously there was only one. Traditional bamboo and thatch village huts have been replaced with concrete block houses roofed with corrugated iron, electricity and water have been installed, outboard motors for their fiber glass and aluminum "run-abouts" (small open boats) are standard, Christianity and education are very strongly espoused, and further manifestations (among many) of their Westernization is their fluency in the English language and acceptance of these dress standards. They are involved with a five-star resort owned by Japanese interests.

Sustainable tourism development

Each case study represents a different picture of the longevity of involvement in tourism development. They range from a continuing successful enterprise over 30 years to complete failure of the venture after only several years. In Solomon Islands, the government's national tourism development plan failed to make any lasting impact and at the provincial and local levels it resulted in few (if any) measurable benefits after 10 years. In terms of community, the three case studies demonstrate markedly different outcomes.

Anuha Island Resort: This multi-million dollar development collapsed within five years, and virtually all trace of it disappeared within 10 years. Its failure was spectacular and highlights many of the issues of powerlessness and empowerment. It will be argued that the lack of empowerment was a major contributing factor to its failure.

Sa village: These communities have been running a successful tourism venture based around one part of their traditional ceremonies since the 1980s. It is controlled and directed by the village owners in such a way that tourism supports and promotes traditional culture. A feature of this venture is the degree of active support it receives from the national Vanuatu Government that nevertheless does not control the venture. Indeed the analysis indicates that any attempt by the Government to assume control would destroy the venture: community empowerment appears genuine in this instance and a major factor in the sustainability of the venture.

Mana Island Resort: This property has been operating continuously for 30 years and has experienced very strong community involvement throughout this period. The community has split into two because of differing benefits that have accrued from their involvement in tourism development. The rivalry is substantial and has the potential to spill over into the smooth running of the resort operations.

Each of the case studies exhibits different characteristics and opens up to detailed analysis the process of empowerment for tourism development.

Case Study Fieldwork

The case studies are derived in large part from what may be described, under the aegis of participant observation, as a blend or combination of methods and techniques that mirror some of the qualitative methods of ethnographic fieldwork strategy. These include protracted interaction in the field with the subjects of the research, direct observations of relevant events, both formal and informal interviewing, and access to secondary sources (documents and other relevant material). A limited degree of systematic enumeration (for example, a survey by questionnaire in the case of Mana Island) is integrated with the qualitative data. Several case studies, such as the *ghol* ritual in Vanuatu (Chapter 8) and Mana Island Resort in Fiji (Chapter 9) constitute what the ethnographic literature describes as "a situational analysis" that exhibits "the morphology of the social structure" (Gluckman 1958; Mitchell 1984), from which inductive analysis proceeds. Ethnographic techniques are extensively utilized throughout. The Vanuatu study also benefits by drawing upon extensive fieldwork by Jolly (1982, 1992, 1994), Bani (1989) and de Burlo (1987, 1996).

The case of Anuha Island Resort in Solomon Islands represents longitudinal or extended investigation. Whereas the analysis of a social situation is limited to a single one or at most to a restricted set of events located in the same

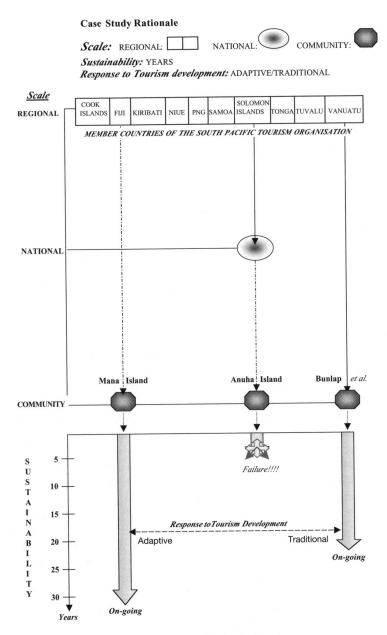

Case Study Rationale

Scale: REGIONAL: ☐☐   NATIONAL: ⬭   COMMUNITY: ⬡

Sustainability: YEARS
Response to Tourism development: ADAPTIVE/TRADITIONAL

Figure 1.1: Case Study Rationale

situation, an extended case study recounts events over a relatively long period of time, typically several years. This contributes both historical and dynamic dimensions to the account. Both the Mana Island and the South Pentecost cases incorporate historical data from a range of sources to reveal the processes at work over several decades.

The Anuha Island Resort case for example examines the rise and fall of a foreign venture over a 10-year period. For the first three years of its genesis, the author was resident in Solomon Islands and played a minor role in facilitating negotiations among the traditional landowners, the Solomon Islands government, and the Australian investor. Throughout the next ten years the author frequented the Solomon Islands for periods varying from two weeks to three months.

The issues surrounding the development and operations of the resort were discussed with all major participants and key figures over the 10-year period during which material was gathered. They included three Solomon Islands Prime Ministers, seven national government ministers, two premiers of Central Province, the Chief Justice of Solomon Islands, the Anglican Archbishop of Solomon Islands, two Australian High Commissioners, one British High Commissioner, the Police Commissioner, the village "bigmen", the principal Australian developers, investors, and more than a dozen senior Solomon Islands government civil servants. Discussions were open-ended rather than structured interviews with a set of pre-determined questions, although in each case a core of central issues was canvassed using "discussion starters" and focusing comments. These are designed to ensure that discussion flows readily, allowing flexibility for issues to be pursued in as much depth as desired by the interviewees and for as long as interest is maintained by them (Moser 1988).

Participant observation was a significant method of data collection and periods of between one to three weeks at a time were spent in the village and at the Resort over the decade that developments unfolded. "Convenience opportunities" were taken during these periods for open-ended discussions with the succession of resort personnel and village community members.

Attendance at formal institutional proceedings where the issues were being scrutinized included parliamentary debates and court hearings. Other secondary sources were tapped, such as High Court records, government files, and the Solomon Islands parliamentary record, *Hansard.* Newspapers, regional monthly magazines, and an Australian television documentary were lively sources of additional information.

Triangulation was a necessary technique to assist in diminishing the subjectivity invariably present in qualitative research. The propensity for Melanesian subjects to provide inconsistent information over a period of time as they respond to varying circumstances, particularly when the issue concerns customary ownership of land, necessitates "data source triangulation" (Stake 1995:113). This protocol is designed to increase accuracy by cross-checking all information with two or more primary sources (or secondary sources if it can be ascertained that they were not derived from the same or single source). Hence, many of the same questions were put to different participants as the events of Anuha Island evolved.

Similar techniques were utilized for the case studies of Mana Island Resort and the *ghol* ceremony of south Pentecost. The author lived in both countries for a period of time (see below) and was intimately familiar with both ventures. Subsequently, three fieldtrips were made to Fiji and Vanuatu, each over a three-year period to undertake additional research, although it was only possible to visit Pentecost on one of those occasions and then at a time when the *ghol* was not being performed.

Interpretation of the issues and problems of development in the South Pacific has been assisted by almost 20 years of living and working in the region, often in a privileged position where access to confidential sources of information was possible, for example as Australian High Commissioner, Solomon Islands; Acting High Commissioner, New Hebrides (which was re-named Vanuatu on independence in 1980); Deputy Director, South Pacific Forum Secretariat, Fiji; Acting Chairman, Tourism Council of the South Pacific. Periods of continuous residence included almost four years in Solomon Islands, two years in Fiji, periods of six months in Vanuatu, and four months in New Caledonia. Numerous multiple visits for field research, consultancies, conferences, workshops, and project supervision to another 12 Island countries for periods ranging from 1–16 weeks were undertaken. A combined period of nine years has been spent in South Pacific countries in the past two decades, and to that may be added another two and a quarter years as Director of the South Pacific Section, Department of Foreign Affairs, Canberra, responsible for the day-to-day oversight of Australia's ten diplomatic posts in the region with combined development assistance programs of about $100 million per annum (all amounts throughout the book are quoted in US dollars).

Methodology and Concepts of Time

The lengthy time frame of close involvement in tourism development in the South Pacific by this author has been particularly useful in terms of a methodology that has avoided some of the restrictions and deficiencies of "conceptual time-capsules" described by Wilson (1993:32), when a longitudinal dimension is lacking. These include difficulties in appreciating the underlying dynamics of a situation since many elements will change over time. An historical perspective may assist by uncovering what went on before the period of research commenced; but a finite, single field trip will tend to focus only those aspects dominant at the time. It will not necessarily assist in unraveling the underlying forces shaping the way in which a situation is moving, changing, adapting, and being amended. These forces, however, may be manifested and revealed over a longer time span.

The longitudinal approach adopted in this study for several of the case studies thus avoids what Hitchcock, King, and Parnwell (1993:6) have termed "snapshot pictures" of a particular period in time that fail to capture the underlying reality of the situation. They note in this context Picard's studies of tourism in Bali which have clearly contributed "to a historically grounded understanding of the transformations of local cultural forms in relation to tourism development" (Picard 1987b, 1993). Picard (1997) has himself written about the way his own views changed over two decades of continuous involvement and observation of the effects of tourism in Bali. Wilson was particularly critical of "one-off" studies providing polar viewpoints based on interpretations and conclusions that were in fact deficient because of the lack of an adequate time dimension. Some of these studies "have nevertheless gained seminal status in the anthropology of tourism literature because of their utilization of provocative new concepts" (Wilson 1993:36).

In this context Wilson cited two studies. The first was Greenwood's 1977 account of the Alarde Festival, Fuenterrabia, in the Basque Province of Spain that became "commoditized" by tourism and fell into terminal decline (this study introduced to tourism literature Greenwood's concept of commoditization). The second was Buck's (1978a) study of "boundary maintenance" among the Amish in Pennsylvania, USA, in which Buck postulated that a total separation of Amish "backstage" life from tourists reinforced and revitalized their traditional culture (Wilson 1993:36–40).

Other researchers began to utilize Greenwood's example of commoditization so that it became one of the most powerful indictments of the corrosive effects of tourism and one of the most often quoted. For instance, Cohen's use of Greenwood's material in his 1988a paper on "Authenticity and Commoditization in Tourism" helped to perpetuate Greenwood's thesis. Buck's study of the Amish also attracted influential support. In his 1988b paper on "Traditions in the Qualitative Sociology of Tourism" Cohen described it as "one of the more important studies" based on MacCannell's work on authenticity.

Wilson subjected the Alarde Festival and the Amish involvement with tourism to a revisit by research students 10 years after the original research by

Greenwood and Buck because of concerns that there were inconsistencies in their studies. Greenwood had found that the Fuenterrabia municipal council, in attempting to exploit the tourist, had ordered the festival to be performed twice a day. In Greenwood's interpretation, this imposition had deprived the festival of its excitement and spontaneity. It became "an obligation to be avoided. . . . [The decision to make] their culture a public performance took the municipal council a few minutes; with that act a 350-year old ritual died" (Greenwood 1977:137). The concept of commoditization attained validity.

In 1988, however, Young discovered a thriving festival, "a vibrant and exciting ritual which took place in a town alive with expectation and emotion . . . the people, far from feeling that the Alarde was an obligation to be avoided, were enthusiastic in the preparations and enactment of the week long festival" (cited in Wilson 1993). Her investigations suggested that the festival had fallen into temporary decline during Greenwood's visit not because of the commoditization of the event by a tourist invasion but because the municipal government had been viewed then as corrupt, undemocratic, and dominated by Spanish bureaucrats. Accordingly, the inhabitants had withdrawn their support for the festival in opposition to the council's decision. Young considered that the current success of the festival lay in the politics of that original decision, which had turned the event into a symbol of Basque nationalism: "the men no longer march to celebrate a famous Spanish victory over the French but rather to state their Basqueness" (cited in Wilson 1993). Her conclusion was that Greenwood's fundamental premise that the development of tourism had led to the commoditization of the Alarde and thence its cessation was inaccurate. Like reports of Mark Twain's death, Greenwood's pronouncement about the demise of the Alarde Festival was also premature. Greenwood himself subsequently accepted the revised analysis of the festival's temporary demise and its ensuing resurgence.

Buck's premise was in many ways the opposite of Greenwood's — that the Amish had been able to maintain their way of life despite a tourist invasion of very considerable proportions into their midst. They had not been commoditized but had achieved "protection" for their culture by the erection and maintenance of a rigid boundary that disguised and hid their "backstage" from the tourist gaze. Tourists were provided with access only to staged events on the fringes (artificial front stage) of Amish territory.

Wilson's concern was that there was in fact much more contact between the Amish and tourists than Buck had uncovered. Who, for example, were the cultural brokers staging "authentic" Amish performances along the perceived boundary, Route 30? Who were the "teacher guides", "specialists" and "Mennonite guides" referred to in Buck's study?

North undertook fieldwork among the Amish at Wilson's suggestion in 1992 (cited in Wilson 1993). She established that there were some 800 Amish household farms engaged in direct contact with tourists and that about 400 had been so engaged in 1980. Boundary maintenance was not particularly evident. North found that the Amish were in fact critical of the "English" owners of businesses along Route 30 who exploited Amish culture for their own personal profit. The Amish tended to welcome tourism because it provided additional employment and income for their younger generation. Farms had become unviable with the increase in Amish population over the years, and tourism provided *in situ* employment. The different generations were actively engaged in teaching and learning and then displaying for tourists traditional skills, crafts and occupational tasks. Without tourism, employment would have had to be sought outside the Amish community, a greater evil in the judgment of the elders, than bringing tourism inside their farm gates.

Tourism had thus contributed to the maintenance of Amish culture, community cohesion and family solidarity. This took place not by a policy of exclusion of tourists enforced through boundary maintenance, but by the opposite: the provision of access to the "real" Amish world. Buck had simply arrived at a time when one faction of the Amish had been concerned with boundary maintenance, so that the issue was prominent when he had undertaken his fieldwork; but that situation had changed through time.

Wilson's observation was that these two examples demonstrated how the lack of a time dimension could, especially in the case of "one-off" studies, confuse rather than clarify understanding of the impact of tourism. It is obvious that a longitudinal study has an improved probability of interpreting more accurately just where a particular situation may stand in terms of the various tourism development models that have been designed by researchers such as Butler (1980), Miossec (1976), Doxey (1975), Noronha (1979), E. Cohen (1983), and others. Characteristic of all of these models are steps or stages and a situational study may be only a given historical moment and not reveal the processes at work that might result in a different conclusion being drawn.

All situations are of course dynamic. The point is not that situational studies should not be attempted. They may reveal very insightful understandings and provide what Gluckman has described as "apt illustrations" (1961:7, cited in Wilson 1993) but that caution might best be applied to some forms of conclusions. A series of snapshots over time could provide a technique to chart the transformation of a particular destination through the stages of the various models.

The lack of a longitudinal approach may also result in reliance on what Wilson described as "currently fashionable research strategies" that are "the product of a given historical moment" that may capture a researcher's "entrapment by one conceptual framework" (1993:35). Thus, to benefit from this insight, in terms of the longitudinal analysis of Anuha, originally modernization theory was utilized since it was then at the forefront of anthropological research (Sofield 1990b); this was refined with reference to conflict theory and functional/dysfunctional sociocultural impact assessment (Sofield 1996); thence to social exchange theory; and finally to a re-analysis of the situation by employing the concept of empowerment (Sofield 1997).

Wilson further suggests that a key way to overcome the limitations of some research is not only by longitudinal qualitative research and revisiting previous studies, but also by undertaking multi-location rather than single-site projects (1993:46). This is also an important part of the methodology for this book that the concept of empowerment has been examined from a multi-locational rather than a single site perspective. It is thus unashamedly positioned outside the arena of post-modernist deconstructivist ethnography that resists the epistemologies of the general-in-the-specific.

Chapter 2

Tourism and Development: Theories and Relationships

Development of Tourism

A discussion of tourism and development of necessity requires an examination of the role of the state, of government and often politics, and of their relationship to the many facets of the tourism system. Governments are intrinsically political, and politics, reduced to its fundamentals, is about power. The latter is about who gets what, where, how, and why and the politics of development are also about who gets what, where, how, and why (Hall 1994). It is of interest then that in much of the literature about development theory, the relationship of the state-as-politics to development is absent or subsumed under economic or sociological constructions. For example, some of the literature on modernization theory ignores the politics of governments except in an indirect, general way. Harrison points out the necessity of including, centrally, political structures and the nature of political leadership in any analysis of modernization and development, arguing that too often the emphasis on economics resulted in little or no understanding of the decision-making processes (1988:181).

Much of the literature of tourism development also glosses over the role of government. Ritchie (1993), Matthews (1977), Richter (1983, 1984), Urry (1991), Hollinshead (1992), and others have all deprecated the lack of relevant political science theory in analyses of tourism decision-making, planning and development. Dependency theory, which draws upon analyses of colonialism and imperialism, through the work of authors such as Britton (1980, 1982, 1984, 1987b, 1991, 1996), who consistently sought to relate dependency to tourism development, is an exception to this general observation. Given the general lack of detailed analysis of the relationship between the state and tourism, politics and power, however, it is also no surprise to find that empowerment as a concept rarely enters the literature. Nor is it readily apparent in much of the discourse about development *per se*.

While tourism as an industry is generally regarded as a private sector activity where market forces predominate, in fact the embrace of the state is comprehensive. The strength of that embrace may vary from country to country. By and large, all governments are active participants in tourism development even when their stated policies may be characterized by a *laissez faire* approach. The question tends to be not whether government should have a role at all, but an acceptance that it does have a role, and that it is the nature of that role which requires definition. It will differ across countries depending upon a range of variables of which a major determinant will be the set of values governing policy approaches. However, the differences may not necessarily come with ideological values since governments of varied hues all pursue tourism development with similar degrees of enthusiasm. No matter what type of political structure a country has, there is invariably some form of government involvement in tourism.

> The state is a powerful, resilient, pragmatic and reflexive social structure capable of sustained powerful action across many areas of social activity. It is not inherently a benevolent structure intent on social good; nor is it inevitably a modernizing force working towards desirable forms of progress; nor is it singularly malevolent or motivated by self-interest (Davis, Wanna, Warhurst, and Weller 1993:18).

The state is not synonymous with the government, as governments may change but states will continue to exist. A first step in developing an appreciation of the role of the state is to identify its various institutions. These consist of a central government (whether elected or unelected), including supporting institutions such as ministers of state (the executive), administrative departments (the bureaucracy), the courts and judiciary, enforcement agencies, other levels of government (like provincial, local), government business enterprises, regulatory and assistance authorities, and a range of semi-state authorities (Davis *et al.* 1993).

All of these parts will exercise the power of the state in various ways and most of them will be involved with policy formulation to a greater or lesser degree. Many of their policies will impact directly or indirectly upon tourism development and upon communities located within the boundaries of the state. When one considers the scope of their activities, the potential for direct and indirect interaction with tourism is obvious. Despite its increasing importance for many countries, both economically and socially, some governments have failed to appreciate the size, strength, and growth of tourism and thus it is often not on their political agenda. There is frequently a mismatch between government resources devoted to tourism *vis-à-vis* other sectors. A survey by this author of 10 South Pacific island countries in 1995 revealed that their governments devoted far less resources to tourism than to their agricultural sectors despite the fact that in every case agriculture earned a fraction of the foreign exchange generated by tourism.

As noted above, there is no government, of any particular form or ideological bent that has not embraced tourism development to some degree. At one extreme lies the Peoples Democratic Republic of Korea (North Korea) whose xenophobic government has placed the most severe restrictions on tourism (tourists are rigorously screened and basically it is "Friends of Korea" only who are permitted entry visas). The "Sunshine Policy" introduced by South Korea in 1998, in which tourism based on family reunions as a way to support normalisation of relations had, by mid-2002, seen less than 1000 people cross the border. A special agreement to allow tourists from South Korea to visit sacred Mt Kumgang in North Korea had resulted in several thousands crossing the border in the same years but tourists were restricted to the one site. At the other end of the spectrum are governments with "open door" policies that facilitate visa-free entry (European Community member states that allow nationals to travel freely within the EC countries) and 30-day automatic visa-on-arrival countries (such as New Zealand that has such agreements with more than 20 countries). Following the events of September 11, 2001, when the twin towers of the World Trade Center in New York were destroyed by suicide terrorists, and the Bali bombings of October 2002, governments worldwide have re-focused on visa screening procedures to enhance security. Increasingly the "free-flow" provisions of past decades are being jettisoned as the threat of international terrorism impacts upon travel globally.

Although travel is considered a right and thus a "freedom" enjoyed by the citizens of many countries, democratic forms are not in any way a prerequisite for government involvement in tourism development. In this context, one might note the varied resources and efforts directed towards tourism development by the former socialist countries (Special Issue of *Annals of Tourism Research* on tourism in centrally planned economies 1990).

Other forms of government have also been active in tourism development. In the Philippines, Marcos used tourism in an attempt to legitimize his regime (Richter 1989). In Greece, greater emphasis on tourism development followed the imposition of a military dictatorship in 1967 (Leontidou 1988). A similar emphasis occurred in Fiji in the aftermath of the 1987 coups when General Rabuka introduced a major foreign investment incentives package for tourism to kick-start the economy (Sofield 1990a). The Chinese government, which had viewed tourism as an unacceptable industry under Mao Zedong, has pursued tourism development very vigorously since 1978 (Lew 2000; Li and Sofield 1994; Sofield and Li 1998; Swain 1990b) and it is now one of the "four pillars" for economic development in 20 of China's provinces. The Myanmah (Burmese) military junta has devoted a relatively massive effort to tourism development and promotion since 1993 in an attempt to gain acceptance and legitimization for its regime (Nwe 1993).

Socialist states, especially those with centrally controlled economies, have traditionally instituted very strong control over most forms of economic activity, including tourism development. These governments accepted responsibility for virtually all its facets, from planning to construction of both infrastructure and superstructure; from marketing to the development, management, and operation of all attractions, accommodations, and so forth; from state ownership of most tourism plant and transport to a system of state-employed guides. Such intrusive involvement was often accompanied by strict controls over the movements of both outbound and inbound tourists. In these countries, the industry was often a political tool used to showcase "development and progress".

Many Third World countries also consider that government involvement in tourism development is essential for a range of reasons. Williams and Shaw, in a European context, identified six major considerations that lead to public sector involvement in it: "improvement in the balance of payments, fostering regional development, diversification of the national economy, increase in public revenue, improvements in income levels, and the creation of new employment" (1988:7).

Most of the governments of the micro-states of the South Pacific have actively engaged in tourism development with slight variations on these themes such as the need to generate foreign exchange and employment, to revitalize economically depressed areas, to bring economic development to areas that lack other identifiable resources, to raise the capital for major development that in many of these countries is beyond local investors, to own and control a national airline, and to market the country generically. They have set up not only their own individual national tourism administrations (NTAs) and their own airlines but have also initiated *regional* action by setting up a joint tourism council that has wide responsibilities for tourism development, and the Association of South Pacific Airlines (ASPA) for coordination of air services. The micro-states of the Caribbean have also been very active in tourism development and some of the first studies into its economic and social impacts centered on case studies from this region. A major reason for the readiness of the Caribbean governments to develop their tourist industries lies in the lack of alternative resources and "the very limited economic possibilities with which they are faced" (Bryden 1973:3).

Swain has argued that for ethnic tourism development by minorities to be sustainable there needs to be a land ownership base coupled with some politically sanctioned power (1989:33). In an analysis of ethnic tourism in

Yunnan, China, she explored the articulation of state political economy, tourism capitalism, and local ethnic group economy in promoting ethnic group maintenance. Without the active support of the state (through its "Law on Regional Autonomy of Minority Nationalities 1984" and their gazetted reserve land rights) she considered that the expanding role of the Sani minority community in controling tourism businesses and the local economy would not have been possible. Swain developed a model for indigenous tourism development that specified the active and legitimizing role of the state (1989:37).

Developing countries elsewhere have followed similar patterns of direct and major government involvement in tourism development. In 1970 the Mexican Government, for example, established the National Trust for Development of Tourism (FONATUR: *Fondo Nacional de Fomento al Turismo*) that has responsibility for all developmental aspects of national tourism development, including planning, land acquisition and expropriation, foreign investment incentives, infrastructure coordination, marketing, and community relations. It is "the catalyst and coordinator of new development by the tourism industry" with a record of five major developments: Cancun, Ixtapa-Zihuatanejo, Loreto, Cabo San Lucas and Las Bahias de Huatulco (Long 1991:207). The Indonesian Government played a similar role in developing major resort destinations such as the billion dollar investment in Nusa Dua, Bali, which it is currently utilizing as the model for another nine projected developments around the archipelago (Sofield 1995). It is probable that this situation will change. After the Bali bombings in which terrorists killed more than 180 international tourists in October 2002, many governments listed Bali and Indonesia on their travel advice warnings as destinations to be avoided. Tourism numbers decreased dramatically and are likely to remain depressed for quite some time. As a consequence work on the nine tourism projects may cease, or at least slow their rate of development. According to Smith: "Government agencies at every level from the international down to small towns have adopted a progressively more active role in the use of tourism as a development tool . . ." (1989:22).

The active and expanding role of governments in tourism development in Third World countries provides a stark contrast to the trend in many western countries for a contraction of involvement. The role of a number of these governments in tourism development has been affected in the past decade by what Davis *et al.*, identified as three principal reasons: "Governments are interested in: reducing the dependency on public enterprises on public budgets, reducing public debt by selling state assets, and raising technical efficiencies by commercialization" (1993:24).

An approach based on these tenets has left local authorities to take up tourism development without any national framework in some countries such as Italy, the Netherlands, Switzerland (Gilg 1978), and Germany (Pearce 1992). The United States' tourism industry and state and local authorities are currently confronting the action of the US Government by disbanding its federal tourism administration completely. The New Zealand Government, which for many years played a major entrepreneurial role in tourism (developing attractions such as Rotorua, the Waitomo Caves complex, Mt Cook National Park and ski fields, the Milford Track, and many more, as well as running hotels and chalets, travel agencies, coach and rail tours, etc.) has since 1984 withdrawn from most developmental and operational activities and now concentrates only on marketing and promotion.

In the United Kingdom, especially under the reductionism of Prime Minister Thatcher, policy rhetoric indicated a disengagement by government in tourism development. But in fact so deep was that involvement — through a wide range of governmental and semi-governmental bodies actively pursuing the kind of objectives identified by Williams and Shaw (1988) and generating much-needed revenue for government coffers — that extricating government was by and large neither possible nor desirable. The result was that most of the involvement remained but without strong government direction, because a policy framework for that involvement was replaced by expression of a policy avowing dis-engagement. Provincial and local agencies of government faced difficulties implementing integrated strategies.

In countries such as Australia, the role of the federal government as tourism developer/entrepreneur is also subdued. It has withdrawn from airline ownership, is in the process of selling its airports, and, in March 1996, the incoming gov-ernment disbanded the Department of Tourism and incorporated it into another department. However, it remains committed to support tourism research (it estab-lished the federal Bureau of Tourism Research several years ago), and tourism promotion and tourism marketing. State and local governments in Australia also engage in these activities. At the provincial level there may be very active participation in tourism development in stark contrast to the federal sphere. The state government in Queensland charged the Queensland Tourist and Travel Corporation (QTTC) to "develop and market tourism to maximize the economic benefit of the tourism industry to Queensland" (Queensland Government 1979), and "to assist the tourism industry to develop at a faster rate and in a more beneficial manner than it would do without the benefit of government assistance" (QTTC 1993). The QTTC's current successor, Tourism Queensland, remains committed to a pro-active role in development. Further, the Northern Territory Tourist Commission (NTTC) also plays a direct role, its Act being amended in 1992 to emphasize its responsibilities as a "facilitator for tourism development" (NTTC 1993). The New South Wales Tourism Commission Act of 1985 also gave that state a major entrepreneurial role in tourism development, so much so that one commentator observed that its annual report for 1985–1986 was more of "a manifesto of entrepreneurial interest [than] an exposition of legislative responsibility" (Hollinshead 1990:46). These examples emphasize the point made by Williams and Shaw that "the study of tourism policy formulation is made more complex because the aims of the local state may diverge from those of the central state" (1988:230).

Common to all governments of whatever political persuasion is the fact that they shape the economic climate for the tourism industry, they help to provide infrastructure, they provide education and training, and they legislate the regulatory climate for business operations (Hall 1995). While many western governments may have withdrawn from previously more active roles in tourism development as privatization of government operations has entered their agendas, most nevertheless accept a major responsibility for environmental and social mitigation of the possible impacts of this industry. In Australia, the first manifests itself in a variety of ways such as the establishment of World Heritage Sites together with management strategies to integrate environmental values with tourism; bi-partisan support of the broad principles of sustainable development and tourism; and legislation on environmental impact assessment. With reference to the social impacts, federal government involvement finds strong expression in its developmental policies for Aboriginal communities (Commonwealth Government National Strategy for Aboriginal Tourism 1994); and for heritage values, where it provides funding for a wide range of activities from restoration and conservation of historic buildings and sites to construction of museums (such as the National Maritime Museum), to publications about heritage and history, and so on.

The use of tourism as a tool for economic development by governments is now well established, although the focus of much of the early literature on the promise of it as an economic panacea has been tempered by more accurate analysis of real benefits and costs, a better understanding of the leakage factor, social costs and opportunity cost (Bryden 1973; Jenkins 1980; Pearce 1989; Sofield 1993; Tisdell, Aislabie, and Stanton 1988).

Development Theory

There is a vast literature on development that has spawned a variety of meanings and interpretations of the term. It has been used to describe both a process and a state, and different disciplines will utilize the term to mean different things. When referring to social and economic change it is defined as a process.

When it refers to a condition (for example, a country may be classified as "developed" or "undeveloped"), it is used to describe a state of being. Often these interpretations will be used interchangeably and care must be taken to examine the context in which the term is placed. Bernstein (1973) considers development as the progressive transformation of society. Friedmann considers that it has a structure, since it is always "development ... *of* something particular, a human being, a society, a nation ... often associated with words such as *under* or *over* or *balanced*; ... which suggests that development has a structure and [the analyst] has some idea of how this structure *ought* to be developed" (1980:14; italics in the original).

Sociologists, social anthropologists and political scientists (Bernstein 1973; Eisenstadt 1966; Geertz 1963; Nisbet 1972; Varma 1980), less so economists (Hirschman 1959, 1975; Rostow 1960), have drawn a distinction between economic growth and development. The former is quantitative, the latter qualitative. O'Dowd makes the same distinction: growth is "a quantitative process, involving principally the extension of an already established structure of production, whereas development suggests qualitative changes, the creation of new economic and non-economic structures" (1967:153).

Mehmet also draws a distinction between economic growth and development, but changes the emphasis somewhat by referring to the two terms as a shift from elitist to egalitarian principles. For him, the former has a narrow focus and refers to "the expansion of national income or production, most typically measured as GNP or GDP per capita, as a result of increased capital formation and input utilization". Development, on the other hand, has a much broader meaning and refers to "a general improvement in the material and social well-being of the society as a whole" (1978:175). A higher per capita income is only part of a general improvement in living standards: reforms in the institutional or quasi-economic framework are also required. These include a more equitable distribution of the benefits of progress, and wider accessibility to educational, health, and welfare facilities. They may be achieved through sound economic planning. Mehmet also advocates greater political participation in the national decision-making process as an integral feature of development, because in his view an open society is a prerequisite to more equal opportunity.

The elitist/egalitarian differentiation is also made by others, based on the fundamental difference between the rate and pattern of economic change in a society. Statistically, a less developed country (LDC) may achieve an impressive GNP growth; yet this growth may reflect a lopsided, uneven pattern with the mass of the population receiving marginal benefits or even being more disadvantaged than before, while a small privileged elite increases its wealth and power.

As early as 1957, Myrdal emphasized the need to transcend the then conventional segregation of economic and noneconomic factors in order to understand development in dynamic and relational terms, rather than as a static condition of backwardness. Inherent in his analysis is the notion of circular and cumulative causation, in which "market forces, rather than having a positive distributive and stimulating effect in fact sustained and even intensified existing unequal relationships" (1957:25).

Bernstein, agreeing with Myrdal, states that "The distinction between underdevelopment and development denotes the transformation of given historical conditions; and the question of how this is to be achieved, as well as particular outcomes, will reflect the often conflicting conceptions and interests of different social groups" (1973:20).

He considers it necessary to get away from the notion that development is a process and underdevelopment is conceived in a static fashion as a state: that "underdeveloping" is also a process, as a phenomenon that has emerged historically. This notion aspires to and is inseparable from development. The historical perspective enhances an awareness that the forms of development of one period can become those of "underdevelopment" of another period. Amin (1974) critiqued underdevelopment theory, arguing that it was as much a process as development. Balandier points out that research devoted to "backward" societies disrupted by the introduction of modern technology and forms of economy "capture an evolutionary moment which differentiates essentially the various types of global societies" (1965:87), and this approach may lock a country into a particular perception of its development which belies the dynamic nature of the process. Thus development and underdevelopment must be analyzed longitudinally.

Douglas Pearce (1989) provides an overview of the ambiguity associated with the usage of the concept, quoting from a wide range of sources. One source is Rostow (1960), whose widely cited views focus on development as a linear evolution through five successive stages of economic growth — traditional, transitional, take-off, maturity, and high mass consumption. Another is D. Smith (1977), who noted that "development was frequently assumed to be an economic condition" commonly measured by the economic indicator, GNP per capita, but which should be extended to broader, less technical factors such as "welfare improvement". A third source is Seers, whose two seminal papers (1969, 1977), assisted in moving the definition away from the narrow confines of development as economic growth to incorporate social concerns such as poverty, unemployment, inequality (1969), and subsequently, self-reliance (1977). These elements brought the meaning of development to the point of Bernstein's social transformation, stressing the interrelationship between production and distribution, between developed centers and under-developed peripheries, linking it closely to dependency theory. As such it was a critique of the capitalist mode of production and its call for transformation in the realm of Marxist ideology became a call for revolution. Fourth is Mabogunje (1980), who having identified the concept of development as moving through four successive but coexisting definitional stages of development as economic growth, as modernization, as distributive justice, and as socio-economic transformation, then added his own fifth notion, that of development as spatial reorganization. There is according to Mabogunje,

> the need for a pattern of social relations which can inculcate new processes of production requires the reconstruction of spatial structures both in the rural and urban areas of a country . . . certain types of spatial arrangements can be expected to make a relatively better contribution to the attainment of specified goals than others . . . thus spatial reorganization is seen as synonymous with development (1980:65–68, cited in Pearce 1989).

A more detailed examination of the major theories of development over the past 50 years will facilitate discussion in Chapter 3 of the place of empowerment in the development debate. Included here are the "widening gap" theory, "take-off" theory, the "big push" theory, modernization theory, dependency theory, articulation theory and — the most recent to join the stable — sustainable development. It will be seen that there has been some movement towards concepts such as self-determination and self-management that reach out towards empowerment; but for the most part empowerment has yet to be accepted as a fundamental component of development. However, it is increasingly finding its way into discussions about community development in the context of self-assertion over destiny.

The thrust of the following examinations of various development theories is oriented towards Third World countries (a term that is becoming increasingly difficult to define) since the island countries of South Pacific are so classified. For this reason it also does not explore in any detail Keynesian theory which is more related to economic developments in mature, industrialized capitalist societies, nor classical Marxist theory related to the ideology of centrally-controlled economies, although both are mentioned where relevant.

Development in the Aftermath of World War Two

As the global economy began to revive in the aftermath of World War Two and countries set about the tasks of reconstruction and development, the desired objective of many was to progress toward the economic standards to be found in the most advanced societies of the modern world. Out of this cauldron of concern came the body of work collectively labeled as "development theory": a wide range of various social science approaches that have tried to explain and understand the process of societal change in Third World countries that took place in the postwar period.

Socialist countries of the communist bloc pursued Marxist philosophy that went beyond the more materialistic objectives of capitalism. It encompassed concepts of welfare and equality in which the resources and the means of production were owned and managed by the state in a centrally-controlled economy. For capitalist, western countries, the model they pursued was variously known as "modern society (modernization)", industrial society, mass society, and so on. The world was divided into those countries that were advanced or developed, and those that were not. Undeveloped countries would progress towards this model as soon as they eliminated certain social, political, cultural, and institutional obstacles. These obstacles were represented by terms such as "traditional societies", feudal systems or feudal residues. Imperial powers would pay their part in securing the economic progress of advancing their colonies to higher standards of living.

Economic planning for the less developed countries became a growth industry, initially promoted by western countries motivated by a multiplicity of objectives. Some of these motivations were commercially based, some were strategic, some even military in nature, and some were humanitarian. Rivalry developed between the two competing ideologies of capitalism and communism and aid for development became a tool of the "Cold War".

Varma called these two competing models of development "the revolutionary model" (Marxism) and "the evolutionary model" (capitalism and modernization) (1980:22). Initially, the communist countries had little capacity to provide funding for economic development (revolution came first), and Marxism as a globally valid paradigm was simply to be applied to Third World countries and their development needs without any real modification. The outgrowth of development theory thus took place in the western social sciences.

Whatever the foreign policy objectives of major powers involved in delivering development assistance, the economic rationalization was the "widening-gap" theory (Myrdal 1965, *Rich Land and Poor Land*; Ranis 1972, *The Gap Between Rich and Poor Nations*; Ward, D'Anjou, and Runnals 1971, *The Widening Gap: Development in the 1970s*; Zimmerman 1965, *Poor Lands, Rich Lands: The Widening Gap*). This was predicated on the argument that the advanced industrialized countries of the west were becoming richer while the underdeveloped countries of the Third World were becoming poorer. In western eyes the gap could be closed over time by the injection of sufficient amounts of capital, in exactly the way that the Marshall Plan had laid the foundations for the miracle of post-war reconstruction in Europe. Development was synonymous with economic growth, and it was to be fostered by rapid industrialization built on technology and know-how imported from the western world and "advanced" communist nations.

Little attempt was made to adapt the idiomatic European footings of the theory (embedded in the value systems, political and other institutions of western "civilization") and to rework concepts in transferring the formulae to the environments and circumstances of the LDCs. As Mehmet noted:

> The appropriateness or the capacity of political and social insti-
> tutions to absorb large inflows of foreign funds, or to manage
> a controlled process of rapid change were rarely taken into
> account. The efficiency of the governmental machinery and
> bureaucracy to implement and monitor large scale development
> projects was seldom questioned. Neither was the moral commit-
> ment of the leadership to economic and industrial expansion
> doubted. It was as if there existed only one single constraint on
> industrial expansion: capital shortage. Given generous foreign
> aid programs and foreign investment, rapid industrial take-off
> was only a matter of time (1978:17).

Rostow (1960) was the principal proponent of the take-off theory. To trans-form a stagnant, low-income LDC into one experiencing a steady growth path would, he argued, take only one or two decades of assistance. It would achieve maturity and consolidate its position as a developed nation through high levels of mass consumption.

Take-off could be accomplished by "the big push" (Rosenstein-Rodan 1963). Its theorists argued that all resources should be concentrated on industrialization. Scarce development funds should not be dispersed across other sectors since the "growth poles" were to be found only in the manufacturing and non-agricultural sectors. The maximum impact in the shortest possible time could only be achieved through a single-minded concentration on industrialization. Some even advocated the deliberate use of inflationary financing through such tactics as forced savings or by printing more money, on the assumption that a higher level of national output was only a few years ahead that would bring it under control. For this reason, all other social needs and reforms, such as education and man-power development, administrative modernization, and agrarian development, could be postponed until industrialization was sufficiently advanced to become a self-sustaining process. "In short, industrialization, with aid and technology, was the panacea to break the poverty trap in which the countries of the Third World found themselves, owing to their largely stagnant subsistence sectors" (Mehmet 1978:18). Income maximization via industrialization became the target of development as proposed by the take-off and big push theorists.

The typical development plan in the early post-war period was a macro model based on certain key aggregate relationships between employment, output, and investment. For example, the 1955 annual meeting of the United Nations Economic Commission for Asia and the Far East (UNECAFE) declared that "The rate of economic growth may be analytically considered as being the function of two factors: the rate of capital formation; and the capital/output ratio. Accordingly, development policies may be described as aiming to increase the former, reduce the latter, or do both" (UNECAFE 1955:7).

This approach to development was flawed in that theoretical assumptions about fixed input-output relations (often impossible to measure accurately in Third World countries) created an intolerable degree of inflexibility in prescribing methods of production. India's planning experience is a good example of the difficulties of this approach. Its first three five-year plans were based on the "grand strategy" of developing heavy industry first, centered on the creation of a self-sufficient Indian iron and steel industry, and over time achieving optimal sectoral linkage. Thus, while heavy industry was given priority, agricultural production was not accorded the same attention and the import of foods and agricultural machinery led to a severe balance of payments crisis and a slow-down in the rate of economic growth.

Other LDCs experienced similar difficulties with the industrialization approach to development. They may have recorded impressive aggregate rates of growth of manufacturing output during the 1950s and 1960s, but employment in the manufacturing sectors increased on average by only about half of the output growth rate. Indeed, in some countries (such as Thailand and Algeria) the level of employment in manufacturing actually declined as capital intensive, mechanized technology proved more efficient (Morawetz 1974). The drive for industrialization was in many cases an inappropriate strategy for providing adequate opportunity for burgeoning labor forces and the resulting frustration posed constant threats to political stability. In other words, the neoclassical growth theory in which unemployment was regarded as "an essentially transitory problem" that would disappear with growth in output, failed in many LDCs where very high population growth rates confounded theoretical formalism (Bettelheim 1961:294).

Adelman and Morris (1973) in their work linking social, political and institutional factors with economic data considered that maldistribution of income in LDCs arose from "socioeconomic dualism" reflecting unequal allocation of political, economic, and social opportunities in those countries. They examined 35 independent variables for 43 countries ranging from the level of GNP to "the degree of social tension", "the extent of leadership commitment to economic development", etc., and converted them to numerical scores on a cardinal scale ranging from 0–100. Their initial (arbitrary) gradings were subsequently submitted to a group of 30 independent experts involved in planning work in LDCs, who validated virtually all of their grades. The results of the Adelman and Morris study indicated that those who derived the most benefit from post-war economic growth were those already in the wealthiest income groups. As a whole, the richest 5 percent received an income share of 30 percent, and the poorest 60 percent had an average income share of only 26 percent. Their overall conclusion on the impact of post-war development (that is, economic growth) for the 43 countries was that:

> development is accompanied by an absolute as well as relative decline in the average income of the very poor [and that] . . . hundreds of millions of desperately poor people throughout the world have been hurt rather than helped by economic development. Unless their destinies become a major and explicit focus of development policy . . . economic development may serve merely to promote social injustice (1973:189, 192).

While these findings were criticized by a number of observers (including Rayner 1970; Lal 1984), others such as the International Labor Organization (ILO) and the World Bank supported their conclusions. Chenery in a study for the World Bank stated that "It is now clear that a decade of rapid growth in underdeveloped countries has been of little or no benefit to perhaps a third of their population" (World Bank 1974:xiii).

The flaws revealed in the application of the neoclassical theory of growth confronted western economists with a fundamental conflict between two major themes: efficiency in production and equity in distribution of that production.

A major ethical problem was that western ideals of democracy espoused equity issues, yet the development processes being pursued — even where they did lead to growth in GNP — was accompanied in most cases by greater income concentration in the top layer of the socioeconomic pyramid with mass poverty at the bottom (Meade 1961). Mehmet put it succinctly: "Equity was sacrificed for the sake of [economic] efficiency" (1978:18).

Given the record of increased inequality that economic growth brought to a significant number of LDCs, the ideals of social or distributive justice (welfare economics) began to find a place in development planning in the 1970s.

The first tentative steps toward empowerment may be identified with the use by Mehmet and others of such terms as "egalitarian planning", "self-reliance", "reduced dependency", "decentralized action" and the need for "equity principles" to embrace a form of development that allowed "the masses" to participate in decision-making processes. In the late 1960s and even in some quarters into the 1970s however, equity considerations were not usually accepted as integral elements of "development".

The ILO in its 1976 Declaration on Employment Growth and Basic Needs (World Employment Program, Geneva), constituted one of the first indications of a growing international acceptance of the link between economic development and equity principles. The United Nations General Assembly Declaration and Program of Action on the Establishment of a New International Economic Order (NIEO 1985) was not accepted with the same degree of approval, and launched an acrimonious debate between the "have" nations of the North and the "have-not" nations of the South (the so-called "north–south dialogue") that continues to this day, albeit in a more orderly form than first enjoined. The principal premise underlying the NIEO was that sustained domestic development in the Third World could not be achieved until the existing mercantilist system of international trade was restructured drastically to promote equitable global distribution of incomes and resources.

Modernization Theory

The development paradigm that encompassed these various approaches to economic and sociopolitical change at the national level came to be known as "modernization theory". It took shape in the 1950s and 1960s. It draws *inter alia* upon the work of social science theorists such as Weber, Durkheim, Main, and Tonnies. While the nation state is the primary unit of analysis, modernization theory also accords importance to institutions and collective patterns of behavior. In essence, the theory postulates two types of society: traditional and modern. These societies form consistent coherent wholes and are positioned at opposite ends of a graduated spectrum whereby over time the traditional society would progress, via the development process, to the status of a modern economy epitomized by capitalist, western characteristics. This change would be gradual and internally rather than externally generated (Rostow 1952). It was a highly Eurocentric view of the world: the European nations were developed, the others were not.

Following Weber (1930, 1978), Durkheim (1933, 1961), and others, traditional societies in the context of modernization theory were perceived as exhibiting low social, economic, and political differentiation where "social relationships are based on kinship, religious affiliation, regionalism and ethnic identity" (Friedmann 1980:16). In these societies, generally status is ascribed rather than achieved (note the contrast here between the hereditary, royal lineages of Polynesian and Micronesian societies and the achieved status of "bigmen" in Melanesian society). Face-to-face relationships are vital because individuals play multifaceted roles depending upon the social context.

Economic effort tends to be inflexible in the sense that the network of over-lapping reciprocal obligations and social relationships in which each individual is bound, makes it difficult to engage in new sorts of economic activity. Economic risk is minimized rather than opportunities for potential benefits being maximized, so change is slow. The society is seen as basically static. Political authority is vested in custom — "traditional legitimacy" as Weber (1978:19) described it — in which sacred power and supernatural forces shape world-views rather than rational, mechanistic explanations. Thus, social, eco-nomic, and political order tends to acquire sacred legitimization (Durkheim 1961).

By contrast, modern societies (according to modernization theory) exhibit very different characteristics. They are highly differentiated socially, politically, and economically, with many degrees of specialization. Role play is conse-quently limited as individuals do not have to interact with one another across multiple contexts. Status tends to be achieved rather than ascribed, society sets goals based on certain principles of universality so individuals are able to acquire positions on merit rather than kinship ties or inheritance. Economic activity is flexible since the individual is not bound by strong communal ties to share and distribute the products (and profits) of his labor. The nuclear family unit predominates over community. Legal (constitutional) forms constitute the basis for political authority and a public service bureaucracy is central to systems of administration. Often rapid change may be favored by these insti-tutions of the state, by communities and by individuals, and the prevailing secularization promotes a pragmatic world-view that encourages rational deci-sion-making in many fields of endeavor. Entrepreneurship is seen as a positive contributor to development.

The early proponents of modernization theory defined the process in terms of structural functionalism (Parsons, Weber, Smelser, Rostow, and others). They conceived of it as a one-way ("neo-evolutionary") street in which the superior economic and technological complex of the developed society was adopted. Further, by an inevitable process of diffusion ("the imperatives of compati-bility" as Parsons termed them) all the accompanying structures of the modern society — cultural beliefs, legal institutions, patterns of family organization (the nuclear family unit replacing the extended family), and political institutions — are also replaced by their traditional counterparts.

Smelser (1964) focused on the structural discontinuities of the modernization process. This included the problems that arise during the period of transition when old social orders are disintegrating and the new "compatible" ones are slow in being institutionalized. Others have advocated the simultaneous transfer of political, social, and cultural structures with the diffusion of the economic/technological complex as a means to facilitate the transition.

A number of planning practitioners such as experts from UN agencies and the World Bank have often in their economic development plans recommended the re-organization ("westernisation") of social and cultural institutions as "prerequisites" for economic growth and as "conditions" to be met before the delivery of their aid and "development" loans. Some have proselytized about the advantages of underdeveloped countries being able to "modernize" without having to undergo the century-long trauma of a British industrial revolution; and from the other side of the coin some have lamented the destruction of idyllic forms of traditional social solidarity and the disappearance of tribal social values (Crocombe 1987; Hoogvelt 1986).

With the differences between traditional and modern societies thus sharply delineated, modernization theory posits the thesis that the nature of traditional society is both an expression and a cause of underdevelopment. As such, tradition forms a barrier to development. Major and fundamental change must occur across social, cultural, political and economic values, institutions, and patterns of action if modernization is to occur. There are four main components of the modernization paradigm:

- Development is a spontaneous, irreversible process inherent in every single society.
- Development implies structural differential and functional specialization.
- The processes of development can be divided into distinct stages showing the level of development achieved by each society.
- Development can be stimulated by external competition or military threat and by internal measures that support modern sectors and modernize traditional sectors (Hettne 1995: 50–51).

Rostow's (1952) evolutionary stages of development fitted comfortably into the modernization paradigm, since he postulated that western countries had

progressed from an initial stage of underdevelopment, supposedly characteristic of all traditionally oriented societies, to their present, developed stage.

The evolutionary element of modernization makes Marxism in a sense a variation of modernization because this form of development emphasizes the linear
transition of traditional and feudal societies to higher stages through internal
class struggle. Development is assured because of Marxist support for the
modernizing of traditional sectors through the scientific application of knowledge. Therefore, all transitions to a new stage are evidence of progress and
"development" (Hettne 1995).

The deficiencies of a structural functionalist approach to modernization are
now more clearly understood. There is no longer acceptance that diffusion is
inevitable, that "westernization" is inescapable and that non-western institutions
are incompatible with the economic and technological superiority of developing
societies. Japan is the example *par excellence* where its progress to becoming
one of the world's most advanced powers has been accomplished with the retention of a full measure of its own social and cultural institutions. China is
currently displaying a similar capacity to retain traditional forms despite the
rapidity of its modernization.

By the 1970s modernization theory was squarely in the sights of a number
of writers who *inter alia* considered that it was Eurocentric by its insistence on
measuring development progress in terms of a country's proximity to the institutions and values of western models (Nisbet 1972). Modernization theory was
also questioned by critics such as Frank (1966) and Wallerstein (1974) as being
historical and an apologia for colonialism. That is, there was no stage prior to
underdevelopment; so all traditionally oriented societies had no history before
their colonization, yet all western countries had advanced from underdeveloped
to developed. There was thus no account taken by modernization theory of the
influences exerted by Europe's imperial powers from the 16th century to the
present on their colonies. These intrusions, according to critics of the modernization theory, forced the "superiority" of the western, capitalist model on the
"inferior" institutions of the traditionally oriented society and accounted for
their structure of underdevelopment. Frank (1966) argued that modernization
was empirically untenable, theoretically deficient, and in a practical sense incapable of stimulating development in the Third World. It could not account for
the strong particularistic characteristics of many such countries. It was from
arguments similar to these that dependency theory evolved.

Weiner (1969) commented that modernization theorists tended to confuse
two separate concepts of tradition. The first defined modernization analytically
as the opposite of modernity. The second defined modernization empirically as
whatever is inherited from the past. Traditional culture was thus held up as a

radical contrast to modernity and because of the strength and persistence of its staying power was seen as a barrier to change requiring a "powerful anti-dote" to counter it if a society was to "progress" or modernize. Varma, for example, stated that the barriers to modernization were many, stemming mainly "from traditional folkways and mores, such as familism and casteism, to attitudes such as fatalism or other-worldliness. These traits develop over centuries and the socialization of the young takes place in terms of these values" (1980:3–4).

Weber (1976) was probably the most influential of a stable of writers who advocated the need for a carefully planned strategy to counter this barrier. Other writers sought a more unequivocal attack on the barrier, a strategy variously described as "a sledge-hammer reform model" (Peacock 1986), or "the sociology of pain" (Davis 1987). Varma called for ways to raise the level of aspirations of people in underdeveloped countries because "the success of modernization depends very much upon how high a level of aspiration among the population is transformed into new kinds of motivation" (1980:4).

In a similar vein to Varma, Weber and others, Hapgood and Bennet (1968) writing about the *raison d'être* for the American Peace Corps, noted that the people of most undeveloped societies saw change as a threat. They tended to be inflexibly bound to their traditions and resistant to the new: "If in fact the character patterns of people in developing countries had already evolved sufficiently to make change a positive value . . . there would be little need for a Peace Corps" (1968:28).

This view quite clearly followed the prevailing thought of the time that modernization was a unilinear evolution from the "backward", underdeveloped, traditionally oriented society to one espousing and implementing the values and patterns of behavior of "modern" societies. Despite expressed concerns about the capacity of tradition to stall modernization, the early theorists of the latter considered that the passing of tradition was in fact inevitable (Lerner 1958; Levy 1966). Such researchers were both unilinear evolutionists and convergence theorists: there would be global convergence towards western capitalism. Some saw no cause for regret in this: the sooner the world modernized the sooner world poverty and misery could be alleviated. Others saw great dangers in the destruction of traditional societies and a gradual move to conformity.

The threat that tourism posed to traditional societies in this view of modernization was the thrust of much of the early anthropological and sociological literature about tourism. Valene Smith, for example, commented that most of the contributors to her seminal volume "Hosts and Guests" considered the impacts of tourism "to be more negative than positive" (1977:14). Jafari (1990) characterized the tenor of this approach to tourism studies as the "cautionary platform". This was one of four research positions Jafari defined and in his view it grew out of a rejection of the claims of the "advocacy platform" that preceded it and that extolled the benefits — economic, social, environmental and developmental — prospects of tourism. By contrast, writers of the "cautionary platform" focused on the undesirable consequences of tourism, alleging *inter alia* that its economic benefits were over-rated and that it

> generates mostly seasonal and unskilled jobs, that it benefits only tourism firms and big corporations, that it destroys nature and scenic formations; that it commoditizes people and their cultures; and that it disrupts the structure of the host society (Jafari 1990:34).

Cohen (1988a), drawing upon the concepts of authenticity (especially the work of MacCannell 1976) and commoditization (Greenwood 1977) produced a paradigmatic case for this negativity. He argued that common to the analyses of MacCannell, Greenwood, and others was the assumption that tourism commoditized culture and in the process destroyed its authenticity: the latter was replaced with "staged authenticity".

It is of interest that both modernization theorists and critics of tourism's perceived impacts held similar views about the nature of the process of cultural change, the incompatibility of traditional and modern cultures, and the greater force of the latter (Wood 1993). They tended to differ, however, in their value judgments about whether such change was to be welcomed or lamented.

The broad generalizations about the anti-developmental qualities of traditional societies were subsequently modified by area specialists who progressively entered the debate. They disputed the sweeping assumptions of the early modernization theorists, noting how tradition could be reconstructed, adapted and even harnessed for development and modernity (Apter 1972; Eisenstadt 1966; Geertz 1963; Gusfield 1967; Huntington 1968; Rudolph and Rudolph 1967; Singer 1972). Geertz (1963) particularly was influential in developing a much more sophisticated exploration of modernization that moved away from equating it with "development" at a national level to a more nuanced and complex process of counter-tendencies in which aspects of traditional society asserted themselves over or adapted aspects to control modernity and the pace and form of change.

Then came the dependency theorists (and Marxists) whose attack on modernization in the late 1960s and early 1970s reinforced the views of those positioned in the cautionary platform. They moved beyond writers such as

Geertz, who had already modified the basic tenets of modernization, to demolish the distinction drawn between tradition–modernity. They argued that what the modernization theorists called "traditional" was not simply compatible with modernity but was in fact modern, in the sense of being a creation of, or an adaptation to the modern world capitalist system. They challenged the equation between modernity and development and argued that the relationship between tradition (which they defined as the outcome of the incorporation of the periphery into the world capitalist system) and modernity (capitalist imperialism) had produced not development but "underdevelopment".

Dependency theory incorporated prevailing analyses of imperialism and colonialism, in which dominant powers exploited colonies at the periphery to further develop their own metropolitan economies at the expense of the latter. Implicit in this analysis was the notion that development and underdevelopment could only be understood in the context of global capitalism (Hettne 1995). Given that all South Pacific countries were colonies (several, such as American Samoa, New Caledonia, and French Polynesia, remain under metropolitan tutelage) the issue of colonialism is enlarged before the focus is returned to dependency theory.

Colonialism

Colonialism as a feature of conquest has a recorded history of many centuries, stretching over 5000 years of Chinese governance and more than 3000 years of Middle Eastern and European history. The focus of this review, however, is basically on the post-1945 situation, although of necessity it must incorporate elements pre-dating this time.

Van den Berghe (1982), in surveying theories and ideologies of ethnic relations and development, suggested that colonialism saw virtually all ethnic groups move through three stages based on the regulation of competition for scarce resources by means of territoriality and specialization (before the advent of independent states as the global norm, when many countries were colonies and tribal affiliations were the extent of ethnic cohesion) to a fourth stage where coercion and hierarchy played (and continue to play) a salient role in ethnic relations. Dominance, exerted through a hierarchical structure that resorted to a range of coercive practices, determined in any individual state the order of access of different ethnic groups to resources. For van den Berghe, this group stratification evolved with the modern state, "a collectivity headed by a group of people who exercise power over others in order to extract surplus production for their own individual and collective benefit" (1982:61).

The ideology most often used to legitimize the *status quo* of colonial governance in pre-industrial countries was paternalism: the conquerors were by definition of their victory superior and those conquered were inferior. Colonies were often characterized by extreme social distance between masters and subjects, rigidity of ethnic boundaries, by exploitation and domination, bipolarity of living standards, and elaboration of self-serving ideologies (Balandier 1970a). Stereotyping of superiority/inferiority could be found in phrases such as "they" are simply not like "us"; "they" are "primitive and savage" while "we" are "civilized".

For van den Berghe:

> The essence of the [colonial] state is intraspecific — indeed, intrasocietal parasitism. The state [in effect the ruling class, the parasitic class] is the coercive apparatus used by the few to exploit the many. ... Plunder and predation between human societies existed long before the rise of the state. With the emergence of the state however, parasitism was extended within societies (1982:60).

Colonies were often distinguished as those of settlement or of exploitation (Bernstein 1973; van den Berghe 1982). Temperate areas that had been colonized by Europe — such as the United States, Canada, Australia, New Zealand and Argentina — involved the movement of people. In effect they were extensions of Europe where Caucasian settlers displaced the original inhabitants (whose populations tended by comparison to be small, and often nomadic) and quickly became the majority. These areas developed as "colonies of settlement" and the pattern of agriculture that emerged was significantly different from that in the tropical countries where mainly capital and enterprise were involved in the movement from the metropole to produce "colonies of exploitation" (Bernstein 1973:121).

White settlers may have chafed at their treatment by their metropolitan powers but they remained by and large kith and kin of the home population. Therefore, relations were "always of the intra-ethnic type and exploitation and domination were restrained by law, custom, religion and countless civilities" (van den Berghe 1982:87). Rebellions there were (like the American War of Independence), but they were managed (and fought) with a degree of civility lacking in the brutal suppression of non-European ethnic rebellions (such as the Zulu Wars).

Even in the tiny South Pacific countries, signs of unrest could unleash relatively massive retaliations. The French brutally suppressed a Kanak uprising in New Caledonia in 1903, killing more than 1000 out of a total Kanak population of about 22,000; (there were, according to Cler (1987) 21,768 at the time of the 1901 population census). An attempt by a small band of Malaitans (about 50) in Solomon Islands in 1927 to refute colonial control, that resulted in the deaths of an Australian district officer, a British doctor and 14 Solomon Island policemen, drew a massive response from the British Government. During a six-month campaign it sent a cruiser to bombard villages, an army of 600 from Australia, and a special local conscript force of 100 to hunt down the perpetrators. They burned numerous villages, destroyed crops and livestock, killed "about" 65 men, women and children, and captured and hung nine warriors (Keesing and Corris 1980).

In colonies of exploitation, development constraints were of a different kind from colonies of settlement. They were characterized by the colonialists remaining a small (often very small) elite among much larger populations of "natives". In addition to capital and enterprise, the plantation structure was often characterized by imported labor, first slavery, then indentured labor. Thus, the rubber plantations of Malaya and Sumatra drew most of their labor force from China, Java, and India. Hawaii's sugar plantations relied on Chinese, Japanese, and Filipino labor. Sri Lanka's tea plantations relied upon imported labor from Tamil Nadu in southern India. Fiji's sugar industry was built on indentured labor from India. Queensland's sugar industry utilized the "blackbirding" of Pacific Islanders for its labor force. Imperial domination was thus compounded by immigrant ethnic domination in some countries. For example, at the time of the military coup in Fiji in 1987, Indo-Fijians were the majority ethnic group with 51 percent of the population and Fijians only 44 percent; in New Caledonia, French policies of inward migration have reduced the local Melanesian (Kanak) population to less than 43 percent of the total (Sofield 1992).

The main task of the colonialists was to transfer the resources and wealth of the territories back to the metropolitan power as expeditiously as possible. The principal constraints were those imposed by distance from the metropolitan power, lack of adequate staff and budgets to administer often large territories, the capacity of the local populations to avoid exactions (who were often quite astute at avoidance), and in some cases a lack of natural resources in the colonies. For example, in the South Pacific with the exception of Nauru and Banaba (phosphates), New Caledonia (nickel) and to a lesser extent Fiji (gold), the island colonies lacked mineral resources. The mineral wealth of Papua New Guinea (copper, gold, and most recently oil) was only exploited in a major way after World War Two.

Agricultural resources of the South Pacific islands were limited basically to coconut plantations, some tropical timber, and after 1880 sugar in Fiji. The relationship between the "home" colonial office and their "native" populations were fundamentally different from those enjoyed by colonies of settlement. European political control was obtained and maintained largely through superior technology for warfare and of transportation. Whether the colonizers were British, French, German, Dutch, American, Australian, or New Zealanders, the exploitation of native, tropical populations by small Caucasian minorities, followed the same basic pattern and produced the prototypic colonial situation (Balandier 1970a; van den Berghe 1982). Their economies were predicated on the same conception of their function: colonies existed to produce raw materials for European industry and agricultural commodities for European consumption. They also served as a market for cheap European manufactured goods.

Three key economic policies followed logically from this concept. One was the maintenance of a constant supply of cheap labor, with the control of it most often achieved through coercion. Throughout the South Pacific the imposition of a head tax guaranteed a continuous supply of labor, since the subsistence villagers were outside the monetized economy. "Work", as defined by the colonial administration, was for many the only way to pay the head tax — either by wages or by a term of labor deemed equivalent to the value of the tax. In some colonies labor supply was guaranteed by dispossessing the indigenes of their land to open up the areas for large European-controlled plantations or ranches. But while some of this occurred in the South Pacific, in most cases alienated land constituted less than 10 percent of the total. New Caledonia was an exception; less than 1000 French farmers hold title to one third of the land; mining companies hold title to another third; the government has alienated a further 20 percent; and the Kanaks have been compressed into *tribus* (reserves) occupying only 10 percent of the land (Sofield 1992).

The second key policy was a monopoly by the metropolitan power of all trade with its own colonies, to the exclusion of rival colonial powers. This was a trade pattern common to all parts of global colonial empires. The third was the deliberate fostering of economic dependency of the colony on the metropolitan power. Self-sufficiency, except at the subsistence level, was discouraged. Diversification of exports was rarely pursued and so-called mono-economies were a characteristic of many colonies including copper in Zambia; sisal in Tanganyika (now Tanzania); cocoa in the Gold Coast (now Ghana); coffee in Kenya and Brazil; sugar in the West Indies, Mauritius, and Fiji; copra in Samoa, Tonga, Solomon Islands, and New Hebrides (now Vanuatu), with the products being tied to artificially low prices imposed by the metropolitan power. These economic policies were underpinned by a sharp dichotomy of social roles in which colonialism maintained inequality along ethnic boundaries.

Fundamentally, the plantation system was international in character. It was derived from external stimulus and enterprise. It produced for external markets.

It was, and often still is, largely underwritten by external finance. Its marketing has been international. The transport of produce to world markets (shipping) has always been externally controlled. Thus, while there are many references to "the plantation economy" as if it were a complete and separate system, in fact plantations are only part of a much wider economic system: the financial and industrial centers are usually in regions remote from the plantations themselves (Britton 1977, 1980, 1982).

The extent to which the plantation system is dependent upon the center revolves around the degree to which the latter exerts control. This control usually takes two forms: property ownership, and/or political power that impacts upon prices, tariffs, and loan funds. Direct political control may no longer be exercised as in colonial times, but indirect forms may today still govern the pattern of resource allocation and production in countries where plantations are located (Britton 1980, 1982). Such indirect controls may take the form of a monopoly over production, quarantine regulations imposed by the importing metropolitan country, financial control through foreign exchange and banking system legislation, control of shipping, and the specifications of quality and volume demanded by the manufacturing/refining plant in the metropolitan country. It is this form of control over economies where plantations predominate that has led to the derogatory term "banana republics" to denote that they are independent in name only.

Structural features of the plantation economy typically include foreign ownership, export orientated effort, low skill content of plantation labor forces (making it difficult to transfer them into other sectors when plantations become increasingly mechanized), unequal distribution of incomes, transfer of profits, and a rigid, often racially-based social structure (Beckford 1973:149). The particular characteristics of plantation enterprises, especially where they are multinational corporate enterprises, and the dependent nature of the economies dominated by them, suggest that inefficiencies are perpetuated and the potential for development is limited. Allocative inefficiencies arise from the structural characteristics of plantation enterprises, in particular the vertical and horizontal integration across national boundaries, and the high degree of capital specificity that is typical of the production process.

Trade expanded dramatically throughout the decades of colonialism, but very uneven development occurred in the peripheral countries. The major contribution to and the beneficiaries of the dynamism of capitalism were in the metropolitan countries into whose economies the colonial ventures were integrated. Only when the type of enterprises called for the absorption of a large number of wage earners — such as the tea plantations in Ceylon (now Sri Lanka) — did the effect of the capitalistic organization on the local economy become of major importance. Mining as in Rhodesia accounted for less than 5 percent of the total local labor market and ranching even less.

Where colonialism was accompanied by improved health services and burgeoning populations, if the export sector remained stationary that population growth could lead to an enforced reduction in the average real wage level and a decline in per capita income. Ghana and some of the plantation economies of the Caribbean and the South Pacific exhibited this process of underdevelopment. Indeed, in countries like Solomon Islands, Kiribati since the cessation of phosphate mining on Banaba Island, and Vanuatu, this process may be recognized today. An annual population growth rate of more than 3.5 percent has seen Solomon Islands' population rise from 265,000 at the time of the 1976 census to more than 420,000 in 2000, while the estimated per capita income has decreased by 35 percent over the same period of time. In the Polynesian countries of Western Samoa, Tonga, the Cook Islands, and Niue, the same would be true. But because overseas remittances from very large proportions of their populations who migrated permanently have in fact led to per capita income increases of the remaining resident populations. In the case of Niue, only 2000 residents remain, with some 12,000 now living mainly in New Zealand. For the Cook Islands the figures are about 17,000 to 30,000, respectively.

For economic growth to occur, diversification from the original narrow base of colonial export-oriented activity is required, with horizontal integration into the domestic sector. If this begins to happen, the economy may "progress" from underdevelopment to a developing economy. However, if diversification takes the form of a local industrial nucleus producing goods designed for the consumption of the foreign ventures operating in the country (that is import substitution), which is of course a form of horizontal integration, underdevelopment may still result. That part of the country affected by development remains minor and there is only a very slow decline in the subsistence sector. This explains why some countries may have an active local industrial sector (like India), but still exhibit a dual economy with a pre-capitalist occupational structure and a large proportion of its population cut off from the benefits of development.

Malaysia, once dependent upon tin mining and rubber plantations, is an example of a Third World country that was for a long time caught in underdevelopment. But, in the past four decades, it has witnessed strong economic growth as diversification — in which tourism has played a major role — with the dual economy transformed into an integrated modern capitalist economy. However, underdevelopment is not a necessary stage in the process of formation of a modern capitalist economy. In dependency theory, it is interpreted as historically caused by the restricted type of penetration of modern capitalistic enterprises into traditional non-monetized societies.

Nash described tourism as a form of imperialism: the expansion of a state's interests abroad, imposed on or adopted by an alien society and evolving inter-societal transactions "marked by the ebb and flow of power" (1977:34). In Nash's view, tourism is generated by advanced capitalist societies (metropol-itan states) where the level of incomes and material possessions permit patterns of behavior that encompass the "consumption" of leisure: tourism arises when people use the technology of transport for leisure-time pursuits. Often the "centers of production" will select and/or create destinations and attractions away from the metropolitan power in subordinate places and countries (the periphery). Tourists participate in the touristic expansion and thus the imperi-alism of such centers. The United States and the Caribbean island countries serve as a model for Nash's thesis.

Dependency and Underdevelopment Theory

According to Friedman (1988), Martin (1991), Hettne (1995), and others, dependency theory grew out of a search by Latin American social scientists looking for an alternative theory of underdevelopment, following the failure of major development programs run by the United Nations Economic Commission of Latin America (ECLA). It viewed underdevelopment and development not as different historical stages in a linear progression but as two coexisting parts of the world economy, with a causal link whereby the underdeveloped Third World was largely a creation of the process of global capitalist expansion. Imperialist policies supported the rapid industrial growth of the West by annexing the "periphery countries" to supply raw materials to the "center" (Portes 1976). Third World countries thus became underdeveloped because of their incorporation into the modern, capitalist world economy.

In 1973, Dos Santos proposed a theory of underdevelopment as dependence. In his view, the dual economy that was characteristic of many colonial entities was in fact a particular case of embryonic capitalism, a system in transition towards capitalism that happened to take on the form of a colonial exporting economy at the time that Europe was passing through a transition towards the capitalistic mercantile manufacturing period. Therefore, underdevelopment, rather than constituting a state of backwardness prior to capitalism, was seen as a consequence and a particular form of capitalist development: dependent capitalism.

Dos Santos then described dependency as

> a conditioning situation in which the economies of one group of
> countries are conditioned by the development and expansion of
> others. A relationship of inter-dependence between two or more
> economies becomes a dependent relationship when some coun-
> tries can expand through self-impulsion while others, being in a
> dependent position, can only expand as a reflection of the expan-
> sion of the dominant countries, which may have positive or
> negative effects on their immediate development (1973:76).

In other words, the growth of an underdeveloped country was conditioned by and
subjected to the external hegemonic power center in an unequal relationship. In
this context, it could be described as neo-Marxist, the major differences being
that Marxism views imperialism from a center perspective, dependency theory
sees imperialism from the periphery vantage point. Further, Marxism, caught
perhaps in the time-warp of its 19th century origins, holds the view that the concept of scarcity is a bourgeois capitalist invention, whereas neo-Marxism integrates ecological concerns into its view of development (Foster-Carter 1994).

The perceived dependence had to be recognized as susceptible to change
since the hegemonic structures and the dependent structures themselves change.
Such changes need not cut off the relationship, but simply redirect it; and much
of the South Pacific demonstrates this kind of dynamic. It is when the formal
ties of dependence are loosened and power is devolved that one may then begin
to discuss empowerment.

The mechanisms by which this dependence was imposed, according to the
dependency theorists, included maintenance of a cheap source of labor (first
through slavery and then through indenture schemes); the imposition of head
taxes that could only be met by entering the monetized economy of the plantations, mines, or other imperialist ventures; the mercantilist export of
agricultural and other resources from the colonies; maintenance of control in
the expatriate imperial society prohibiting the rise of an indigenous entrepreneurial class; and the export of goods from the center back to the periphery,
preventing the development of import substitution industry (Asad 1973;
Britton 1984; Harrison 1988). Thus, the poverty and economic stagnation of
the periphery could not be explained as due simply to internal factors as
claimed by the proponents of modernization, but by metropolitan domination
over satellite colonies.

Furtado (1973) suggested that underdevelopment was a distinct historical
process linked to the expansion of developing capitalism through colonialism.

He drew on the idea of dual economy, that is, an unbalanced and unintegrated economy characterized by the coexistence of a dynamic "modern" sector of production, typically export-oriented, and a "traditional sector" of subsistence agriculture inhibiting the development of an internal market.

In Asia, Africa and Latin America, the penetration of the traditional society by the capitalist enterprise under colonialism was typically at the margins (like mining and plantations), resulting in limited modifications of the prevailing economic structures. This was because the volume of the labor absorbed by the enterprise(s) was in many cases less than 10 percent of the available workforce; the wages offered were based on the local living conditions without any precise connection with the productivity of labor in the new economic activity; the profits generated tended not to be integrated into the local economy but exported overseas; and the level of local taxes (certainly in the beginning when all kinds of incentives were offered) were minimal. In other words, as the capitalist ventures' connection with the region was almost exclusively as a wage-generating agency, the payroll had to attain a relatively substantial level before modification could occur in the underlying traditional economic structure.

This coexistence could continue in a state of static equilibrium for a long time. In such cases, the result according to Furtado (1973) was chronic underdevelopment because there was an insufficiently large wage-earning group to raise the overall level of aggregate income and lead the society into mass consumerism.

Geertz (1973) pursued Furtado's line in examining the economy of Java with his focus on the exploitative relationship between the dual economies; the "traditional" nature of the indigenous sector was maintained by the Dutch colonial authorities in order to provide cheap inputs, above all labor, for the modern sector.

Britton (1984) applied dependency theory to an examination of the economy in Fiji and found that more than 80 percent of all business turnover in 1973 was attributable to foreign companies. The tourism industry was controlled by an informal conglomerate of big business, expatriate communities, transnational companies and foreign airlines controlling routes and dictating access. He considered that the establishment of a tourism industry in a peripheral economy could not occur from evolutionary processes within the economy, but only from exogenous foreign interests. The peripheral economy provided the setting, the metropolitan companies determined the shape of the industry.

> Metropolitan companies determined the organization and operation of tourism through a series of "system determinants" including ownership of national transport, the wholesaling of

package tours, overseas tourism investment, and the manipulation of tourist preferences and expectations ... the tourism
industry because of the predominance of foreign ownership,
imposes on peripheral destinations a development mode which
reinforces the characteristics of structural dependency on, and
vulnerability to, developed countries (Britton 1984:12–13).

Critique of Modernization and Dependency Theories

By the 1980s the pendulum was again swinging, and many of the certainties
of the dependency theorists were under critical scrutiny. In common with the
early modernization theorists, dependency theory was criticized for attempting
to make universal generalizations that failed empirically; there was a corresponding lack of attention to explaining variation (Wood 1993:54). The
implication of a continuous polarization in income and welfare between developed and underdeveloped countries that was inherent in the theory of
underdevelopment was too simplistic and the growth patterns of countries and
per capita measures have belied the presumed polarization.

The concept also proved difficult to apply empirically. Trying to distinguish
dependent from nondependent countries was problematic. In reality, all
countries — even those normally not considered as underdeveloped, such as
Japan — import technology, import raw materials upon which they may be
dependent for their energy and industry, are dependent on exports, emulate
consumption patterns in other countries, contain their own mix of undeveloped,
disadvantaged and developed regions, and so on. It also became clear in the
1970s that a number of Third World countries were industrializing rapidly
although, according to dependency theory, their development was blocked.

In addition a growing band of writers suggested that "at every stage from
external imperialism to decolonization, the working of European imperialism
was determined by the indigenous collaborative systems connecting its
European and Afro-Asian components" (Robertson 1972:38) and was not
just a matter of exogamous influence. Hegemonies within the economy of
Third World countries were not necessarily structures of dominance and subju-
gation imposed externally, but required collaboration from host elites
(Hollinshead 1992).

The critical review of dependency theory reduced the sharp opposition with
modernization and under such writers as Hoogvelt (1986) the two concepts
found some common ground. In the words of Evans and Stephens, "the earlier
sociologies of development have evolved into a new comparative historical

political economy" (1988:744). In this context, one approach was to conceive of modernization "as an historical process of westernization due to the dominance of western civilization during a particular period of history" (Hettne 1995:65).

Others took the opposite tack and "de-westernized" it. Thus, for Moore (1979) modernization was reconceptualized as "rationalization" not linked into any comparison with European economies, this way avoiding the Eurocentric connotations of the original concept. Nash redefined modernization as "the growth in capacity to apply tested knowledge to all branches of production" (1984:506), leaving open the question of the appropriate form of social structure to follow (essentially modernization without westernization).

Interdependence theory, often called global interdependence, also emerged, stressing the need to coordinate development globally because of the interrelatedness of economies, markets, capital, communications, and countries in multifaceted networks. This combined elements of both modernization and dependency, but it was also vague and ambiguous and attracted the same criticism of impractical universalism as modernization and dependency.

Hoogvelt boldly stated that:

> Development theory is in something of a muddle. Societies which were previously classed together as featuring the same conditions and as subject to the same laws of motion, have demonstrated a disorienting divergence of development performance and experience. This has undermined our confidence in generalizing theories. The Third World or Less Developed World as a unified, homogeneous object of enquiry no longer exists. With its disappearance has gone the grand competing theories at one time majestically erected to explain the causes of its poverty and to chart the path to its prosperity. Worse still, detailed empirical scrutiny of the successes of some countries and the failures of others has contradicted and refuted the theoretical predictions and policy prescriptions of the main opposing paradigms (1990:352).

Thus, some Third World countries that based their development policies on an acceptance of the tenets of dependency theory and the presumed exploitative relationship with its First World mentor(s) and then followed the prescribed socialist strategies of self-reliance (such as Tanzania and Zambia), recorded "embarrassing failures" (Hoogvelt 1990:353). On the other hand, some of the then success stories of the so-called newly industrializing countries (NICs), such as Korea, Taiwan, and Singapore, whose development at first sight would appear to have been due to modernization through the application of policies of free and unhindered diffusion of western capital and technology and support for free capitalist enterprises, are precisely those in which the state has intervened in a direct and commanding way. The government has

> seized the commanding heights and has regulated its [trade] with the world capitalist system in a manner wholly at odds with the structural functionalist preferences and neo-evolutionary directions of the modernization prospectus. Indeed, these policies of corporate statism are more in keeping with the general thrust of ... dependency theory (Hoogvelt 1990:353).

To explain these apparent contradictions came the 'delayed development' or neo-Listian theory of development (Senghaas 1985). This is based upon the policies of the 19th century economist, Freidrich List, on economic nationalism, and draws a parallel between the swiftly industrializing European economies of 100 years ago with characteristics of NIC states such as Singapore, Taiwan, and Korea. Delayed development incorporates such elements as "temporary disassociation" of economy and society from international competition, protection of infant industries, strong state intervention in the economy, a readiness to discard ideological commitment to either socialist or capitalist strategies in favor of total pragmatism, and a capacity by the state to politicize issues in pursuit of narrow nationalist objectives (for example, the move by Third World countries to be exempted from the internationally obligated emission controls arising from the Rio Earth Summit of 1992 on the global environment). Delayed development is becoming increasingly difficult in an increasingly interconnected globe, however, and the role of international capital cuts across national boundaries. The placement of huge sums of international capital in selected countries has given rise to a new source of uneven development.

Harrison (1988) was one of the first to point out that modernization theory and underdevelopment/dependency theory should not be seen as polar opposites, nor as separate paradigms, but that elements of both found expression in linkages with the component parts of the world system (thus foreshadowing the globalization debate). He noted that "It was the contrast of 'tradition' and 'modernity' which led some writers to refer to the dualism of Third World societies". While there was no agreement on a definition of "development", neither modernization nor underdevelopment theory should be viewed as necessarily contradictory. Rather, it was "reasonable to regard development as a far-reaching, continuous, and positively evaluated process of social, economic and political change which involves the totality of human experience. Individuals and collectivities will be affected, most dramatically, perhaps in the Third World, and existing changes will be evaluated and measured according to the actors' and observers' standpoints". He suggested that development could be seen as "movement towards a valued state, which may or may not have been achieved in some other social context and which may not be achievable. [Modernization] is a similar process. It is what is actually happening, for good or ill: a series of patterns with consequences that can be described, argued about and evaluated" (1988:149, 155, 156).

Harrison further stated that in any assessment of development, it was invalid to propose a dichotomy between internal and external "variables", although the impact and influence of them would rarely be of equal importance:

> Clearly there are countless examples of the immense effect of colonialism, trade or direct invasion on specific societies or regions. Nevertheless, it should also be evident that the nature of domestic social, cultural, political and economic institutions will have a crucial bearing on the processes of modernization and development. Apart from anything else, they help to determine how social change will be instigated, accepted, rejected, acted upon, acted out or altered by indigenous people. Crude arguments that see class structures or cultures as pale reflections of metropolitan interests do less than justice to the vibrant variety of cultures that is found in the Third World. In effect they brand whole nations, and sometimes the working class in metropolitan countries, as cultural dupes. Similarly, insofar as [some] modernization theorists concentrated on the nation-state . . . they have ignored key features of modernization and development. And theorists of all persuasions have often failed to recognize the ability of actors to bring about change, individually and collectively, even in the face of overwhelming odds (1988:163).

Emerging from these criticisms of generalized theories is a new emphasis on trying to understand the diversity of development experience. Power/dependence relations and modernization both have elements that provide some of the better approaches to understanding certain situations. However, rather than trying to force or fit individual situations into a unified, universal, explanatory theory, there has been a quest for concrete empirical examination of specific local social structures and change. This in turn has resulted in a renewed interest in anthropological, ethnographic, and historiographic work.

As a corollary, culture and cultural values are being accorded a new place of importance in shaping locally specific responses to processes of induced economic development and social change (the case studies in Chapters 7, 8, and 9 explore the cultural dimensions of development in detail). This is particularly relevant with reference to dependency theory that neglected the most crucial level of anthropological inquiry: the local community. What happened at the local level was simply regarded as unimportant, a reflection of processes going on in a remote peripheral area.

Dependency theory, had it persisted, may have eventually got around to considering empowerment of the nation state as a way to break the chain of dependency; but it would not have incorporated community empowerment in its thesis.

One response from Marxist anthropologists has been to advance the theory of articulation as development. This established a link between the anthropological concern with community and dependency theory. It accepts that the local level has its own dynamics and in Third World countries its pre-capitalist modes of production articulate with capitalism in different ways. The outcome of this articulation may be characterized by "development" or "underdevelopment" (Beaud 1984 as cited in Hettne 1995; Foster-Carter 1994; Hyden 1983; Oxaal, Barnett, and Booth 1975). However, it too has been difficult to verify empirically, and the theory of interdependence, that assumes that there is only one mode, a world mode of production, makes its focus on an array of modes irrelevant.

As early as 1984, Worsley considered that an understanding of the role of culture in the re-emergence of a (modified) modernization theory was missing, and Harrison (1988), Weiner and Huntington (1987), and Wood (1993) shared this view. Hitchcock *et al.* (1993) believe that an examination of the developmental processes at work in Third World countries has brought about a very marked shift in conceptualizing cultural change resulting from tourism. Much of the research and debate on tourism in Third World countries "has focused on whether its effects are beneficial or negative, whether they are developmental or anti-developmental" (Hitchcock *et al.* 1993:5), but there is an emerging consensus that it is too simplistic to argue that sociocultural effects are either "good" or "bad". Sociocultural change is also difficult to measure accurately and interpret objectively, and the use of terms by authors in Jafari's cautionary platform such as cultural "degradation", cultural "corruption", loss of tradition and ethnicity, may defy rational measurement. The result is a reconceptualization of such key concepts in anthropology as culture and ethnicity.

Recent approaches to culture in the sociology of development have reflected that found in modernization theory, with a move away from universal generalizations towards documenting and explaining variation in the cultural consequences of tourism. Beginning in the 1970s detailed studies of the impact of tourism in Third World countries challenged the mostly negative critiques of the cautionary platform that had dominated the field. Researchers such as Graburn (1976, 1983), Lansing (1974), and McKean (1976, 1977) argued that tourism is a positive force for combining economic development with support for tradition. The work of Picard (1996) in Bali over two decades has contributed to a better understanding of the transformations by the Balinese themselves of local cultural forms in relation to tourism development.

Graburn described societies such as Canadian and Alaskan Eskimos, the Maori of New Zealand, and the Kamba of Kenya as ones where the production of art for outsiders heightened self-identity and self-esteem; the ethnic minority used

> its special skills to its advantage, surpassing the efforts of the larger society", [knowing that the white man] "could not or would not carve soapstone as well as they [the Eskimos] can. The same might be said of Navaho jewellery and Maori wood-carvings (1976:467).

Graburn proposed a typology of the "portable arts" for cross-cultural analysis, ranging from functional fine arts (with great contemporary cultural and social significance for the people themselves); commercial fine arts (whose artistic merits are superior and whose market would be serious collectors); souvenir arts (made for sale to wider tourist audiences); to assimilated fine arts (where non-traditional techniques and materials may be utilized in the production of works that retain essentially ethnic qualities). To these Graburn added "airport art" which he saw as part of souvenir art but with emphasis on simplification, standardization, and mass production. These various manifestations of artwork were indicative of a special economic relationship between the ethnic artists and craftsmen on the one hand, and the capitalist world, on the other, in which tradition was strengthened and yet adapted to the tourist market (1976:465–66).

McKean's work in Bali (which has extended over a 25-year period) was influential in determining tourism planning for the island. He detailed the adaptations made by the Balinese themselves to manage the impact of tourism on their traditional culture (arts, dance and music), and the nature of their linkages between the two component parts of the dual system, one that was modern and one that was embedded in tradition:

> The sacred realm authenticates and legitimates Balinese craft, dance and drama [while] these aesthetic creations simultaneously receive economic encouragement from tourists. This

involution illuminates the peculiar characteristics of classic tradition and modernity which combine to strengthen the Balinese cultural productivity and self-identity (1977:104).

McKean's research has also been influential in tourism literature. It was one of the first comprehensively analyzed instances of a society that was not passive to the impacts of tourism but which has responded dynamically to the changing situation. Picard (whose research into tourism and culture in Bali goes back to the 1970s) agrees with McKean, arguing that it is "asking the wrong question" to seek to understand the impacts of the industry on Balinese culture, as if tourism were "the irruption of an external force striking Bali from without". Rather, the appropriate question would consider it as "a process transforming Bali from within". In short, this culture "is the product of a dialogic interaction between the Balinese people and significant others" that "has rendered the Balinese self-conscious about their 'Balinese-ness' while compelling them to explain what it means to be Balinese to a foreign audience" (Picard 1993:72–73). In the process the Balinese have proceeded to a series of conceptualizations about their art and culture pertaining to what is traditional, religious, artistic, political, or touristic.

Wood (1980:565) takes the ballistic simile a little further by suggesting that too many researchers have conceived of tourism in terms of the "billiard ball model": a static sphere (culture) is hit by a mobile one (tourism). In fact, as the research of McKean, Picard, and others demonstrates, the recipients of tourism are rarely if ever passive and will respond in a variety of ways to it.

A theoretical point that has been taken up by anthropologists and rural sociologists engaged in research on peasant communities in their own regional, national and international economic contexts (Friedman 1988; Mehmet 1978; Nash 1981) is that people who are faced with forces not of their own making do not simply receive them passively but respond actively to them. Friedman stated that in the case of St Lucia, their reactions were

> based on their particular circumstances as well as their common position in export economies . . . in an economy dependent upon tourism. There are no single uniform responses to conditions imposed from outside forces. Rather the variety of local conditions generates a variety of responses to forces which may lie outside the reach or control of individuals (1988:8).

Pi-Sunyer added a different complexion to the issue. He noted that "tourism did not invariably lead to external economic control, the decay of local institutions, and negative attitudes towards outsiders. Some societies seem to have flourished in a tourist milieu". He placed Austria and Switzerland in this category where in his view the Swiss and the Austrians had, for the most part, adapted to tourism in a manner that brought both economic benefits and little or no social disharmony. In the context of mass tourism to the Costa Brava of Spain, however, he considered that this development had led to negative stereotyping and reinforced the gulf between locals and outsiders. But if elements of the culture of the locals had been commoditized by tourists, the locals had retaliated by categorizing tourists "as a resource or a nuisance rather than as individual people". They kept a major part of their culture intact "by erecting largely insurmountable barriers to genuine human relations" (1977:149, 155). Tradition was maintained in spite of tourism, from which profits were reaped.

Nunez and other anthropologists who have examined host–guest relations echo the view that this relationship "is almost always an instrumental one, rarely colored by affective ties, and almost always marked by degrees of social distance and stereotyping that would not exist among neighbors, peers or fellow countrymen" (1977:212). The process of acculturation is the framework within which these researchers tend to place the asymmetric exchange that is characteristic of most host–guest interactions. However, this very asymmetry means that it is too simplistic to label traditional societies as subordinate and modern societies as dominant (the error of most of the early anthropological analyses of tourism), because in some instances the locals will pipe the tune to which the tourists dance. Thus, researchers should "resist the temptation to condemn tourism as unnecessarily intrusive . . . and deculturative . . . and indigenous people as unable to adapt and assimilate to a changing world" (Nunez 1977:215).

The earlier view of unlimited economic growth as some kind of natural law that could be supported by increasing sophistication in technology has now been replaced by acceptance that there are limits to resources and that intergenerational equity imposes a review of current levels of consumption. This includes both non-renewable resources (such as minerals) and the four main biological systems (renewable resources): oceanic fisheries, forests, grasslands and croplands. The deterioration of these four present serious problems, since in many instances their carrying capacities are being exceeded. When coupled with global warming and possible climatic change, the impacts on the productivity of the various ecosystems could be adverse (catastrophic according to some). In the words of Brown, "[n]either the old nor any new international economic order will be viable unless the natural biological systems that underpin the global economy are conserved" (1991:205).

Sustainable Development

To bring systematic analysis to these complex issues, the development theorists have advanced the concept of sustainable development. It has grown out of the fundamental issue of how much and what kind of development can be sustained over a relative time perspective. The construct of "sustainable development" first gained global prominence with the publication of the World Conservation Strategy in 1980 by the International Union for Conservation of Nature (IUCN). Its international significance lay in the fact that it brought the thinking of the conservationist into a dialogue with the growth-oriented but sometimes insensitive or unheeding developer through the participation of some 450 government agencies from more than 100 countries that wrote the report (Hall 1995). Its definition of sustainability encompassed the relationship between economic development and the conservation and sustenance of natural resources.

The concept of sustainability was cast in its present shape by the World Commission on Environment and Development (1987). It collated a wide range of views on ecologically sustainable development (ESD) which it set out in the so-called Brundtland Report, *Our Common Future*. This included both biophysical and cultural spheres and enunciated a set of principles which in the South Pacific have been adopted by many governments, including Australia, New Zealand, Fiji, the Cook Islands and others.

There are four fundamental canons for the World Conservation Strategy that emerged from the World Commission on Environment and Development as follows:

- *Ecological sustainability.* Development must be compatible with the maintenance of ecological processes, biological diversity and biological resources.
- *Economic sustainability.* Development must be economically efficient and equitable within and between generations.
- *Social sustainability.* Development must be designed to increase people's control over their lives and maintain and strengthen community identity.
- *Cultural sustainability.* Development must be compatible with the culture and the values of the people affected by it.

These four elemental points have been applied in a number of countries. For example, a review of development options for Bali was based on them and resulted in a set of seven criteria by which to assess the sustainability of tourism development: social and cultural sustainability, community and "integration-balance-harmony" were given a prominent place (Wall 1993:55). Combined, the seven criteria suggested for Bali's development path reinforce the notion that sustainable development is an integrated, holistic concept in which all four of the tenets outlined above are inextricably linked together. The Australian Government set up a Task Force in 1989 to examine the issues with a view to achieving a balance between economic and ecological requirements. It assigned the following 12 principles to sustainable development. One, *inter-generational equity or development* is development that "meets the needs of the present generation without compromising the ability of future generations to meet their own needs" (WCED 1987:43). Two, *conservation of biological diversity and ecological integrity* may entail constraint on certain kinds of economic activity. The non-evolutionary loss of species and genetic diversity needs to be halted and the future of evolutionary processes assured. Three, *constant natural capital* (such as biological diversity, healthy environments and freshwater supplies) must be maintained or enhanced from one generation to the next. Four, *anticipatory and precautionary policy approach* is designed to ensure that policy decisions should err on the side of caution where scientific evidence of the impacts of development is lacking or where uncertainty exists. A demonstration of ecological sustainability is desirable for development to proceed. Five, *social equity* is regarded as a key principle in a sustainable society. Six, *limits on natural resource use* have two key elements, the first being the capacity of the environment to supply renewable resources, and the second the capacity of the environment to assimilate wastes. Seven, *qualitative development* is designed to put the qualitative dimension of human welfare first rather than the quantitative growth of resource throughput. Eight, *pricing environmental values and natural resources* involves setting prices of natural resources to recover the full social and environmental costs involved in their extraction, production and use, while trying to find ways to set appropriate values on environmental aspects (clean air, wilderness, etc.). Nine, *global and regional perspectives* is acceptance of the responsibility that the actions of one country or one region may impact environmentally on another country, region or globally. Ten, *efficiency of resource use* must become a major objective in economic policy, with wastage being minimized or eliminated. Eleven, *resilience* relates to the need for economic policy to develop a resilience to external economic or ecological shocks: a resource-driven economy is unlikely to be resilient. Twelve, *community participation* is advocated as a vital pre-requisite in planning and developing ecological sustainability (Commonwealth Government of Australia 1992).

The issue of community participation is a theme repeated in many models for tourism planning, but often that involvement is "in effect public relations rhetoric that permits the local community to do little more than *react* to plans, proposals and developments that will be implemented" (Macbeth 1996:2). Constantino-David (1995) drawing on case studies from the Philippines, suggests that non-governmental organizations have a better record than most in terms of empowering communities, but this too can be challenged. This matter will be explored further in the next chapter.

The paradigm of ESD presents a major challenge to conventional paradigms of development. It questions, *inter alia*:

- The positions of countries in the developmental hierarchy as determined by modernization, dependency and neo-Listian development theories. Its values for measurement of "development" are radically different.
- The values of consumerism (or growth) on which economic analyses of development tend to be based.
- The negation of universalism in the context of the removal of any model that a country can follow, since it is to shape its future from its own unique ecology and culture.
- The primacy ESD gives to ecological (environmental and cultural) values over other values.

It has become highly contentious in many countries as the application of its ideals challenge vested interests particularly in the extractive and manufacturing sectors such as mining, logging and refineries. Tourism development has not been exempted from sometimes stringent criticism about its lack of commitment to the principles of ESD.

Sustainability does not imply a static situation and the need is to strike an appropriate balance between economic development and ecological conservation. In developmental terms it should mean a strengthening of decision-making among local, regional and national levels of society because of their interdependence; but this is contrary to the pattern of centralization of power at the national level in most developing countries. This issue will be taken up in the next chapter on empowerment.

It is important to recognize that "tourism as sustainable development" is not the same as "sustainable tourism". In terms of the first, it would be "developed and maintained in an area [community, environment] in such a manner and at such a scale that it remains viable over an indefinite period, and does not degrade or alter the environment [human and physical] in which it exists to such a degree that it prohibits the successful development and well-being of other activities and processes" (Butler 1993:29). Sustainable tourism, on the other hand, would only have to maintain its viability as a profit generating activity for an indefinite period of time to be regarded as such. In other words, to qualify for the first definition, tourism activity needs to combine "long term economic sustainability within a framework of long term ecological sustainability, and with an equitable distribution of the costs and benefits of development" (Woodley 1993:136).

But this review of the development literature would not be complete without some passing reference to "another development". This phrase first gained currency with the publication of the Dag Hammarskjöld Foundation's report *"What Now?"* (1975). "Another development" (sometimes referred to as "alternative development") is not a theory, but as a concept it has captured much attention. It focuses on the content rather than the form of development. Its main constituent parts are:

> it is needs-oriented (being geared to meeting human needs, both material and non-material); it is endogenous (stemming from the heart of each society, which defines in sovereignty its values and the vision of its future); it is self-reliant (that is, each society relies primarily on its own resources, its members' energies and its natural and cultural environment); it is ecologically sound (utilizing rationally the resources of the biosphere in full awareness of the potential of local ecosystems as well as the global and local outer limits imposed on present and future generations); and it is based on structural transformation (so as to realize the conditions of self-management and participation in decision-making by all those affected by it, from the rural or urban community to the world as a whole, without which the goals above could not be achieved) (Nerfin 1977:10).

The appeal of "another development", with its emphasis on small-scale solutions, ecological concerns, popular participation and the establishment of community, etc. has been greater in developed than in Third World countries. Hettne (1995) attributes this to a greater acceptance among rich nations of its ecological dimensions (in this context the linkage to ESD is obvious) and to planning approaches that in many such countries encompass community consultative arrangements as a normative part of development. There is also an element of power sharing inherent in this approach that may be opposed by the elites running many Third World countries, particularly when it incorporates ethnic minorities.

Globalization, Modernity, and Development

There has been an explosion in the rhetoric of globality, globalization, internationalization, and so on, in the past decade. The literature spawned by the topic of globalization is far too extensive to attempt a survey of its major scholars and the many divergent lines of research they have pursued in this short chapter. It is necessary, however, to provide a brief overview of the main themes and issues. This summary of globalization leads into a questioning of the place of tourism in the process of globalization, the world economic system, the formation of identity and image of place and people (society), and from there to the role of tourism in the development of so-called global culture, modernization, and the interconnectedness of the world.

According to Featherstone (1995a, 1995b), King (1991) and others, two particular representations of globalization simultaneously vie for pre-eminence. The first entails the outwards expansion of a single, homogeneous, dominating culture that integrates and incorporates all less robust cultures. This homogeneity is perceived in a single global economy, that is dominated by western-style capitalism, and there is a sameness in terms of the development of infrastructure, markets, and business culture. It is perceived in a global technology based on western computerized technology and telecommunications with faster and easier access to increasing amounts of information (mass media such as radio, terrestrial and satellite TV, and communications technologies such as telephones, faxes and the Internet). Developments in the technology of transport (air, road, rail, and sea) facilitate "the binding together of large expanses of time-space not only on an intra-societal level but increasingly on an inter-societal and global level" (Featherstone 1995b:7). Further, this process is perceived in a global culture that increasingly has the English language as the medium of communication worldwide, and the expansion to virtually all countries of western styles of dress, food and recreation. It is a world "of diaspora, transnational culture flows and mass movements of people" (Gupta and Ferguson 1997:38) where a homogenizing globalization is, in the view of some, demolishing difference and moving everyone closer to the establishment of the so-called "global village" (Urry 1991). It is thus perceived to be an agent of modernization in the development process.

The second image focuses on "interconnectedness", the way in which cultures formerly held apart are brought into contact and juxtaposition. Cultures pile on top of cultures in a heap that appears to have no organizing principle beyond the fact that the "culture" of communications, abetted by the ease with which contemporary information technology and telecommunications reaches every country and its messages are accepted and absorbed at least in part by each of the separate cultures. This interconnectedness is supported by the mass movement of people that is facilitated by modern transport technologies, so that over time a certain degree of commonality evolves and echoes of different cultures will be found in every other culture (Sofield 1999a, 1999b).

There is much talk in the popular press of "Americanization" and "Disney-ification". Paris and Tokyo have their Disneylands and in 1999 Hong Kong reached agreement for another Disneyland near its new airport. MacDonald's hamburgers may be found throughout Europe, Asia, Africa, and Australasia. Such manifestations lend support to the contention that the processes of Western modernity constitute an inescapable universalizing force: that development, as noted above, would see societies move from the traditional to the modern through a range of specific phases: "industrialization, urbanization, commodi-fication, rationalization, differentiation, bureaucratization, the expansion of the division of labor, the growth of individualism and state formation processes. In effect, western history is universal world history" (Featherstone 1995a:87). Despite elements of commonality, in reality few observers would adhere to the belief that the endpoint of historical development would be a single, homoge-neous, integrated world culture bereft of linguistic, social and cultural differ-ences. Economic differences may be lessened, political sharpness and national contestation may eventually be subdued, but certainly at the present time, in sharp contrast to the first image, the second image suggests greater clashes of cultures, with greater complexity in assertions of identity than the first image permits. There is "a spiral of relativization of culture through increased contact" where not only integration but also increased conflict has occurred: rather than the emergence of a unified global economy and culture "there is a strong ten-dency for the process of globalization to provide a stage for global differences not only to open up a world showcase of cultures in which the examples of the distant exotic are brought directly into the home, but to provide a field for a more discordant clashing of cultures" (Featherstone 1995b:13). Fissiparous tendencies in the former Soviet Union (now Russia), in the Balkans (formerly united Yugoslavia) and Indonesia attest to this process.

There is now a discourse of globality, but within it there are many problemat-ics. While there is some common ground on its contents, the interests that sus-tain the discourse vary tremendously from society to society and also within societies. The discourse itself has become an important part of globalization and of contemporary global culture. Increasingly as the process of globalization has gathered strength, nations and other entities have been faced "almost continu-ously with the problem of response to the wider, increasingly compressed, global context" in which they exist (Robertson 1991:88). The ways in which such entities have simultaneously attempted to learn from one another and adopted elements of the wider world while sustaining a sense of identity — or have attempted to isolate themselves from the pressures of contact — also constitute an important aspect of the creation of global culture. China under Mao elected to isolate itself from the world in many ways in contrast to the "Open Door" policies pursued since 1978 when Deng delivered China's new outward approach to the world. As Robertson noted, "even more specifically the cultures of particular societies are, to different degrees, the result of their interactions with other societies in the global system. In other words, national-societal cultures have been differentially formed in interpenetration with significant others" (1991:89). In this context, the role of the tourism system as "a significant other", interpenetrating societies and cultures across the globe, has rarely been mentioned in the sociological and political science literature of globalization. It is this element of interpenetration that assists a dialogic component in image making for and between tourists and agents of the tourism system on the one hand, and host countries on the other (Sofield 1999a, 1999b, 2000).

The discourse on the nature of linkages between the global and the local reveals that the latter may either enjoy a benign relationship with the global or be subordinated to it. While cultural integration processes are taking place on a global level, at the local level there are increasing pluralistic or polytheistic manifestations (Featherstone 1995a). This situation has been variably described as "a process of cultural fragmentation and collapse of symbolic hierarchies" where there are "shifts in the value of the symbolic power and cultural capital of the west" because of the emergence of competing centers of global significance such as Japan and East Asia (Featherstone 1995b:9); and as "a postcolonial contra-modernity" that captures "the hybrid and syncretic perspectives . . . of those half-inside and half-outside of modernity, a conscious mixing of traditions and crossing of boundaries" (Bhabha 1994:5). Hollinshead (1998) supports Bhabha's contention of "third space" occupied by "halfway people". Postmodernism can be understood in the way it points to the decentring of culture and the introduction of cultural complexity (Featherstone 1995a, 1995b), paradoxically away from the very universalism inherent in the concept of globalization. Rather than contrasting autonomous local cultures (original, centered, authentic) with an opposing global cultural ecumene (that is seen as new, external, artificially imposed, inauthentic), the challenge for ethnographic theory is to seek out the ways in which connectedness between the two occurs, and the ways in which dominant cultural forms may be picked up and used — and significantly transformed — by communities and nation-states in the midst of the field of power relations that links localities to the wider world (Gupta and Ferguson 1997).

Tourism provides a milieu for examining this interstitiality of local–global phenomena in the context of what Wallerstein (writing about economic and cultural processes not tourism) has called the simultaneity of particularism and universalism (Wallerstein 1974). Tourism is simultaneously a contributor to and part of the process of globalization. It is a major utilizer and consumer of the instruments of information technology and telecommunications, but it goes beyond their "virtual reality" to concretize the travel experience. In doing so, as Urry (1991) expounds in *"The Tourist Gaze"*, it contributes to the globalization process by *inter alia* its dissemination of homogeneous management systems; universal applications of service quality; repetition of touristic architectural styles in different countries around the world; touristic marketing, promotions, and presentations; the spread of western values both through its business activities, personnel training and management; and of course through the contact tourists have with local peoples everywhere. Paradoxically, because tourism is about *difference*, at the same time it contributes to the maintenance and retention of cultural diversity (Sofield 1999a, 2000).

The ubiquitous nature of tourism as a major agent in and for globalization and its dominating role in the development of some small countries and/or destinations has seen it likened to forms of economic and cultural dependency, another form of imperialism and neocolonialism. Thus Crick (1989:322) has argued that tourism may be characterized as "leisure imperialism" and Britton (1991) also sees tourism as an agent of capitalist modernity. Hall, however, notes that

> the extent to which power is able to be exercised, and hence development controlled in any nation by an external agency, is somewhat problematic as a more complex notion of globalization has replaced simplistic ideas of imperialism . . . a fuller understanding of the totality of cultural, economic and social change needs to be located in an understanding of the process of globalization as an inevitable outcome of modernity. Indeed, one of the paradoxes of globalization is that it implies the decay of previous imperial powers (1998:147).

This is not to deny that a certain degree of global cultural homogenization is occurring; rather, "the world system is in fact replacing one diversity with another: and the new diversity is based relatively more on interrelations and less on autonomy" (Clifford 1988:17). Development theory may thus be seen to be entering a new phase, where, as ever, orthodoxy is challenged as new understandings about the complexities and paradoxes of globalization lead the analyst in new directions.

Chapter 3

What is Empowerment?

The aim of this chapter is to examine the concept of empowerment and determine its utility for understanding tourism development particularly (although not exclusively) at the community level. No discussion about empowerment can avoid an examination of power concepts. However, this dissertation is not about power in all its manifest forms. It is about *social* and *political* power in the context of tourism development. Thus, the work of the behavioral psychologists in examining interpersonal power, for example, is not pursued.

The last chapter briefly examined politics as power and its direct relationship to development. This chapter will extend the examination of power into society because it is contended that empowerment of and by communities cannot occur without social forces at some point in time combining with political forces of the state to arrive at a new balance of power relations. Of relevance for the purposes of this study is the literature of political science, social anthropology, and sociology where power is examined in terms of stateless societies (where power lies in pre-political circuits — those created by kinship, religion and economics); the unified society (political unit); the state (exercise of political control over a resident population within a specified boundary with the capacity to defend that boundary against external forces); and power and subordination, and social exchange (the bases of the social order) (After Balandier 1970a:30–32).

Power exists and may be identified and recognized in every human society, whether it is "primitive" or technologically advanced and highly differentiated (Mair 1970). It will entail characteristics of both internal determinism (the need to sustain social order and a general level of equilibrium within a society) and external expression (the need to maintain a society's cohesion and capacity to function against external danger, real or imagined; Sutton 1959). Power also implies an asymmetry in social relations. As Balandier noted, "if those relations were established on the basis of perfect reciprocity, social equilibrium would be automatic and power would be doomed to perish" (1970a:37).

Students of formal organizations have tended to focus primarily on the hierarchical manifestations of social and political power either between superior and subordinate positions and roles (such as village "bigmen", village council chief, district superintendent, province governor, national president), or between the various levels of organizational structure (local council, provincial legislature, national parliament). There appear to be relatively fewer studies of horizontal power relations among organizations, although social exchange theory (Emerson 1972, 1976, 1981 and his concept of power/dependence relations) has attempted general conceptualizations about power relations in social collectivities. Bacharach and Lawler (1980, 1981) emphasize the role of internal politics and relative powers of bargaining in their analyses of power in organizations. For purposes of this overview it is accepted that political groupings are but one form of social collectivity and so are not distinguished as a separate entity.

One of the most widely accepted definitions of power is that of Max Weber. Power is

> the probability that one actor within a social relationship will be in a position to carry out his own will despite resistance, regardless of the basis on which this probability exists (cited in Gerth and Mills 1948:180).

Recognizing that this definition was restricted because it functions in terms of individual propensities, and in response to criticism Weber subsequently broadened its application to incorporate groups and larger bodies, including states, as the actor(s) involved. He introduced the concept of "domination" into this broader definition: "the probability that a command with a given specific content will be obeyed by a given group of persons" (1978:53). In his typology of domination, he drew a distinction between legal domination and legitimate domination. The latter is not necessarily dependent upon the existence of the state and is expressed through "traditional domination" in which personal relations are used as support for the political authority. It takes some five globally recognized forms. One, *gerontocracy* links power with seniority as in most traditional Aboriginal societies in Australia. Two, *patriarchalism* maintains power within a particular family. Three, *patrimonialism* (inheritance through male lines) is the most widespread, its norm is custom, regarded as inviolable, its mode of authority is essentially personal and its organization entails no administration in the modern sense. It employs dignitaries rather than functionaries and there is no separation between the private and the public sphere. Four, *charismatic domination* is another form of domination, which is extra-legitimate. It is an exceptional type, a revolutionary form of power that can operate against regimes of traditional or legal character. Five, *legal domination* can only occur in states with a legislative framework, and domination will be exercised by a combination of the executive and its bureaucracy (Weber 1978:53). These concepts will be utilized in analyzing several case studies in later chapters.

Power and Society

In scanning the anthropological, sociological, and political science literature, five main themes or models of social power emerge. First, the *reputational* model assumes that power in a given social context will reflect the way it is distributed among those with a reputation for power and influence. A reputation for power will be an important resource. Second, associated with this model is the *positional* approach in which "powerholders are defined as those who occupy formal positions of leadership and management" (Jacobsen and Cohen 1986:107). In the South Pacific context, the Melanesian "bigman" system is a reflection of both models: a reputation for power and influence enhances the acceptance of an individual or group of individuals as "bigmen". Once acknowledged as "bigmen" there will be occasions when that position will translate into acceptance of their power and authority to take decisions and actions on behalf of the community. The major deficiency in this duality is its neglect of covert power brokers who have neither a reputation for power nor a position of leadership. In some countries, this phenomenon is common: behind the formal and openly recognized positions of leadership will be backroom powerbrokers who avoid publicity but exercise influence over decision making.

Third, the *decision-making* model views social and political power as "the ability to make decisions and have them implemented, irrespective of other people's wishes". This is an operational view of power, in that "it compares outcomes with prior decisions of the actors: the powerful are those whose decisions constantly match the outcomes" (Jacobsen and Cohen 1986:107). While this model has been criticized because it ignores the nondecision mode, where power is used to prevent an issue from ever reaching the decision-making stage (Lawler and Bacharach 1986), its basic idea is sound: power is only as effective as its application. This model will be used later in the consideration of empowerment. Fourth, the *control* model (Tannenbaum 1981) analyzes control within organizations (as distinct from interpersonal relations), defining power as "any process in which a person or group of persons or organization of persons determines, that is, intentionally affects, the behavior of another person, groups, or organization". The limitations of this model relate to its concentration on Weber's notion of domination, or vertical power relations only. This has been interpreted by some to mean that Tannenbaum considers that power "rests solely on the subjective perceptions of those being controlled, as if power only exists when it is felt by those over whom it is exerted (Jacobsen and Cohen 1986:108). However, a closer examination of Tannenbaum's work indicates that manipulation of subordinates can occur without them realizing it. In other words, control can be effectively exercised even if subordinates are not aware of the imposition of controls. Finally, the *resources* model "compares the potential power of the sides in a power relationship by their respective access to resources which are desired or required by either party" (Jacobsen and Cohen 1986:108). This is the model most often utilized in political science and by economists and market researchers to analyze power relationships. However, in this form it is limited because it equates resources with power. It needs to be rounded by specifying that power requires the capacity to mobilize the resources; access is insufficient. This expanded model is still flawed, however, in that it does not specify under what conditions such mobilization will or will not take place. It is this juncture that suggests the application of the concept of empowerment; and this will be explored in detail in due course.

In summary, the five main models of social and political power point to useful, but different, indicators of the characteristics of power. But each has inadequacies and thus provides an incomplete picture of power in social collectivities. Jacobsen and Cohen (1986) have attempted an integration of the models that hinges on a clear distinction being drawn between power resources and power potential. They argue that this is necessary to explain why potential power is translated into action in some situations but not in others; why groups with relatively poor power resources can at times impose their will on others who are much more richly endowed; and, conversely why "social collectivities with immense resources sometimes find themselves impotent and at the mercy of groups with much more modest resources" (Jacobsen and Cohen 1986:109).

An example of this is the way in which a number of traditionally oriented village communities along the Fly River in Papua New Guinea were able to achieve a compensation package for pollution from Australia's largest company, mining giant Broken Hill Proprietary Ltd, after eight years of negotiations and legal action. The villagers had claimed that the waste disposal operations of its Ok Tedi mine had polluted the river to the extent of destroying traditional fisheries and other resources and disrupted their traditional river usage (*Sydney Morning Herald*, 15 June 1996:2). The villagers' grievances attracted international attention and received legal support from an Australian law firm that pursued recompense through the Australian courts (since the parent company BHP is registered in Australia).

The company attempted to circumvent the legal challenge by utilizing its influence with the Papua New Guinea government to have the government introduce legislation making it illegal to pursue damages claims outside the country (Australian High Commission to Papua New Guinea, personal correspondence 1997). This gambit failed. The transparency of the company's attempt to avoid litigation drew negative comment in the media and reinforced the moral stance taken by the villagers. It eventually reached an out-of-court settlement that has been reported as costing the company more than $75 million. Although the villagers had virtually no funds, they were able to obtain very substantial compensation, with BHP paying the villagers' legal fees of $5 million in addition to the compensation claim (*Sydney Morning Herald*, 1996). The villagers had previously won the concession of a tailings dam being constructed to contain the pollutants, in environmental terms the most important compromise made by the Broken Hill Proprietary nationally and internationally.

Braithwaite (1992) in an exploratory paper on "weak power" also argued cogently that "the hegemony of the majoritarian model" can be successfully challenged by the weaker public interest group, although his rationale applies a different emphasis from Jacobsen and Cohen. If battles were fought purely in economic terms, the powerless would invariably be beaten because the stronger interests would always prevail. But the powerless may be able to take their cause into the public and political arenas in a confrontation with a powerful player by seizing the high moral ground. And if they can link that to a perception that their cause is also in the national interest, then the powerless may unsettle the powerful. Obviously the rich and powerful can access and utilize more, better, and stronger resources; and, conversely, the allocation of resources to the weak can lead to empowerment (such as anti-discrimination legislation). But if general disapproval against the powerful can be mobilized and articulated, weaker interests can broker a shift in political support in their favor.

For example, the objective of national development may see a multi-million dollar tourism resort as contributing to that objective by generating foreign exchange earnings, creating employment, and providing infrastructure. But if that development dislocates traditional landowners, alienates their lands, and pollutes their fishing grounds, then the national identity that "we are a country which values village life and traditions and we do not want that happening in our village" may have wide support. Dispossessed landowners may be able to force powerful actors to make a choice — support a foreign, rapacious multinational or their own citizens and the ideals of national identity. "The very visibility of the international money power of the transnational can be a deficit" (Braithwaite 1992:469).

The Broken Hill Proprietary's Ok Tedi result may be viewed as an example of the fallacy of the "capacity-outcome" approach, which assumes that the outcome of a struggle can be determined by identifying the resources available to both sides (Hindness 1982). The eventual outcome of the confrontation between the traditional landowners and the Anuha Island Resort in Solomon Islands (examined in detail in Chapter 7) provides another example. In other words, it is not simply a case of power equated to resources and conversely powerlessness/lack of resources that constitutes the determinant of outcomes. Even without material and financial resources, the powerless can move through a process of empowerment that allows them to redress the original power imbalance and achieve an outcome favorable to their objectives.

Where resources of the dominant party are linked to dependency, however, subordinates will demonstrate greater powerlessness and a lesser capacity to act in ways designed to redress the imbalance of power. Where the subordinate party has a degree of autonomy, the less the need for the powerful party and its resources, hence a greater capacity to reject its power and to enter into relations with others (Lawler and Bacharach 1986). In the Ok Tedi dispute, those villages located downstream from the mine and not directly dependent upon it for wages, welfare, education and other services, were not in a dependency relationship with Broken Hill Proprietary. Therefore, it may be accepted that they had the freedom to act independently of it. But for the Papua New Guinea government, which had a shareholding in the Ok Tedi Mines Ltd company it sponsored to exploit the gold and copper deposits, and for whom the company is its single largest supplier of royalty payments, there was a strong element of inter-dependency. Its interests in this case were not readily compatible with those of the downstream villagers, hence its apparent readiness to consider legislation to prevent them from taking court action against BHP in Australia. (In 2002 BHP announced a phased withdrawal from its Ok Tedi operations because of the increasing costs of environmental safeguards.)

In terms of power/dependence relations, the former is regarded as "a function of structural position in a network of actors, that is, as control over rewards or punishments for another *relative* to the control exercised by alternative partners" (Molm 1989a:1393). Early theorists (Bierstedt 1950) conceptualized power as coercive in nature and exercised by the application of threat or force; but exchange theorists such as Blau (1964) and Emerson (1972) proposed that power is derived from the mutual dependence on rewards that is the basis for social exchange. Subsequently, Lawler and Bacharach (1986), Molm (1989a), and others integrated both of these approaches to demonstrate that power/dependence relations may "structure control over both positive outcomes [rewards] and negative outcomes [punishments]" (Molm 1989a:1393).

Findings by Molm (1989a and 1989b) raised the interesting prospect that in an unequal power relationship punishment was the most likely power strategy the weaker actor would resort to where expected rewards were not forthcoming, and where the disadvantaged party lacked the capacity to substantially increase its rewards to the dominant party to improve reciprocal benefits. However, resort to punishment by the weaker party could be constrained where there was a high reward dependence. A punishment power strategy by a weaker party was only effective where it increased the other actor's reward exchange and shifted the asymmetry of reward exchange in favor of the weaker actor. If in fact it brought punitive retaliation rather than reward, then it would serve to consolidate and reinforce the domination of the stronger actor. Some acts of terrorism may be interpreted in this context where the weaker party, lacking the power to confront an adversary on equal terms or militarily, resorts to suicide bombers, for example, in an attempt to punish the dominant party and redress the power imbalance through violence.

Location of the actor in a network is, according to Conger and Kanungo (1988), a key determinant of power differentials between and among actors. Structural location, (or those advantaged positions that have a capacity to exercise the greater power in exchange relations, rather than strategic actions), can determine outcomes — sometimes by positive action and sometimes by negative actions. By the latter is meant the capacity to exclude others from the process and benefits of the outcome: the power to keep other actors out of a situation; out of exercising any control over resources; out of control over negotiations; and out of exercising control over outcomes. This capacity of exclusion is evidence of both empowerment (by those doing the excluding) and powerlessness (by those being excluded).

A fundamental proposition of Jacobsen and Cohen (1986) is that all power relationships present themselves through contended issues. These are defined as issues that are important to both sides and on which there is disagreement. If there is no disagreement, power will not be evidenced; if the issue is unimportant to one side, there will be no exercise of power for the other party to achieve its end; and if both parties consider the issue unimportant, it is unlikely that either would resort to power. As such, power resources are seen as the pieces on the board, the chessmen in a power/dependence relationship, that those engaged in issue resolution will use. The ability to actually use those resources to achieve a desired outcome regarding specific contended issues will determine where the balance of power lies. Jacobsen and Cohen define power resources as "anything tangible or intangible, which either side can muster to its aid in a confrontation with one another" (1986:110).

According to the latter source the ability to use resources effectively will depend not only upon the amount and type of those resources but also the position of one party relative to the other to bring more or less of its resources to bear on the issue at hand. They will be "strategically placed: physically, socially, politically" in order to apply those resources effectively. There will be both a temporal and a spatial dimension to position. One must be in the right place at the right time to convert resources into effective action and thereby achieve control to ensure the desired outcome. But by themselves neither position nor resources are sufficient to conceptualize power: "resources which cannot be applied to contended issues leave their owner impotent, while a position of strength without adequate resources to hold it under pressure is a temporary illusion of power, not its reality" (1986:110).

In this approach, position is the structural element of potential power, denoting the point at which power may be exercised; and resources are the dynamic element, denoting the processes influencing the situation. To understand a given power relationship and more specifically the likelihood of potential power being converted into enacted power, the ratio of resources to position of both sides needs to be assessed. Other writers suggest that resistance rather than contention leads to a more accurate assessment of a power/dependence/domination situation. To understand the difference between contention and resistance we need to examine the concept of powerlessness, the notional opposite of empowerment.

Powerlessness

Atkinson and Delamont (1990) utilize the concepts of technicity and indeterminacy to characterize powerlessness. For them, each job is located in a two-dimensional social space of technicity and indeterminacy — technicity being the "explicit, rule-governed, codified part of a job" and indeterminacy the "hidden curriculum of job performance" (1990:106). To illustrate this concept, they provide the example of the London taxi driver for whom technicity is the knowledge of London's road system, knowledge of the regulations governing taxi operations, and the ability to pass the license test; indeterminacy is the ability to deal with drunks, bewildered "lost" tourists, a mix of customers from quite different social classes, and other cab drivers. All of the uncodified "things" are referred to as the "habitus" of an occupation. A person may achieve technicity but without indeterminacy (mastery of habitus) will be powerless. The concept of Atkinson and Delamont (1990), conceived in the context of personal empowerment, may be extended to societal groups. Such groups are also located in social space and mastery of both technicity and indeterminacy could provide the tools necessary to negotiate their way through the power brokers occupying that surrounding social space. If successful they would be able to determine their own future and one might say that they had achieved empowerment.

Some of the sociological literature on urban redevelopment focuses on the powerlessness of residents (Bramham, Henry, Mommaas, and van der Poel 1989; Cameron 1989; Mommaas and van der Peol 1989). The decisions to undertake contemporary transformation of a "slum" area, a dilapidated, under-utilized city center or industrial area may be made without consultations with those most directly affected; they will already be marginalized, with little power. The elected representatives of a city council, concerned about economic development, the state of the city's finances, and possible re-election (the politics of the situation) may see redevelopment as having many advantages for them; and they will be supported by a range of business interests (often deeply integrated into local councils) who see commercial advantage in the exercise.

Often redevelopment will be designed to present a new image of a city such as the redevelopment of Birmingham, the London Docks area, Fremantle, Western Australia (at the time of the Americas Cup Yacht Race) in the context of tourism. The new facilities thus tend to be consumed by tourists and other well-to-do pleasure seekers rather than integrating the disadvantaged (and relocated?) groups into their space. Elites from within and without take control of the facilities (Roche 1991). The politics of power predominate and citizen disempowerment rather than empowerment would seem to be a more accurate picture of the urban environment in many instances.

Those who are powerless are alienated or marginalized. The sociology of alienation is divided into two world-views, the unidimensional and the discrete. The former presupposes that different concepts of alienation are subsumed under the umbrella of a general alienation, while the latter consider that alienation is situation-specific. Different concepts of alienation represent unique, particular phenomena: many contextual factors rather than a few general forces engender alienation. General forces in society are mediated by the values, perceptions, and relations of individuals and groups (communities). Thus, it is not plausible, in the view of the discrete school, to attribute each dimension of alienation to a general syndrome.

Powerlessness will underlie some forms of alienation, when the social actor(s) lack the power "to wipe out the discrepancy between *what is* and *what ought to be*" (Travis 1988:65). For the unidimensional school, powerlessness is equated with meaninglessness (of life): the more powerless, the more meaningless. Those in the discrete school, however, would argue that powerlessness does not necessarily lead to meaninglessness, that in any power relationship there is a two-way relationship and that there are often reactions and responses to powerlessness that will attempt to mitigate its effects. While power relations imply acceptance on the part of those subject to them, paradoxically they also imply "resistance" (Barbalet 1985). This is because acceptance by social actors of the legitimacy of power over them does not mean that they cannot attempt to modify its effects. Resistance may limit power and influence the outcome of power relations. Therefore, powerlessness and meaningless will be either unrelated or negatively related according to the discrete school of thought.

Acceptance of power because of pragmatism or expediency may include a significant "resistive element", either because of a lack of interest in the goals that the authority is trying to attain, or because of hindrance, overt or covert, of the operations of the authority (Barbalet 1985:532). The integral nature of an element of resistance to power relations is in fact embodied in Weber's definition quoted earlier. Other writers have also treated resistance as an irreducible element of power relations, such as Dahrendorf (1968), Foucault (1980), and Gouldner (1960). Even Thomas Hobbes in 1651 acknowledged resistance as a component of power relations in his claim that:

> because the power of man resisteth and hindereth the effects of the power of another, power is simply no more but the excess of the power of one above that of another (Hobbes cited in Tuck 1991:57).

The notion that conflict follows from power that is resisted has wide currency. When resistance has to be overcome then power implies conflict: otherwise power and conflict are not linked. For Talcott Parsons, for example, the problem of coping with resistance "leads into the question of the role of coercive measures, including the use of physical force" (Parsons 1966:352).

However, a distinction could be drawn between resistance that is "frictional" (when two bodies come together there will be friction between them) and "intentional" that suggests conflict. Power about which there is consensus may still be faced from time to time with frictional resistance that could arise from indifference, for example, rather than any conscious or directed opposition. In such circumstances, the exercise of power to overcome such resistance would most likely be neither coercive nor forceful: in other words resistance could take many forms some of which may not necessarily be associated with conflict. Nadel has referred to the resolution of resistance and tensions that do not amount to conflict as "consociation" because of the interdependency of the protagonists (1963:181).

What the different forms of resistance will have in common will be the imposition of some limits on power, and it is these limitations that allow resistance to contribute to the outcome of power relations. When that resistance produces a transfer of some power, one may say that the process of empowerment has commenced. This could be the case in both "friction resistance" and "conflict resistance". The former could be an acknowledgment that friction could be reduced by a sharing of power, redistribution of responsibilities, etc. With directed opposition, its aggressive nature (conflict) could force a sharing or redistribution of power resulting in empowerment. Thus, empowerment may be granted, it may be taken, or it may be a compromise between the two extremes.

Resistance emphasizes the fact that power relations are characterized by both asymmetry and reciprocity. All relations of autonomy and dependence are reciprocal however wide the asymmetrical distribution of resources involved: all power relations express autonomy and dependence in both directions (Giddens 1976). The different components of the societal group will all be engaged in doing something essential for the existence and maintenance of power; both those issuing the orders and those obeying. Subordinate parties will not necessarily be obeying simply because of the "clout" of the "master" but for a wide variety of reasons. The exercise of power is thus made up of a capacity to influence and carry others in accepting a decision or situation. In short, power is not the cause of collective action but an outcome, and its source must be sought in the constellation of interlocking relationships and attributes of resources that make up a societal group. As Lukes (1974) noted, power as an asymmetrical relation can be conceptualized in terms of control, dependence, or inequality and Weber's "celebrated" definition of power is compatible with all three. Implicit in empowerment is a shift in the balance of power/powerlessness, dominance/dependency and thus changes to patterns of both asymmetry and reciprocity.

The Definition of Empowerment

Empowerment has entered the popular vernacular as a generic term denoting a capacity by individuals or a group to determine their own affairs. However, the lack of a clear definition has resulted in a proliferation of usage where different authors define the term in the context of their professional experience or a particular situation. The Australian Concise Oxford Dictionary defines "empower" as

> to authorise, license (person to do);
> give power to, make able, enable, to commission (Sykes 1987:339).

The concept of empowerment currently has much wider application than its original roots in political science. It has been found as relevant to all kinds of situations in many disciplines. For example, in education, empowering teachers in the management of schools and universities, and/or empowering students (Apple 1995; Fagan 1989), is seen as relevant to improved quality of staff teaching and student learning. It is regarded as an important concept in sociology and anthropology, where empowerment of minorities and marginalized groups is viewed as a prerequisite for their successful adjustment to the dominant society or their capacity to withstand mainstream values (Deloria and Lytle 1983; Hokansen Hawks 1992; Kymlicka 1995; McConnochie, Hollinsworth, and Pettman 1988; Pettman 1992; Ross 1992).

Criminologists, in analyzing the generally significantly higher rates of criminal activity by, and jail populations of, disadvantaged ethnic minorities also draw upon empowerment as a solution to part of the problem (Cuneen 1987, 1992; Hazlehurst 1987, 1993, 1995; Smandych, Lincoln, and Wilson 1995). Other areas of minorities studies, such as the women's movement (Minkler and Cox 1980; Wheeler and Chinn 1989), the Black Power movement (Minkler and Cox 1980), gay rights and people with AIDS (Haney 1988; Epstein and Coser 1981), the aged and the disabled (Rose and Black 1985), have adopted empowerment advocacy to counter perceived discrimination and advance their perceived rights.

The field of nursing is beginning to examine empowerment of nurses within the total health system, and empowerment of patients as contributing to their recovery (Gibson 1991; Hokansen Hawks 1992; Katz 1984; Minkler 1989). Gibson's (nursing perspective) definition recognizes three primary factors of empowerment: attributes that relate to the client (patient); attributes that relate to the nurse; and attributes that belong to both client and nurse. Here, empowerment is a social process that is designed to facilitate people controlling their own lives. It achieves this by recognizing, promoting, and enhancing people's abilities to meet their own needs, solve their own problems, and mobilize the necessary resources. Even more simply defined, "empowerment is a process of helping people to assert control over factors which affect their health" (Gibson 1991:359).

Business management has adopted empowerment in terms of a devolution of authority and decision-making from top level executives to workers on the factory floor (Jones and Davies 1991). This is expanded a little in the section below on empowerment in the commercial sector, including hotel management. Political science views empowerment in terms of a re-assignment of power to a group or community or nation whose power had been alienated by force (Boldt 1993; Dyck 1985; Green 1995; Hall and Jaques 1991; James 1992; Lijphart 1995). This element of a *return* of power because of prior disempowerment–empowerment is lacking in most other disciplines' consideration of the concept. For other disciplines the conferring of power or granting of rights to groups that may never have experienced real authority previously (such as factory workers, hotel staff, patients, pupils) is seen as empowerment.

Simmons and Parsons have a summary definition of empowerment as "the process of enabling persons to master their environment and achieve self-determination" (1983:199). They consider that empowerment may occur through individual change, interpersonal or interactional change, or change of social structures, that have an impact on the individual. Onyx and Benton define empowerment as "the taking on of power at both the individual and social levels" and when it "is located within the discourse of community development [it is] connected to concepts of self-help, participation, networking and equity." They consider participation is a vital part of empowerment since such involvement in decision-making affecting people's lives opens the door to "confidence, self-esteem, knowledge and [the development of] new skills" (1995:50). Rappaport (1984) points out that because empowerment is a process it is difficult to operationalize and no single measure can capture it adequately. However, each measurement, intervention, and description in a particular context adds to the understanding of the construct.

The question that much of the discussion on empowerment leaves ambiguous is the degree of self-reliance or self-sufficiency necessary for empowerment to have occurred. At one end of the spectrum are those writers who consider that it is essential for self-help to be total, with minimal outside intervention or assistance. At the other end of the spectrum are those who consider that involvement in decision-making is sufficient (McArdle 1989). An immediate problem with the purist's approach is that often it is those most in need who have the least resources and capacity to help themselves. This has proved the case in many community development programs in Third World countries. There has been a high failure rate of such programs because of the fallacious assumption that communities in poverty had the capability to help themselves once the opportunity was presented to them: external assistance was to be occasional or "one-off" lest the community become dependent upon that outside source of support (Kotze 1987). There is also the problem that such communities may lack even the basic knowledge to set an agenda for discussion of appropriate development and in a sense be disempowered prior to any consideration of the issues because of their inability to control the agenda.

The difficulty with accepting the other extreme view is that except for involvement in decision-making, everything else is left to the experts and the professionals. It can be criticized as tokenism, particularly because it fails to recognize the fundamental proposition that as long as the process is controlled by others who have access to the resources then the process is actually one of disempowerment (Rose and Black 1985). People faced with conditions or circumstances introduced or imposed by external forces do not simply receive them passively but will tend to respond actively. As Friedman said in respect of plantation economies in the Caribbean, "There are no single uniform responses to conditions imposed from outside forces. Rather the variety of local conditions generates a variety of responses to forces that may lie outside the reach or control of individuals" (1988:7).

Similarly, Y. Cohen (1983) asserts that what is observed within may have its source without, meaning that individuals make endogenous decisions based largely on exogenous pressures. The range of responses and adaptations will be designed to exert a degree of control by the local actors over the situation. They may be more, or less, successful depending upon the tools available to assist in attaining that objective. There may be a structure, for example, that allows them to facilitate their capacity to exert certain rights; or to exercise certain decisions. Indeed, the very process of challenging, adapting, reacting, responding, may set them on the path towards empowerment. In other instances, lack of a structure to facilitate the implementation of decisions may frustrate desired action and thereby prevent desired outcomes. In such circumstances, the lack of empowerment may generate resort to action outside legal sanction.

Self-Development Through Empowerment

Kieffer perceives empowerment in an individual's development as a process of moving through four stages of human life. The first stage, the "era of entry" parallels the developmental stage of infancy. In this stage, the participation of the individual "is exploratory, unknown and unsure while authority and power structures are demystified" (1984:12).

The "era of advancement", the second stage, parallels late childhood. It is

> characterized by a mentoring relationship as well as supportive peer relationships. Opportunities exist in this stage for collaboration and mutually supportive problem-solving. A critical understanding of the situation is gained with the assistance of an external enabler. The individual develops mechanisms for action and accepts responsibility for choices. Additionally, rudimentary political skills are developed (1984:13).

The third stage is termed the "era of incorporation" wherein "activities are focused on confronting and contending with the permanence and painfulness of structural or institutional barriers to self-determination. In this phase, organizational, leadership, and survival skills are developed." This stage parallels adolescence. The fourth stage, the "era of commitment" is a period "in which the individual integrates new personal knowledge and skills into the reality and structure of the everyday life world" (1984:13, 14). This stage parallels adulthood.

Kieffer's model may be seen as more evolutionary than revolutionary, where the individual, through a labor-intensive process, integrates into the existing structure. Other concepts of empowerment may be considered revolutionary because the focus will be on changing and reforming the structure of society: empowerment by gay rights movements, women's liberation groups, and so on, may be seen in this light. These may involve individuals in personal growth and development, but the action by individuals in securing their common objectives as a coherent pressure group is a form of community empowerment, that Minkler and Cox refer to as "functional conscientizing" (1980:22).

Empowerment may thus be regarded as a developmental concept, both at the level of the individual and of the community. Individual, family and community growth and potential are enhanced by empowerment and it may be viewed as either a process or an outcome. In a broad sense empowerment is a process by which individuals, organizations and communities gain mastery over their own lives (Rappaport 1984). Part of the difficulty in defining empowerment is that it takes on different forms in different contexts (Wallerstein and Bernstein 1988). Therefore, empowerment of the individual (for example, a patient in a health care situation) will be qualitatively different from empowerment of an organization (say a gay rights association that is given a legal identity by government legislation). The implication is that empowerment will be possible in many competencies given a variety of niches and opportunities (Rappaport 1984). In other words, while one may be able to identify some general principles, empowerment will be amenable to definition not in a single way but according to the contextual situation.

Empowerment as a Transactional Concept

Because empowerment is a process that involves relationships between individuals and/or communities and others, it is a transactional concept nurtured by the effects of collaborative effort (Kieffer 1984). In this context Katz (1984) views empowerment in education within a synergistic paradigm: the interrelationship involves a sharing of resources, and collaboration is encouraged by the process. According to Gibson, the process "entails mutually beneficial interactions that strengthen rather than weaken the mediating structures between the individuals and the larger society" (1991:355). Simmons and Parsons (1983) make much the same point, and Hess (1984) notes that power is both taken and given. Hegar and Hunzeker (1988) define empowerment as being both dynamic and democratic because of this element of sharing power. There is a need to consider not only how the "powerless" take power but how the "powerful" release power. Collaboration theory is weak in this aspect (Reed 1997).

Nursing science literature has as a constant theme the need for those in power (doctors, hospitals) to "release" power to nurses, and to patients (Gibson 1991; Hokansen Hawks 1992); health is not the kingdom of doctors and hospitals (Anderson 1990; Labonte 1989); although nurses and doctors have a responsibility to promote health they do not have a monopoly on health (Dunst, Thrived, Davis, and Cornwell 1988; Hegar and Hunzeker 1988; Labonte 1989). The nurse is challenged to expose power imbalances that prohibit patients from achieving their full potential (Butterfield 1990).

Some authors (Gibson 1991; Watts 1990; Wheeler and Chinn 1989) have defined empowerment in terms of "male" and "female" concepts of power. A female view has power conceptualized as "a condition of being able to achieve some object in cooperation with others" in contrast to "a male view of power where there is a limited supply that must be struggled for and defended against others" (Gibson 1991:355). This interpretation, suggesting that empowerment involves a redistribution of power, may be seen as advancing social justice. Conflict and tension are seen as inextricable elements of the process of empowerment when pursued from the male perspective; growth and sharing more likely outcomes of the female approach. For Katz (1984) divergent and conflicting solutions to problems are viewed as essential components of the process of empowerment because "old" problems can be seen in new ways and may cease to be problems; out of negative tensions may rise positive solutions.

But to be effective, empowerment requires more than actions to increase self-esteem, or one's efficacy, or promoting positive behavior of different kinds: it will normally require environmental change as well (Wallerstein and Bernstein 1988). Stated another way, there will be intrinsic and extrinsic connections between those ostensibly being empowered, those "doing" the empowering, and a range of economic, political and social forces that shape situations (Butterfield 1990). Often, for empowerment to be effective there must be accompanying change in one or others of these areas since empowerment is a multi-dimensional concept (Kieffer 1984).

The Murrell-Armstrong empowerment matrix (Murrell and Vogt 1990) provides a model for analyzing empowerment in which it is viewed as an inter-active process with two or more people. Designed originally for organizational management it has been applied to areas as diverse as education (Apple 1995), public administration (Labonte 1989) and nursing (Hokansen Hawks 1992). The matrix incorporates five settings of interactive empowerment: dyad, small group, organization, community and society. Six categories of empowering methods are described: educating (the sharing of information as well as helping others to learn, use and create new information); leading (involving others in the decision-making process); mentoring/supporting (the provision of support and guidance to others to help them achieve their goals); providing (resources are found and supplied); structuring (includes promoting organizational arrangements that allow or limit activities); and actualizing (builds upon the previous methods and involves the individual and the organization as the individual performs what he or she is best prepared to do at the highest level).

Regardless of the orientation of application, most sources refer to empowerment as providing opportunity and resources to build, develop, or increase the ability and effectiveness of others (Freire 1970; Imai 1986; Kymlicka 1995; Lijphart 1995; Pettman 1992; Smandych *et al.* 1995). Freire, writing in the context of Latin America and oppressive military regimes, in outlining his concept of "conscientization" (1970:64–69) refers to the need for "the silence of the masses" to be broken by "naive transivity" in which there is a passage from ignorance and marginalization to popular consciousness. As conscientization begins to expand through literacy and education and there develops a clear realization of the obstacles preventing the masses from attaining more equal rights and benefits accruing to other levels of society, "cultural action" for freedom (revolution) emerges through praxis — the "authentic union of action and reflection" — and challenges the power of the elite (Freire 1970:68). For Freire, conscientization and praxis could provide the building blocks for increasing the capacity of the masses to challenge the conceptual and cultural domination that prevailed in the slums and villages of Latin America.

Excepting violent revolution or other means of force, in order for empowerment to succeed as a process of *sharing* of power, both parties (the one that empowers and the one that is empowered) must share a common purpose. If indigenous participation in tourism development is the goal, then it must be a vision shared equally by those who define the parameters of development and the village communities themselves. Mutual goal-setting and decision-making will be present. Both parties must exhibit commitment to the process: the party that has power must be willing to devolve authority, provide choices and encourage involvement in decision-making; and the party being empowered must be prepared to assume responsibility and participate in goal-setting and decision-making (Hokansen Hawks 1992). In a case of genuine empowerment the lines distinguishing the "empowerer" from the empowered will be somewhat blurred because the emphasis will be on achieving the common purpose, not on control over others. The result is one in which the empowered community will have an increased ability to set and reach goals for its own ends.

Indigenous Minorities and Empowerment

The literature about indigenous communities and empowerment is summarized briefly because, in the context of the South Pacific tourism case studies examined in this book it is considered to have particular relevance. There is a considerable literature on the phenomena of indigenous people and indigenous tourism, of which V. Smith's seminal collection of essays entitled *Hosts and Guests* (1977) is perhaps the most widely quoted, and that could claim to have legitimized indigenous tourism as "a pursuit of scholarly research" (Butler and Hinch 1996:6). The concerns expressed in these essays included the potential for marginalization of indigenous communities and indigenous entrepreneurs, domination by interests from the developed world, problems of commoditization and authenticity, the impacts of acculturation and tourism's role in that process, and tourism as a new form of colonialism. A more recent volume of essays edited by Butler and Hinch entitled *Tourism and Indigenous Peoples* pursues many of the same themes. Their definition of indigenous people is:

> races of people who are endemic or native to a destination region. As such this group may represent either the majority or a minority group in the destination. The terms is inclusive and global in its application (1996:9).

This definition is consistent with that adopted by the United Nations for its 1993 International Year for the Indigenous Peoples of the World. Indigenous people are:

> minorities and tribal populations with special problems related in particular to discrimination and deprivation of basic human rights, and with special needs concerning education, health, economic development and the environment (United Nations General Assembly resolution 46/128 of 17 December 1991).

While noting that indigenous communities around the world vary greatly in demographic, economic, cultural and other terms, the United Nations Development Programme Report stated that:

they share several common characteristics which taken together, define indigenous people as vulnerable groups often living in extreme poverty. These characteristics are: a subordinate position within national societies; marginal and inhospitable territories; subsistence economies; languages which are, for the most part, unwritten; cultural marginalization; maladjustments due to migration from rural to urban areas; and threatened ancestral habitats, particularly rainforests (UNDP Report 1992:2).

It is of interest that while the United Nations devoted significant attention to the plight of indigenous peoples and asserted the need for consultations and a process of self-determination, it did not utilize the term "empowerment". In effect, however, it was moving in that direction with statements such as that made by the UN Technical Meeting on the International Year for the Indigenous Peoples of the World:

Foremost among these [characteristics of indigenous peoples] is the special relationship which indigenous peoples have to the land and nature. This special relationship may have numerous implications at the policy level, for example, by making projects involving displacement from historically occupied territory, even with monetary and land compensation, unacceptable to indigenous people. Alternatively, projects which are imposed without the sometimes lengthy consultations with traditional decision-making institutions based on debate and consensus characteristic of many indigenous communities may bring dissension rather than improved conditions. A knowledge of these and other features of indigenous society are necessary for the successful planning and implementation of projects. . . . [It is] important to involve indigenous peoples in the planning, implementation and evaluation of projects affecting them (Report of the United Nations Technical Meeting on the International Year for the World's Indigenous Peoples, 9–11 March 1992:17).

Butler and Hinch also did not specifically use the term "empowerment" but they confronted the lack of ownership by indigenous peoples in their definition of indigenous tourism, that is:

tourism activity in which indigenous people are directly involved either through control and/or by having their culture serve as the essence of the attraction. The factor of control is a key one in any discussion of development and tourism development is no exception to this rule. Whoever has control can generally determine such critical factors as the scale, speed, and nature of development (1996:9).

Empowerment as a theoretical concept has been applied to explore the marginalization of indigenous communities following colonization usually in the context of law and order issues and the destruction of traditional social structures. The argument is that because control of their own destinies has been removed from them, typically through dispossession of their traditional lands, there has been a breakdown of indigenous societies (McMullen and Jayawardene 1995). Much of the literature on indigenes and empowerment thus focuses on asserting the value of indigenous autonomy as both a necessary foundation and a vital ingredient of future justice strategies. However, many of the same arguments could equally be applied to the issue of development for such communities.

The inter-connection with dependency theory, center–periphery constructs, colonialism and also modernization is obvious. Development paths, patterns, and forms may be dictated by dominant outside authorities, often in terms of models imported from overseas with no regard for "fit" with the local community structures. The involvement of indigenous peoples by way of consultations, appointments of advisors, employment into new "indigenous" positions, training courses in indigenous cultural and social perceptions and values, etc., by the contemporary, dominant systems are often seen as merely diverting resources, personnel, and attention in the wrong direction, away from the creation of indigenous models.

Conventional state-sponsored and state-controlled development strategies in countries with indigenous minorities (such as Australia, Canada and New Zealand), are based on one assumption. A regime that utilizes colonial constitutional and legislative instruments can effectively implement development at micro community levels if only it undergoes a relatively painless "sensitization" process with minimal adaptation. This assumption has been criticized as fallacious by Cuneen (1992), Dyck (1985), Hazlehurst (1995), among others.

Havemann (1988) and MacNamara (1995) in commenting on Canada's indigenous peoples and the Canadian legal system both reached similar conclusions. Reform of the police and justice systems was criticized as being directed towards social control (for more effective policing) rather than self-determination, with only lip service being paid to indigenization. Havemann commented that "indigenization has emerged as an ameliorative policy within the criminal justice system . . . which compounds the net-widening effect of the hybridized social service and order-maintenance policing which indigenous people experience" (1988:81). Social control, not self-determination, was the main concern.

MacNamara (1995) suggested that until strategies were introduced within the context of an exercise by aboriginal communities of autonomy, effective reform would not take place. These strategies would need to address dispute resolution processes between aboriginal communities and the wider society to offer the possibility of genuine alternatives for dealing with matters of social harmony, the maintenance of order, and development in aboriginal communities. Autonomy was necessary to overcome the underlying reality of dispossession. "The first step is to recognize that tinkering won't work and what will work is empowerment. Until the [Canadian] justice system can accommodate the reality of self-determination it can hardly begin to deal with the situation" (1995:2).

Policies of assimilation, paternalism, and the top-down imposition of decisions may be replaced with empowerment of communities and the development of policies designed to support rather than pre-determine a range of community-based initiatives. The views of Havemann, MacNamara, Hazlehurst and others emphasize the need for empowerment to be based on a constitutionally recognized right. This is possibly because they are approaching the topic from an analysis of perceived shortcomings in the legal system. This legal basis is essential for the capacity of the "pioneer space empowerment" concept, outlined in Chapter 7, to provide the alternative approach. In traditional societies, before the advent of a state, empowerment could be achieved through a sharing of power between parties that was sanctioned by the social mores of the society in the absence of a formal legal foundation.

Swain's model for indigenous tourism (1989) also emphasizes the necessity of some politically sanctioned power if tourism development is to be sustainable. Swain does not use the term "empowerment" in her analysis of the Sani minority in Yunnan Province in China, although she does touch upon aspects of power relationships between the state and minority communities. This is similar to and in common with other authors who have analyzed indigenous and minority communities involved in tourism, such as Altman (1989), and the Australian Aborigines, Hall (1996) and the NZ Maori. Power, dependency, exogenous control and the need for greater autonomy are often characteristic terms, but the concept of empowerment is not linked in to their analyses and explored.

Incorporated into Swain's model is the notion of the nation state as the key actor required to create an environment conducive to ensuring that the community has the capacity to act upon its decisions and sustain them. In the particular case of the Sani people in China, it was legislation that created land rights and granted limited political autonomy. The 1984 Law on Regional Autonomy of Minority Nationalities provides a mechanism for empowering (this author's term) a local community to make decisions in its own right, rather than as a unit subsumed within a generally applicable and uniform tourism development regime. It requires authorities responsible for development to accept *and respect* the right of the community to make a decision for or against its involvement and the use of its resources in tourism development; and then to have the power to carry out that decision.

Swain's analysis demonstrates the way in which the minority community has been able to move into Sani-controlled tourism ventures in a significant way even though at times there is a contradiction of policy in terms of state regulations, ethnic rights, and the need to counter "museumification" of Sani culture by the Yunnan Province's tourism marketing authority. This latter occurs, she suggests, because of the paradox between conservation and change in the process of development, the standardization of ethnic culture controlled by the state for tourist consumption with staged "authentic" events, and with tourists themselves having expectations of their ethnic hosts being "quaintly non-modernized" or "museumized" (1989:37). A "restructuring of political relationships" occurred as the state, that once suppressed minority cultures as uncivilized during the Maoist regime, became the promoter of cultural forms while also validating ethnic group awareness and legal rights (1989:38).

A paradox remains, however, as the modern Chinese state needs cultural pluralism for successful ethnic tourism (Swain 1989; Sofield and Li 1998) while political and economic infrastructure integrates minority groups into majority society. "Control that the Sani may have in tourism is contingent upon the national political climate" (Swain 1989:38). If the concept of empowerment is applied to Swain's analysis, the conclusion to be drawn would be that the devolution of a certain degree of power from the state to the minority group has produced an element of cooperation in tourism development between the Sani and the state that constitutes a rationale for continued ethnic identity, indigenous rights, economic independence, and cultural diversity, i.e. sustainability.

Empowerment in Rural Development

There is a vast literature on rural development, originating from sources as varied as the United Nations, the Commonwealth of Nations, and other international agencies; financial institutions such as the World Bank, the International Monetary Fund and the International Bank for Reconstruction and Development; government development assistance bureaus (such as USAid) that are run by all First World countries as part of their foreign affairs policies, international diplomacy (and often trade); special ministries within most "Third World" governments and often special divisions within ministries devoted to the rural poor; non-governmental organizations; development workers; and academics.

A common theme throughout much of this literature is the need for rural communities, especially the most impoverished and/or oppressed sectors, to be given a greater role in determining their future. One influential writer (but by no means the only one) is Chambers, probably best known for his two books on the need to "put the last first" (*Rural Development: Putting the Last First*, 1983; and *Whose Reality Counts? Putting the First Last*, 1997). In these two volumes, Chambers argues that in most approaches to rural development the course of any project or program of development will be determined in the main by "outsiders" who, no matter how well-intentioned, will often inevitably distort the flow of benefits to the target communities, or deliver (or not deliver) programs with any lasting benefits. The very terminology used to describe rural communities, such as "remote", implies this outsider domination, because of course such communities are only remote from urban, developed, civilized centers. "What to do" has similar connotations: it implies action taken from the center, channeling resources outwards and downwards to the remote and powerless. Chambers (1983) has termed this "the paternal trap of core–periphery perception and thinking". "At the end of the day, however much the rhetoric changes to 'participation', 'participatory research', 'community involvement' and the like, at the end of the day there is still an outsider seeking to change things. Marxist, socialist, capitalist, Muslim, Christian, Hindu, Buddhist, humanist, male, female, young, old, national, foreigner, black, brown, white — who the outsider is may change but the relation is the same. A stronger person wants to change things for a person who is weaker" (Chambers 1983:141).

There is no complete escape from this paternalistic trap: the poor are poor because they lack the resources (material, economic, educational, human, etc.) that are controlled by Chambers' "outsiders" and they must therefore rely to some extent upon assistance from the center. Even a decision not to act by the center must be seen as action impacting upon the poor because they can be affected as much by what happens as what does not happen. In order to lessen this paternalistic dependency, Chambers argues, the approach to rural development must be reversed: the desires and objectives of the rural poor must be put first and the capacities, views, and values of the professionals held in abeyance and only harnessed to assist in bringing to fruition those desires and objectives of the poor. Chambers in effect is arguing for the emic to replace the etic in analyzing and implementing rural development (his application of the core–periphery approach), and for empowerment of rural communities.

Despite more sophisticated approaches to rural development assistance, many projects fail to achieve their potential because of neglect to take account of political factors. There are two main aspects to this. The first concerns the need to ensure that the project design is compatible with existing policies and/or political institutions. One national tourism policy plan formulated for the Kingdom of Tonga by a group of international European experts was never opened beyond page one of its Executive Summary by its recipients because of this issue. The plan proposed the abolition of "the nonsense of Sunday observance" so that tourism could function seven days a week. In this devoutly Christian kingdom, Sunday observance is manifested with the closure of all public services including a ban on all flights (power, police, and hospitals operate with emergency staff only), and virtually all private businesses. In addition, leisure activities such as swimming and sunbathing at beaches on the main islands are banned, with non-stop church activities the order of the day. This tradition is backed by current legislation and dates back to the 1860s when the then king of Tonga declared his entire kingdom Christian and adopted the old English edict of "rule by divine right", with the royal household the center of all authority and of Sunday worship. The tourism planners, in proposing the abolition of Sunday observance, were in effect not recommending economic reform for more efficient tourism but calling for a revolution in the governance of the kingdom (Sofield 1994).

The second aspect of failure to take full account of political feasibility occurs when planners and rural community development workers do not ask the crucial question: who gets what, when, where, and how? When this question is not addressed, projects and programs will run the risk of being "intercepted, distorted, and captured by powerful interests and local elites" (Chambers 1983:161). Some programs result in augmenting the wealth and power of the already rich and powerful. Many outsider agencies and institutions turn a blind eye to such an outcome because they are rewarded by those actions that yield quick and visible results: utilizing and/or involving local elites opens doors and facilitates delivery of aid that might otherwise be obstructed. By contrast in many cases, poverty alleviation is a long-term rather than a short-term outcome. There is thus often a need to confront powerlessness and plan around entrenched interests. Chambers has produced a table to illustrate the relative acceptability of different types of approaches to rural development by elites and governing institutions (Table 3.1).

Various participatory development methodologies have been designed to encompass a greater degree of involvement by the recipients of poverty alleviation. But unless there is a real devolution of power down to the local level in perhaps the majority of instances, most methods will remain under the control of outsiders. In the early 1980s, Rapid Rural Appraisal (RRA) was suggested as one way of reducing outsider domination and ensuring that planners and developers tapped into local knowledge bases through a bottom-up learning process from the target communities (Chambers 1983; Collinson 1981,

Table 3.1: Acceptability of Rural Development Approaches for Local and Other Elites

Dimension to rural deprivation	Examples of direct approaches	Acceptability to local and other elites
Physical weakness	Eye surgery camps Feeding programs Family planning Curative health services Emergency relief	**HIGH** ⬆
Isolation	Roads Education Extensions	
Vulnerability	Seasonal public works Seasonal credit Crop insurance Preventive health	
Poverty	Distribution of new assets Redistribution of existing assets	
Powerlessness	Legal Aid Enforcement of liberal laws Trade unions Political mobilization Non-violent political change Violent political change	⬇ **LOW**

Source: Chambers 1983: 164

Hildebrand 1981, Rhoades 1982). The main approach was to utilize a multi-disciplinary task force (a team might, for example, include an agricultural economist, an anthropologist, a sociologist, a physical planner, a demographer, and a statistician). The team might spend only one or two weeks in the field with the community (hence "Rapid"). Team members would combine their expertise to sit with, listen to, and learn from members of a target community using a variety of techniques such as open-ended and structured interviews, workshops, simulation exercises, participant observation, and questionnaires. The greatest weakness of RRA is that since consultations take place over a short period of time the dynamics of processes may be missed; its strength lies in its multidisciplinary input combined with input from the local community. RRA is not intrinsically empowering because of its dependency upon the attitudes and behavior of team members. But if the inherent tyranny of outsider domination can be modified, then RRA may be considered as contributing to empowerment. However, by itself this is only one part of a multifaceted process.

Towards the end of the 1980s Participatory Rural Appraisal (PRA) appeared (Chambers 1997). This approach places even greater emphasis on professional planners and experts being facilitators rather than implementers and exploring in greater depth indigenous technical knowledge. PRA is characterized by seeking power reversals between the "uppers" (outside experts) and "lowers" (local people) when properly executed. Moving from a closed experts' superiority to an open sharing between the uppers and lowers "restrains the normal dominance of the etic, and encourages expressions of emic reality" (Chambers 1997:155). There is a reversal in roles, with the local people accepted as experts and teachers and the outsiders placed in a learning mode. Analysis has shifted from the urban office to the rural village. PRA has the local people involved in drawing up budgets, monitoring progress, and evaluating outcomes. Where RRA is primarily directed towards research for data gathering, quantitative measuring, and analysis by outsiders, PRA is more specifically directed towards comparing understandings, so that local realities are not obscured but fore-grounded through visual representations and self-analysis. There is a reversal from the written to the verbal and the visual, in order to empower local communities by circumventing the need for formal literacy: many PRA techniques are visual, relying upon the local participants to draw maps, diagrams, and/or pictures (on the ground, with sticks and stones, on bark, etc.). The information that arises from the process is seen as owned, analyzed, and used by the local community, a major reversal from the RRA approach that is more extractive than empowering. Where RRA is a short-term technique for amassing a variety of data quickly, PRA is much more measured and may be spread out over a relatively longer period. In fact, according to some practitioners it should be an ongoing process.

However, PRA may be no more empowering than RRA if it follows the tendency to involve those local people already more attuned to involvement since they will in a relative sense already be empowered — "the better-off, local elites, officials, local leaders, men, adults, the healthy, rather than the worse off, the underclasses, the vulnerable, lay people, women, children, the disabled and the sick" (Chambers 1997:155). For example, because of the workloads invariably carried by women in many rural communities, trying to find undisturbed blocks of time long enough to allow their meaningful participation is difficult. It is also virtually impossible for the facilitator not to influence the outcome(s) no matter how sensitive he/she may be. As Cornwall and Fleming noted; "If PRA is to have a meaningful influence on mainstream development practice, radical institutional, personal and professional changes are needed" (1995:11). PRA is incomplete as an empowering process unless there is substantial environmental change whereby there is actual/genuine devolution of power and responsibility to the rural community.

Empowerment in Business and Organization Management

The management literature on empowerment interprets Western business management as being traditionally dominated by top-down accounting and decision-making to control the operations of the company and the behavior of employees. The latter will impose restrictions that govern the employee relationship with the customer; quality satisfaction of customer needs may be subordinated to the need for performance measures imposed on employees by management. Where accountancy management dominates, cost centers proliferate and control every part of production or operations. Although a particular service may be attracting customers (such as the provision of free cups of coffee during waiting periods), seen in the isolation of cost center accounting the coffee is a cost that may be interpreted as thereby reducing the profit margin on the process for which the customers are waiting. In this type of management there is a restricted flow of information from the top down, and employees at the non-managerial levels are kept out of the decision-making process. Similarly, the capacity of workers at the coal face to provide information to management (upwards or reverse flow of information) is often difficult.

This *modus operandi* is contrasted with the Japanese style of operating businesses where *kaizen* (empowerment) as it is understood in business operations and management is held to have originated (Imai 1986). Accounting information is used to track financial results and to plan the extent and financing of a company. But the purpose is not to control business operations or to direct and control workers — or managers (Johnson 1992). In Japan, empowerment is characterized as being process-oriented rather than results-oriented management (Imai 1986).

The bottom-up empowerment cycle of business management and operations is one in which ownership of information is disseminated to both the workforce and the customers, where the end result is greater customer satisfaction that then translates into improved trading performance and profitability. The effective operation of a company practicing empowerment encompasses actions generally described under the rubric "TQM" (total quality management). TQM specifically refers to

> company-wide programs to empower workers and managers to solve problems scientifically with an eye to constantly improving customer satisfaction. Driven by a strong customer-focused mission, all personnel in a TQM environment pursue a well-defined improvement process, such as the highly publicized strategies articulated by Motorola and Xerox. TQM should be seen as a people-oriented way of running business, not just another way to achieve better results by pursuing business as usual (Johnson 1992:6).

However, actions consistent with TQM usually conflict with what is prescribed by conventional western management accounting controls. The challenge for many western companies is to make the paradigm shift from the one to the other.

In terms of the tourism industry, the concept of empowerment is occasionally considered in the context of hotel management (Huyton and Baker 1992). This is a variation on business management concerns rather than on tourism development *per se*. Empowerment in the hotel sector is "basically about pushing responsibility and decision-making down the organization to those employees closest to the customer" (Jones and Davies 1991:213). The Marriott Hotels Group has been a leading proponent of this form of empowerment in this sector for more than a decade. There appear to be few studies, however, that focus specifically on empowerment and tourism development outside the business sector.

Non-Governmental Organizations and Empowerment

In the past decade, structural adjustment programs intended to encourage Third World countries to pursue market-led export-oriented development have become the central feature of development as prescribed by the World Bank, the International Monetary Fund and other such agencies. Increasingly this approach has been challenged because of its emphasis on utilizing existing systems of control and economic, political and social structures that has resulted in a further concentration of wealth and power in the hands of political and economic elites (often one and the same). The objective of spreading development to all sectors of the population and especially to the rural and urban poor has not been achieved, with conspicuous consumption by the elites expanding and lesser benefits reaching the masses. Disparities between rich and poor in many countries have increased rather than narrowed. This has been exacerbated by a global trend to reduce state spending on welfare programs, to downsize government and reduce state responsibilities while promoting alternative solutions based upon private market forces and increased community contributions (Mishra 1990).

In response to criticism about the failure of structural adjustment programs, organizations and agencies for development have been "discovering" community participation, although many non-governmental organizations (NGOs) have been involved in "grassroots" participatory activities for several decades. The World Bank has recently recognized that community participation is "a means for ensuring that Third World projects reach the poorest (people) in the most efficient and cost-effective way, sharing costs as well as benefits, through the promotion of self-help" (Craig and Mayo 1995:2). The United Nations Development Program, commenting on challenges confronting development in Third World countries, stated that:

> The best route is to unleash people's entrepreneurial spirit — to take risks, to compete, to innovate, to determine the direction and pace of development. It is fitting therefore that this year's Human Development Report has peoples' participation as its special focus. Peoples' participation is becoming the central issue of our time (1993:1).

This report defined participation as "access to decision-making and power" as well as in terms of economic participation (UNDP 1993:21). It is thus moving towards embracing empowerment, although it does not go so far as to set out strategies for achieving this end. This institutional support for community participation contains the same weakness in scope that we find in planning literature advocating greater "community consultations", "self-help", "self-reliance", "self-management", and similar phrases: it lacks explicit recognition of the need for empowerment if development is to be sustainable.

Even the Brundtland Commission is deficient in this respect. While it concluded that "effective citizen participation" is one of the main prerequisites for securing sustainable development, it did not specify empowerment as the ingredient in participation that is necessary for "effectiveness". If attention is drawn to the most recent paradigm in development — sustainable development — one finds the same shortcoming. The Australian government, for example, in the report of its Task Force on Ecologically Sustainable Development, enunciated a set of principles, several of which emphasize the need for community consultation and community participation in decision-making (Commonwealth Government of Australia 1992); but taking the next step of empowerment is absent from its report.

Non-governmental organizations tend to have a better record (certainly at the micro-level) than governments and international agencies in promoting community participation that extends to empowerment (Constantino-David 1995; Galjart 1995). However, the jury is still out on whether these interventions are effective in terms of alleviating poverty in a sustainable way (as distinct from augmenting incomes over the duration of a project) at a national level. Galjart quoted a Dutch evaluation of NGO activities in six developing countries which concluded that there was no evidence at the national level that there had been a redistribution of resources or income because of NGO-supported empowerment (Zaal, *Impactstudie Medefinancierings-programma 1991*). However, this report provided examples of grassroots organizations acquiring access to resources and services at the local level. Van Niekerk's (1994) appraisal of NGO projects in Bolivia and Peru indicated the success of such assistance at the village level in the Andes. A similar study of 16 British sponsored NGO projects concluded that while they achieved a certain degree of success, in many cases the monetary costs of intervention were greater than the economic outcomes.

It is of interest that 10 years ago, NGOs were often portrayed as radical in a political sense, partly because of their pursuit of empowerment which was seen as posing a challenge to existing power structures. They are now often seen as more effective implementation agents than governments. They are considered to be more cost-effective. They target rural and urban poor, other disadvantaged groups (such as women) and uneven characteristics of economic and social growth in very direct ways as beneficiaries of their efforts. They do not require large bureaucratic support structures. They appear to have highly motivated personnel prepared to work in village environments without expensive expatriate housing, motor cars, allowances, etc. They remain for relatively long periods of time in close contact with the local population, encouraging their active participation in decision-making. Since their successful projects imply some reliance upon and thus incorporation into and acceptance of the prevailing economic order, that very success contradicts the NGO radicalism that the order is unjust and must be changed; the perception that such institutions constitute a political threat dissipates (Sofield 1997).

Further, as the World Bank has noted, communities that do not have projects imposed on them but participate because of their own decisions are less likely to "deconstruct" those projects or set alternative goals (Bhatnagar and Williams 1992). People become more willing to contribute to the realization of a project and to be less ready to see it fail. Thus agencies such as the World Bank have given increasing support to NGOs engaged in development work in Third World countries.

There is one element in the NGO support for community participation and empowerment in development that requires elaboration. As agents of change, NGOs do not automatically carry out the informed wishes or desires of the target group. They tend to operate by consensus which means that either side has the power of veto over the other. An agreed plan will almost certainly be a combination of endogenous and exogenous components arrived at after lengthy discussions (that may be presented as consultations although in fact "negotiations" may be a more accurate description of the process). During these discussions, community participants may agree on a particular plan of action not because it is in fact their preferred option for development but for unrelated social reasons, such as an unwillingness to publicly oppose the views of a prominent village elder. In this context, social representations theory (Pearce *et al.* 1996) could be aptly utilized to analyze community views.

The need to access resources controlled by the NGO may also sway them to move in a certain direction that may in turn induce a degree of reliance upon the NGO. There may also at times be conflict and tension between the NGO technical expert and the more socially oriented value system of villagers; and the fact that NGO professionals may be more accountable to their donor agency than to their clients. All of these circumstances have been experienced by this author while working with village communities in Solomon Islands, Vanuatu, and Fiji to introduce development projects. Empowerment in these situations may be less than complete.

There is also the possibility that NGOs' ideals may not be shared by the village community as the recipient of their attention so that they may pursue alternative action to that desired by the community itself. The NGO program may be presented as giving the community a choice of services tailored to their needs. But the way this process is carried out often remains firmly under the control of the experts, whose knowledge base is privileged over the life experience of community members. As Onyx and Benton noted, "This kind of approach to empowerment attracts the criticism of tokenism. It fails to recognize that as long as the processes are controlled by others who have access to the resources, then the process is actually disempowering" (1955:51).

Today we have an increasing number of governments, politicians and officials in many countries promoting "empowerment" — indeed, there is a certain global acceptance of the slogan. Rahman states however that "such growing endorsement notwithstanding, participatory development is far from being adopted in practice anywhere in a way that leads to major structural reforms and the transfer away from those vested interests that control dominant social and political structures towards underprivileged people" (1995:26). There is an element of political correctness that seems to account for many governments talking glibly about "empowerment" but not implementing it in any real way — because implementation of course would require at least a sharing of power and in some cases perhaps a transfer of power. Governments have historically been slow to take such steps. It is suggested that in fact this current orthodoxy (of expressed government support for empowerment) conceals very divergent interests and meanings (Craig and Mayo 1995).

Empowerment in Tourism Development

When the application of empowerment is considered in the context of tourism development literature, it is conspicuous by its virtual absence. Self-determination, community participation, and community consultations tend to fall significantly short of empowerment. Murphy advanced the notion of a pluralist conception of the tourism policy-making process through community-based planning, an approach he termed "community-driven tourism planning" (1985:18). Krippendorf (1987) argued for a new approach to tourism planning more sympathetic to local concerns with community social elements given equal weighting to economic aspects. Britton (1984, 1991) pursued a structuralist conception of politics that would involve communities. Hawkins listed 19 major issues for tourism planning and development that included as its eighth item: "Resident responsive tourism is the watchword for tomorrow: community demands for active participation in the setting of the tourism agenda and its priorities for tourism development and management cannot be ignored" (1993:186), but took it no further.

Following on from Hawkins, Ritchie identified key tourism research topics needed in his view "to encourage and facilitate resident-responsive tourism" (1993:208). But an examination of his topics suggest that again there is a certain advocacy of tourism that is accepted as a given. The need, it would appear, is in fact to persuade residents of the benefits of tourism rather than to empower them to make their own decisions. For example, his sixth topic is "to assess the ongoing implementation of a program to enhance resident reception of visitors" (Ritchie 1993:208). Poon (1992) in a discussion of tourism planning advocated what she termed "new tourism" in which *inter alia* the emphasis would shift from host communities as passive recipients of tourism to becoming the managers themselves of guests and associated infrastructure. Her concept of management extended to ownership, with control being manifested through the exercise of management.

In a stimulating analysis of the value of social representations theory for examining community involvement in tourism, Pearce *et al.* (1996) emphasize the importance to be attributed to the role of community. Social representations are "the concepts, statements and explanations originating in daily life in the course of inter-individual communications" (Moscovici 1981:181) and the theory "focuses on both the content of this social knowledge and the way this knowledge is created and shared by people in various groups, societies or communities" (Pearce *et al.* 1996:31). What people think about tourism, what they expect from it, and how they should interact with tourists are all aspects of social representations, an important point being that their views (or "public opinion") may not be based on an accumulation of factual knowledge or any particular capacity to apply such knowledge in an expert way. Social representations according to Pearce *et al.* can be used to understand how different community groups think about tourism and the results can then be taken into account in the tourism planning process. They provide considerable detail about the processes that may be associated with that involvement. They advocate the value of social representations theory to foster "a more sophisticated understanding of how communities react to the burgeoning phenomenon of tourism" and how the need is to develop greater awareness of "community reactions to tourism" to assist and improve its planning. According to the authors "In any discussion on community involvement in tourism development decision making, the question of power and influence becomes a dominant consideration" (Pearce *et al.* 1996:183).

However, there is no advocacy by Pearce *et al.* of the primacy of a role for the empowerment of community in considerations of tourism. In their detailed discussion of community participation in tourism planning of some 30 pages, the word "empowerment" does not appear, although their definition of community involvement is one in which members are to be part of the decision making and implementation process (1996:181). In the same vein, their opening chapter is entitled "Why Do We Need to Understand *and Manage* the Tourism-Community Relationship?" (italics added). This question has a pre-emptive tone that seems to deny empowerment of communities and thus follows the pattern of much of the tourism planning literature. According to these authors, "The final form of the tourism product is a statement of the powers and degree of cooperation among the interacting political, community and business parties" (Pearce *et al*. 1996:181), but again this seems to preclude the implementation of a community decision that may wish to not proceed with a tourism venture or other form of involvement in it. It seems that social representations are presented rather more as a technique by which to better manipulate communities to accept and acknowledge the benefits of tourism development decided by agendas formulated from "outside", than as a means by which to empower communities: "the social representations framework can thus provide . . . conceptual support for what mediation attempts to achieve in the more conflict-oriented tourism decisions" (Pearce *et al*. 1996:197). However, the theory could be a potent force for empowerment if utilized to assist communities to understand themselves and their attitudes towards tourism.

All of these approaches are predicated on policy formulation taking place within quite different value orientations and perspectives with varying degrees of community participation, but they appear more concerned with process rather than outcome. Community support for tourism development rather than control by community of development is expounded. In this context, the concept of sustainable development must also be treated with caution where its emphasis on consultative processes falls short of any real devolution of authority because it does not embrace empowerment.

Empowerment is about political and social power, and development (as noted in Chapter 2) is about political power. We turn full circle then from development as economic growth to development for social justice and equity, which is where it is suggest empowerment may be implanted into the politics of tourism development. There are five generally recognized major elements to politics, all of which impinge on the process of empowerment: the activity of making decisions in and for a collection of people, whether a small group, a community, an organization, a nation, or a group of states acting in an international grouping (such as the United Nations, World Tourism Organization); the various policies and ideologies that help to establish the various choices that affect decisions; the question of who makes the decision (one person, a group of people, an elite) and how representative they are in terms of the situation about which they are making decisions; the processes by which decisions are made; and how decisions are implemented and applied to the community (after Jaensch 1992).

In other words, politics is about control, and power governs the interplay of interested parties at all levels, whether local, regional, national, or international, trying to influence the direction of policy, policy outcomes and the position of tourism in the political agenda (Hall 1994; Lyden, Shipman, and Kroll 1969). As Sabatier and Mazmanian (1983) noted, the substance of policy, (or the general focus on data) needs to be connected to the processes of policy making including the relationship between power, structure and ideology. Analyzing the network of interaction between dominant groups and ideologies operating within a political and administrative system will lead to an understanding of whether power is being shared (empowerment) or withheld.

This use of the concept of power is "inextricably linked to a given set of value assumptions that will predetermine the range of its empirical application" (Bernstein 1973:12). In this context the case studies presented in subsequent chapters will probe the politics of tourism development in an attempt to understand the limitations that empowerment (or lack thereof) imposes on the scope for decision-making and implementation.

Much of the literature on tourism development does not address questions of power and values. Rather, development issues are examined from a technical-rational or managerial perspective that excludes substantive questions of politics (Hall 1994). Where the literature on development does include an excursion into politics often the argument is couched in ideological terms (such as capitalism versus Marxism) where the values of the researcher are intrusive, such as Britton (1984) whose views are transparent in his critique of tourism development in Fiji as being shaped by the forces of dependence. Of course, no researcher is entirely objective, devoid of feelings, emotions and ideology in pursuit of intellectual endeavors, but balance as a desirable trait is sometimes difficult to attain.

As outlined in Chapter 2, the varied resources and efforts directed toward tourism development by most countries demonstrate that a democratic form of government is not a prerequisite for government attention/involvement in tourism development. It is considered necessary to touch on this issue briefly because the value system accompanying democracy incorporates the ethical issue of the rights of individuals in a way that not only permits but often encourages and supports various forms of equity and empowerment. Therefore, some might be inclined to argue that empowerment cannot take place outside such states.

It is probably true to say that empowerment of communities for tourism development is more likely to occur in democratic countries than in dictatorships, military regimes, and centrally controlled economies. However, the failings of some democratic countries in extending empowerment to communities has been documented on numerous occasions (one has only to consider the current debate in Australia about Aboriginal empowerment, especially land rights, to appreciate this).

On the other hand, empowerment may occur in communist regimes. For example, the 1978 "Open door" policies of China resulted in hundreds of thousands of private companies, both community and individually owned, being established and operating in sectors previously restricted to the state (Sofield and Li 1998). Legislative reform in 1984 made individual rural households responsible for meeting production quotas, in effect disempowering the Communist Party cadre who formerly controlled all production in each village and hamlet throughout rural China. Swain's (1989) research among the Sani minority also confirms that these transfers of responsibility demonstrate that a communist regime may implement a form of empowerment.

In many countries state involvement will not lead to empowerment. Despite the attention that may be paid to tourism policy, planning, and development by a national government, the practicality, application and implementation of those policies, plans and developments must often be placed in the context of the local levels of authority and their communities. This is the crux of empowerment. Without empowerment at the local and community levels, there will be failures in transmitting national effort to development on the ground. In the 1968 "Bellagio Declaration on Planning" (OECD 1968:8) the OECD stated that "Planning . . . must be performed at the lowest effective level to make possible a maximum of participation in the planning itself *and in its implementation*" (emphasis added). As Wanhill (1987:54) noted: "At the end of the day the implementation of any tourism strategy on the ground rests with the tiers of local government." Community whose "closest" representative in government is the local council is not mentioned.

This key element is often overlooked. Hall begins to approach the problem when he states that "In nearly all political systems and especially in federal systems, there are overlapping levels of policy formulation and implementation. Such a situation can often lead to problems in translating tourism policies from the national to the local level and vice versa" (1994:154). He goes on to describe community-oriented tourism planning by writers such as Murphy (1985), Blank (1989), and Getz (1991) as posited on a pluralistic approach in which decision-making is shared by all in a community. However, as Macbeth noted, these models and Hall's own model for tourism planning "foreground" the planners not the community because there is no transfer of power. "Most of the (community) participation is essentially reactive and consequently the agenda is set and the decisions are made elsewhere" (Macbeth 1996:7).

Painter (1992), citing Pateman (1970), has drawn a distinction between "pseudo", "partial" and "full participation" based on assessments of the potency displayed by community participants. Pseudo participation is restricted to providing information and seeking endorsement of what has been decided elsewhere, and is said to offer a sense of being involved but in fact is lacking in real substance. Partial participation provides community members with a capacity to exercise some influence but the final decision making power rests with an external authority. Full participation describes a situation where each individual member involved in the decision making process has equal power to determine the outcome.

In reality, there will rarely be equal opportunities for all parties within a community to participate in the decision-making process. Citizen empowerment will in fact be deficient. In most instances, some groups will be excluded from the decision-making process, such as when communities may be denied any right to veto the hosting of a major tourism event. Governments may use their power to make decisions without any comprehensive public information about the spread of costs and benefits, so that communities may be led — deliberately or inadvertently — to acquiesce in decisions. Those exercising power may thus be able to exert a significant degree of control over what people care about (perhaps the Victorian Government's decision in 1995 to host the Grand Prix races for 10 years in Melbourne is a case in point, since no community consultations were established as part of the decision-making process). In short, the agenda is set outside the community. In Lukes' (1974) terms, the power lies with control of the agenda.

Often there may in effect be a situation of "non-decision making" that may not be revealed by adopting the pluralist approach to community decision-making analysis. That is because this approach proceeds to identify all those groups involved in reaching actual or concrete decisions; by definition, non-decisions are excluded from consideration. There is thus a danger that non-decision-makers will be overlooked and conclusions may be drawn indicating that there is empowerment because clearly defined groups will have roles that can be mapped in the decision-making process. In fact, power elites with a capacity to push their points of view and to protect their interests may be excluding significant components of a community population. Power behavior may also include deliberate decisions not to act; those with power may use their power to create or reinforce barriers to prevent an issue being placed on the agenda, or simply by their inaction prevent a decision on an issue being reached (Hogwood and Gunn 1986). O'Gorman (1995) made a similar point with reference to empowerment of communities in development projects in Brazil.

It is of interest that the World Tourism Organization (WTO) in its definitive study of tourism planning basically ignores the politics of tourism. In doing so in a sense it seriously weakens its planning efforts because it ignores questions of power and empowerment, that are essential to implementation. The stated aim of the WTO's 1994 publication is to outline "concepts of national and regional planning and the basic approaches, techniques and principles applied to these levels". The first part explains planning concepts and describes planning and marketing methodologies. The second part consists of 25 case studies of tourism policies and plans. Both parts of the publication "reflect the WTO's basic approach to planning for the integrated and sustainable development of tourism in its global technical cooperation activities" (1994:viii, ix).

The World Tourism Organization includes sustainable development as an important principle underlying tourism development, but the emphasis on its advocacy role is evident throughout the book. For tourism to develop, development is regarded as synonymous with growth: more facilities, improved infrastructure, greater diversity of attractions, staging of special events and finding alternative uses for facilities in low seasons, increasing economic benefits, expanding efforts to educate host communities about the positive side to tourism, and so on. Public involvement in planning is mentioned — but in the context of accepting that while people "should be involved in the planning and development of tourism in their areas" if they are so involved "and if they understand the benefits tourism can bring — they will more likely support it" (1994:9).

The World Tourism Organization makes it clear that it prefers the "top-down" approach:

> The "bottom-up" approach involves holding meetings with local districts or communities to determine what type of development they would like to have. These local objectives and ideas are then fitted together into a national or regional plan. This approach achieves greater local public involvement in the planning process. *But it is more time-consuming and may lead to conflicting objectives, policies and development recommendations among local areas.* These conflicts need to be reconciled at the national and regional levels in order to form a consistent plan (1994:10; emphasis added).

In its case study of the national tourism development plan that the WTO prepared for Sri Lanka in 1992, emphasis *was* placed on community involvement in tourism. It proposed that its Sri Lankan model serve as the archetype for other countries wanting to manage community involvement in tourism development. However, the proposal is bureaucratic, "top-down" and requires an unrealistic input from the private sector.

Under this model, local tourism committees would be established in all areas of resorts or where substantial tourism activity exists or is proposed, with the private tourism business sector providing support (including funds) because they would recognize it was in their interests to do so. The composition of these committees is prescribed for the communities concerned. They will be composed of persons representing tourism-related businesses, other business interests directly or indirectly affected by tourism, local police, representatives of community interests (there is no comment on how these representatives might be selected or elected), and social and community liaison workers who are to be appointed to each major project and paid for by the developers. The work of the committee is not to provide input into proposals for the national plan (that had already been formulated in the case of Sri Lanka), nor to assess the impacts of proposed tourism developments. Rather "there should be a public relations campaign to inform local residents of what to expect in tourism development, and how to take advantage of the new business coming into their area" (WTO 1994:213).

In areas of "high social vulnerability where major tourism projects are proposed, a tourism community liaison officer should be appointed by the tourism committee" and "his salary would be borne by the developer of the tourism project". Although this officer would be paid by the developer "he should represent the interests of the community, including low income and socially vulnerable groups". There is more along the same lines: tourism operators should commit themselves to supporting the local committees, they should commit themselves to respect and promote local culture and small businesses in the areas in which they operate (even if they are in direct competition?), they should underwrite the costs of setting up "local community tourism centers" in their resorts and hotels that would provide a range of services (some of which would probably be in direct competition, such as craft and souvenir shops and information on competing resorts), and so forth. The office of the tourism liaison officer should be located in these centers and "encouragement should also be given to establishing a branch of the tourist police in each resort area". The serious question of conflict of interest is not mentioned. The WTO Sri Lankan plan for proceeding with these ideas for community involvement is that "after government adoption of the community tourism proposals (in the plan), the next step is implementation. This will require organizational initiative, technical assistance and some funding" (WTO 1994:214–215).

In short this proposal is about managing community involvement in a way that will seek community support for planning already put in place from outside (top-down), and to assist in minimizing adverse community reaction, rather than genuine community involvement in determining for itself the role of tourism development in its community. It is more concerned, it would appear, with a public relations exercise than real commitment to community involvement — what Arnstein (1971) referred to as "tokenist participation". The WTO's definition of sustainable development paradoxically does not extend to empowerment, which would seem to have no place in the WTO design of things. It is perhaps little wonder that the Sri Lankan government had to establish a Working Committee to work out how to make the National Tourism Plan work; and after two years they had still been unable to effect implementation (Sofield 1995).

Mowforth and Munt (1998) make similar stringent criticisms of the jointly sponsored World Travel and Tourism Council (WTTC)/WTO/Earth Council's (1995) response to the Rio Summit on global environmental concerns in their report entitled "Agenda 21 for the Travel and Tourism Industry: Towards Environmentally Sustainable Development." While it contains "all the right words" it is seen as platitudinous in the extreme, with the emphasis on harnessing environmental interests and concerns to maximize benefits for tourism in ways that do not allow communities the right to choose not to participate in tourism development. Like the WTO's model planning attempt, it is seen as prescriptive.

Collaboration theory has been applied to tourism specific planning recently (Jamal and Getz 1995; Selins and Beason 1991) and would appear at first glance to represent a significant step towards empowering communities. "Collaboration offers a dynamic, process-based mechanism for resolving planning issues and coordinating tourism development at the local level". Collaboration theory is "a process of joint decision-making among autonomous, key stakeholders . . . to resolve planning problems . . . and/or to manage issues related to policy and development" (Jamal and Getz 1995:187–188). This definition "emphasizes the ability of individual actions to engage in purposeful activities for mutual self-interest" and it suggests that the planning process should focus on "defining where the optimum balance of interests lies among competing sections (of a community) and on using specific techniques to bring it about" (Reed 1997:568). Jamal and Getz view power as an instrument to be managed and balanced to ensure optimal solutions and that collaboration can overcome power imbalances by involving all the stakeholders in a planning process that meets their needs.

There are shortcomings in this approach, however. Collaboration theory tends to assume that "the planning and policy process is a pluralistic one in which people have equal access to economic and political resources" (Reed 1997:567). This is patently absurd. It is nevertheless at least an implicit assumption in ecological models of tourism planning such as that advocated by Murphy (1985). Second, when collaboration fails it tends to seek causation solely "in individual processes rather than considering broader structural features within which the processes are embedded" (Reed 1997:568) such as prevailing power structures.

Third, it does not explain how and why those with power would be willing to redistribute it to other stakeholders to ensure collaboration produced an optimal solution. In this context, Jamal and Getz suggest that a local government agency could act as arbiter; that this "suitable convenor" should be appointed early in the process of collaboration, when power is not initially equal, to bring about a necessary balance (1995:190). Jamal and Getz address the issue of power, and indeed have developed a table suggesting that power relations must be dealt with at all stages of the collaborative planning process. But government authorities have their own agendas, particularly at local community levels where they are often elected from the local business community; they often act formally as regulators and controllers of development; they operate informally as agents of influence; and they cannot therefore be regarded as automatically neutral and thus able to play the role that Jamal and Getz advocate (Hollinshead 1990; Macbeth 1996; Reed 1997).

Finally, the question as to exactly who are legitimate, key stakeholders may be a contested issue. Also, who should represent "the community" is often vexatious. Blank (1989), for example, notes that "community leadership is heterogeneous, drawn from a number of power bases" (1989:54) and Reed points out that "resistance to building a community tourism product may come from political leaders, a dominant industry, the Chamber of Commerce, and others" (1997:568).

It is obvious that some writers and researchers into community participation in tourism planning and development do not avoid considering dimensions of power; but empowerment as part of that consideration is a concept about which they tend to be silent. Reed (1997), for example, investigated the inability of a voluntary group representing the community of Squamish, British Columbia, Canada, to have their community tourism development plan implemented although it was formally accepted and approved by the local council. She concluded that "power relations are an integral element in understanding characteristics and consequences of community-based planning where tourism is emergent" (1997:588). In advocating greater attention being paid to power imbalances in the context of community involvement, she stated that "theories of collaboration must incorporate power relations as an explanatory variable that demonstrates why collaborative efforts succeed or fail, rather than as an instrumental variable that suggests how power can be balanced or convened" (1997:589). Interestingly, she did not refer to the concepts of the implementation gap or empowerment in her analysis of Squamish.

More genuine involvement of community is advocated by Brass (1994) in his "Community Tourism Assessment Handbook" that starts with the assumption that tourism is not necessarily good, and that communities should have the right to reject (and thus effectively prevent) tourism as part of their development strategy if they wish. Macbeth has developed an eight-step "process model" for involving communities in tourism planning, the starting point of which is that the model "does not assume that tourism is good for or will be chosen by a community but rather assumes the right and responsibility of the community to make some choices" (1996:11). This approach grew out of research into a rural community in Victoria, Australia, that was in effect disempowered by a state government decision to abolish its shire council and amalgamate it into a larger, centrally controlled administrative unit. The model proposed by Sofield and Birtles (1996) for indigenous peoples' consideration of their cultural resources for tourism also underpins the right of local communities to reject any involvement and supports empowerment at the grass roots level. The Indigenous Peoples Cultural Opportunity Spectrum for Tourism (Sofield and Birtles 1996) incorporates ways to operationalize community decision-making in a meaningful way, stripping back the rhetoric and focusing on freedom of choice, allowing a community to move either towards or away from tourism. It is specifically described and formulated as a mechanism for community empowerment.

Construct of Empowerment for Tourism Development

In summarizing the review of the literature about empowerment, four themes emerge to define empowerment: those based on a distribution of power (Ellsworth 1989; Emerson 1972; Kanter 1977) with both political science and sociology as milieus for this approach to empowerment; those meaning to enable or make possible (Hokansen Hawks 1992; Hazlehurst 1995) with the analysis of indigenous peoples and political processes such as decolonization and Third World country development included here; empowerment as professionalization (Maeroff 1988); and empowerment at the level of the individual; self-empowerment as self-development (Kieffer 1984). The third lies outside the scope of this thesis; and the fourth is summarized only in the broad and not accorded detailed discussion because of its focus on the individual rather than community. This is not to say that within community empowerment there will be no self-empowerment. Indeed, those in a community leadership role will often display strong personal growth as a result of the empowerment of their community (*vide* the case of Yaro Levu village, Mana Island, Fiji, in Chapter 9). Empowerment may thus be regarded as a developmental concept, both at the level of the individual, of the community and of larger units including countries. Indeed the exercise of independence and attainment of sovereignty may be seen as empowerment in process.

While the emphasis is on empowerment as a process, it may also be regarded as a concept, as outcome, and as a dynamic for two-way exchange. Empowerment as a concept rests on a philosophical base (the acceptance of equity principles and social justice). It is regarded as "good", as "right", as "correct". The presence of equity principles and social justice in empowerment thus introduces ethical considerations (what is "right", what is "wrong", what is "good", what is "bad"). In a search of the tourism literature one finds that several areas in particular have focused on this issue of ethics such as those writers examining: the sociocultural impacts of tourism and advocating humanistic and socially responsible responses; the environmental impacts of tourism, and most recently, those advocating ecotourism where "green codes of behavior" are being proposed; the area of sustainable development that also integrates ethical issues, apparent from its definition as development capable of meeting present needs without compromising future generations' ability to meet their needs; and a fourth area related to marketing, where a need for greater social responsibility is advanced.

It is within this general framework that community support for and involvement in tourism development is strenuously advocated by many writers. However, while "meaningful community input" is said to be essential (Hall 1995:190) and virtually all models of tourism planning incorporate public and community participation, most of them are market driven, and could be described as "reactive and containment public participation" (Macbeth 1996:8) because they tend to be placed in the context of *how* to achieve tourism development plans, rather than permitting communities real choice. Even noted tourism planners such as Gunn (1993), Inskeep (1991), and Murphy (1985), while rightly giving community participation a high profile in their planning models, foreground the planners, policy professionals, financial interests, and government authorities. Empowerment as the strategy for achieving a meaningful degree of participation has been found in only a few instances such as those mentioned above (Brass 1994; Macbeth 1996; Sofield and Birtles 1996).

Empowerment of communities for tourism development requires a political framework that is either supportive (proactive) or at least neutral, not obstructionist. In situations of dual systems, (traditionally oriented communities located in the social and political space of a modern state) there must be effective means whereby empowerment embedded in Weber's traditional or legitimate base can be transformed into legally sanctioned empowerment if it is to be a vehicle for sustainable development. There must be a shared willingness by community, individuals, and external entities (authorities) to initiate and undertake the processes leading to empowerment (the so-called "environmental change" of Wallerstein and Bernstein 1988). A fundamental tenet is that it must be able to counter dependency. If it cannot/does not, then it cannot be defined as genuine empowerment. As Jacobsen and Cohen state,

> resources which cannot be applied to contended issues leave their owner impotent, while a position of strength without adequate resources to hold it under pressure is a temporary illusion of power, not its reality (1986:110).

These comments emphasize the necessity for positive support emerging from the public sector, working in partnership with peoples' organizations, if a project is to be sustainable. The concept of empowerment thus includes as an essential characteristic the wider issue of the role of the state. As Craig and Mayo write:

> Without engaging with the state and with political processes at different levels, localized community actions risk remaining marginalized, if occasionally incorporated. The importance of developing strategies to link local projects into wider strategies and movements for change at both national and international levels is clearly defined. ... This issue is critical in relation to longer-term goals for transformation. If community participation and empowerment are to contribute to such longer-term goals, then strategies need to be formulated ... to engage wider political processes and to be set within a framework of (existing) economic, social and political structures (1995:9–10).

In the context of tourism development it is proposed that empowerment be regarded as a multi-dimensional process that provides communities with a consultative process often characterized by the input of outside expertise; the opportunity to learn and to choose; the ability to make decisions; the capacity to implement/apply those decisions; acceptance of responsibility for those decisions and actions and their consequences; and outcomes directly benefiting the community and its members, not diverted or channeled into other communities and/or their members.

This concept of empowerment by and of communities is at once both a process and an outcome. It is an amalgamation of several different emphases, although a key component is the decision-making model that encompasses application or implementation of decisions. This concept is derived in part also from the social exchange theory literature, especially Emerson (power/

dependence relations, 1962); Blau (dependence, subordination, prestige and power in social exchange, 1987); and Molm (linking power structure and the use or non-use of power, 1988, 1989a).

Another key element resides in the first two points. Many communities, especially those in developing countries, will lack any real understanding of what it is they are supposed to be making decisions about. Often they will make decisions in ignorance — "unconscious incompetence" (Romm and Taylor 2000:283) — and often from positions of relative weakness when confronted with multinational and/or government forces arraigned against them. The first two points admit external expertise: to assist a community's understanding of the real meaning of a situation and the decisions they are being asked to make; and to achieve a modicum of balance in the power relationship. They constitute a manifestation of the adage that "Knowledge is power" and are regarded as essential to empowerment.

Empowerment of communities may be considered a social phenomenon, in contrast to many studies of the exercise of power, and of the topics often studied in surveys associated with tourism. People's attitudes, decisions on destinations, career achievements in different sectors of the industry, tourism satisfaction, motivations for visiting different attractions and engaging in different activities, all of these are certainly socially conditioned and influenced, and many are oriented toward other people; but these factors themselves refer to the acting and thinking of individuals and not to a social process.

Equally, individual empowerment may be analyzed in terms of the individual's behavior, and conflict can be dissected according to the motives of the adversaries. However, in the construct of empowerment, as with social exchange, attention is centered "directly on the social process of give-and-take in people's relations" rather than on the psychological motivation of those involved in the process (Blau 1987:85).

Social exchange theory "dissects the transaction process to explain the interdependent contingencies in which each response is dependent upon the other actor(s) prior action and is simultaneously the stimulus evoking the other's further reaction" (Blau 1987:85). It is thus a particularly appropriate tool for analyzing reciprocity and relationships in Melanesian society. It does not focus on ego's prior conditioning, experiences or attributes but rather on the alternating reciprocities underlying the social interaction: the motivation of the participants is taken as given. It ignores psychological reductionism to concentrate on the social processes of the exchange relationship. Similarly this concept of empowerment may be considered an outcome of the social processes of social exchange where those processes result in a change of the power balance between the actors.

The concepts of empowerment, tourism development (especially involving indigenous communities), and sustainable development in the context of political and socioeconomic environments have been synthesized and the following propositions formulated:

- That without the element of empowerment tourism development at the level of community will have difficulty achieving sustainability.
- That the exercise of traditional or legitimate empowerment by traditionally oriented communities will of itself be an ineffectual mechanism for attempting sustainable tourism development.
- That such traditional empowerment must be transformed into legal empowerment if sustainable tourism development is to be achieved.
- That empowerment for such communities will usually require environmental or institutional change to allow a genuine reallocation of power to ensure appropriate changes in the asymmetrical relationship of the community to the wider society.
- That, conversely, empowerment of indigenous communities cannot be "taken" by the communities concerned drawing only upon their own traditional resources but will require support and sanction by the state, if it is to avoid being short-lived.

The case studies that follow provide specificity in examining the validity or otherwise of these propositions. Each of the case studies exhibits different characteristics and opens up to detailed analysis the process of empowerment for tourism development.

Chapter 4

Tourism Development in the South Pacific

This chapter provides an overview of tourism development in the South Pacific, especially in the context of the economies of the Island states in order to place the succeeding case studies in perspective. In geopolitical terms an area is normally described as a region if it meets the three major criteria of common borders, contiguity and compactness (Herr 1985b). There is one area of the globe, however, covering more than 17.5 million sq miles (about 28 million sq km) of ocean which meets none of these criteria, but which is nevertheless referred to as a discrete region. It encompasses more than 20 countries which are characterized by insularity, an absence of common borders, smallness of the entities concerned, and dispersal (Herr 1985b). Their combined land mass is only 551,000 sq km — and if the largest polity (Papua New Guinea) is removed, the total is less than 65,000 sq km (Fairbairn 1985).

The South Pacific region (Figure 4.1) contains some of the world's smallest micro-states and is loosely defined as including all those island countries east of Australia from New Caledonia to the Cook Islands and French Polynesia, and north from New Zealand to Kiribati, the Marshall Islands, the Federated States of Micronesia, Palau, Guam, and the Northern Marianas. Easter Island and the Galapagos Group are not included, nor is Hawaii. These are considered part of the Americas because of their political associations rather than their geographical locations. While Papua New Guinea is included, for the purposes of this text Irian Jaya (which since its incorporation into Indonesia has been regarded as part of South East Asia) is not.

This definition is predicated on membership of the pre-eminent political regional organizations, the South Pacific Forum based in Suva, Fiji, and the South Pacific Commission (re-named the South Pacific Community in 1999) based in Noumea, New Caledonia, together with their associated technical agencies such as the Tourism Council of the South Pacific, the South Pacific Regional Environment Program and the Regional Civil Aviation Council. Thus, unless otherwise qualified, in this chapter the term "South Pacific region" incorporates the countries and territories of American Samoa, the Cook Islands, the Federated

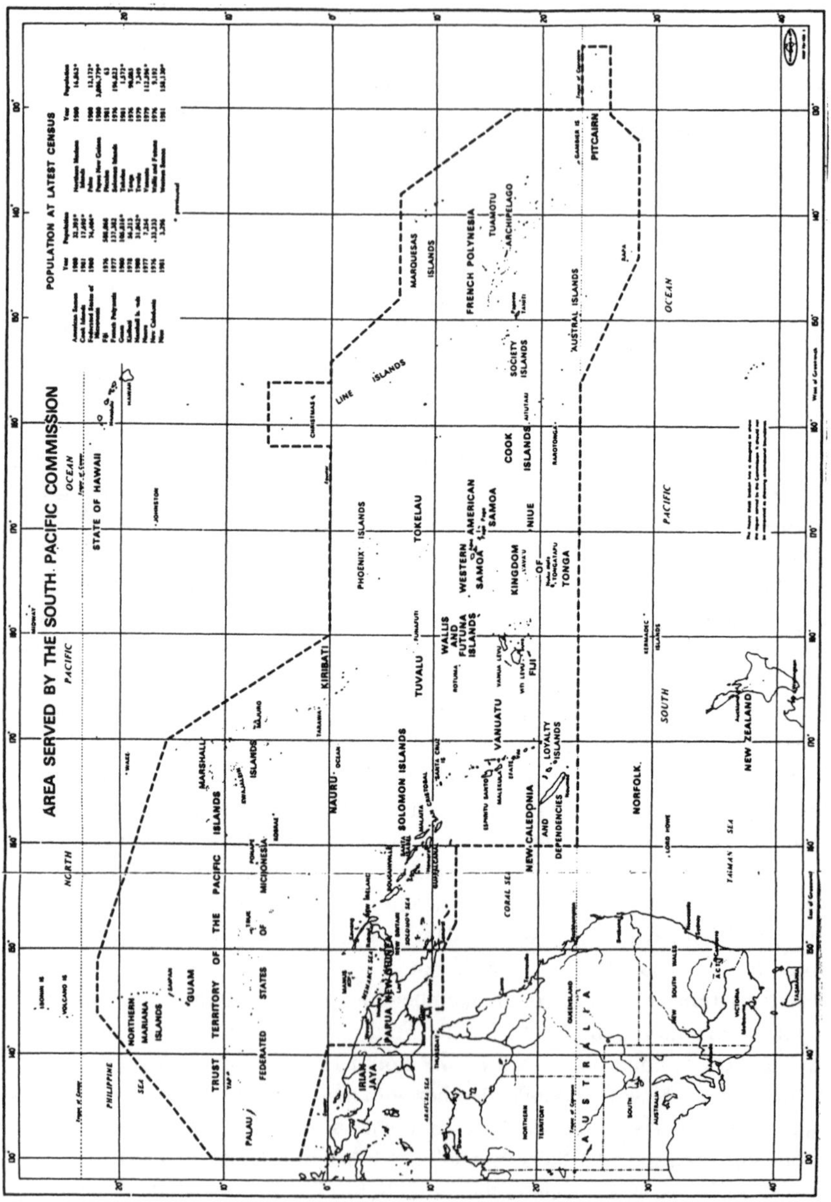

Figure 4.1: The South Pacific Region
Source: South Pacific Commission

States of Micronesia, Fiji, French Polynesia, Guam, Kiribati, the Marshall Islands, Nauru, New Caledonia, Niue, the Northern Marianas, Palau, Papua New Guinea, Pitcairn Island, Solomon Islands, Tokelau, Tonga, Tuvalu, Vanuatu, Wallis and Futuna, and (Western) Samoa (renamed just "Samoa" in 2000). Pitcairn Island, a British possession, and Tokelau, a New Zealand Trust Territory, have no tourism facilities, although both receive the occasional "adventure" tourist and cruising yacht.

Tourism and the Micro-States of the South Pacific

To understand the particular role that tourism plays in the South Pacific it is essential to have an appreciation of the smallness of these states of the region. Their very micro size works against their economic viability because of the impossibility of achieving economies of scale in many instances and this characteristic heightens their vulnerability (Pollard 1987). They exhibit many of the same characteristics of Third World tourism in general, but island tourism economies have their own special problems (Britton 1987a; Sofield 1996).

Several of the South Pacific countries vie for the honor of being the smallest.

Tuvalu (formerly the Ellice Islands) has an estimated population of 10,450 (2000). Its nine coral atolls have a total land area of only 24.4 sq km. They stretch in a winding chain for 580 km and are dispersed over 1.3 million sq km of ocean. Their highest point above sea level is less than five meters.

Niue, with a current population of 2000, has the smallest population although with a land area of approximately 190 sq km it is eight times larger than Tuvalu. It is an uplifted coral atoll with its cliffs reaching a maximum height of about 55 meters.

Nauru is also a single uplifted coral atoll of 22 sq km and 7000 people (about 4500 Nauruans and 2500 non-permanent migrants). Because of its phosphate reserves it has the largest per capita income in the South Pacific and for a number of years was ranked third in world per capita incomes after Brunei and the Gulf States. However, the extraction of phosphate has created a "moonscape" for 80 percent of the island by exposing the underlying base of coral rock, reducing habitable areas to a narrow coastal strip and a very limited area around the perimeter of a small inland lake which was once fresh but is now contaminated and saline. By 2001 phosphate mining had almost ceased as the deposits were exhausted.

The *Cook Islands* has a resident population of about 17,000 and a land mass of 240 sq km for its 15 atolls and islands. Some 25,000 Cook Islanders have migrated permanently to New Zealand and about 5000 others reside in Australia and the United States.

Kiribati consists of 33 atolls totalling only 710 sq km, with the highest point only four meters above sea level and the widest point less than 500 meters excluding the uplifted atolls of Banaba and Kiritimati (Christmas) Island and shares the honor of being the lowest and the narrowest with Tuvalu. At the other end of the scale, however, its tiny land mass generates one of the largest 200 nautical mile economic fisheries zones in the world — more than 3.5 million sq km. It has a population of about 82,000 (2000).

At the other end of the scale is *Fiji*. With a population of around 720,000, a total land mass for its 300 islands of 18,200 sq km and a GNP of approximately $600 million, Fiji is the largest of the small island countries of the South Pacific. Most of its land mass consists of high islands of volcanic origin with only several small atolls in the east.

Papua New Guinea, while geopolitically part of the South Pacific region, has a land mass of almost half a million square kilometers and a population in excess of four million. As such it is not classified as a small island state.

These variations of smallness find a reflection in the size of the annual budgets of the micro-states and the paucity of resources they are able to devote to tourism. Four of them, Nauru, Niue, Tuvalu, and Wallis and Futuna, have no separate tourism authorities. Niue and Tuvalu have but two designated positions within a relevant ministry with responsibility for tourism issues. The annual operating budgets of three of the region's national tourism authorities are less than $100,000. Another three have annual budgets of less than $0.5 million. Six of them have a staff of less than ten. Only American Samoa, Cook Islands, Fiji, New Caledonia and French Polynesia maintain a tourism promotion office overseas.

Niue has one hotel with 20 beds. Tuvalu has one hotel with 26 rooms. Kiribati has one hotel with 60 beds and two resorts with 30 beds combined. Only Fiji has more than 5000 beds. French Polynesia, Papua New Guinea and New Caledonia have more than 1500 beds. The Cook Islands has about 1000 beds. All other states and territories have less than 500 beds. In 1999 Fiji received more than 400,000 tourists, but this dropped significantly in 2000 because of political instability. At the other end of the scale, with air services to Niue supplied by charter flights Niue received less than 1500 visitors in 2000 of whom less than 1000 were genuine tourists.

Constraints of Smallness

Island micro-states have a number of unique development constraints. One such set concerns the limited natural resources that are relative to their size. The smaller a country the more limited the range of natural resources is likely to be and hence the narrower the range of options for development. Despite the once-enormous size of its phosphate deposits, Nauru has no other resource. Exploitation of the phosphate deposits has destroyed 80 percent of the landscape. With only limited resources remaining, mining is expected to cease within five years. The mono-economy of Nauru is locked into such an economic, sociocultural and environmental dead-end that mass emigration is an option that has and continues to receive serious consideration. Such a precedent was set by Banaba (Ocean Island) in Kiribati, whose entire population was resettled on Rabi Island in Fiji when the island was despoliated upon exhaustion of its phosphate deposits.

Atoll environments like Tuvalu in particular have finite limits to their capabilities for production. They lack sufficient water resources for any large hotel, resort or other development. No coal or other fossil fuel exists for power generation and they cannot generate hydro-electricity. The combination of low soil fertility, tropical climate and scarcity of land acts as a severe constraint to their capacity for tourism to develop backward linkages into the local agricultural economy. Atoll environments cannot support extensive tracts of timber. There is a general paucity of construction materials beyond coconut palms and pandanus for timber and thatch, and coral boulders for floors and walls. Their future may be even more restricted than at present if the concerns about global warming result in rising sea levels.

As populations have burgeoned in most of the South Pacific's small island countries, increasing strain has been placed on these resources to meet their communities' traditional needs of housing and agriculture. Environmental degradation is a major problem in most of them (Baines 1987). The geophysical structure of atolls also places considerable technical and environmental constraints upon development and when combined with vulnerability to periodic cyclones, earthquakes and *tsunamis* (tidal waves) these factors impose design and construction limitations and significant additional costs. Carrying capacity (amount of beach to tourists, home-stays in villages, etc.) will also be limited.

One of the dilemmas for small island states is that western approaches to resource management are not always applicable to their fragile, spatially specialized environments and sociocultural structures. But in a modern world, traditional ways are often also no longer appropriate for sustainable use of resources (Prasad 1987; Sofield 1991a). Kuilamu (1995) identified a range of traditional Fijian farming, fishing and other practices that in the contemporary context have adverse impacts on the environment and may impede sustainable ecotourism ventures. Modernization has impacted upon tradition to modify outcomes in a negative way.

In the South Pacific, despite often large annual population growth rates in excess of 3 percent (Connell 1984) and continually increasing allocations of funding to education, the tendency is for a lack of experienced managerial staff and trained workers. Increasing birth rates have not resulted in higher percentages of trained manpower (Fairbairn 1991). These limits on supportive resources may extend to a lack of additional finance to optimize initial investment because of the general subsistence level of the economy and thus a lack of domestic savings. They are in the main "reliant on foreign powers to provide capital for economic development and the transport links that enable the export of goods and services" (Hall 1998:146).

The isolation of most South Pacific destinations constitutes another constraint to development and tourism in particular. There are time constraints: how much time is available versus travel time to some destinations, how much time can be spent at the destination, and does seasonality shorten the length of the tourism season? In the case of the Federated States of Micronesia, Kiribati, Marshall Islands, Nauru, Palau and Tuvalu, no direct flights are available from any of the Pacific Rim countries. For instance, Tuvalu has access either from Fiji (by turbo prop aircraft twice per week) or from the Marshall Islands (via Kiribati to Tuvalu on a twice-weekly flight to Fiji). Depending upon when the tourist departs from Marshall islands or Fiji, the waiting time for the flight to Tuvalu could be between one to four days. Spatial attributes, including proximity and accessibility to source markets, place most of the South Pacific Island states at a disadvantage in tourism terms (Britton 1987a).

There are also constraints of indivisibilities caused by smallness (one cannot fly half an aeroplane even if it is only half-full). Many of the air routes in the South Pacific are classified as "light" where aircraft face light loadings because of low demand (Tucker, Halcrow and Associates 1985). The island nations generate less than 6 percent of inter-island traffic so that small aircraft flying long distances with low yields result in some of the highest per kilometer fares in the world (Tucker, Halcrow, and Associates 1985). Fiji, with its relatively well-developed tourism industry and its central location, is serviced by "heavy" routes, most of the traffic for which comes from direct access to Pacific Rim countries like Australia, Japan and the United States. But Tuvalu, as noted, has no direct flights and the potential for tourism-generated growth is thus restricted (Tucker *et al.* 1985; Sofield 1991b).

The tyranny of distance also affects the capacity of many of the small South Pacific countries to attract cruiseships to their waters. The Caribbean Islands are geographically much closer to each other and also located relatively close (a few hundred kilometers) to the United States with its population of more than 260 million from which to source tourists. The resort islands of the

Mediterranean have a similar geographical advantage. By contrast Tuvalu is more than 4000 km from Australia which has a population of only 19 million, and 3000 km from New Zealand which has just over 3 million. It is rare for more than one or two cruiseships to visit Tuvalu annually. Niue is entirely surrounded by cliffs and lacks both beaches and harbours: it cannot accommodate even the smallest of cruiseships.

The type of small island economy which has been shaped and determined by the scarcity of resources has been characterized by Bertram and Watters (1985) as "the MIRAB economy". That is, one of *Mi*gration from the outer islands to the centre, and then from the centre overseas; "de-agriculturization" as more and more of the population ceases active farming linked to a growing dependence upon *R*emittances from abroad (which in turn supports further migration from the outer islands to the urban centre); a significant *A*id input; and a large government *B*ureaucracy which serves as the major employer.

Tuvalu in this context is typecast as a MIRAB economy. Almost 50 percent of its population has now migrated from the outer islands to the capital, Funafuti. About one fifth of its population has emigrated permanently. Its subsistence farmers produce only one sixth of the output recorded 20 years ago. About 2000 Tuvaluans working abroad regularly send remittances back to their families and this is Tuvalu's second largest source of foreign exchange after aid grants.

Budgetary aid from the United Kingdom, granted on an annual basis, was essential to underwrite Tuvalu's budget for the first 10 years (1978–1987) of its independence. Interest earned from a $21 million Trust Fund established in 1987 by a coterie of aid donors (Australia, United Kingdom and New Zealand which each gave about $6 million, plus Japan and South Korea which gave smaller grants) provides the source for most of Tuvalu's recurrent budget. The cost of all major new works and capital expenditure is met by aid grants since Tuvalu cannot generate sufficient domestic capital itself. In terms of the bureaucracy as employer the government provides jobs for some 90 percent of all Tuvaluans engaged in salaried and wages labor (Tuvalu's Fifth National Development Plan 1992–1997).

Niue, the Cook Islands and Kiribati exhibit similar MIRAB characteristics. With regard to out-migration, as noted above, an estimated 25,000 Cook Islanders now live overseas, leaving only 17,000 still resident in their homeland. The case of Niue is even more extreme: some 11,000 have departed permanently leaving only 2000 still resident in the island. It is an aged population with a dearth of skills, requiring the provision of a significant level of social services which cannot be supported by the local economy. Kiribati and Tuvalu have been less affected by out-migration, although over the past three decades more than 16,000 i-Kiribati (as ethnic people from Kiribati are called) have settled elsewhere (8000 to Solomon Islands; some 3500 to Nauru; the 1000 inhabitants of Banaba to Rabi Island in Fiji; and another 4000 to the Marshall Islands, Vanuatu, New Zealand, Australia and the United States), leaving about 80,000 in Kiribati.

Agricultural production has declined steadily in all four countries and once-viable export industries have ceased. The Cook Islands 15 years ago had thriving orange groves on Rarotonga, pineapple plantations on Mangaia, and its own fruit juice factory exporting its canned products to New Zealand and Australia. The factory closed 12 years ago as remittances and aid flows acted as disincentives to local labor and production. Niue in the late 1970s developed a thriving export industry of passionfruit, which contributed more than $0.7 million to its annual budget — by far the dominant economic activity (outside government) on the island. But it was dependent upon hand-pollination (with school closing at 2 p.m., a daily task for the children was to pollinate the day's flowering), and with the depopulation of Niue the industry has withered. All four countries are now heavily dependent upon imports for foodstuffs and other basic necessities.

A review of the original MIRAB hypothesis 12 years after the original research (Bertram 1999) raised the interesting proposition that as both remittances and aid flows had been sustained the result effectively challenged the orthodoxy of modernization theory. In other words, that export-led tradable production and private sector investment were essential if small island economies were to avoid regressing to lower living standards and economic performance. Bertram argued that the classical economic theory of the development model transferred from mainland Asia categorized the South Pacific island economies as "dependent" and "unsustainable". Such an analysis resulted in aid policies designed to force these countries away from "their natural and preferred pattern of resource allocation" (1999:105–106). Development planning and economic policy initiated by donor countries and agencies ignored the main locomotives driving the MIRAB economies, leading to aid intervention which attempted to "trigger export-led growth fuelled by private investment ... away from, rather than toward, strengthening and developing that [MIRAB] status quo." Despite relatively massive aid flows "a decade of very little economic growth was the result". According to Bertram, as the 21st century began, some of the Polynesian and Micronesian countries of the South Pacific continued to exhibit "the empirical anomaly ... of higher standards of living than is predicted by classical economics, modernization or dependency growth models". These models focus on gross domestic product as the key economic growth indicator because convention dictates that expenditure can only be sustained on the basis of local, geographically bounded output. But the continued out-migration from countries such as Tonga, Samoa, Cook Islands and Niue (reducing over-population within these territorially limited small states) is combined with sustained levels of remittances and foreign aid. MIRAB island countries "sustain levels of expenditure that run consistently and apparently sustainably ahead of gross domestic product". Bertram reasoned that "Pacific Islander populations became globalized long before most of the rest of the non-OECD world" and "in a MIRAB economy the indigenous populations maximize their material well-being by management of the globalization process". The population remaining in the islands, generally, has an insurance floor guaranteed by non-alienation of their customary land and thus a capacity to maintain production at a level providing for basic needs, and potentially some small cash income. What differentiates their economies from less-developed nations in Africa and Asia is the outward movement of family members to other countries which opens the way for inflows of higher income than is possible from local resources, a kind of "transnational corporation of kin" (Bertram 1999:105–106, 107, 125). There are "globalized communities consisting of two or more population nodes separated by large distances while apparently maintaining similar social relations of rights and obligations as would be operative in a previously geographically bounded system" (Hayes 1991:9; cited in Bertram 1999).

In the context of tourism and smallness, atoll countries, more so than the high island countries, may face a relatively restricted inventory of "things to see and do". This lack of "critical mass" (Sofield 1991b) impedes the capacity of the atoll countries to develop a multi-attraction destination. They tend to exhibit characteristics of "parachute tourism". Tourists simply drop in and then fly out of the one place because no excursions or alternative sites are available or accessible.

Despite these very real limitations and often concomitant vulnerability to natural disasters (such as Fiji's sugar crop to periodic cyclones) alternative options for development are so few that the small states of the South Pacific have all turned to tourism, with varying degrees of commitment and caution, in an attempt to increase economic security (Hall and Page 1997; Sofield 1991b; Tisdell and McKee 1988). The facilities required for tourism development occupy only a relatively small proportion of land, and most of the countries have a range of attractions related to sun, sea, sand and coral reefs which globally are of a high quality. Their peoples have a reputation for friendliness which can be a partial substitute for the lack of hospitality-related skills and training. In this sense tourism may superficially make an appropriate "fit" with the smallness of most of the micro island states.

Such small countries often experience difficulties in providing the necessary inputs for international tourism from their own resources. Britton (1987a) explored the ramifications of this in respect of the Cook Islands and Fiji and found that one major outcome was a dependence on foreign capital and exper- tise and the exacerbation of some structural inequalities. The tourism sector can require a disproportionate share of the country's infrastructure. Resident foreign companies can be relatively so large in the overall economy of a developing island micro-state that their operations give them significant commercial and political power (Crocombe 1987), which in turn may weaken national economic and political sovereignty. These factors can produce divisiveness which will find reflection in domestic political tension.

Economic profitability may also be a short-term factor and some forms of tourism development will prove unsustainable over the longer term. Atolls with their fragile environments should pay particular regard to the principles of sustainable development, with equal emphasis on both biophysical and socio- cultural elements. Too often, however, the immediacy of perceived economic advantages appears to outweigh longer term considerations. Baines (1987) comments on these issues in a sharp critique of tourism in the South Pacific aptly titled "Manipulation of Islands and Men". Tourism for a small economi- cally disadvantaged state can be a two-edged sword.

Tourism Analyses

There is a growing literature devoted to the underdeveloped countries of the South Pacific, with increasing emphasis on the immediate effects of economic and technological progress on their traditional societies. Systems which were able to prevail in a rural environment where communities were restricted in size, where social units were well integrated and dominated by direct personal relationships, are giving way to the new social and cultural systems inherent in industrialization and urbanization. The new value systems often focus on material things, on modern economic relations that involve social differentia- tion and individualization. Tension develops, imposing strain on traditional structures; antagonism may become common; specific cultural traits are eroded; and relations between individuals are broadened and become more indirect (Balandier 1970b:361).

Much of the literature on tourism development reveals a dichotomy of approach between the "advocacy" and the "cautionary" platforms of Jafari's conceptual framework for analysing views on tourism (1990). There is less work from Jafari's knowledge-base platform. Many writers tend to highlight the adverse impacts of tourism development, both in sociocultural terms as well as in economic and environmental terms (Clarke 1987; Farrell 1977, 1979; Finney and Watson 1975; MacNaught 1982; D. Pearce 1980; Prasad 1987; Rajotte 1982; Ranck 1987; Varley 1978). Tourism practitioners, whether they are governmental, semi-governmental or private sector developers, tend to highlight the positive benefits of the industry. This tendency is not unnatural given that their existence as stakeholders is predicated on the continued development (growth) of tourism.

The impact of tourism development refers to the sum total of all the social, cultural, economic and environmental influences that come to bear upon the host society as a result of this development. The magnitude of the impact is dependent upon a number of factors such as "the nature of the society, its flexibility or resilience to change, the size of the host population relative to the number of visitors, the degree of dependence of the society upon tourism" (which will determine the extent of contact and the exposure of the society in terms of the influx of tourists), "and the economic state of the society" (Prasad 1987:10). In the micro-states of the South Pacific that influence can be significant in producing changes in the structure of a country's economy, society's behavior and/or the transformation of traditional institutions and culture.

To ascribe only adverse and destructive effects to tourism development in the societies of the South Pacific countries and advocate alternative forms of development, as some researchers have done (Crocombe 1987; Prasad 1987; Rajotte 1982), is to ignore the fact that there are very few states which do not aspire to modernity in which tourism is seen to play a key role. Conversely, to ascribe only beneficial results to tourism development is equally unbalanced. Change is inevitable. But it is the pace of change and the direction of change, not change *per se*, which is of concern to most of the governments of the micro-states of the South Pacific. Value judgments on whether tourism development is "good" or "bad" should be avoided in preference to examining conceptual issues such as conflict, coexistence and symbiosis to reach an understanding of tourism development (Sofield 1990b).

Conflict is the manifestation of verbal and non-verbal behaviors symbolizing opposition. Because conflict is universal among human beings the genesis of conflict may be found in the general characteristics of the societies humans create. Conflict may be exogenous or endogenous. The circumstances and situations in which individuals, groups or societies display behaviors which are interpreted as symbols of opposition are collectively labelled "strains". Relative power will determine the way in which conflict is resolved, as noted in Chapter 3.

Coexistence refers to the situation where two or more disparate units occupy the same spatial environment with little or no interaction. The term here refers to tourism development on the one hand and communities of the host society on the other. It is a situation that is rarely static, particularly if there is rapid growth in tourism-related activities. Therefore, according to Budowski, it is followed either by a mutually satisfactory relationship, symbiosis, or by conflict (1977:3).

Symbiosis is a mutually beneficial partnership between organisms of different kinds. In the biological sense, it usually refers to an association where one organism lives within the other. In this chapter it is used to refer to the situation where tourism, tourists and the host society (or part thereof) benefit from a continuing interrelationship. Here a limited analogy may be drawn between the impacts of tourism development on host societies and the biogeography of islands. The five fundamental processes of biogeography are dispersal, invasion, competition, adaptation and extinction (MacArthur and Wilson 1967:4).

The biological colonization of an island is a dynamic process, accompanied at all stages by a turnover in species. During the build-up of species of a given taxon toward its saturation number, the immigration and extinction rates vary as a function of the number of species present. The immigrant species may find an ecological niche with minimum competition from established biodata and coexist; they may enter into vigorous competition for available resources and exist in a degree of conflict with established species; they may form a mutually dependent or symbiotic relationship with established species; or they may take over and eliminate entirely the prior established species (extinction) — or themselves be eliminated (MacArthur and Wilson 1967).

The processes of biogeography can be applied to tourism; its dispersal from source regions; its "invasion" of new countries; competition in several forms, including between the foreigner and the host; adaptation by both parties to ensure survival; and elimination of traditional institutions and practices when the values of the developer prevail. The analogy with biogeography is used in an attempt to move away from the often emotive comments of those observers who fall victims to an ethnocentric tradition and describe change arising out of tourism as "destructive" or the tendentious advocacy of industry practitioners and national tourist authorities who describe everything as "positive". A more objective analysis of conflict, coexistence and symbiosis recognizes that societies and culture are dynamic, that change is inevitable.

This analogy is not belabored: there is a fundamental difference between animals and humans after all. As Marx noted:

> In contrast to all animals which can only passively adjust to nature's requirements by finding a niche in the ecological order which allows them to subsist and develop, man is active in rela-

tion to his surroundings. He fashions tools with which to transform his natural habitat. Man begins to distinguish himself from animals as soon as he begins to produce his means of subsistence . . . (1995:53).

The sociologist Park (1952) made much the same point, maintaining that the processes which characterized the growth and development of plant and animal communities applied to human communities as well. Taking the Darwinian model of evolution as his point of departure, he conceived of a biotic order common to plants and animals to which he applied the term "community". In his community all individual units live in a relationship of mutual interdependence that is symbiotic rather than simply occupying the same habitat in an unorganized fashion, being interrelated in the most complex manner. But while human communities exhibit an ecological or symbiotic order similar to that of a non-human community, they also participate in a social and moral order that has no counterpart on the non-human level (Park 1952:148).

Sociocultural Change and Tourism

Much of the literature on tourism development in the South Pacific focuses on modernization, describing the process of socioeconomic change in which tradition-bound villages or tribal-based societies are compelled to react to the pressures and demands of the modern, industrialized, urban-centered world (Smelser 1964). Many observers have viewed modernization as socially destructive, often singling out tourism as a prime negative agent. For example, Crocombe of the University of the South Pacific writes:

> the trend is for tourism to turn the (South Pacific) islands into a giant Disneyland and the Islanders into well trained puppets whose life and behavior are fashioned to fulfill the dream expectations of the traveling public from the richer nations.
>
> The tourism industry . . . invests vast sums in the planned creation of largely spurious images of primitiveness, condescending notions of simplicity and the exaggeration of differences. . . . The artificial myth of exotica which provides a validation for the purchase of the status [of tourist in a culturally new environment] receives a fallacious fulfillment in the presentation of pseudo-traditional performances in the hotel lounge, the purchase of evidence of "cross-cultural" contact in

the handicrafts from the Toorak lathes [an inner district of Suva, Fiji] and in the polychrome postcards (1987:30–31).

Crocombe noted that tourism has the potential to be both positive and negative but that the short-term demands for maximum profit determine the shape of the industry in the South Pacific. Many tourism investors, he asserted, were adopting practices which were likely to be destructive of traditional cultural assets:

> The travel industry is alas corrupt. Not in the sense of money bribes perhaps, but in the deeper sense of distorting, twisting, falsifying, cheapening in order to increase its income (Crocombe 1987:99).

Crocombe suggested that aspects of the travel industry would come to be regarded in the same light as pirates and blackbirders; both in their respective heydays were regarded as respectable businesses and rewarding occupations financially and socially, but are now regarded as criminal.

As the wide sweep of modernization's generalizations have proved difficult to apply in many situations, the term was modified by a series of subsequent formulations in which concepts such as "urbanization", "social mobilization", "development" and "industrialization" narrowed the analysis to the particular. Indeed, modernization as outlined in Chapter 2 was strongly attacked by the dependency theorists as a justification of center–periphery dominance and underdevelopment (Britton 1984). Nevertheless, the modified concept remains useful in a restricted sense and is a relevant tool to apply to the analysis of change that accompanies tourism development in the South Pacific.

Urbanization, literacy, education, monetary reward for labor and its accompanying access to consumer goods, education and the mass media all expose the traditional person to new forms of life, new standards of enjoyment and new possibilities of satisfaction. These experiences break the cognitive and attitudinal barriers of the traditional culture and promote new levels of aspirations and wants. This process of new-want formation has been termed "social mobilisation" (Hoogvelt 1986:143). However, the ability of the transitional society to satisfy these new aspirations grows much more slowly than the aspirations themselves. Consequently a gap develops between aspirations and expectations, between want-formation and want-satisfaction. This gap in turn generates social frustrations and conflict (Hoogvelt 1986). Tourism is considered to play a major role in this process by many writers.

Cohen has challenged the popular notion that tourism is a major factor of sociocultural change, or that the impact of tourists is necessarily negative (1979:

28). The anti-tourism stance is a view which tends not to take account of other factors present such as the general intrusion of a cash economy, its concomitant payment for labor and the rise of a consumer society, the impact of telecommunications, and access to video and television, advertising for all sorts of non-tourism products, and so on. In some instances, it is valid to argue that tourism is a symptom not a cause of change.

There is a danger that the critic of alleged changes caused by tourism may gloss over the fact that all societies reveal "a continuous process of destructuring and restructuring" (Balandier 1970b:362). To ascribe only adverse and destructive effects to tourism development on the societies of the South Pacific countries is to commit cultural imperialism (perpetuating the idea of the noble savage happy in his primitive state) because it ignores the fact that all of the states aspire to forms of modernity. It is a stance that also carries the implication of a value judgment, that industrial societies are "bad". Yet traditional societies exposed to the processes of economic and technological development have opportunities for reorganization which can be beneficial. Once the transitional period is over, new systems of equilibrium begin to function. Objectively one cannot regard in a solely negative (or positive) way the social and cultural changes that characterize those countries undergoing industrialization and urbanization. Change is inevitable. But it is the influence of tourism development on the pace of change and the direction of change, not change *per se*, which is of concern to most of the governments of the micro-states of the South Pacific as they strive for economic development as "modern" countries among others (Sofield, 1991a).

In this context, it is necessary to distinguish between temporary maladjustments, which can create antagonism and conflict in the short term, and those which threaten the future of a society. It would be erroneous, for example, to treat conflict in Papua New Guinea caused by secessionist sentiment on Bougainville (which poses a threat to national law and order) in the same way as conflict arising from an attempt by youths to set up a village guest house which can challenge established "bigman" leadership roles and clan equilibrium (Iowa 1989).

With reference to tourism development in the South Pacific, conflict arising from discongruent interests is to be expected given the coexistence of two very different world visions. One is shaped by traditional Melanesian, Polynesian and Micronesian values and the other by mainly European (Australian, New Zealand, French and American) and Japanese investors/developers. Adverse tourist ratios are more quickly reached and have the potential to be more disruptive the more traditional the host societies are. There is a continuous tension between these ideologically divided groups, with the governments of the South

Pacific countries sometimes in support of their own people and traditional values and at other times (when pursuing "planned" development) in support of the foreign investor. Empowerment of the concerned local communities as a mechanism for managing the tension is rarely considered.

A distinction is often drawn between conflict that is functional or adaptive in the sense that it contributes to the efficient working of society and the long-term survival of its membership, and conflict which is dysfunctional or maladaptive. Competitive games such as Samoan village cricket are generally regarded as functional, since they can be rationalized as displacement of aggression in a socially accepted way, as training for war, or as character-building activities. Factionalism or conflict within a society is generally regarded as dysfunctional to the extent that it disrupts normal productive activities, but functional to the extent that it leads to adaptive changes in the organization of the society (Beals, Hoijer, and Beals 1977:452).

While there is consensus on the distinctions drawn between functional and dysfunctional conflict there is sharp disagreement over the interpretation of whether a given situation of conflict is one or the other. According to the time-frame utilized by a participant or an observer, such as short-term or long-term, the situation can be interpreted in either direction. According to whether one benefits or not from the situation, so it may be interpreted as functional or dysfunctional. Thus, conflict arising from the modernization processes accompanying tourism development may be labelled "good" or "bad" (Sofield 1990a).

Britton (1980, 1984) took the notion of conflict further by positioning it firmly within the concept of underdevelopment. In this view the colonial powers participated in a global conspiracy to pursue capitalist objectives in ways which maintained the dependency of former colonies on the metropolitan powers as sources of cheap goods and resources. As noted in Chapter 2, Britton applied dependency theory to an analysis of Fiji's tourism more than a decade ago when control and ownership of much of the hotel sector was in the hands of non-Fiji interests and the international airlines and cruiseship companies dominated the industry. While there is greater diversification in the hotel/resort sector today, and the national airline, Air Pacific, has emerged as the dominant carrier, core–periphery dependence still has a certain degree of validity.

Other studies of island tourism have also viewed tourism development in core–periphery terms (Bryden 1973 and Friedman 1988, with reference to the Caribbean Island states). Bryden considered that attempts to diversify out of traditional agricultural exports into the export of manufactured goods was frustrated mainly because of the protective tariff policies of the industrial countries and limited domestic markets of developing countries. Tourism, on the other hand, appeared to be less amenable to the operations of restrictions by industrial countries, although restrictions are not unknown. The vested interests in industrial countries which might lose by an expansion of international tourism are perhaps less entrenched, less vocal, than is the case with agricultural producers or manufacturers (Bryden 1973:4).

Bryden's most useful contribution related to his ground-breaking work in social cost-benefit analysis, using the Caribbean states as a case study. He argued that the net returns from tourism for the Caribbean Island states were less than normally stated. The high level of foreign ownership of hotels and the relatively high numbers of expatriates in executive and skilled positions resulted in considerable repatriation of profits. Furthermore, the tourist consumption pattern was based on a high level of imported goods resulting in significant leakage. Bryden thus argued that net foreign exchange earnings were less; that there were disparate benefits as between nationals and expatriates; that regional development had an opportunity cost often not factored into arguments about decentralisation; and that labor was drawn away from agriculture and provided competition for the agricultural sector during planting and harvesting seasons in particular, to the detriment of agriculture. The concomitant social costs of tourism development needed to be accounted for.

In this context, a major impact of tourism development in the South Pacific is socioeconomic conflict which may have its roots in opposing attitudes, culturally derived, about the purpose of tourism development and its utilization or take-over of resources. The most obvious area concerns differing notions of ownership of land. It highlights the clash between traditional values which give custodial rights in perpetuity to clans and tribes based on ancestral occupancy, and those of the innovating, contemporary, monetized society where land is a commodity which can be bought and sold for profit by any individual.

Colonial powers had very different concepts of land rights from their subject peoples and created various categories of land which did not exist in the traditional Melanesian, Polynesian and Micronesian societies they governed. Such categories as Crown land, freehold title, park land, reserve land, waste land and catchment areas were foreign concepts which could not be easily accommodated in the traditional land tenure systems.

Foreign investors (and in some countries, local indigenous ones) took advantage of these imported concepts to establish new ownership of land and utilization of land and resources with legal backing through the imported legislative and court systems. Traditional landowning groups in the region have long been manipulated by those wanting to use indigenous resources and labor for commercial profit (Baines 1987). Some of the small islands now functioning as tourism resorts (such as Wakaya Island in Fiji) came into the possession of Europeans in the 19th century when they manipulated the traditional presentation of gifts for rights to use land. The Europeans chose to interpret their gifts as the price for unconditional purchase. The indigenous people, however, could not conceive of that notion and the gifts exchanged were for rights to use, but not to own, the land. The latter, its adjacent reefs and lagoons, and the resources there-in, together with the people, were a single integrated entity (Baines 1987:21).

With political independence, however, came a capacity by the South Pacific states to restrict the foreign manipulation which characterized their colonial status. To a large degree they can exert political control (although more limited economic control) over the pace of tourism development and can attempt planning regimes aimed at lessening the introduction of "foreign" values and practices perceived by the Islanders to be inimical to their own sociocultural systems. Yet, as Baines wrote, "manipulation continues in new forms, aided by naivete, carelessness or at worst corruption among some members of indigenous communities" (1987:21). The centrality of land-related traditional values to tourism development in Vanuatu may be noted in this context. The British and French colonial powers had very different concepts of land rights from their subject peoples and applied these categories to alienate much "customary" land.

Following independence in 1980, the Vanuatu Government accrued the power to restrict the foreign manipulation which had characterized its colonial status. Accordingly, on independence all alienated freehold land except that owned by the government reverted to customary ownership (chapter 12 of the Vanuatu Constitution). There are now only three categories of land in Vanuatu — leased alienated, urban and *kastom* (customary) owned. Alienated land comprises about one fifth of all holdings in Vanuatu. It is land for which compensation had been paid, boundaries surveyed and title registered, usually as freehold land, prior to independence and is now held on a maximum 75-year lease, with customary ownership to be determined at some time before the lease expires. Urban land refers to land inside the town boundaries of Vila and Luganville and is not owned by custom owners. Most of the urban land has been registered and titles may be bought by and sold freely to ni-Vanuatu and residents. The government has ultimate control over this land. *Kastom* land is controlled by landowning units such as clans, with members of the unit having usufructuary rights. This land cannot be bought or sold: in effect it is held in perpetual trust by the present landowners for future generations.

In the first flush of nationalism immediately on independence there were a number of incidents as *kastom* owners pursued their claims on the basis of rights restored under the constitution. In Port Vila harbor the clash between traditional values and commercial tourism resulted in indigenes stoning tourists snorkelling and diving on "their" reef which a tour operator (expatriate) had been using for years. Compensation (rent) was demanded as they reasserted their traditional rights suppressed under colonial rule. "The conflict was economic not racial" (Baines 1987:19). Furthermore, while urban land may have been incorporated into the constitution as beyond valid customary claims, it still led to conflict — indeed violence — as witnessed by land rights protests in Port Vila in 1987 when the residents of Ifira Island laid claim on customary grounds to all of the capital. The Ifira Island marchers resorted to violence in street demonstrations and were suppressed by police counter action. Their leaders were arrested and jailed.

In this instance an indigenous government committed to upholding traditional rights found it could not entertain claims which would have destroyed its capacity to function as a government and to pursue national economic development. Empowerment had been extended by the former colonial powers to the new independent state and its government. But that empowerment, despite apparent constitutional guarantees, in practice did not extend to individual tribal communities.

Conflict may also be endogenous and in Melanesian communities where there are many "levelers" to prevent one individual or clan getting too far ahead of others, intra-clan and inter-clan rivalry may create major problems for tourism. Ranck (1987) in his case study of autonomous village guest houses in Tufi, Papua New Guinea, catalogued the tensions which tourism development engendered in the area between competing guest house owners. Similarly, Iowa's 1989 study of guest house development in Buna, Papua New Guinea, outlined inter-clan and inter-generational tension. This author has detailed other examples in the latter country, Solomon Islands, Vanuatu, and Western Samoa (Sofield 1991b).

In 1999, major conflict erupted in Solomon Islands between the tribes of the two main islands, Malaita and Guadalcanal. The key factor was the purchase of alienated lands on Guadalcanal by Malaitans, which had the effect of removing any future access to those lands by the Guadalcanalese *kastom* owners who would otherwise have been able to assert their ownership rights when the lease on those alienated lands expired. This was because the Lands and Titles Act (1984) permitted Soloman Islands nationals the right to purchase alienated land as not just 75-year leases but as titles "in perpetuity". Over the 20-year period from independence in 1978 to 1998 several thousands of acres of former plantations on Guadalcanal, which had been owned as freehold by colonial settlers and which had reverted to 75-year leases in 1978, were purchased by Malaitans in a mass migration from their own overpopulated island. This was a new form of alienation, practiced by Soloman Islanders on fellow Soloman Islanders, since the practical effect of the transactions was to bar the *kastom* owners of Guadalcanal from ever reclaiming these traditional lands. Unable to remove Malaitans regarded by Guadalcanalese as illegal squatter settlements under customary law and frustrated by the imported legal system which protected this new wave of "outsiders", the Guadalcanal tribes reverted to violence to occupy their alienated lands. Some 25,000 Malaitans were forced off their Guadalcanal holdings and fled for safety back to Malaita. With the conflict spreading as law and order broke down, in large part because the Police Force could not divest itself of tribalism within its own ranks, a Malaitan militia group seized control of the capital, Honiara, and its international airport by force and compelled the Prime Minister and his government to resign. All resorts on Guadalcanal were destroyed in the ensuing warfare and tourism, which had been paralyzed, came to a complete halt. Despite various attempts to resolve the intertribal conflict through mediation by Australia and New Zealand, and agreement to hold fresh elections which resulted in the formation of a new S.I. government in December 2001, the peace remained fractured; violence has remained endemic and it is likely that it will take many years for its tourism industry to recover. Similarly, in Fiji another coup in May 2000 resulted in the overthrow of that government and brought its burgeoning tourism industry to a grinding halt. A number of resorts were taken over by indigenous Fijians demanding land rights. Tribal rivalries and inter-ethnic tension between the indigenous Fijians and Indo-Fijians were at the root of the unrest. Peace was finally restored and a new government elected following a democratic process in 2001 but visitor numbers remain depressed as political instability and an intermittent judicial process aimed at bringing the perpetrators of the coup to account undermined confidence in public safety.

Small countries which rely on tourism can also become locked into a situation of requiring ever-increasing numbers of tourists to sustain growth; and thus they are susceptible to exceeding their "saturation levels" or capacity to absorb or cope with very high tourist-resident ratios. In Rarotonga in the Cook Islands, for example, there were 82,000 tourists in 2000 "hosted" by a local population of only 9500. With an average length of stay of 10 days there were at times up to 6000 tourists on the tiny 32 sq km island and their presence was, not unnaturally, highly intrusive (Ra, Cook Islands Tourist Authority Marketing Manager, personal correspondence, 2000). Alienation between tourists and locals will be more acute the greater the social and cultural distance between them (Britton 1987a:175).

These aspects of tourism cannot be isolated from a strong nationalism in small island states in the South Pacific (Crocombe 1987; Sofield 1991b). They gained political independence despite limitations in resources which restrict their capacity to be economically independent. The right to political self-determination and cultural separateness were goals which overrode other considerations. Countries such as the Cook Islands, Niue and Kiribati in particular appeared prepared to accept a situation of semi-permanent reliance on foreign aid; on high rates of out-migration; stagnating production sectors (especially agriculture); and an increasing reliance on imported goods and foodstuffs as the price for sovereignty and the preservation of traditional lifestyles (Sofield 1991b). The core–periphery dependency theory of Britton and others retains a certain validity.

Economic efficiency as defined by the western model of development is not necessarily accepted by some communities in some of the micro-states of the South Pacific region, since other values counter the desire for an industrialized, urbanized, secular society. So-called *kastom* groups such as the Kwaio of Malaita in Solomon Islands, the John Frum Movement of Tanna and the "pagan" villages (their description of themselves) in South Pentecost in Vanuatu who have deliberately turned their backs on western values and the "benefits" of contemporary development, are not uncommon in Melanesia. However, even for these communities the contact situation and some acculturation and modernization cannot be avoided (Balandier 1970b). As modern forms of communication (television, videos, radio) and education, provided and supported in many cases by aid programs, reach more and more of the people, they contribute directly to the changing (the cautionary platform writers would say "undermining") of traditional values and practices. The demonstration effect (to which tourism contributes because of the exposure to local people of western patterns of consumption and behavior by tourists) also plays a part and may motivate individuals to acquire the accoutrements of "modern" society.

Political leaders of the micro-states must come to terms with the fact that the espousal of policies designed to attain western levels of material affluence are increasingly necessary if their constituents are to support them at the ballot box (Sofield 1991b). In this sense, tourism appears to some of the region's political leaders as one of the few "easy options" by which the small states can pursue economic development because it appears to be capable of generating much-needed foreign exchange, creating new employment, reducing reliance on aid, and contributing to national development.

But the expansion of tourism and the "invasion" of a small country by relatively large numbers of tourists is a significant agent of change which can threaten the further erosion of time-honored traditions and values. Nunez's observation about the development of tourism in Third World countries in general is pertinent in the case of South Pacific island countries:

> the situation indicates an interesting irony: in order to survive
> and perpetuate their cultural identity and integrity, emerging new

nations . . . caught up in a competitive world economy encourage and invite tourists, the most successful agents of change (short of political or military agents) active in the contemporary world (Nunez 1977:209).

It is realization of this which has produced a reluctance by some of the South Pacific states to embrace tourism enthusiastically. Rather they have taken a cautious approach to the development of a viable tourism industry, insisting that it be based on respect and support for traditional values and customs. The tourism policy of the Solomon Islands Government, which will be examined in detail in Chapter 7, clearly reflects this standpoint. It was developed over a three-year period from 1987–1990, involved extensive consultations with seven provincial governments, and has survived several changes of national government. The policy document commenced with seven "guiding principles", of which no less than five insist on harmonizing tourism development with the sociocultural heritage of Solomon Islands.

Sustainable tourism has recently appeared as a topic of some importance for the further development of tourism in the small island states. Their general paucity of resources has encouraged the consideration of sustainable development principles, and its philosophical approach about inter-generational equity in many ways mirrors the traditional Melanesian, Micronesian and Polynesian concepts of holding their lands in trust for future generations. There have been several major conferences on sustainable development and related tourism subjects since 1992 (such as the "Conference on the Business of Ecotourism in the South Pacific", Auckland, October 1992) which have spawned numerous papers.

The South Pacific Regional Environment Program has consistently included tourism issues in its agenda for the past 10 years. These have strongly favored definitions of sustainable tourism which incorporate cultural values equally with biological values, based on Islanders' perceptions of the indivisibility of humankind and nature and their own close association at the community level with their terrestrial and marine environments. Island governments and aid donors are both beginning to direct development efforts in this direction (for example, the Australia South Pacific 2000 Programme (*sic*) announced by the then Prime Minister Keating at the South Pacific Forum summit meeting in Papua New Guinea in 1995 which provided a total of about $500,000 aid grants for ecotourism projects over the five-year period to the end of the millennium). By the very nature of ecotourism, projects tend to be relatively quite small. Parenthetically, in the growing literature and educational activity about sustainable tourism in the South Pacific, while self-reliance and community-level action are proselytized, the notion of empowerment as being essential if that development is to be sustainable has yet to filter through.

Economic Impacts of Tourism

In approaching an assessment of the economic impact of tourism on a regional basis, it is axiomatic that because the overview of the industry is necessarily broad, caveats must be drawn for individual countries. For example, the level of tourism activity, the size of the industry, the degree of foreign participation, and the rate of tourism development all differ markedly from country to country. Thus, Kiribati receives fewer than 2500 tourists per year but Fiji in 1999 received 160 times more — over 400,000 (as noted above, Fiji's tourist numbers crashed dramatically after the May 2000 coup attempt and have yet to recover to pre-1995 levels). In New Caledonia, foreign (non-Kanak) ownership of tourism plant and attractions is 98 percent with only a handful of village guest houses owned by the indigenous people. But in Tonga there is little foreign ownership with only one major resort and one hotel owned by foreign interests (Britton 1987a; Sofield 1991b, 1997). Tahiti, Guam and Fiji have several five- and four-star hotels each; Niue, Tuvalu, Solomon Islands and Kiribati have none.

Economic measures for tourism include the current level of tourism development and projected investment in the sector, direct and indirect employment, types and amounts of tourist expenditures, the multiplier effect, types and amount of government revenue received from tourism, amount of foreign exchange earned, and import content and leakage factor of foreign exchange (Milne 1988). In order to determine the economic impact of international tourism on the national economies of the South Pacific countries it is necessary first to measure the amount of expenditure and how it is expended in different categories. Inadequate studies exist to attempt an estimate however, although the Tourism Council of the South Pacific has undertaken a series of surveys in eight countries. One estimate a decade ago, based on WTO figures for nine island countries, suggested an extrapolated figure for total receipts for all 21 countries and territories of the region would be in the order of $2.42 billion (Sofield 1991b). Given that tourist numbers around the region increased by about one third in the past decade, it is reasonable to assume that this estimate would be considerably higher; but in the absence of real data and widely different expenditure patterns for different countries, it is difficult to put forward a figure with any confidence. The former Director of the Tourism Council of the South Pacific wrote that in 1996 the tourism industry of the South Pacific had generated gross earnings of $9.246 billion (*South Pacific Tourism* 1997:5) but no statistics were provided to support this figure.

The overall growth in regional tourist numbers has occurred despite individual countries experiencing uneven patterns of visitation. Fiji, for example, attained some 240,000 tourists in 1986, then experienced a sharp decrease to fewer than 180,000 in 1987 and 208,000 in 1988 as a result of two military coups in 1987. By 1999, that figure had increased to more than 400,000 (*Islands Business* 2000), but visitation was again decimated following political instability in 2000. The South Pacific Tourism Organisation reported that in June 2000 daily arrivals had fallen to 455 from an average of 1280 per day in June 1999, an average daily revenue loss of about $650,000 (*South Pacific Tourism* 2000:12). Similarly, Vanuatu received more than 30,000 tourists per annum from 1979 to 1983, which fell in 1985 to only 12,000 when direct flights between Australia and Vanuatu ceased. By 1989 that figure had risen to 24,000 and in 1990 the total visitation for the year was again back at the 30,000 mark (ASMAL *Pacific Report* 1991). By 2000 it was approaching 40,000 plus another 20,000 cruiseship day visitors (*South Pacific Tourism* 2000:10). Tourists to the Cook Islands peaked in 1994 at 57,000, struggled to reach 50,000 per year for the next five years, but reached an estimated 82,000 in 2000 (*Pacific Magazine with Islands Business* 2001:16).

The Micronesian countries of Guam and the Northern Marianas experienced the most dramatic growth as they responded to surging Japanese demand. In 1980, Guam received only 203,000 tourists with the greatest number coming from the United States. By 1990, that figure had spiralled to almost 774,000 with more than 650,000 (80 percent) originating from Japan (Guam Economic Research Center 1990). By 1995 it had reached one million, mostly from Japan (*Islands Business* 1996) and it has continued to attract similar annual levels of visitation despite fluctuations in demand attributable to the so-called Asian meltdown from 1997 and a concomitant drop in outbound Japanese tourist numbers. By the end of 2000, Japanese numbers were expected to have exceeded 1.1 million, with Koreans and US tourists contributing another 200,000 (*Islands Business* 2000:38). However, the new wave of Japanese are younger and less affluent than their middle manager predecessors, per capita expenditure is less, and total tourism receipts are down about 10 percent from five years ago (*Pacific Magazine with Islands Business* 2001:18).

Similarly, in 1980, the Northern Marianas received only 117,000 tourists. In 1985, the total was 142,000. They contributed $106 million in total receipts for the Northern Marianas, constituting approximately 37 percent of the country's GNP (School of Travel Industry Management 1987). By 1990 the total number had risen to 435,454 of whom some 80 percent were of Japanese origin (*Islands Business* 1991). Receipts exceeded $260 million, more than 50 percent of GNP. Both Guam and the Northern Marianas have benefited from the development of direct air services with and their geographical proximity to Japan. By 1995, the figure was in excess of 550,000 (*Islands Business* 1996) and more than 650,000 by the end of 2000 (*Islands Business* 2000:38).

The World Tourism Organization (WTO) input–output analyses of nine countries (referred to above) took place between 1985 and 1988 and revealed some of the difficulties inherent in inadequate national databases. All of the WTO surveys covered situations that lacked information about tourist expenditure and data illustrating inter-linkage between sectors. There were inadequate household surveys on the induced effects and a lack of basic tourism trade statistics. The WTO researchers employed a variety of techniques to overcome these deficiencies and managed with varying degrees of success to construct input–output models for the small island states of the Cook Islands, Kiribati, Palau, Papua New Guinea, Niue, Solomon Islands, Tonga, Vanuatu and Western Samoa. The 1985 economic impact survey of Vanuatu, for example, used an input–output table from Fiji for 1977 because of the lack of Vanuatu data, justifying it on the grounds that the two economies were "not totally dissimilar, both being small island countries" (UNDP/WTO 1985). However, a 1988 WTO study on Vanuatu produced much more reliable data.

The input–output analyses carried out under WTO auspices suggested (despite the limited availability of data and reservations about the adequacy of some of the research techniques adopted to overcome that limitation) that some regional patterns could be discerned in terms of the economic impact of tourism. Thus, with reference to a first-round propensity to import, handicrafts in all countries surveyed exhibited a propensity of nil to less than 5c in the dollar. Handicrafts are produced by local people utilizing local materials and sold in the main through locally owned outlets. (With reference to the latter, Fiji was the exception, selling most of its handicrafts through "upmarket" outlets such as souvenir shops in the large resort/hotel sector and duty free shops in Nadi, Lautoka and Suva.) Locally owned guest houses demonstrated a propensity to import which was only a fraction of that experienced by the larger, expatriate-managed luxury hotels and resorts. Foods in guest houses, for example, tended to be locally produced rather than imported. Both of these activities (handicrafts and locally owned guest houses) exhibited nil or a low level of leakage.

Locally run guesthouses also exhibited strong income and employment generation qualities. The development of such guesthouses, as was the case in Tonga and Western Samoa in particular, provided high economic multiplier effects and permitted a greater role for indigenous ownership within an industry which is dominated in most of the South Pacific countries by foreign interests. The development of local tours, often built around traditional elements of the indigenous culture, also reflected many of the same advantages as locally run guesthouses. Such tours can be especially important in spreading the benefits of tourism horizontally and into areas which would otherwise be outside the tourism industry.

The WTO analyses suggested that with reference to employment generation, for every $10,000 of tourist expenditure direct employment would rise by between 0.92 (UNDP/WTO, Vanuatu 1986b) and 1.95 (UNDP/WTO, Solomon Islands 1986a) standardized (full time) jobs; and that for every new job created in the tourism industry (for instance, in a hotel), the total employment — that is, jobs created in other sectors to absorb the demands for goods and services required by first-line tourism establishments — would increase by a factor of between 1.6 (Tonga) and 2.2 (Papua New Guinea). This impact is designated the degree of backward linkage. The local income generated by each tourist dollar in the countries analyzed varied from 42c for Tonga to 87c for Papua New Guinea. The surveys indicated the relative importance of tourism as a government source of income, with multipliers ranging from a low of 0.21 in Vanuatu to 0.50 in Papua New Guinea.

The Australian National Centre for Development Studies (1988) investigated the linkage between the agricultural sector and tourism in 1986 and 1987. This report obtained information from a total of only 15 hotels (six in Fiji, four in Vanuatu, three in Tonga, and two in Western Samoa). While these figures represented the total number of hotels in the last three countries, they also have numbers of resorts (for example, nine in Vanuatu, including three co-located with the four hotels inside the boundaries of Vila, the capital; four in Western Samoa; three in Tonga and more than thirty in Fiji). The sample size and restriction to hotels thus suggests caution in wider application of the results.

Nevertheless, the report supported a number of expectations, reflecting local conditions. For example, Vanuatu which has a well developed beef cattle industry and is a net exporter of meat imported only 5 percent of speciality cuts. At the other end of the scale, the two major hotels in Western Samoa imported 83 percent of their meat requirements. All four countries demonstrated an import content of around 50 percent for vegetables and more than 20 percent for fruits. While Fiji grows a range of suitable vegetables, quality control and regularity of supply proved a hindrance to decreasing the level of reliance on imports. Fiji, Tonga and Vanuatu were almost self-sufficient for chicken and seafoods but Western Samoa had an import content of 31 percent for these items. Imports of beverages were naturally enough very high for wines and spirits but Fiji, Tonga and Western Samoa have their own breweries so that these countries exhibited significantly lower import requirements than Vanuatu. As with the WTO reports, the research by the Australian National Centre for Development Studies (1988) revealed limitations and deficiencies in data. Because of the generally incomplete level of understanding of the interaction between tourism and the local economies of most of the South Pacific countries, and because of limitations identified in other analyses, the Tourism

Council of the South Pacific (TCSP) embarked on its own economic impact analysis exercise in 1988/89. The initial approach was to review existing literature, including those input–output analyses carried out under WTO auspices. While acknowledging the value of input–output analysis as the best way to approach the South Pacific countries, the TCSP considered that the resources made available for the WTO studies were too scarce to result in a profound level of analysis (for example, very short data collection periods, in one case only eight days). A greater degree of disaggregation and more comprehensive surveys as the major tool for data collection were required; adapted Keynesian multiplier models utilized by the WTO researchers were judged unsuitable for national tourism planners to continue to collect data and to improve on the planning tools. The TCSP emphasized the fundamental importance of obtaining accurate expenditure patterns to be used for tourism planning purposes.

The TCSP commenced a series of "visitor surveys" of its member countries, aiming at 1000 comprehensive air passenger interview/questionnaire respondents for each. *Inter alia*, these have been particularly useful in obtaining details of tourist expenditure. Thus, the 1990 visitor survey for Solomon Islands (TCSP 1991), which was conducted over a nine-month period from December 1989 to September 1990, revealed that the average daily expenditure per tourist was $40 and the average per capita expenditure per visit was $480. The survey indicated that a total of $3.8 million in foreign exchange was earned from the 9171 arrivals to Solomon Islands for the year 1989/90.

The TCSP continued further surveys in every member country to update previous ones carried out until 1997 when decreasing aid funds restricted its research capabilities. They still provide the most comprehensive information available for international air visitation to those eight countries which receive European Community aid to participate in the TCSP programme, and the data is applicable for input–output analyses. Despite intentions to the contrary the TCSP did not take its activities in economic impact assessment beyond the visitor surveys.

Tourism Development and Resource Allocation

Much of the early enthusiasm for tourism in developing countries centered on its potential as a vehicle for economic development which would provide a number of specific advantages such as securing foreign exchange, increasing employment, widening the export base, and assisting in decentralization. A review of recent literature over the past decade is more critical and suggests that in the South Pacific tourism has: contributed little or nothing to decentralization;

generated less indigenous employment than often anticipated; led to "de-agriculturization"; was characterized by problems of seasonality and dangers of sole source market dependency; had unwelcome distributional consequences; and exaggerated hopes for a country's balance of payments because leakage has often been high (Sofield 1997).

All of these contentions may, in specific cases, be accurate. But to generalize about the adverse impacts of tourism *per se* in respect to some of them is misleading and overlooks the interplay of concurrent factors in some of the South Pacific countries. There is often a mis-match between resources allocated for tourism development *vis-à-vis* other sectors which in fact are less productive. Australia's aid program to the South Pacific is reviewed in this context and a significant imbalance between tourism and less productive sectors is revealed.

Decentralization

Rural–urban drift has been a constant factor in the economic and social development of all Pacific Island countries since colonial regimes replaced the decentralized village-based societies with a centralized administration (Douglas 1996). The consequent changes in demographic patterns were historically present well before the advent of tourism on any scale. Tourism has not played a major role in speeding up this shift, contrary to the view of Rajotte (1982) and others, since the capitals of the South Pacific states are not dominated by tourism activity. There are many other economic and social elements exerting much greater "pull" in attracting increasing numbers to the urban centers of the South Pacific than tourism. The capitals do of course serve as obvious locations for the business tourism (only a small percentage of the total number of arrivals for most countries — less than 10 percent), for international airport entry and customs services, for communications services, for travel agency services and for related activities such as tour operators. Backward linkages may be significant. But to the extent that many resorts in the South Pacific are located outside the capitals, then tourism may be held to have made a positive contribution to decentralization.

A case in point is the proliferation of resorts in the Mamanuca Islands chain west of Nadi in Fiji. In 1995 11 island resorts employed more than 1500 people directly, whose activities provided additional indirect employment and income for another 500 families and were largely responsible for maintaining a population of more than 6000 on the islands. When the resorts of the Coral Coast and Pacific Harbour, Viti Levu (12), of Denarau, south-west of Nadi (3), of

Savu Savu, Vanua Levu and Taveuni (8) and eastern island resorts (5) were added to the Mamanucas for a total of 39 with 3014 rooms, and contrasted with the number of hotels and apartments in the Suva/Nausori area (14 with 493 rooms), it could be deduced that in fact tourism had made a significant contribution to decentralization in Fiji.

Even when Nadi (160 km by road from Suva, and location of the international airport) with its 10 hotels and guest houses totalling 595 rooms was combined with Suva for urban tourism plant, the ratio of urban to rural/off-shore islands was still 3:1 (Fiji Hotels Association 1995). However it could be argued that since Nadi's development as an urban centre was tourism-dependent (its growth was predicated on the services which grew incrementally out of its site as the country's international airport) then in fact it is more aptly classified as regional and its figures should not be included with those of Suva.

De-agriculturization

The concept of a rural population being lured away from traditional farming pursuits because of tourism is (based on 30 years of this author's experience with development projects in countries as diverse as Tanzania, Sri Lanka, Nepal, Indonesia and most of the Island countries of the South Pacific) a major fallacy. The single greatest factor in this trend in the South Pacific has been the result of contact with western civilizations and the concomitant introduction of their styles of education and religion (Christianity). Where once children went through an informal schooling process (or for special skills through a form of apprenticeship) in which they accompanied adults during farming and fishing activities and so absorbed the major elements of their traditional technology, the advent of formal lessons for six or eight hours per day five days per week divorced the new generations from traditional learning processes and isolated them for significant periods per day over a number of years from their parents and other adults. The new knowledge was in most cases inapplicable in the traditional society. In addition, Sunday observance (that is, no labor on the Sabbath) has been rigidly enforced in a number of South Pacific countries (Tonga, Western Samoa, Fiji, Niue, for example, where legislation supports the "Sabbath-rest-day" ethic) so that all sections of the population have been divorced from traditional agricultural pursuits according to a timetable at variance with traditional needs.

In short, western education and Christianity have fostered several generations of Pacific Islanders who are less able to understand and participate in traditional agricultural practices, whose societies are in transition and where a new set of values and aspirations has been inculcated which downgrades both village society and physical labor as a satisfactory lifestyle (Sofield 1993). Tourism has been only one factor in the modernization process since the 1950s whereas western educational and religious systems have been at work modifying traditional society in the South Pacific for 200 years. Where agriculture cannot provide an avenue of employment which makes use of western education, employment in the tourism industry often can make such a contribution. In this context, tourism cannot be interpreted as a cause of "de-agriculturization". Rather, as with the issue of decentralization, "de-agriculturization" may be seen as a manifestation of the process of modernization with tourism as only one factor in the equation (Sofield 1993).

The other side of this coin is that tourism demands greater supplies of agricultural produce and so may contribute to increased village income when such supplies are sourced locally. Vulelua Island Resort, some 70 kilometers east of the Solomon Islands' capital Honiara, for example, between 1989 and 1999 put more than SI$1 million into the local economy of three mainland Guadalcanal villages from which it drew its labor, most of its fruit and vegetables, all of its fish, and much of its chicken and pork requirements. This was only a small three-star resort of 36 beds but its contribution to the three villages of Aola, Nazareth and Mpare, with a combined population of about 200, alleviated poverty almost completely. Tambea Resort, about 80 kilometers west of Honaira, put about three times that amount into the local villages surrounding it over a longer period of operations (1960–1999). Both resorts were forced to close in 1999 because of tribal unrest, and have not reopened (Sofield, 2002).

Aid Policies

This issue raises the complex question of whether the relatively large amounts of development assistance directed toward the agricultural sector in the South Pacific have been misplaced to a degree. The issue also needs to be addressed in the context of the relatively scarce land resources of most of the island countries and the limited capacity of current village-based societies and technology to be adaptive and serve as a vehicle for economic development. The adverse long-term environmental implications of moves to transform essentially small hand-worked bush garden plots into more productive units, especially plantation type agriculture, have only belatedly been recognised. They are rarely taken into account in the design of development assistance for agricultural projects.

The sociocultural factors which inhibit development have been recognised for much longer. For example, the Government of Western Samoa in a 1982 policy document outlining its development strategy and assistance needs noted that the traditional land tenure system effectively prevented unused land being acquired not only by non-Samoans but by

> local people who are short of land or want to increase produc-
> tion. . . . [The land tenure system] also limits the amount of
> land available for commercial plantations, means arable land lies
> uncultivated and restricts the movement of capital and potential
> planters from the commercial to the primary sector where the
> opportunity exists for the development of the land and the
> introduction of new techniques (Western Samoa Government
> 1982:2).

The government also drew attention to resistance to innovation at the village level because of sociocultural characteristics:

> Under the Samoan system, goods and services are transferred
> on request as gifts or assistance and carry with them an obliga-
> tion on the part of the recipient to reciprocate at some time in
> the future. Gift giving adds to social prestige. . . . Although this
> system may ensure a fairly equitable distribution of wealth it
> also acts as a disincentive to accumulation [of wealth]. On the
> whole the villagers are not orientated to the monetised economy
> (Western Samoa Government 1982:3).

In Samoa and the other Polynesian societies of Tonga, the Cook Islands and Niue, motivation to produce more from village land is also blunted because desired consumer goods are obtainable through the flow of remittances from relatives overseas, as noted in the discussion of MIRAB economies.

The appropriateness of the subsistence sector for national economic development has sometimes been questioned and is an area that is often inconsistently addressed in the literature and by these countries' national planners and decision makers. Thus, on the one hand, the concept behind many economic development programs, sanctioned by orthodox growth theory, is that a modern, urban-based industrial sector is essential to achieve both expansion of employment and economic dynamism; and on the other, "rural development" by subsistence societies is advocated to transform the economy into thriving 20th-century consumer-oriented communities.

Fairbairn (1985), a Samoan economist, presents an image of this dichotomy in *Island Economies*, for in Chapters 8, 9 and 10, he presents three models which suggest that subsistence economies cannot sustain economic growth of the kind favored by development plans, especially those which depend upon capitalist, export-oriented industries. Such plans, he comments, run the risk of disruption (perhaps even destruction) of the subsistence sector and thus of traditional society in the longer term without providing for an enduring replacement (Fairbairn 1985). Yet, in subsequent chapters, Fairbairn argues that rural development should replace the plans of the "growth economists" for national development and that there is a large reservoir of untapped potential in subsistence village communities. Indeed, in respect of Western Samoa, he states that "with no proven mineral wealth or any other compensating advantages, *the economic future of the country depends essentially on progress in this* [*the subsistence*] *sector*" (Fairbairn 1985:350; emphasis added).

There is no suggestion by many economists that attempts to change the present land tenure systems of the Melanesian, Polynesian and Micronesian societies of the South Pacific, and to increase agricultural and marine resources productivity at the village level may have serious environmental impacts. Rather "progress" is to be achieved by "greater emphasis on commercial agriculture and fisheries, more productive use of land, high value-added industries, technical innovation and a greater effort by the subsistence sector" (Fairbairn 1985:322). The economic rationalist sees unused customary land as "available" for exploitation without consideration of the impact of semi-permanent or permanent loss of rainforest cover, erosion, siltation of streams and waterways, downstream impacts on coastal marine life and off-shore reefs, etc. In short, the ecosystem is not seen holistically.

But it is not only change induced from outside which may cause serious environmental degradation. A study in Solomon Islands suggests that with population growth in north Malaita in the past two decades, the traditional slash-and-burn cycle of 50-plus years has in some areas retracted to less than 10 years. Large areas of low secondary growth and grasses are being burned rather than small plots of more mature rainforest, with consequent increases in soil erosion, decreases in soil fertility, and a lesser nutritional value of crops. Malnutrition is appearing apparently for the first time (Sofield 1986).

In this context it is suggested that a detailed study of the impacts of non-traditional agriculture might well indicate far greater adverse impacts on both the physical and sociocultural environments than tourism development. One has only to look at the acreage of land now under non-traditional agricultural use in the South Pacific and to compare it to the relatively tiny amount of land utilized for tourism development to appreciate this point. The Australian aid-funded Kolombangara cattle project in Solomon Islands, for example, utilized 5000 hectares of clear-felled former tropical rainforest. To maintain soil fertility and pasture growth, hundreds of tonnes of fertilizer were utilized each year, with nutrient-enriched run-off draining into a fringing lagoon-reef system more than 10 km in length. In addition, some 60 streams which drained the slopes exhibited severely eroded gullies because of the deforestation, contributing large amounts of detritus and soil to be deposited in the lagoon. By contrast, all tourism plant in the Solomons occupies less than 100 hectares. In evaluating nine of the fourteen agricultural projects completed under Australian aid funding in the period July 1989 to December 1990, an analysis of the "Project Completion Reports" revealed, *inter alia*, that:

> the potentially far-reaching environmental effects of project activities were not always taken into account. Not only the effects resulting from the project itself must be considered but also the possible effects of environmental degradation on sites not involved in project implementation. For example, in one project salinization from aquifer recharge on a geographically removed site affected the viability of crop and pasture species selected for the project site (AIDAB 1991b:10).

A detailed analysis of Australia's aid programs to the South Pacific for the 14-year period between 1976–1990 indicated that a total of more than $310 million had been directed towards the agricultural sector, and only $1.5 million towards tourism (Sofield 1993). The 10 years from 1991 to 2000 saw a similar injection of development assistance into the agricultural sector and associated rural development by AusAID (Sofield 2002). Yet in every island country agricultural production continued to decrease throughout the period and receipts from primary produce continued to decline, while tourism consistently outperformed agriculture with upward trends. This aid program tended to follow the path of large, technically sophisticated schemes directed toward import substitution and production for export, and multisector rural development schemes ($2.5 million for the "Simbu Rural Development Project", Papua New Guinea). This approach is a seemingly logical path to follow if the limitations of increasing village-based productivity are accepted. But many of those projects and much of the expenditure have been less than successful.

In Tonga, for example, a desiccated coconut factory provided by the Australian Government cost more than $4 million and after numerous problems was decommissioned in 1989. During its operations, Tonga's total output of desiccated coconut fell in value from $0.5 million to $0.25 million per year in five years (National Reserve Bank of Tonga, Annual Report 1990), not exactly a profitable rate of return. A major input ($1 million) into onion cultivation in Western Fiji collapsed after two years because costs outran returns.

In Solomon Islands the "Cattle Under Trees" project at Kolombangara was closed after eight years of investment totalling more than $3.5 million, having accumulated losses of more than $4 million and failing in its objective of producing a national cattle breeding herd. In Samoa, a cocoa rehabilitation project costing more than $2 million saw not one single bean harvested after its completion because of a collapse in world prices of cocoa prior to the start of the project. In Papua New Guinea a coffee research project between 1991 and 1995 consumed $3 million in aid from Australia, with virtually no impact on smallholder practice, and a micro-propagation unit capable of producing one million coffee plants a year "proved not to be needed by the industry. Capital costs and operating costs of the unit were high, suggesting a net economic loss to PNG", and five years after project completion the extension service it had set out to establish had collapsed (AusAID 1998, pp. 18–19).

A comparison of the total foreign exchange earnings of Fiji's four major sectors — tourism, sugar, coconut products and gold — between 1970 and 1991 revealed that tourism had outperformed sugar in eleven of those years (Sofield 1993). During the next 10 years, 1991–2000, annual tourism receipts totalled more than twice those earned by sugar, with a lower leakage factor. Yet sugar still receives massive Fiji Government assistance, while tourism receives little by comparison. In 2000, the Fiji Ministry of Civil Aviation's Tourism Division and the Fiji Visitors Bureau together employed fewer than 45 officials. The Ministry of Agriculture had more than 600 extension officers and others working directly with the sugar industry.

While Australian aid to the agricultural sector of Fiji continued to increase despite its lesser position in the national economy and especially in terms of foreign exchange earnings, tourism was virtually ignored. During the period 1975 to 2000 Australian aid to the agricultural sector of Fiji totalled $45 million. During the same period, assistance to Fiji's tourism was about $480,000, a ratio between agriculture and tourism of 98:1.

A similar situation is found with reference to Samoa. A review of its gross export earnings from all agricultural products and gross foreign exchange receipts from tourism between 1985 and 2000 revealed that the latter grossed 125 percent more than agricultural exports. Australia contributed an estimated $15 million to Samoa's agricultural sector between 1985 and 2000. By contrast it contributed only $25,000 directly to Samoa's most successful export industry, tourism (short-term training scholarships). Agricultural exports behaved erratically, while tourism receipts rose steadily each year. In 1999, tourism generated an estimated $34 million in foreign exchange, while agriculture produced less than $5 million. In Samoa, contrary to the general picture often painted of tourism in the South Pacific, it is this industry which has demonstrated a degree of stability superior to that of the agricultural sector.

In a review of the Australian aid program, the Aid Bureau acknowledged from a study of 16 evaluations of agricultural projects made over the period 1985–1990 that the agricultural sector had proved to be a difficult one in which to design and implement successful projects (AIDAB 1991b). This was especially so when alleviation of poverty was also a major objective along with the purely agricultural ones.

According to the Australian Aid Bureau, key lessons which emerged included:

- There was a lack of proven technologies for improving rain-fed agriculture. Recommended practices must be of low risk to households with limited capital and land resources, and real benefits at the farm or operational level must be demonstrable.
- There was an over-emphasis on institutional research rather than operational activities related to the socio-economic environment of target groups.
- Inadequate attention was accorded to extension, which was invariably the weak link in the technology transfer chain. Where support was provided for extension, the strategy was often inappropriate.
- Projects often promoted technology that did not generate attractive financial returns. This was often the case in projects promoting the introduction of large ruminant animals.
- The provision of subsidies to encourage the adoption of a new technology had an inhibiting effect on sustainability (1991b:6–7).

Subsequent Evaluation Reports by AusAID in the last decade indicate that while some improvements in project delivery have been accomplished, the agricultural sector remains a problematic recipient of aid donor funding.

A scan of the aid programs to South Pacific countries of other aid donors (New Zealand, the United Kingdom, France, the European Community and Japan, for example) and the work programs of the South Pacific Commission and the South Pacific Forum over the past two decade reveals that they directed more than $250 million towards a variety of agricultural projects in the South Pacific states in addition to Australia's largesse. The projects undertaken share similar characteristics to those funded by Australia. Large amounts of aid are spent on the agricultural sector sometimes with little return.

In Fiji, a coconut oil factory built under European Community aid in Lakeba in the Lau Province closed down after six years of operations, because its running costs were greater than its earnings, for example. In Niue, more than one million New Zealand aid dollars were spent on passionfruit and lime production; the processing plant closed in 1983 having absorbed large losses, as noted above. Similar attempts by New Zealand to underwrite agricultural export production in the Cook Islands (pineapples and oranges) also failed.

The Leakage Factor

As noted by AIDAB (1991a), much of the development assistance for agricultural development has been toward the high technology end of the spectrum, not involved with large numbers of local people and not generating mass employment or greater efficiency in traditional practices, mainly because of its inability to be applied at the village level. As a result, much of it carries a high leakage factor, since it requires importation of fertilizers, pesticides, machinery and equipment, fuel, and expatriate expertise.

In several of the region's major cash crops (such as sugar in Fiji, coffee and palm oil in Papua New Guinea and Solomon Islands, beef cattle in Vanuatu) the leakage factor is deemed to be high although very few studies appear to have been carried out. One study of the Fiji sugar industry in 1989 indicated that it had a leakage factor of 49 against 57 for tourism. In other words, for every dollar earned by sugar, 49 cents was expended on imports while 57 cents in every dollar earned by tourism left the country for that industry's requirements (Sawailau 1989).

However, this study failed to take into account the costs of transport (mainly by trucks and railways) of the cane to the crushing mills, and when these costs were added in, the leakage factor of the sugar industry was at par with tourism. Since that time, backward linkages by tourism in Fiji have improved, especially with the establishment of thriving textiles and furniture sectors, and the leakage factor for tourism is now rated at less than 50. However, costs for sugar production have inflated as tractors and trucks have replaced bullocks as the main motive power in the fields and imports of fuel, chemicals and fertilizers have incurred price increases in line with global movements. The leakage factor for sugar is now higher than for most resort tourism.

In fisheries development projects, a similar leakage factor may be observed, especially where hi-tech purse seine trawlers and canneries are involved (for instance, Solomon Islands, Kiribati, Fiji; the continuation of all three projects is in doubt). Even in village-based fisheries projects there is an often unrecognized but significant leakage factor present. Locally made craft may be used, but items such as outboard motors, nylon nets, and diesel-fueled generators to power ice-making machines, with fiberglass coolers for transport of the catch to more distant markets are often standard equipment. These of course are imported and require foreign exchange.

Such fisheries projects are typical of community assistance to most South Pacific countries by Australia, New Zealand, United Kingdom, Japan, the European Community and Germany. Ranck (1987) noted that in the Tufi area of Papua New Guinea, a New Zealand aid-funded village fisheries project encountered a number of problems, a significant one being the inability of the villagers to raise sufficient capital from their catches to cover necessary replacement of the imported materials and equipment.

Two crops — copra and bananas — have received particularly high levels of aid funding in the South Pacific. Numerous efforts have been made over the years to revitalize the copra industry, the backbone of indigenous cash cropping throughout the region. More than $50 million has been expended by a variety of aid donors on coconut-related projects in South Pacific countries in the past 25 years. The South Pacific produces only 6% percent of the world's copra supply and is totally dependent upon foreign-controlled (largely European Community) markets for its exports so that it can exert no control over global prices (South Pacific Bureau for Economic Cooperation 1996). Despite the concerted efforts of both aid donors and recipient South Pacific governments the coconut industry has been in constant decline throughout the region for a number of years. Bananas have suffered a similar decline.

Seasonality and Market Source

In considering development in tourism and agriculture, governments are often cautioned by advisors about the seasonality of tourism and the dangers of "putting all one's eggs into the tourism basket". The same cautionary advice is rarely heard *vis-à-vis* agriculture. This is of course understandable given that subsistence agriculture is an integral feature of the socioeconomic environment of the island countries. Yet one has only to consider the seasonality of agriculture and the greater comparative vulnerability of crops to cyclones and droughts in the South Pacific to query whether some of that advice may be misplaced. In terms of seasonality, crops may be harvested only once per year (with the exception of copra, oil palm, and some root crops). While tourism registers seasonal fluctuations, it retains the capacity to continue generating a cash flow throughout the year. Unlike crops, tourism can maintain income earnings in off-peak periods by specific marketing strategies such as discounted fares and reduced-price accommodation packages.

Some tourism employment may be seasonal, but so is agriculture (including tuna fishing), a point that is often overlooked when tourism is being criticized. While tourism's seasonality may be a disadvantage in terms of a continuing cash income, it is not necessarily so for those who can return to their home villages during the off-season and help in local rural activities including farming and fishing (Tisdell *et al.* 1988). In the South Pacific countries this pattern of a return to the village is a general one for seasonal employment, and is not confined to the tourism industry.

Historically, it is difficult to penetrate new markets for agricultural exports. But in the case of tourism, a downturn in the economy of a major source market which might affect tourist inflows (such as recession in Australia) may be countered with a promotional campaign in a new source market (such as the United States) which will mitigate the economic impact quickly and effectively. The agricultural sector does not have the capacity or flexibility to recover either from natural disasters or from difficulties with source markets in the same way as tourism.

A graphic example of this was witnessed during the 1987 coups in Fiji which saw the national occupancy rate plummet below 20 percent (Fiji Hotels Association 1990) as the main source markets of Australia and New Zealand were turned off, both governments advising their nationals against traveling to Fiji. While the events in Fiji were given very full coverage in the Australian and New Zealand media over a six-month period, the coup dropped out of media reporting in the United States after two weeks. Taking advantage of this, an enterprising resort in Savu Savu, northern Fiji, ceased all Australian and New Zealand promotion, switched its entire marketing budget to the United States and in October 1987, only three weeks after the second coup, its occupancy rate was 95 percent — all of them (with the exception of this author) being Americans. That occupancy rate, based on the American market, was maintained for the next six months. The most recent coup, in May 2000, also saw a similar rapid flight of tourists from Fiji, and non-harvesting of the sugar crop as a form of protest by Indo-Fijian sugar cane farmers. Tourism receipts have recovered more quickly than sugar-related income since there is a move (spear-headed by India) to enforce a global ban on Fiji's sugar exports until it returns to democracy. Elections were held in Fiji in late 2001 but despite a constitutional requirement to include Indians in the Government the Fijian nationalist regime by mid-2002 had refused to countenance court orders to do so.

Tourism, Agriculture, and Natural Disasters

In terms of natural disasters, tourism has some advantages over agriculture. Crops such as sugar and coconuts take at least one year to recover from a cyclone (provided the coconut tree is not uprooted, in which case it takes five to six years for a replacement to become productive). Breadfruit trees and oil palms take from six to eight years. Niue's small beef herd has had to be reduced by slaughtering every six or seven years because of drought. In Tonga a prolonged drought in 1987/88 decimated agricultural production and thus agricultural exports and there was a drought-induced 2 percent fall in real GDP. By contrast Tonga's tourism receipts in that drought year maintained their 1986/87 level (National Reserve Bank of Tonga 1990). A severe cyclone in 1995 decimated Samoa's coconut trees and it took five years for them to come back into production.

There are two main areas of advantage for tourism. First, construction standards for commercial buildings in Fiji, Vanuatu and other countries are generally high following the introduction of cyclone and seismic resistant standards based largely on those from Australia and New Zealand (Favell 1986). In recent times tourism constructions have demonstrated a better capacity to withstand cyclonic winds and earthquakes. Tourism is also largely unaffected by drought. Fiji's resorts in the Western islands of the Mamanucas, for example, receive an annual average of only 35 cm of rainfall and the very dry conditions with high sunshine hours are regarded as conducive to the beach and sea sport-based tourism product of that area. It is difficult to perceive of agricultural inputs which could replace the income generation levels of tourism for these dry islands.

Second, in a disaster situation, tourism has a capacity to respond flexibly in a way which agriculture cannot. For example, cancellations (which are invariably the initial response to news of a natural disaster by potential tourists) can be countered by putting in place a range of strategies, such as cut-price fares, or special accommodation packages. Fiji has become expert at such promotions — *vide* its strategy to counteract Cyclone Sina in November 1990, for example, when it evacuated tourists from the affected Western area to resorts in the north and east untouched by the cyclone and undertook an international campaign to advertise those resorts with discounted air fares, while the Western resorts which had suffered some damage were swiftly repaired. Damage to tourism plant and loss of earnings was estimated at around $15 million. Losses to the sugar harvest from Cyclone Sina were estimated at around $63 million (*Fiji Times*, 6 November 1990). As previously noted, earnings for Fiji from tourism in 1990 amounted to a then record $210 million but only $112 million for sugar. Despite Cyclone Sina, visitor arrivals in 1990 achieved a then record total of 280,000 (Sofield and Donaghy 1991).

In Western Samoa, in January 1990, Cyclone Ofa, described as one of the most devastating cyclones to hit the country in the 20th century, caused widespread devastation. Agricultural production was severely affected, with exports down by more than 30 percent. Earnings from all the major primary export products recorded sharp reductions. For the first six months of 1990, the volume and average price of coconut oil exports dropped by 18 percent and 28 percent, respectively; cocoa by 11 percent and 43 percent; copra meal by 39 percent and 23 percent; taro by 68 percent and 9 percent; and timber by 60 percent and 21 percent. In addition to these losses, food imports doubled in 1990 over the 1989 figure because of the shortages of locally produced items (Central Bank of Samoa 1989, 1990).

In the first six months of 1990, gross tourism receipts declined by only 3.4 percent over the same period for 1989 or $12.6 million as against $13.06 million (personal correspondence with Western Samoa Visitors Bureau). In part this was explained by the arrival of several hundred short-term relief workers arriving and taking up most available accommodation. By the end of the year, Western Samoa had achieved its then highest ever gross foreign exchange earnings from tourism: some $21 million (Tourism Council of the South Pacific 1991). This experience illustrates the differential impacts of cyclonic activity on agriculture and tourism, with the latter weathering the storm rather better (Sofield 1993). By 1995, Western Samoa's tourism receipts were more than $26 million (TCSP 1996). In 1999 they were estimated by the Samoa Visitors Bureau at $34 million following record visitation of 85,120 (*Islands Business* August 2000:17).

Agriculture and Tourism Production Shifts

There is danger in concluding that the expansion in the tourism industries of the South Pacific countries during the past two decades has been achieved at the expense of agriculture, since they occupy the same time frame for their respective rise and fall. This argument has in fact been advanced by a number of sources (such as Crocombe 1987; Kent 1975; Rajotte 1982). Caribbean studies by Bryden (1973), Brown (1974), Friedman (1988), George (1987), and Hudson (1987) suggest that tourism attracted labor away from agriculture, and that capital intensive tourism affected the price of agricultural land to a point where (in the case of Jamaica, for example) it resulted in "the sterilization of agricultural land and so a process of underdevelopment of the country" (Clarke 1987:3). However, a close examination of the situation in the South Pacific suggests that the interaction of a large number of factors accounts for the decline in earnings from agricultural exports and that tourism, if it is a factor, is only a minor one.

Foremost is the global decline in commodity prices, particularly for agricultural products, which has affected both the agricultural sectors and the whole economies of most developing countries. For South Pacific village communities the price of copra is the single most important determinant of output. High prices, as in 1979, cause production to rise dramatically; low prices as has been the norm for the last 10 years, result in an instant decrease in output. When the other major village-based cash crops of the region (such as cocoa, bananas and coffee) follow similar downward movement in prices, so production spirals downwards too.

As previously noted, the educational systems introduced into the island nations more than 100 years ago provide, generally speaking, little support for continuation of a village lifestyle. Aims, ambitions and expectations are raised which cannot be fulfilled by the younger generations following in their parents' path of subsistence agriculture. Employment in tourism may provide an avenue for achieving those objectives, but it would be erroneous to conclude because of this that the industry is responsible for enticing the younger generations away from traditional farming. Education has been the primary cause, changing value systems the supporting cause and tourism simply a consequential option for satisfying the new wants generated by societies in transformation.

Nor can the argument be sustained that the capacity of this industry to pay relatively high levels of wages and salaries has had the result of making unpaid agricultural work for the family unit so unattractive as to be abandoned. Such argument ignores the pre-existing attraction for five decades of employment in the former colonial administrations and their present-day successors, the government public services of the independent states, where some of the highest salaries in the region may be found. Prior to 2000 the Solomon Islands public service employed approximately 10,000 persons; resorts and hotels employed fewer than 400. In 16 states and territories throughout the region (American Samoa, the Cook Islands, the Federated States of Micronesia, French Polynesia, Kiribati, the Marshall Islands, Nauru, Niue, Palau, Solomon Islands, Tokelau, Tonga, Tuvalu, Vanuatu, Wallis and Futuna, and Western Samoa), the government is the single largest employer in the monetized economy (Sofield 1991b). In Tonga, the civil service salary bill consumes more than 60 percent of the annual government budget (*Islands Business* 2000:17).

The argument against tourism also ignores the fact that in some of the South Pacific countries (such as American Samoa, New Caledonia, Niue, French Polynesia, Papua New Guinea, Tonga, and Western Samoa) tourism operates at a lower level of remuneration than other sectors, including the public. In others, such as Fiji, Solomon Islands and Vanuatu, basic or minimum rates have been set by their governments and apply equally to both the public and private sectors. In either case, it is erroneous to single out tourism for criticism.

One could suggest that in the case of Cook Islands, where tourism is now the largest employer after the government, this industry has drawn workers out of the agricultural sector. But when it is considered that some 25,000 Cook Islanders have migrated to New Zealand for the far higher wages there, it is tourism which can be seen as providing an incentive for some Cook Islanders to remain at home. The decline in Cook Islands agriculture — and indeed, almost every other industry in this country — is due in large part to an inability to retain a skilled laborforce because even the lowest wage scales of unskilled factory workers in New Zealand are considerably higher than local levels. Much the same situation prevails in respect of Tonga, Niue and Western Samoa.

The Melanesian countries lack out-migration opportunities to mitigate the dramatic population explosions experienced in the past three decades. For instance, in the Solomon Islands population has grown from 176,000 in 1976 to 285,000 in 1986 to an estimated 420,000 in 1999 at an annual rate of 3.5 percent (Solomon Islands Government statistician, personal correspondence). Thus it may be surmised that in fact agricultural output for local consumption has increased. Imports of food have increased to the Melanesian countries in recent years but domestic production to meet the needs of the burgeoning populations appears to have resulted in increased total production even if lesser volumes are being exported. However, more study is required into this question before a definitive statement can be made.

In the Polynesian countries of Western Samoa, the Cook Islands, Niue and Tonga, an increased volume of food imports has displaced a large measure of traditional foodstuffs and thus contributed to a decline in levels of domestic agricultural output. This has been attributed largely to the remittance of monies from relatives working abroad (as noted above). To lay the blame at the foot of the demonstration effect of tourism would appear to be drawing a rather long bow.

These comments should not be interpreted as an attempt to write out development assistance to agricultural ventures. The South Pacific countries obviously continue to have very substantial needs in this sector. Some 70 percent of their populations currently live in rural villages. Rather is it an attempt to question accepted orthodoxy about development assistance and to provide a perspective on tourism which tends to be lacking in much of the literature and in the planning processes of both aid donor and recipient. Linkages between agriculture and tourism need to be actively investigated, since there is an un-realized potential in virtually all of the South Pacific countries for local agricultural effort to provide a much greater proportion of the food and beverage requirements of the industry. Export agriculture has declined in the South Pacific countries and so has traditional agriculture in the Polynesian countries and in some of the other islands where national income has risen, but none because of tourism. According to Lattimer (1985) "correlation is not causation". Bryden's and Friedman's case studies of Caribbean islands would seem not to hold for the South Pacific.

There is a need to debunk some of the myths surrounding tourism as a form of development that may or may not be appropriate for small island states. Some of these relate to the perceived "superiority" of other sectors *vis-à-vis* tourism; and the agricultural sector in particular. It is suggested that this emphasis may be partly historical. In pre-independence times, as colonial regimes dealt with the "problems" of rural modernization, village-based societies whose livelihood and lifestyle were dependent upon an agricultural subsistence economy, it seemed — and almost certainly was — appropriate to focus on ways to build upon that base by improvements in quality, quantity and crop diversification. In countries like Papua New Guinea where more than 85 percent of the population remains directly dependent upon subsistence agriculture with some cash cropping, agriculture remains an ideal vehicle for widely distributing the benefits of economic growth.

In post-independence times, the ministries of agriculture of most South Pacific countries have remained among the largest and the oldest of their ministries, in many cases supported by commodity boards, statutory marketing authorities and development banks. They have within their ranks one of the largest sectoral corps of tertiary graduates in the region. Over time they have developed a strong corporate identity with considerable political influence, a not unexpected outcome given that more than 90 percent of the politicians in South Pacific governments come from rural not urban electorates.

This depth of human resources and political clout contrasts starkly with government attention to the tourism sector. Most of the countries (such as Federated States of Micronesia, Kiribati, Marshall Islands, Nauru, Niue, Palau, Papua New Guinea, Tonga, Tuvalu, Vanuatu, Western Samoa) do not have ministries of tourism but have small visitors bureaux or tourism authorities. One consequence is the inability of government planners and decision makers to focus on tourism. The impact of this historically derived bureaucratic and political alliance should not be underestimated.

Another result is that concentrated effort has been put into often non-productive or counter-productive agricultural development without the opportunity costs of investments in other sectors, such as tourism, being fully considered. Certainly it is a pattern of activity by both donor and recipient governments that has — and continues to be — operative throughout the South Pacific. There

have been many successful agricultural projects as well as many expensive failures; and this fact should be examined in the context of the long-term decline
in production and prices of major village-based crops such as copra and other
agricultural exports of the South Pacific countries. The economic effects of this
situation are serious and donors, including Australia, "must acknowledge their
implications in the design of programs and projects" (AIDAB 1991b:3).

As change proceeds apace in the smaller island countries, the situation
requires reassessing. The lessons of slow progress (and in some cases regres-
sion — as with copra, cocoa and bananas) appear to have been discounted. The
high leakage factors inherent in much agricultural and fisheries development
and their environmental implications appear not to have been seriously
addressed. The appearance of a new industry such as tourism with potential for
making a significant contribution to individual and national incomes has in
most cases not received donor and recipient government interest nor financial
investment and support commensurate with its current economic role.

Writers such as Britton have suggested that the international characteristics
of tourism development have introduced structural inequalities into the small
economies of the island South Pacific; but the historical evidence points to
those inequalities having been introduced well before the advent of tourism in
any significant way. The contemporary situation thus constitutes a major impediment in the ability of governments to address the needs of tourism because of
those inbuilt structures and institutionalized norms which continue to focus on
more traditional economic sectors. The power structures of governments (their
executive legislatures and their bureaucracies), which control the who gets
what, how, where, and when, continue to channel resources into those sectors
despite the obvious imbalances and the fundamental needs of what is for 10 of
the island countries their primary foreign exchange earner and greatest generator of paid employment. Inertia in undertaking necessary restructuring of the
bureaucratic structures is another factor contributing to this situation.

Conclusion

While the topic of tourism development in the South Pacific has attracted a
substantial degree of attention, much of the published work has focused on its
sociocultural and economic impacts. Empirical studies dominate. Here, the
concepts of both modernization and core–periphery dependency have been
applied to an understanding of the region's tourism industry. But, with the
exception of Britton, Sofield, and, to a lesser extent, D. Pearce and Hollinshead,
few theoretical issues from political science are explored in any depth. The

issues of tourism development in the South Pacific (and indeed in the Third World generally) have political ramifications of far-reaching significance. Some of the non-governmental organizations' literature deplores the mix of politics with humanitarian assistance. But it is naive idealism which sees development as somehow being "above" politics since this sentiment, however laudable, disregards the entrenched nature of much community powerlessness.

The same is true of the technocratic approach that sees the achievements of development as dependent upon the abstract rationality of economic and technical inputs "free from political interference". Both views are misconstrued and may divert analysis away from effective policy formulation. In effect, social development is inseparable from economic development and therefore politics. For 10 of the small South Pacific island countries, tourism is now their single largest industry in terms of foreign exchange earnings; and governments are deeply and directly involved. But the role of the state in development, and hence politics and power, tend to be lacking from the literature on tourism issues in the small island countries. The principles of sustainable development have recently received a significant degree of attention; but the notion of empowerment as a political and social process essential for sustainable community tourism development is absent.

Tourism development highlights the issues of adaptation to and interconnectedness with the global economy, perhaps more so than other sectors because of the direct interaction with a large number of global players, including international airlines and cruiseship companies, hotel and resort chains, travel agencies and tour companies, and of course the tourists themselves. The need to examine macro-economic factors and their linkage with internal socio-economic processes and the distribution and exercise of power in South Pacific countries is embedded in the international character of tourism. Thus, it draws on the political economy to analyze strategies of response to the exogenous pressures which tourism imports. It examines the articulation of community with the larger national, regional and international systems; the periphery with the center; and the dominant–subordinate relationships of the dependency theorists — but with an assertion that, rather than a repeating pattern of asymmetry and exploitation, empowerment can break that "chain of determination" (Bateson 1985) and lessen the dependency upon exogenous forces. Case studies can best examine these issues in the context of empowerment in South Pacific settings at the international, national and community levels.

Chapter 5

International Cooperation
or Disguised Dependency?
The South Pacific Region

Much of the material in this chapter came from confidential government
sources which were made available based on the fact that the author had
been a senior Australian diplomat in charge of the South Pacific Section of
the Australian Department of Foreign Affairs (1980–1982), serving in several
South Pacific countries as Head of Mission, and Deputy Secretary General of
the South Pacific Forum Secretariat from 1985–1987. It was during this
latter period that the Secretariat was directed by the Forum to establish the
South Pacific Tourism Development Program with the Tourism Council of
the South Pacific. Access to this material has permitted an authoritative account
of the historical chronology of moves by the South Pacific to establish a
regional tourism program not available from any other source. However, the
confidential classification of some material has meant that at times only
generalized references to documents could be provided. As already noted, in
1999 the Tourism Council changed its name to the South Pacific Tourism
Organisation.

To begin with the theme of this chapter, over 30 years ago in 1971, as the
first of the small island countries of the South Pacific gained their independence, they established an intergovernmental regional organization (IGRO), the
South Pacific Forum, to pursue inter-regional development. Although this move
was couched in economic terms, it was in fact a highly political attempt to
throw off colonial domination and assert the primacy of their national interests
over those of their metropolitan mentors. Because of the lack of domestic
markets of any size and the difficulties of achieving economies of scale, Island
leaders considered that only by combining their efforts and cooperating on a
region-wide basis could they attain a degree of economic development.
Through economic independence they would be able to assert political independence (Piddington 1986).

In order to understand the emergence of the South Pacific Forum, it is necessary to step back to 1947 and contemporary concerns in the aftermath of World
War Two. At that time, the strategic importance of the island countries to the

future defence and security of Australia and New Zealand was stark, given the way in which the Japanese armed forces had used them as stepping stones to advance southwards into the Pacific. As the Cold War began to develop a head of steam after 1945, it was also considered that the small island countries could be vulnerable to ideologies deemed dangerous to the western cause. Accordingly those colonial powers with territories in the South Pacific region at that time — Australia, New Zealand, United Kingdom, France, the Netherlands and the United States — decided to institutionalize links between their various colonies in an umbrella organization which would provide a modicum of economic and social development to their indigenous populations. This would demonstrate the commitment of the metropolitan powers to their welfare and lessen the attractiveness to Islands peoples of ideologies considered hostile to western security needs. This was meant to make it difficult for communist powers to expand their interests in the region (Sofield 1990a).

The vehicle the metropolitan powers established to meet their strategic concerns was the South Pacific Commission (now called the South Pacific Community) with the signing of the Canberra Agreement in the Australian capital in 1947. Its membership consisted of the six colonial powers and 22 non-independent island entities. The Netherlands was included because of its territory of Dutch East New Guinea. It subsequently withdrew when its colony was incorporated into Indonesia as the province of Irian Jaya. While the Commission grew to deliver a quite impressive range of economic and social programs to the island countries, and in this way became an important agency in their overall development, its rationale and continued funding levels were dependent upon the assessment of strategic concerns of the metropolitan powers in the first instance. Its charter was restricted to economic and social issues narrowly defined by the colonizers, and any topic considered political was not permitted by them within the Commission. Its agenda was set firmly by the metropolitan powers and they exercised total budgetary control in its early years (Sofield 1987, 1990a).

With the accession to independence by several of the island members of the Commission during the 1960s and onwards, however, the metropolitan powers were forced to step back somewhat from total, overt control. Consultations and negotiated programs became accepted but the metropolitan powers still wielded decisive influence and authority. The newly independent island states became increasingly disenchanted with the Commission as they chafed under what they perceived as paternalism and sought ways to exert control over their own destinies. Particularly frustrating to them was the proscription on the discussion of French atmospheric nuclear testing on Moruroa. Decolonization was another topic of intense concern to Islanders but the Charter of the Commission precluded such issues being considered and provided the island states with no platform for expressing their views.

Of almost equal concern to the island states was the approach of the Commission to economic development. It was regarded by them as paternalistic. The budget of the Commission was rigorously controlled by the metropolitan powers, and its programs at times appeared more concerned (particularly on the part of the French) with trying to duplicate metropolitan living standards for expatriate residents in some of the territories than with real economic advancement for the indigenous populations. For example, in New Caledonia priorities for development by France in the 1970s and 1980s included *inter alia* the provision of automatic telephone exchanges, television, and sports facilities such as floodlit tennis courts. All of these were of central interest to the expatriate French but of marginal interest to the Kanaks (who owned less than 5 percent of the telephones in 1985 and less than 8 percent of television sets). The approach to economic and social development was in the view of Islanders exacerbated by "solutions" to problems which had little relevance to the capabilities and resources of the small independent states. They lacked indigenous trained personnel for the most part, and they could not, for example, draw on an agricultural department of 5000 staff to tackle a crop disease problem as the metropolitan powers could (at least not without seeking aid funds). Expatriate technical expertise dominated the approach to planning and policy, often without regard for the sociocultural determinants of the indigenous peoples.

Tourism development was a case in point, with two major areas of concern for the island states in the 1960s and early 1970s (and which remain as continuing significant concerns today). They were/are foreign investment and cultural impact. Acknowledging the capital intensive nature of tourism, the island states considered control over foreign investment to be of particular importance if they were to be masters of their economic futures. But for the metropolitan powers, infusion of American, Australian, British, French or New Zealand investment capital into their colonies was to be encouraged since it reinforced their control. If other foreign investors wished to participate in development schemes, then the metropolitan powers had the resources to be able to ensure that no threat to their interests arose from such investment and that authority remained firmly in their hands.

With regard to the second area of concern — the cultural impact of tourism — again there was (and still remains) a sharp demarcation of interests between the metropolitan powers and the island states. The United Kingdom, France and the United States especially were spending large sums to advance their own cultures into South Pacific societies through such agencies as the British Council and the Overseas Service of the BBC (British Broadcasting

Corporation); Alliance Française and Radio France International; and the United States Information Service and the Voice of America. These agencies were supported more insidiously in all their territories by the colonial powers' imported educational systems based on their metropolitan curricula. In the former British colonies, indigenous students studied the kings and queens of England in their history lessons and learned about the cities, rivers, and mountains of Europe in their geography courses. The French colonies still retain almost unadulterated metropolitan curricula. Millions of dollars were expended in these directions by these powers, with only token gestures toward South Pacific cultures (for example, by way of financial contributions to the participation of their territories in the quadrennial South Pacific Festival of Arts). In this context, the cultural impact of tourism on the indigenous societies in the territories of the colonial powers was of minimal concern to their metropolitan governments. Only as the island countries gained independence could they begin to focus their school curricula on national and South Pacific concerns, a process in which both Australia and New Zealand actively participated through their aid programs.

The three areas of colonial domination of the political, economic and cultural may be interpreted as manifestations of dependency theory. Dos Santos, focusing on the economics of development, described this as "a situation in which a certain group of countries have their economy conditioned by the development and expansion of another economy to which the former is subject" (1972:71–72). Erisman (1983) enlarged the definition to encompass both political and cultural dependency as two equally major points with the economic in an essentially triangular relationship. Other writers (including Britton 1987a, 1987b; Crocombe 1983, 1987; de Kadt 1979; Matthews 1977) have argued that the plantation societies of island countries in the South Pacific and the Caribbean have been subjected to continued dependence on metropolitan powers and that characteristics of tourism in such countries (predominance of overseas investment capital, expatriate management and control, repatriation of profits) have contributed to this in no small way. Matthews' (1977) intrusion model of international tourism to the Caribbean has some elements of commonality with the situation faced by the newly-emerging independent countries of the South Pacific in the early 1970s.

The South Pacific Forum

In a climate of considerable frustration with the colonial powers, five Island states (Fiji, Nauru, Tonga, Western Samoa and Cook Islands) met in Wellington in 1971 to develop a mechanism to consider regional issues and development unencumbered by the global concerns of the distant metropolitan powers controlling the South Pacific Commission. After considerable debate among themselves, they decided to invite Australia and New Zealand as South Pacific, albeit non-small-island, non-developing countries and co-founders of the Commission as colonial powers, to join them in their first "Forum". The activities of these two countries were held to be sympathetic and supportive of island aspirations. This restricted grouping by its "pure" South Pacific nature would be able to focus in a qualitatively different way from the Commission on regional issues and concerns. In the words of the first communique of the South Pacific Forum:

> The talks were essentially exploratory. Those present discussed, as neighbors and partners, a number of problems which concern them and possible ways of solving them. They concentrated on matters directly affecting the daily lives of the people of the islands of the South Pacific, devoting particular attention to trade, shipping, tourism, and education (South Pacific Forum 1971:1).

The text then addressed topics of interest, the very first being a strong criticism of French atmospheric nuclear testing. The constraints of the Commission on political agenda items could be forgotten — "for the first time the voice of the island nations of the region could be heard loud and clear on the international stage" (Piddington 1986:8).

On tourism, the communique acknowledged its potential to make a valuable contribution to economic development, and noted that the United Nations Development Program was undertaking a study into the value of establishing a regional tourism body (South Pacific Forum 1971:2).

The general lack of natural resources among most of the micro-states prompted island governments to prioritize tourism as one area capable of sustainable development where the normal constraints of smallness do not always apply. Thus, the Forum included tourism as a key area for regional cooperation, along with trade, civil aviation and shipping, telecommunications and energy in their founding charter. However, it was not until 15 years later that government leaders agreed to establish a regional tourism development program. The reasons for this lengthy delay and the dynamics of dependency, sovereignty and intergovernmental relations are analyzed over the long gestation period, which stretched from the first declaration of intent in 1971, to actual implementation in 1986 through the Tourism Council of the South Pacific.

During those 15 years the Forum registered itself with the United Nations as an intergovernmental regional organization and expanded in size as each of the island countries became independent. The Forum fairly promptly asserted primacy over the Commission as the major regional organization because it met at Heads of Government level, in effect a summit meeting at least once a year. Meetings of the Commission by contrast were normally attended by officials and occasionally ministers, and regardless of their decisions if subsequently Prime Ministers and Presidents decided that the Forum should pursue an issue there was little the Commission could do. Tension between the two organizations developed as the Forum often embarked on areas previously the domain of the Commission. For example, the Commission had been running a scientific program on the South Pacific's tuna resources for about 10 years when the South Pacific Forum established the Forum Fisheries Agency in 1979 in a determined bid to manage the region's tuna resources against depredations by distant water fishing nations (which included the US purse seine tuna fleet). In political matters similar tensions prevailed, such as the Forum's initiative in declaring the South Pacific a nuclear free zone (Rarotonga Treaty of 1985) against very strong opposition by the three nuclear powers, the United Kingdom, France and the United States. The Forum also succeeded in forcing the question of independence for French New Caledonia onto the agenda of the United Nations Committee of Twentyfour (decolonization) against hostile French pressure.

The Forum, by constituting itself as an intergovernmental regional organization through the United Nations, was able to legitimate its authority in global terms. Its member states were able to exercise a degree of control over their own affairs of which membership of the commission had denied and deprived them. As noted in Chapter 2, it is when the formal ties of dependence are loosened and power is devolved that one may then begin to discuss empowerment. The ability of Forum member states to set their own agenda, make decisions and implement them within their own clearly defined sphere of political concerns may be seen as empowerment — the transfer of sovereignty and authority from their former colonial mentors to themselves. However, in economic areas the issue of empowerment is less clear cut and in tourism, as shall be explored, the translucent waters of the South Pacific lose some of their clarity.

Regional Cooperation

In examining the South Pacific's cooperative efforts in tourism, it is necessary first to examine the term "regional cooperation". The adjective "regional" is commonly used to refer to the South Pacific rather than "international" because of its connotations of a single grouping of countries, although it is acknowledged that normal usage would descend from "international" to "national" to "regional" as only a part of a country. However, in this study, the latter is used in its broader, South Pacific envelope.

At least three pre-conditions must be met for such cooperation to exist. First, there must be a sentiment that a particular group of countries constitute a region. Second, the political will to work together must be present. Third, there must be sufficient resources devoted to implementation of regional objectives if the states are to operate at a regional level (Sofield 1987). These are of course interrelated: the sense of belonging to a single region generates a willingness to tackle some issues collectively which in turn leads to the necessary resources being available for joint activities. In the South Pacific, regional intergovernmental cooperation has focused on limited, functional programs in clear recognition of political, economic and geographical constraints which would make the lofty ideal of economic integration pursued by other groups (such as the former East African Community, the Caribbean Community, and the European Community) an impractical goal.

The many manifestations of regional cooperation in the South Pacific include a diversity of both governmental and non-governmental organizations. Insofar as the former are concerned, it may be argued that regional cooperation has been initiated, developed and continued for as long as that cooperation has served, preserved and/or extended national interests. This illustrates very clearly one of the maxims of regional cooperation which most commonly takes place in the South Pacific at the lowest common denominator. When there is consensus on perception of commonality of interest or if a national interest coincides with a regional act, national concerns are most likely to be put to one side and regional cooperation permitted (Sofield 1990a). Where regional cooperation exists it does so because it enables individual governments to pursue national policies and objectives more effectively. The spirit of regional cooperation for its own sake exists more in rhetoric than in reality. As Crocombe, stated: "Regional cooperation is not a virtue in itself. It is justified only to the extent that it is the best option" (1983:212).

In the South Pacific the emphasis of and leadership for regional cooperation has been at the governmental level and the major organizations are all intergovernmental in nature. At first sight, there would seem to be sound justification for asserting that economic rationale underpins regional cooperation since most of the intergovernmental regional organizations were established to achieve developmental (largely economic) goals — *vide* the South Pacific Commission, the South Pacific Regional Shipping Council, the Forum Fisheries Agency, the

Pacific Islands Producers' Association, the South Pacific Bureau for Economic Cooperation, and many more. As the communique of the 16th South Pacific Forum held in the Cook Islands in 1985 stated: "The Forum is founded on the recognition that regional cooperation offers benefits through tackling common economic problems together" (South Pacific Forum 1985:79).

The emphasis accorded by states in pursuit of regional technical cooperation in the South Pacific is very much a functionalist, state-centric view, in contrast to the approaches adopted by the "populist-based idealist" and the "economic reductionist" (Herr 1980). As Herr (1980) has noted the former tends to see regionalism as a mechanism to reduce the divisiveness inherent in much nationalism and thus to promote interaction by non-governmental organizations because they are "putatively closer to the people" (1985b:2). The economic reductionist disregards to a large degree the morality of government, emphasizes the fundamental importance of economic issues and interprets both domestic and international politics in strictly economic contexts.

However the narrow interpretation of the economic reductionist is not wholly tenable for analyzing regionalism in the South Pacific. It gainsays the fact that other motivating forces may be accorded greater prominence in given circumstances by the island countries. They have often sought more than economic benefits through their participation in regional activities. Issues such as regional security, environmental considerations, humanitarian interests and political matters (such as decolonization) have all been actively pursued at times, with economic considerations being relegated to the background. A case in point is the consistent collective opposition over a 30-year period by island countries to French nuclear testing at Moruroa in French Polynesia on environmental, security and humanitarian grounds. This had an "opportunity cost" in the resultant reluctance by France to extend bilateral and multilateral development assistance to some of them. Therefore, it may be interpreted as a very public comment against dependency and about independence and sovereignty by the South Pacific countries.

Another case was the financial support given by South Pacific countries to the Pacific Forum Shipping Line which lost millions of dollars in its first eight years of operations (1976–1984) but where at the time political considerations of regional solidarity and the need to support Prime Ministers who had "nailed their colors to the mast" in setting up their own regional shipping line outweighed rational economic analysis (Sofield 1990a).

Herr has argued persuasively that "for the Islands, regionalism is fundamentally connected with the area's security" even if their "primary aim [appears to be] to promote economic development" (1986:3). There is the belief held by most of the independent island countries of the region that the greatest danger to the free exercise of their sovereignty arises less from direct external intervention than from economic vulnerability. This fear of economic subversion was put with particular force at a special colloquium convened under the auspices of the Commonwealth Secretariat in July 1984 to assess the post-Grenada defence needs of small island states (Herr 1986:4).

Instead of recommendations on defence coordination as the organizers assumed would be forthcoming, the major conclusion was concern that economic dependence could become dependency, a form of neocolonialism that required countering (Commonwealth Secretariat 1984). Thus, "regionalism offers the Islands a means for moderating if not removing the threat to sovereignty posed by economic vulnerability, the primary benefit being the achievement of economies of scale denied the small states individually". By combining to regulate their regional affairs, "the Islands have promoted a stability which reduces the likelihood of extra-regional intervention. . . . The latent political force of effective and organized regional cooperation has not inconsequential security implications for them" (Herr 1986:4, 6). It could thus be argued that by contributing to their security, the island countries were engaging in the process of empowerment. Neemia suggests that for Pacific leaders, other factors such as "perceived cultural affinity, shared historical experiences, aspirations towards political and economic viability as well as collective rejection of neocolonialism, are equally important" as economic imperatives in their acceptance of a degree of regional cooperation (1986:15).

Political considerations of a different sort also define the way in which regional cooperation is manifested in the South Pacific. Countries of the region are divided into independent sovereign states and non-independent territories. This factor has determined the different structures of the South Pacific Community and the South Pacific Forum. The former as noted includes all colonial powers and 22 island polities regardless of their political status. The Forum on the other hand is restricted to regional countries which are fully independent or are self-governing in free association with a metropolitan power. Thus, the Cook Islands and Niue which have constitutional links to New Zealand, and the Federated States of Micronesia, the Marshall Islands, and Palau which share a similar status with the United States, are full members together with the nine fully independent island countries and Australia and New Zealand. But regional cooperation as practiced by the Forum does not extend to the non-independent polities of Guam, the Commonwealth of the Northern Marianas and American Samoa, the British island of Pitcairn, nor the French territories of New

Caledonia, Wallis and Futuna and French Polynesia. Significant institutional stress has been apparent as governments within the region have attempted to address questions of regional cooperation (Herr 1980). This has created diffi- culties and distortions at times — as for example, an attempt at regional civil aviation cooperation in 1985 undertaken by the Forum, which was compelled to omit consideration of and the services provided by France, the United States and their Pacific territories, including the routes linking them to the indepen- dent island countries of the region. Economic rationalism demanded they be included: politics denied them the opportunity (Tucker, Halcrow and Associates 1985).

Regional cooperation in tourism has also been bedevilled by similar strictures. Major funding for the Tourism Council of the South Pacific by the European Community has been restricted to only eight of the Tourism Council of the South Pacific's members which qualify by virtue of being former colonies of European Community member states. Implications of this need to be explored.

Nye (1968) developed a typology for classifying regionalism into five stages, based on the intensity of relationships, interactions and commitments among the actors. At the lower end of the spectrum, "token integration" typifies the first stage: relationships are not intense and involve little more than a rhetor- ical attachment to the idea of a supranational community with no restructuring of national interests occurring. The second stage evidences a strengthening of relationships where a common view of security interests leads to a community "sense of illegitimacy": violent conflict among those on the "inside" is regarded as unacceptable. As with the first stage, this stage involves little direct finan- cial or material cost and provides ample scope for nations to manoeuvre in pursuit of individual political and economic goals which stop short of armed conflict with other community members. The third stage sees limited functional cooperation designed to provide common services, such as a regional airline or a regional development bank. This involves a greater degree of interaction but falls considerably short of stage four, complete economic integration. Stage five, the apex of Nye's ordinal scale, sees "direct political unification". Herr and Neemia, using this typology, have suggested that South Pacific regionalism lies somewhere in the middle to upper end of Nye's stage three. In other words, there is a fairly effective degree of limited functional cooperation (Herr 1980; Neemia 1986).

The Politics of Regional Tourism Cooperation

The cautious approach of the Pacific states to the inclusion of tourism devel- opment into government economic strategy is graphically illustrated by the length of time it took members of the South Pacific Forum to agree to a regional tourism development program. The matter was first raised at its inaugural meeting in 1971. In 1973 the Forum formalized tourism activities as a function of its Secretariat, but only 12 years later did members approve such a program at the Tuvalu Forum in 1984. Much of the following information is drawn from the classified South Pacific Forum Records of Heads of Governments meetings to which the author was granted access.

The minutes of the first Forum meeting (1971) reveal that rather more was said on tourism in discussion than the brief comment in the communique. Australia was the lead speaker on the topic and the title of the agenda item — "Foreign Investment and Tourism" — emphasized the concerns of the small independent island states to avoid dependency. Its representative drew the attention of the Forum to Papua New Guinea's experience of promotion of overseas investment and the establishment of the Papua New Guinea Investment Corporation. The objective of the Corporation was to provide a means for locals to obtain a share in ownership and control of major investment projects financed by overseas capital. The Corporation would hold equities in enterprises for future sale to the people. The Australian representative noted that major tourism development was capital intensive, that a high degree of local participation was difficult to achieve, and that it was a problem to make the most of tourism yet preserve indigenous culture and tradition. Ratu Mara (Prime Minister, Fiji) and Sir Albert Henry (Premier, Cook Islands) both acknowledged the problems that tourism posed for traditional culture, although Ratu Mara ventured the opinion that because 83 percent of Fiji lands were indigenously owned, control of foreign investment could be attained through leasing conditions. Sir Albert said that the Cooks was adopting a very cautious attitude; it was only just constructing an international airport and it would license only two international standard hotels to start with, to control tourist numbers. Western Samoa's Prime Minister, Hon Tupua Tamasese Lealofi IV, observed that tourism was his country's single largest earner of foreign exchange but agreed with others about the possible adverse cultural impacts of the industry (South Pacific Forum 1971).

At the second meeting of the Forum held in Canberra, Australia, in February 1972, the leaders agreed to establish a permanent Secretariat to service them. Among its functions would be the ability to "advise and assist Member Governments with the operation of a regional trade and tourist promotion service" (internal Second Forum Record, February 1972). Tourism was mentioned in the context of trade where it could assist in providing increased market opportunities for handicrafts and the local manufacture of some consumer goods.

The Third Forum in Suva, Fiji, in September 1972, met primarily to consider the Agreement to establish the Secretariat. In the course of discussions on functions to be carried out by the Secretariat, to be called the South Pacific Bureau for Economic Cooperation, New Zealand drew to the Forum's attention a UNESCO pilot project being carried out in Bali on cultural tourism. Prime Minister R.J. Marshall submitted a New Zealand paper on the adverse effects of tourism on culture. This evoked supportive comment from Sir Albert Henry who offered the Cooks for a similar study by UNESCO; from Ratu Mara who expressed grave concerns about the side effects of tourism and said that Fiji should rely on its sunshine rather than "cheapening" culture by frequent repetition of traditional ceremonies; and from the Prime Minister of Western Samoa who noted that his country's tradition and culture were its best attractions but that he had no wish to see them destroyed by tourism. The meeting agreed that the impact of tourism should be put to study before any regional promotion of tourism was attempted (internal Third Forum Record dated September 1972). Subsequently the communique recorded support for UNESCO "to undertake a study of tourism in the South Pacific with particular reference to its impact on the way of life of the islands" (internal Third Forum Record dated September 1972). In fact this study did not eventuate.

The fourth Forum, held in Apia, Samoa, in April 1973, formally accepted the agreement establishing its Secretariat, or "SPEC" South Pacific Bureau for Economic Cooperation – as it very quickly became known. Article VIII set out the functions of the Bureau, and, as had been agreed in Canberra, it included a reference to tourism: [Preamble] "Subject to the direction of the (Forum) Committee, the Secretariat may . . . advise and assist member governments with the operation of a regional trade and tourist promotion service" (1973:2).

In the Forum itself, however, there was no substantive discussion on tourism. Leaders having expressed reservations and urged caution, the Secretariat declined to seek an active direction to pursue the matter. It also declined to list the issue for future agendas, becoming highly reactive in this particular aspect of its work. Partly this was a function of the character of the then Director who by nature was himself a cautious man who perceived his role to be to respond not initiate; partly it was a response to other more pressing preoccupations of member governments (regional shipping and the establishment of the Pacific Forum Shipping Line for example, became possibly *the* dominant issue from 1976 to 1985); and partly it derived from the fact that every year or so another island territory became independent. The new nations had less developed tourism industries than Fiji or even Cook Islands, and tourism was at that time a low priority for them.

For a number of years, following what could be seen as a key input by New Zealand which provoked a negative or lukewarm attitude toward tourism as a priority for consideration by the Forum and Bureau little activity took place. The words of Sir Albert hung over the organization: "Tourism is O.K. but not at any price" (Fourth Forum meeting in Rarotonga in 1974).

Then in 1981 a meeting was held between the European Community and former colonies of its members (the so-called ACP Group, or African-Caribbean-Pacific countries) to discuss development assistance under the Lome Agreement. The Pacific group (Fiji, Kiribati, Papua New Guinea, Solomon Islands, Tonga, Tuvalu, Vanuatu and Western Samoa), accepted a European Community suggestion that financial assistance be made available for regional tourism (Arndell 1989:83). There were mixed views about this among the eight but they acquiesced in the suggestion in the face of strong support from Fiji (the only one with a reasonably developed and mature tourism industry) and Europe's readiness to finance such programs in Africa and the Caribbean. However, they placed a proviso on the aid by insisting that the Forum should approve such a program before submitting a formal request to the European Community. This was in part motivated by a genuine desire to involve all members and not just a select subgroup in a major new regional program which clearly fell within South Pacific Bureau for Economic Cooperation's mandate; partly (by those still wary of tourism) to deflect Fiji from imposing its enthusiasm for tourism on its smaller neighbors; and partly to assert a degree of independence from the European Community.

Thus, in 1982 the Bureau, prodded by the European Community and a resolution from the 1981 Forum meeting, convened a regional meeting to discuss the role of tourism in development and to consider the possible place of the Bureau in regional tourism activities (Bergerot 1982). Again, there were ambivalent signals from delegates concerned about the economic and cultural impacts of tourism and the priority it should have in their development programs. The Bureau also noted that it had no specialist tourism staff in its ranks and thus lacked the expertise to take the matter forward. No firm decision to proceed with the European Community offer was made.

The nexus was finally broken when the European Community (which in 1982 published its own guidelines on "Tourism for the European Community"), through its diplomatic office in Suva announced to member governments in early 1984 that under Lome II there was a pool of unused funds amounting to several millions which could be utilized immediately to establish a regional tourism program. The lure of this largesse proved too much and the Tuvalu Forum meeting in 1984 put its imprimatur on the program, directing a reluctant Bureau to accept a formal decision that "As Regional Authorizing Officer and

Secretariat to the ACP Pacific Group [the Bureau] takes steps to secure funding from the European Community for a regional tourism development program" (internal SPEC Committee Meeting Report, Tuvalu, dated 1984:38). The Bureau was to secure the funding, design the program, appoint a consultant from the European Community to carry out the work on behalf of regional tourism authorities, and monitor its progress on behalf of the European Community and the Forum. This author, as then Deputy Secretary General of the Bureau, held primary carriage for the implementation of the Forum's decision.

The Tourism Council of the South Pacific (TCSP)

Because of the South Pacific Bureau for Economic Cooperation's lack of tourism-specific expertise, the Forum decided to link up with a fledgling autonomous body, the Tourism Council of the South Pacific, and offer it operational carriage of the European Community-funded Pacific Regional Tourism Development Program (PRDP) under the Bureau's oversight. There had been a number of prior attempts to establish regional cooperation in tourism, including one sponsored by the Pacific Islands Development Program which operated out of the University of Hawaii East West Center. However none had succeeded.

The Tourism Council of the South Pacific owed its genesis to these attempts and more specifically to a UNDP/WTO study (1980) into the need for a regional tourism development program. Later in that year, the Visitors Bureaux of Fiji, Tonga, Western Samoa and American Samoa met and formed the Tourism Council of the South Pacific among themselves. Over the next few years five other national tourism administrations joined the Council. It had no permanent secretariat, it met sporadically, its activities were minimal, restricted in the main to exchange of information, and until the Bureau provided funding through the Pacific Regional Tourism Development Program it was close to moribund. It is significant to note that the Tourism Council of the South Pacific was not established under Bureau/Forum auspices and that its members were national tourism administrations not government ministries of tourism. In this context, the Council was an independent autonomous body, able to determine its own rules and regulations without reference to the Forum or its Secretariat.

In 1986, the South Pacific Bureau for Economic Cooperation under a new Director from Tuvalu, and in accordance with the Forum's 1984 directive, obtained about $3 million from the European Community's Global Trade Promotion allocation of Lome II for the Pacific Regional Tourism Development Program, whose Management Board (established by the Bureau) was composed of the Secretariat and representatives of five Council members, to have oversight of it. The board selected one of the nine European firms shortlisted by the European Community, DANGROUP of Denmark, as technical consultants for the program. Subsequently in August 1986 a Financial Agreement for the above amount for a two-year period was signed between the European Community and the Bureau as its Regional Authorizing Officer; and the Council was appointed under the Bureau's auspices to implement the program with technical assistance provided by DANGROUP. This was given explicit recognition in the Financial Agreement for the Program:

> Para 1.4. Implementation will be by the TCSP [Tourism Council of the South Pacific], as administering agency of the South Pacific Bureau for Economic Cooperation (SPEC), the RAO [Regional Authorizing Officer] for the project, together with the technical assistance [DANGROUP Ltd] provided by the project.

Between 1986 and 1988 the Forum Secretariat worked closely with the Council and DANGROUP on the Pacific Regional Tourism Development Program which had six main functional areas: technical assistance to the Council, with the aim of establishing a permanent secretariat staffed by Islanders within two years; development of a database system to link the products of all member states into a centralized, computerized booking service; human resources development, with training covering all aspects of the industry from economic planners to guides to domestic staff of hotels; production of educational and awareness material (such as videos, posters, brochures) both to promote understanding of the South Pacific tourists to the region and to educate Islanders to the pros (less so the cons) of tourism; tourism/development linkages through pilot projects in selected countries; and the production of marketing and promotion material on the region rather than individual countries, including a series of films and videos, with participation in international trade and travel fairs.

From its inception the Council carried out a wide range of activities. Its achievements extended from hospitality training for hotel and catering staff to the formulation of national tourism development plans for some of the eight ACP countries. Its regional marketing strategy benefited the entire region despite being prepared in the first instance for the eight ACP states only, and was highly regarded. Its surveys provided the most comprehensive data available on categories of tourists, motivations for visiting a destination, their expenditure patterns and destination image perceptions. Other activities included the preparation of guidelines for the integration of tourism development and environmental protection in the South Pacific; a review of information technology applications for the South Pacific; detailed surveys of source markets such as North America, Japan, Germany, the United Kingdom and France (but not Australia and New Zealand, the two bread-and-butter markets for the South Pacific countries, which provided more than 50 percent of their visitation until Australia and New Zealand provided separate funding; the EC would not countenance its funds being expended in these countries – another example of politics overriding economic common sense); a series of training manuals (food production, wine service, bar service, front office and reception operations, housekeeping operations, skills for Pacific supervisors, etc.); guidelines for national tourism organizations and their operations; and the development of a database providing comprehensive statistics on the tourism industries of some of the countries of the region. Subsequently it commenced an active ecotourism development project that promised to be particularly relevant for the small, ecologically fragile environments of its member states.

The Council was particularly successful in providing a sharp focus for a regional marketing and promotion strategy with the production of a wide range of multi-media materials and by funding the participation of South Pacific nationals from the eight ACP Pacific countries at travel fairs in Europe, the United States, Japan, Australia and New Zealand (the latter two with non-EC-sourced funding, as noted above) on an annual basis. In 1997 the Council established a "Millennium Coordinating Committee" with the slogan "Crossing the threshold of time", a pun on the fact that its member states lie on both sides of the international dateline, and tourists could begin and end the first day of 2000 in the South Pacific without following the sun all the way around the world. Its marketing advertised that one could see the dawning of the first day of the new millennium in Kiribati, Tonga, Cook Islands and Fiji, and the sunset in Western Samoa. In 1997 (October) the Council conferred its inaugural "Excellence in Tourism" awards at its first annual South Pacific Tourism Conference (held in Tahiti).

In terms of education, in 1989 the Council engaged a well-known British professor to advise on the introduction of a tourism studies program at the University of the South Pacific (USP), and in 1991 agreement was reached with the EC to fund such a Program through the Council. Commenting on this development Harrison noted that:

> As the University serves 12 island states in the region, all of which value the contribution tourism makes to economic growth, and the TCSP is also made up of 12 territories, [nine of which overlap with USP], two of the largest regional bodies in the Pacific were thus committed to cooperation in providing a

course addressed to the tourism needs of the region and potentially able to make a contribution to studies of tourism further afield. . . . This course is now firmly established at USP but not before relationships between the University and the Council were subjected to considerable strain (1997a:3).

The difficulties arose from "dysfunctional fiscal disagreements" between the two institutions over several years which resulted in the EC funding not being forwarded to the USP by the Council (Dowse 1995, quoted in Harrison 1997a). Harrison argued that there were "structural problems inherent in the funding of an academically-orientated Tourism *Studies* Program through the Council, a *promotional* organization" (1997a:9; italics in the original). The difficulties were exacerbated by the fact that the funds earmarked for the University were to be channeled through the Council's training and education sector, which could disburse its funds as it saw fit, and the less it contributed to the USP the more it had for other purposes. The EC itself also displayed little interest in the tourism studies program and in five years made no attempt to support the University in its endeavors to extract the promised funding from the Council (Harrison 1997a:9–11). By 1996 however, the Council had released the funds and in 1998 the University assumed responsibility for funding the program itself.

Empowerment or Disempowerment

In 1988, the Council Secretariat, in a move initiated by its then British national director, relocated out of the Forum Secretariat compound in the university suburb of Muanikau to Suva city's central business district as a demonstration of a greater degree of independence. Again at the initiative of its director it then convened a meeting at Nadi in August 1988 of regional ministers of tourism ("First Meeting of South Pacific Ministers of Tourism", TCSP 1988c) at which a new charter (Memorandum of Association) was accepted, elevating the Council to an intergovernmental regional organization (IGRO). Under the new constitution, its structure was composed of four tiers: ministers of tourism, to meet every two years; the Council, comprising national tourism representatives nominated by member countries' national tourism authorities, to meet at least annually; the Management Board; and a Standing Committee of the Council, responsible for the management of the organization and supervision of the Secretariat (TCSP 1989:17).

With its new-found status as an intergovernmental regional organization the Council was eligible to be appointed a regional authorizing officer under

European Community Lome regulations, and it promptly sought and obtained regional status from the European Community. The second phase of the Pacific Regional Tourism Development Program — for approximately $8 million over the next three years — was then negotiated and signed directly between the European Community and the Council in October 1988 (*TCSP Tourism Topics*, no. 13, February 1989:1). Subsequently, in 1992 a third agreement was signed, granting the Council another $9 million from the European Community. In 1995 that agreement and further European Community funding for the Council was extended to 1999, and then to 2001.

In signing the 1988 financial agreement the European Community attached a number of "Special Conditions", the second of which was that: "The Pacific ACP States shall take over the management of the Pacific Regional Tourism Development Program and the [Council] Secretariat by the end of this (second) phase" (Financing Agreement, document VIII/11167/88-DN:2).

With this agreement, the European Community, the Council and the Pacific ACP states appeared to have exceeded their competence since the Regional Tourism Development Program was "owned" by the Forum and not by any of the signatories to the agreement. While European Community terms and conditions of funding restricted its application to the eight ACP states, it could be argued that the Regional Tourism Development Program as a legal entity was larger than those eight states and required decision by the Forum itself. However, the European Community had been constantly irked by the fact that its funds for the Regional Tourism Development Program were subject to consideration by a body over which it had little control and which was composed of countries which were not ACP members (Australia and New Zealand as well as six island countries fell into this category). The leading role of the (islands-elected) Cook Islands representative on the Council Board of Management, for example, was contested by the European Community on the grounds that as a non-ACP member the Cooks could not participate in determining how the Regional Tourism Development Program should function; and at one stage through the intervention of the European Community delegate in Suva the EC moved successfully to block his election as its chairperson.

The Council's action in setting itself up as an intergovernmental regional organization effectively severed the organic link with the Forum and removed the formal oversight role of its Secretariat, without any consultations with the Forum. It clearly relegated the Regional Tourism Development Program to a subregional activity by specifically excluding the majority of regional countries. It was 12 months before the Forum realized that it had "lost" the Regional Tourism Development Program. Not unexpectedly these developments led to dissension between the Council and some of its members, and with the Forum itself.

In addition to concern about the legitimacy of the Council/European Community action, several governments became annoyed because the Council Secretariat continued to utilize national tourism administrations (statutory authorities) through which it had historically worked, as the channel for communications and decision-making. For as long as the Council work program went through the Forum, governments were apprised of its intentions and activities. But in the new situation they found that decisions affecting their tourism development were being made without their knowledge.

For example, in April 1989 the Council Secretariat, in conjunction with the Solomon Islands Tourist Authority, called for tenders for a nature-based tourism project that did not reflect the priorities of the Solomon Islands Ministry of Tourism. A European consultant employed by the Council had carried out a comprehensive survey of the Solomons' natural resources (Tourism Council of the South Pacific 1988a), recommended certain areas for tourism development, and devised specific projects. The Solomon Islands Tourist Authority had provided in-country support for this exercise. The critical point here is that the Council had made the decision to develop sites to maximize economic benefits without adequate consultations with the landowning communities concerned, and pushed forward with tenders. When the S.I. Ministry of Tourism insisted upon participating in the decision-making process, the TCSP's initial response was to refuse to acknowledge the Ministry's rights and an angry exchange followed. Domestically this also created tension between the Solomon Islands Tourist Authority and Tourism Ministry officials. The matter was raised by the S.I. delegation with other countries at the 1989 Tarawa Forum and the TCSP was in the end forced to accept that governments had primacy over statutory bodies and that Ministries of Tourism, in conjunction with Ministries of Foreign Affairs, could direct the Council as an intergovernmental organization about the official point of first contact. Because of their handling of the issue the DANGROUP consultants and the European Community were perceived at the time by some island governments to be acting arrogantly and riding roughshod over their interests (Solomon Islands Ministry of Tourism, Cook Islands Government, Papua New Guinea Department of Culture and Tourism, personal correspondence).

This situation presented an interesting paradox. The Tourism Council of the South Pacific seized an opportunity to empower itself by elevating its status to that of an intergovernmental regional organization with direct ministerial (governmental) input; yet, at the same time, it disempowered the Forum as the supreme regional organization with responsibility for tourism development. While the Council appeared to have given greater power to its Secretariat its action made it directly accountable to the European Community, thereby dissipating its distance from its funding body and rendering itself more susceptible to European Community direction. In a sense, it replaced its South Pacific mentor from which it was able to obtain prime-ministerial support for its activities from 15 heads of government, with a European funding parent in negotiations with which it could at most employ only ministerial level representations from eight countries.

Another issue that created tension at the time was the closure of the World Tourism Organization office in Suva in 1990. This had been set up in Suva in 1981 and for nine years had been responsible for the South Pacific Regional Tourism Development Planning and Training Project with approximately $0.5 million provided each year by the UNDP. It had thus pre-dated the Regional Tourism Development Program by some five years. Its projects extended to 13 countries, the eight South Pacific ACP states plus the Cook Islands, Niue, and the three Micronesian countries of the FSM, the Marshall Islands, and Palau. Although termed "regional project" the work actually consisted of a series of country projects: "the thrust was individual country assistance, thus clearly distinguishing the UNDP/WTO Project from that of the [Council]" (Atkinson 1988:14). While its funding was much smaller, it had developed a reputation for being able to respond to requests for assistance almost immediately, in marked contrast to the regional development program whose projects often took more than 12 months to initiate because of the cumbersome European Community tendering process. Among other things, the European Community required any European Community-funded tender document to be translated into all its languages and released simultaneously in all its capitals. This bureaucratic mechanism itself could cause a delay of up to three months. The European Community also insisted on employing only its own nationals for consultancies. The WTO office by contrast was able to respond quickly to one-off requests which were country-specific; it could employ in-country experts already familiar with internal tourism environments; and it was thus highly valued by the participating countries.

The UNDP/WTO office had enjoyed an uneasy relationship with the Council under its European Community national director, with the latter constantly striving to position itself as the sole regional tourism development authority. There was little direct cooperation between them despite coordination meetings being convened to avoid duplication of effort. This competitive element intensified after the Council successfully manoeuvred itself into becoming an intergovernmental regional organization and through its European Community connections it pressed the WTO through its headquarters in Madrid to close its South Pacific regional office. Perhaps surprisingly, given that the WTO country projects were qualitatively different from the regional activities of the Council and the fact that the latter could not extend the regional development program outside the eight ACP member countries, WTO closed its Suva office. The three Micronesian states, the Cook Islands and Papua New Guinea were particularly chagrined and the European Community/Council was held responsible for pressing a false claim to being able to provide all of the region's tourism development needs. Another ingredient of tension was thus added to the region's bubbling tourism stew.

These tensions led the South Pacific Bureau for Economic Cooperation, (whose name had been changed in 1989 to the Forum Secretariat and its Director to Secretary General) to re-examine the Council's move away from the Forum. The Secretary General concluded that the Council had exceeded its authority in taking on direct control of the Pacific Regional Tourism Development Program and tried to curtail the autonomy of the Council. At the same time, the latter felt the need to broaden the base of its funding since the agreement under which the European Community funded the Regional Tourism Development Program restricted its application to the eight Pacific members of the ACP group and there was growing dissatisfaction with those limits. It was considered that a closer relationship with the Forum might assist endeavors to obtain additional funding. At the Council's second ministerial meeting, held in Suva in June 1990, the Council adopted the following resolution requesting the Forum summit at its meeting in Port Vila in July 1990 "to note the establishment [of the Council] as a regional intergovernmental organization operating satisfactorily since October 1988; to grant TCSP membership of the South Pacific Organization's Coordinating Committee; and to give favorable consideration to [the Council's] application seeking a reporting relationship with the South Pacific Forum in line with the relationship established with the South Pacific Geo-science Commission" (Record of the Second Ministerial Meeting of Tourism Ministers, Suva 27 June 1990a).

This was not accepted by the Forum. At the private retreat of Heads of Government before the formal summit, some concern was expressed about the degree of influence exerted by the European Community and its European consultants, and a view that membership of the Council should be congruent with membership of the Forum. The Cook Islands in particular (where tourism is by far the most important industry) was highly critical of what it perceived to be European Community neocolonialist control. The Secretary General forcefully demanded that the Council should in effect return to the Forum "family", perhaps with a relationship similar to that of the South Pacific Regional Telecommunications Development Program which was a semi-autonomous division within the Forum Secretariat.

The Tourism Council, however, supported by the European Community, was not about to give up its new-found intergovernmental regional organization status. It resisted this demand (a simple enough task since it was not a creation of the Forum even if its permanent Secretariat and its program had been established under Forum auspices). It sought to enlarge its membership and reach out to non-Pacific ACP states by drawing up proposals for associate government members for other Forum countries and inviting them to join the Council.

Australia and New Zealand in particular found this unacceptable, labeling it as a form of "second class" membership. Consequently, in late 1992 both countries were invited by the Council to become full members on payment of special membership fees; and to contribute to the funding of the Pacific Regional Tourism Development Program. Because of the continued domination of the Program by the European Community, however, Australia and New Zealand considered that their foreign policy and regional interests would not be met and have to date remained aloof. Their preference was to provide discrete funding for specific tourism projects which could be coordinated by the Council but which in effect were outside the Regional Tourism Development Program, thus avoiding the European Community restriction on participation by ACP countries only and European Community control over the use of their funds. In 1997 agreement was reached with the South Pacific Forum for the Council to present a report at the annual Forum summit, but its budget was not supported by Forum funding.

In 1999 the Council changed its name to the South Pacific Tourism Organisation (SPTO) and again attempted to gain Forum support for its program, a pressing need because the European Community had put the new organization on notice that it would cease its funding within another year. Again the Forum declined to provide more than "in-principle" support. Some 12 years after the new organization achieved intergovernmental status the precise nature of its relationship with the Forum remains unresolved and its capacity to function as a fully-fledged regional body remains constrained.

Structural Limitations of the New Organization

As time passed, it became increasingly obvious that while the Pacific Regional Tourism Development Program had made considerable progress in some areas, assistance had been uneven and there were some severe strictures affecting its implementation. The structure of the Regional Tourism Development Program and its funding by the European Community resulted in a number of limitations in delivering tourism development assistance to the South Pacific region.

As emphasized, restrictions in the tied funding of the Regional Tourism Development Program, prevent it from covering the whole of the South Pacific. Neither the European Community nor the eight South Pacific ACP states can move to direct the European Community funding into a central pool to be distributed evenly by the South Pacific Tourism Organisation to other countries in the region because of the terms of the Lome Agreement. Such an arrangement would require all its signatories (more than 55 states) to agree. The political likelihood of African and Caribbean states accepting that non-ACP states — and states moreover which are not fully independent but retain constitutional links with the United States (in the case of the FSM, the Marshall Islands and Palau) and New Zealand (in the case of Niue and the Cook Islands) — should receive some of "their" aid would be slight. African and Caribbean states have no reason at all to agree to European Community funds being diluted by extending expenditures to countries outside their "club".

Because of the constitutional nature of some of the non-ACP countries (the Cooks, FSM, Marshalls, Niue, Palau, American Samoa and French Polynesia) they are basically unable to attract development assistance from the international donor community. They are in the main reliant upon their metropolitan mentors, with Australia and New Zealand being two of the few countries prepared to provide them additional limited assistance. It is thus doubly difficult for them to participate in South Pacific Tourism Organisation projects. Alternative aid donors are not present; and their current aid donors are reluctant to provide funds to match European Community largesse for tourism development because it would be at the expense of development assistance to other sectors such as health, transport infrastructure and education.

The South Pacific Tourism Organisation is sensitive to these limitations and there is a desire by the ACP Pacific countries and the Secretariat of the organization to find ways to extend operations to include the other South Pacific regional countries. Thus, with the series of films made on the various countries, it was able to include the Cook Islands and Niue in its coverage by virtue of additional funds provided jointly by Australia and New Zealand. It should, however, be noted that Australia was responding to the Secretariat representations of the Forum in the context of its bilateral relationships with the Cooks, Niue and New Zealand, rather than the South Pacific Tourism Organisation. In 1998 Taiwan provided $90,000 to the Council to investigate Taiwan as a source market for tourism to the region. (This odd contribution must be seen in the context of resistance by Taiwan to diplomatic efforts by China to have several South Pacific island states withdraw diplomatic recognition of Taiwan and transfer recognition to China). The Council's success in attracting alternative additional funding has been very limited.

Because of the South Pacific Tourism Organisation's tied funding for the Pacific Regional Tourism Development Program it has difficulty working with non-European Community institutions and countries. This means that its relationship with Australia, New Zealand, Japan and Hawaii, all sources of much relevant expertise on tourism in the South Pacific, is somewhat at arm's length. While there is a mechanism which allows European Community principals to subcontract limited work to regional agencies and experts, in practice there have been very few such contracts issued. The Danish firm which was appointed principal technical consultant for the implementation of the regional development program had never previously worked in the South Pacific region. (This was a characteristic common to all but one of the nine European Community firms placed on the restricted tender from which the Forum Secretariat had to select a consultant). European Community nationals have been used almost exclusively for projects. For example, a Danish film-maker with no previous experience of the South Pacific, its geography, peoples or cultures, was utilized to make a series of nine films for tourism education. An Italian with no previous South Pacific experience was appointed to undertake guiding training for South Pacific Islanders (in whose countries, it might be noted, alpine guiding is little practiced). The lack of relevant regional expertise was notable in the report of this exercise which suggested, for example, that lodges were a type of accommodation common throughout the South Pacific and could be described as "a hotel or inn generally located out in the countryside, and frequently providing sports facilities" (Tourism Council of the South Pacific 1988b:14). The term "lodge" may be common in the alpine areas of Italy, but in the South Pacific it is rarely heard outside the French colonies; and while "attached sports facilities" may describe some of the upmarket resorts in the region that offer scuba-diving, deep sea game fishing, and tennis, it certainly does not define traditional houses in villages which may be functioning for tourist accommodation as guest houses and "home stays" and to which the term was referring.

In all aid programs, there is a risk of inappropriate "experts" being selected. With the European Community-funded Regional Development Program that risk was compounded by cultural and linguistic differences and lack of specific knowledge of the region. There are many examples, but one which was particularly inappropriate was the use of Scandinavian architects to design a hotel in ignorance of the island recipient country's cyclone standards, seismic resistance standards, and insulation for tropical heat as distinct from insulation for Arctic cold. The exercise had to be completely revisited. Another project saw $180,000-worth of solar panels installed on the south-facing sides of houses in Tuvalu by a northern hemisphere "expert" who had never worked south of the equator before.

There is obviously a cost to the recipients of such "aid". Not only can it result in ineffectual assistance with potential for social disruption, but the dollar cost of bringing experts from Europe is much greater than the utilization of regional expertise (airfares, per diems, consultancy fee structures, the logistics of support from a European head office, etc.). Therefore, it is not surprising to find among South Pacific governments, tourism authorities and the Forum Secretariat a perception of European Community domination of the Pacific Regional Tourism Development Program and criticism that at least some of its assistance is not cost-effective or appropriate (Morgan 1992; *Pacific Magazine with Islands Business* February 2001). Core–periphery dependence in a new guise is insinuated into the region.

The South Pacific Tourism Organisation's emphasis on subregional development restricts its capacity to meet individual states' needs. Projects can only be justified under its charter if they extend across two or more states and have an identifiable regionality of application. Therefore, much of the database and other information the organization holds is subregional rather than individualized for a member state. This can restrict the value of its data for use in bilateral and multilateral project design for development assistance. In practice the organization has managed several country-specific projects by describing them as a pilot project with potential for other countries (such as a feasibility study for a tropical fruit juice processing plant in Vanuatu to improve backward linkages to the tourism industry) or including them in a region-wide approach (such as individual biennial tourist surveys). Pilot project identification and implementation has been slow.

The European Community consultants were also criticized for not appointing counterparts to localize senior positions on the South Pacific Tourism Organisation's Secretariat in its first two years as originally agreed. That took almost five years to rectify. Currently (2002) the Secretariat is headed by a Tongan, supported by a wide range of South Pacific nationalities, including Fijians and staff from Tonga, Cook Islands, Solomon Islands, Kiribati, Vanuatu and Papua New Guinea. However until 2000 most sections of the organization retained European technical experts who continued to exert influence over its direction and activities.

This is in the process of change. The European Community has indicated a reluctance to continue funding the South Pacific Tourism Organisation's marketing and promotion program and instead will direct assistance to the private sector to undertake tourism development. In response to this pressure, the director of the organization in 1999 proposed an increase in the number of its board members from 13 (who are all official country representatives) to 19, with the additional six members all drawn from the private sector. This move was designed to involve the private sector directly in the decision-making processes of the organization, and in 2000 six industry representatives were appointed to the board. It remains to be seen, however, whether it can carry the private sector with it "across the threshold of time" into the 21st century.

At the end of 2000 the organization had attracted only 150 corporate members (*Pacific Magazine with Islands Business* 2001).

Conclusion

The length of time from the initial adoption of tourism as a responsibility of the South Pacific Forum in 1971 to the implementation of the first regional tourism development program in 1986 underscores a fundamental requirement for regional cooperation: that there must be consensus on a perception of commonality of interest combined with a capacity to further individual national interests. The decision by the Forum to embark on a regional tourism program was reached almost by default. It was due as much to a signal from the European Community that it would fund such a program, and to the persistence of Fiji, as to any felt need by the region's political leaders. A multifaceted program was put in place that subsumed to a certain extent national interests under a regional umbrella. This was a fundamental condition of the European Community funding under the Lome Agreement (only a regional and not a series of national programs could be financed). In this sense, the European Community offer was compatible with the South Pacific Bureau for Economic Cooperation's original mandate which had included tourism as one of its major functions. Within two years, however, the Tourism Council of the South Pacific had cut its organic ties with the Forum and established itself as an independent intergovernmental regional organization. This move inadvertently emphasized that its tourism development activities were in fact subregional only. This resulted in the illusion of greater power and independence for the Council Secretariat but it is suggested that in fact the net result was the loss of some power and a commensurately greater degree of dependence upon the European Community.

In this context, the Council's attempts at regionalism may be considered dysfunctional since they resulted in some stress and tension between regional countries. It is useful to return to the distinction made by Beals *et al.* (1977) between conflict which is functional or adaptive in that it contributes to the efficient working of an organization and the long-term survival of its membership, and conflict which is dysfunctional or maladaptive. A degree of conflict arose between those island countries which benefit from the Pacific Regional Tourism Development Program and those which do not; between the former WTO office and the South Pacific Tourism Organisation; between the latter and the Forum; between the Forum plus some island governments on the one hand and the European Community on the other; and between Australia/New Zealand and the South Pacific Tourism Organisation/South Pacific Bureau for Economic

Cooperation. These may not be major irritants and over time it is possible that ways will be found to remove the causes of dissension. But to the extent that they exist, regional harmony is disrupted. To the extent that the South Pacific Tourism Organisation has not been able to undertake the kind of projects that were formerly carried out by the WTO Suva office, it has been dysfunctional. This inability at this point in time to extend the Pacific Regional Tourism Development Program to the entire region may thus be considered maladaptive in terms of contributing to regionalism, despite the advantages that have accrued to some member countries.

Therefore, the application of Nye's typology for measuring regional cooperation to the South Pacific Tourism Organisation is not straightforward. There undoubtedly is a degree of multilateral functional cooperation: the organization has established more than 30 successful tourism projects under the regional program. However, the elements of conflict and exclusivity have restricted a more complete regional cooperation. If then the organization is to be located in Nye's typology, it can be seen to have elements of stage three, with limited and effective functional cooperation. But the absence of applicability and relevance to a majority of members of the region and the elements of tension which were generated by exclusivity suggest that Nye's typology needs modification to incorporate a situation of subregional cooperation which may involve greater or lesser degrees of conflict with non-participating regional members.

A positive light may be cast on the South Pacific Tourism Organisation's activities since 1986. It brought economies of scale to bear on tourism development and promotion in the South Pacific and provided a wide range of materials and services beyond the scope of any one individual country. Those countries that have participated in the Pacific Regional Tourism Development Program undoubtedly benefited and the South Pacific Tourism Organisation established its presence as a leader in tourism development in the region. There is recognition that, despite the at-times irksome regulatory and other requirements imposed through European Community funding of the Regional Tourism Development Program, the approach offers greater possibilities for minimizing the cost of promotion, marketing and development for their national economies (South Pacific Bureau for Economic Cooperation 1988). It may thus be argued that dependence has been replaced to some extent by increased sophistication on the part of the island countries to maximize the benefits they receive from tourism. Matthews and Richter make the point that "the nationalistic critique of tourism [in the context of dependency theory] has perhaps been moderated" because of the increased capacity of Third World governments to exert greater control (1991:132). Milne would argue that while Britton was correct in asserting that metropolitan-based agencies influence the development of peripheral destinations "it is hard to accept that local governments place foreign corporate interests ahead of those of the local population" and "the failure to acknowledge this fact creates a sense that local populations are 'victims' unable to exert control over their own destinies" (1996:289). This stance may be seen as a criticism of dependency theory and its focus on the global system accompanied by a resultant unwillingness to acknowledge the significance of local factors which may influence development outcomes.

There is an alternative assessment which suggests that the degree of European Community control over the regional tourism development program has itself been neocolonialist, notwithstanding the various achievements of the South Pacific Tourism Organisation. There remains a set of inequitable linkages between the developed European Community countries and the developing South Pacific mini-states, between the core and the periphery. The deeply embedded European Community presence in the delivery of tourism aid funds to the Organization means that the peripheral governments may have little room to maneuver. They are "forced to seek continued reliance on development strategies that revolve around a dependence upon foreign public capital" (Britton 1996:163). The evidence suggests, in contradiction of Milne's view, that at times island competencies have been subjected to European Community direction of their tourism development: *vide* the Solomon Islands nature-based tourism strategy and the blockage of Cook Islands chairmanship of the management board of the organization. A further example was the imposition on Samoa of a village-based model for tourism development which is quite inappropriate and which cost more than $1.5 million for just six bungalows. As a model for other South Pacific communities who cannot access that level of aid it is a nonsense. There are in fact many examples of island authorities placing, or being maneuvered into placing, the interests of external forces ahead of those of their own communities (the Ok Tedi dispute in Papua New Guinea, already referred to, is but one; Chapter 8 on a resort development in Solomon Islands is another). Baines (1987) would note that there are instances of corruption by governing elites where self-interest has been put ahead of local interests, and foreign interests permitted to exploit island resources. Logging in PNG, Solomon Islands, Vanuatu and Fiji was the focus of such activity by corrupt local elements in conjunction with foreign interest throughout the 1990s, and occasional tourism ventures attracted similar criticism.

One may describe the European Community and its Lome Agreement as a supranational institution operating in a global sphere able to influence and in some cases determine economic and political activities in the national sphere. There is a degree of political integration between its member states, but the organization itself is not subject to the laws of any one national government. Supranational organizations operate in many fields and may be private (transnational companies) socio-environmental (such as Friends of the Earth, Greenpeace) or financial (such as the World Bank, the International Monetary Fund). The latter "are dedicated to direct and deliberate involvement in the formulation of national economic policy through money lending activities. Development organizations such as the European Bank for Reconstruction and Development . . . and USAID also wield very considerable power over policies pursued by Third World countries" (Mowforth and Munt 1998:291). The European Community may be less obtrusive in its involvement with the South Pacific than the international banks, but because of its pervasive presence, exercised by its underwriting of the South Pacific Tourism Organisation's Secretariat and work program, its placement of technical experts in-house, and its reliance upon European Community nationals as consultants, the resulting articulation bends the South Pacific's tourism development in directions not always preferred by the recipient countries. Actions and policies desired by national governments may be circumscribed and the form of their tourism development strongly influenced by the supranational organization that provides the funding. "Consultations" may be one-way participatory processes, passive in nature and designed to get communities to accept decisions already made by others. Not only are these Third World countries the recipients of tourists from the First World whose comforts and enjoyment may take priority over activities of greater benefit to local communities, they are the receivers of First World priorities about their tourism development. The agenda for their ministerial Tourism Council meetings may thus be pre-determined, directly and indirectly, to a significant extent by the European Community. There is a form of disguised disempowerment masquerading as empowerment.

In practice, the South Pacific Tourism Organisation has not been able to fulfil the expectations generated by the Head of Government decision at the 1984 Tuvalu Forum to embrace an active program of regional tourism development. The strictures of European Community funding, reinforced by the subsequent elevation of the South Pacific Tourism Organisation to an intergovernmental regional organization, have reduced the Pacific Regional Tourism Development Program to a subregional activity. In the process, a degree of divisiveness resulted and unequal growth in national tourism industries was exacerbated. The goal of true regional cooperation in the South Pacific has proved elusive to date.

Chapter 6

Empowerment at the National Level: Solomon Islands*

Many developing countries show evidence of a colonial legacy in their current legislation, regulations and structures that fail to take due and sufficient account of indigenous practices and values. That legacy may place a series of formidable obstacles in the path of indigenous communities and individuals attempting to participate in various forms of development despite post-independence policies and schemes designed for just such participation. A break may occur between policy intention and actual result, the so-called "implementation gap" (Dunsire 1978), in which a continuing lack of empowerment frustrates effective action. The Solomon Islands' tourism industry provides a case study of such a situation.

A comprehensive tourism development policy was finalized after extensive consultations between 1987 and 1989 by the Solomon Islands national and provincial governments, local area councils and village communities. The consultations consisted of seminars, workshops and village *tok-tok* (literally "talk-fest") sessions, and the outcome was a consensus document in the main. The resultant "National Tourism Policy" contains a broad range of strategies designed to facilitate greater indigenous participation in the industry. To implement the strategies and policies, a "Ten-Year Tourism Development Plan, 1990–2000" (Solomon Islands Ministry of Tourism and Aviation and Tourism Council of the South Pacific 1990) was then formulated. A foreign aid program, the Provincial Development Fund, was designed to provide a source of finance where commercial lending institutions could not assist.

The extensive consultations which produced the Solomon Islands Government tourism policy, its development plan, and the aid scheme were all formulated in isolation from a consideration of the impact on them of existing legislation and accompanying regulations. Those laws and regulations owe their genesis to imported colonial systems which for the most part find no echo in traditional resources, skills and systems. These imported structures were often

* This chapter is an adapted version of an earlier publication in *Annals of Tourism Research*, Vol. 10, No. 4, pp. 729–750.

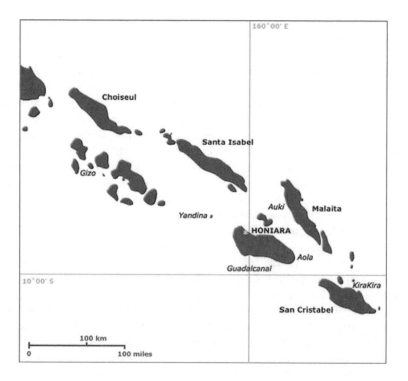

Figure 6.1: Solomon Islands
Source: S.I. Ministry of Trade

inadequately modified (or not changed at all) after independence and can thus continue to militate against village-based development. For instance, the Solomon Islands National Building Code is predicated on western standards which cannot be met by village craftsmen utilising traditional construction methods and traditional materials.

Transition of a society through a pioneer stage where a central authority is lacking, such as American frontier society (Turner 1961), may *inter alia* result in adaptation and innovation across a wide range of practices and systems. The new environment, both physical and social, will often accelerate change which will be manifest in practical and eventually philosophical, governmental and legal structures to support the new systems and models which have developed. Pioneer stages such as those of outback Australia and the Western frontier of the United States, where imported technologies were transplanted without the strictures of rigid codification and regulations, meant that localized adaptations made necessary by prevailing conditions had time to take root. Those that withstood the test of time — non-institutionalized norms — were incorporated into legislation as "civilization" finally came to the pioneer or frontier areas. These adaptations became institutionalized norms.

Solomon Islands had fewer than 150 foreign settlers and missionaries when it was declared a British Protectorate in 1893. The declaration provided a legal basis for British administrative and political centralization of government (Wolfers 1983). Solomon Islands thus by-passed the pioneer stage of development and moved directly from a scattered village-based society with no central power structure to one where the colonial power imposed its authority and created a government apparatus which paid scant attention to traditional practices. Until then, the area had been almost a model of decentralization, having no central governing structure and with power quite widely dispersed among the 87 tribal-linguistic groups living in more than 2000 autonomous villages. These settlements were not hierarchical and each had its own leadership based on the Melanesian concept of "bigman", owing authority to no other.

From 1893 to 1922, administration in Solomon Islands was a system of "severely direct rule" by a small number of government officers acting on behalf of the Western Pacific High Commission which had its headquarters in Fiji (Wolfers 1983:147). In 1922, the "Native Administration Regulation" was introduced which appointed headmen in some areas as government officials. This marked the first step towards employing locals in minor positions of colonial authority. Such power imported its own comprehensive legislation and imposed it usually with little or no modification. As Saemala noted, "As a colonized people we were subject to laws made by the British Government" (1983:1).

Britain established its colonial headquarters first at Tulagi in the central Solomons and then at Honiara in Guadalcanal after World War Two. Like many of the cities of the Third World, neither town grew in response to industrialization, as was the case with many of Britain's cities, but as a result of the impact of a capitalist economy on a subsistence one. As such the towns of Solomon Islands reflected this change from decentralized indigenous social control in small villages to colonial control which introduced the technologies of an alien civilization and foreign exploitation of the indigenous hinterland. Legislation — particularly as it pertained to building standards, health and sanitation, and commercial activities — focused on urban and thus largely expatriate needs. Regulations were designed to support the modern formal sector and reinforced the primacy of alien urban centers over traditionally oriented rural areas and the city's role in the modernization of the Melanesian landscape. Three spatial systems began to coexist, not always in harmony and each serving a different function. They were rarely integrated, even when they shared the same site.

The colonial government created its own spatial system for such specialized functions as administration, commerce, transport and communication. These were based in Tulagi and Honiara. As in other colonial cities like Nairobi, Kenya (El-Shakhs and Obudho 1975) and Suva (Fiji), the rigid designs of the buildings, constructed to imported standards and owing nothing to indigenous heritage, gave substance to segregation policies. Traffic systems, grid street patterns and architectural styling visually reinforced the alien impact. The shops and businesses in these centers served the needs of government officials and expatriate businessmen, planters and traders. Honiara, like many other ex-colonial cities, still reflects the political, economic and cultural structure of its former metropolitan mentor much more than it does the national traits of Solomon Islands society.

The second spatial system was the pre-existing traditional one. It met the needs of the local people, encompassing their communities, village settlements, land and sea resources and their traditional market system. It displayed a tendency, common in other South Pacific countries — such as Fiji, Tonga, Papua and New Guinea (King 1992) — to conflict with the urban primacy inherent in the first spatial system.

The third spatial system was, like the first, an imported one: that of the Christian missions. Mission stations tended to avoid both the colonial centers and the traditional nucleations. They created yet another spatial system focused around the churches as well as schools and hospitals that were often attached to them.

The combined impact of the imported spatial systems was the imposition and institutionalization of western models on Solomon Islands, albeit unevenly, which tended to pre-empt an evolutionary development of change. Government regulations and mission values directed change in prescribed directions. Both imported systems introduced sanctions, one legal and the other moral, to enforce compliance. The result was that the country to a large extent "leap-frogged" the pioneer stage where imported practices and models might have been amended by necessity and combined with local traditional systems and practices to produce a "new" Solomon Islands product. The adaptation that Turner (1961) so graphically described in his seminal essay on "The Significance of the Frontier in American History" was not given the opportunity to occur in Solomon Islands. The constitution promulgated for independence in 1978 specifically incorporated pre-existing colonial legislation to ensure stability and continuity in the legal and legislative processes (Ghai 1983). Structural problems related directly to colonialism thus continue to exist today in Solomon Islands, leaving the country without a system which is conducive to the mobilization of resources for internal as distinct from overseas invest-ment in tourism development. This, as previously noted, is despite the formulation of policies designed otherwise.

Geography, Demography, and Social Structure

Solomon Islands comprises a scattered archipelago of mountainous islands and of coral atolls stretching over 1500 kms in a south-easterly direction from Bougainville in the west (Papua New Guinea) to the Santa Cruz Islands in the east. Australia is approximately 1600 kms to the south-west and New Zealand 2400 kms to the south. The six main islands and island clusters are arranged in a double chain, with Choiseul, Isabel and Malaita to the north, and the New Georgia group, Guadalcanal and Makira to the south. Together with numerous small island groups at either end of the chain, the archipelago covers a land and sea area of approximately 650,000 sq kms, of which 29,800 sq kms is land.

The country is relatively isolated and international air access is possible only by small aircraft such as Boeing 737 from three or four external points (Brisbane and Sydney, Australia; Nadi, Fiji; Auckland, New Zealand; and Port Moresby, Papua New Guinea). Solomon Islands obtained a brief period of noto-riety in 1942 when one of its largest islands, Guadalcanal, was the setting for the initial confrontation between the Japanese and United States armies during the Second World War: the battle for Guadalcanal became known as "the turning point of the war in the Pacific".

The population of Solomon Islands is predominantly Melanesian (approxi-mately 94 percent), although there are smaller Polynesian, Micronesian, Chinese and European communities. Within the Melanesian community, there is a great

deal of cultural diversity exemplified by a range of language and custom variation. The population census in 1986 revealed that 285,796 people were living
in Solomon Islands, of whom 14,000 were enumerated as resident in the small
capital, Honiara. The national total was a 45 percent increase over the 1976
census. Since then the population has continued to increase at an annual rate of
3.5 percent so that by December 2000 the estimated total population was more
than 430,000. There is increasing concern that the country will not be able to
support such a high annual population growth rate, although efforts to reduce
the growth rate run counter to strong cultural and religious beliefs.

Some 80 percent of the people live in small villages of less than 200 persons.
Honiara, the capital and only truly urban area has a population of about 80,000
(2000 estimate). There are only three other centers with a population of more
than 1000. It is probably true to state that as yet there are very few urbanized,
"de-villagized" Solomon Islanders since Honiara did not exist prior to 1943.
Its harbor at Point Cruz was established as a naval base for the American armed
forces in 1943, a site where there was no traditional village. There are thus very
few Solomon Islanders above the age of 30 who were born into and have spent
their lives in an urban environment. Traditional values remain paramount even
among many of the younger educated elite.

While English is the official language and Pijin (Melanesian Creole
language) the *lingua franca* for the majority of people, there are still many,
especially women, who can speak only their local language, one of the 87
languages recorded for Solomon Islands, most of them of Austronesian origin.
This multiplicity of local languages, with the largest single group being spoken
by some 45,000 people, adds to the communication problems already made
difficult by the geography of the country.

According to the Solomon Islander anthropologist, Leonard Maenu'u (1984),
the structure of Solomon Islands communities was traditionally triangular in
form and nature (Figure 6.2). The three main elements which bound the people
together were ancestral gods, land and the tribe. Each could not be divorced
from the others. The land was peopled by both living tribal members and by
ancestors in an unbroken line, with the present population being custodians
of the land and its resources for future generations. The boundaries of tribal
land were determined by pioneer settlement and contemporary custodianship is based on genealogies linking the ancestors with living individuals
grouped together patrilineally or matrilineally. The tribe was the administrative
body and within its boundaries individuals strived for status, wealth, influence
and power.

Traditionally, Melanesian society rarely had a leadership hierarchy of hereditary chiefs. It operated most often under a relatively flat system where a series

of "bigmen" achieved their leading status by the accumulation of wealth, traditionally based on their excellence in different fields of expertise. Their hold on authority, influence and power was not guaranteed and the society was characterized by a robust competition where a fierce sense of egalitarianism found expression in socially sanctioned ways of reducing the status and wealth of "bigmen". Individuals could (and did) exercise individual rights, but where any group action was proposed it was a society in which the entire clan or an even larger group were usually all required to agree (consensus, not decision by the majority) before any action would be taken.

In this fluid social system the importance of *wantok* affiliations should not be underestimated. *Wantok* is a Pijin term widely used throughout Melanesia to denote a close relationship. Literally translated it means "one talk" or "same language". In the Solomons it is applied to a range of relationships depending upon circumstances. In the first instance, a person's closest *wantoks* will be his/her extended family. Beyond that it will be members of the same clan; then members of the same tribe; then all members of the same linguistic group. More broadly, it will then be applied to members of the same geographical locality (like all people of Malaita, or of Guadalcanal, or of Isobel, as in a debate in

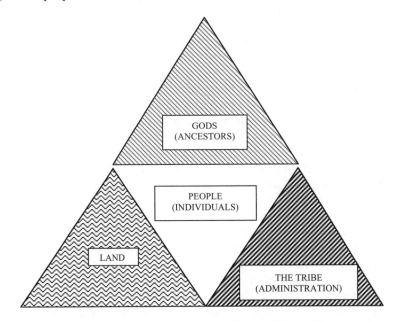

Figure 6.2: Structure of Indigenous Solomon Islands Communities
(after Maenu'u 1984)

the National Parliament when a member of Parliament will distinguish between his/her province and other provinces). When Solomon Islanders are overseas, all Solomon Islanders present, regardless of linguistic affiliation or geographical location, will refer to each other as *wantoks* (such as all Solomon Island students at the University of the South Pacific in Suva, Fiji). Depending upon the situation, one "bigman" will be able to prevail over another not on the basis of comparative individual merit but on the basis of the *wantok* support he is able to muster. The use of the male pronoun here is not sexist but a reflection of the values of Melanesia as a male-dominated society where there might be important women but they could not aspire to the title of "bigmen". As far as this author is aware, none of the 87 linguistic units of Solomon Islands have a comparative word to describe an influential woman, and there is thus no feminine form of the label which carries the same connotations of leadership and excellence as the term "bigman".

Solomon Islands Melanesia is a conservative society in which custodianship of land is so central to the culture that any new idea which impinged on customary land rights would be — and continues today to be — greeted with caution. The traditions of the Melanesian villagers are so interlinked with their forests, coastal reefs, and associated habitats that they are regarded as their most important social and economic resources. Individual, family, clan and tribal status and wealth are equally derived from these resources, as well as subsistence. Some 80 percent of land holdings are owned by indigenous villagers under customary rights. The government owns only 8 percent of so-called "alienated" land. The remaining 12 percent is also alienated land, some owned by Solomon Islanders with an in-perpetuity lease and the remainder (about one tenth) owned by non-nationals on maximum 75-year leases.

In this situation, the strength of the traditional land tenure system is such that the government's capacity to introduce and implement management policies is limited. This limitation is not constitutional since the Land and Titles Act (Solomon Islands Government, 1984a, Part V, Paragraphs 70–84) empowers the national government to compulsorily acquire land in the national interest. Rather, it is political in the sense that every politician in the national parliament is there because of the support of his/her village. Political parties are still at an embryonic stage and political platforms have little electoral appeal. Village-based affiliations (the *wantok* network) and village issues, including the relative "bigman" status of competing candidates, are the decisive factors in every electorate in Solomon Islands, including the two urban electorates in the capital, Honiara. Most villagers are traditionally oriented and the values of the people must be reflected in the actions of the elected representative if he/she is to remain in parliament. In fact, in every national and provincial government election since independence in 1978, there has been a rejection of between 60 to 80 percent of sitting members by the voter.

The political power of customary rights is clearly demonstrated by the fact that not once since independence has a national government used its powers to compulsorily acquire land or resources (Sofield 1991b). In a *de facto* sense it has granted the power of veto over the national parliament to the village. The national government, on any question concerning *kastom* land may find itself in conflict with its people. Thus, although the government may introduce policies designed to manage the nation's resources in a sustainable way (Solomon Islands Government Forest Policy Statement 1989a), its ability to implement those policies is heavily circumscribed. McMaster (1993) and others have described this as the "strong society, weak state" concept.

The twin advents of Christianity and colonialism introduced their own economic, social and political structures and imposed them from above, impacting upon many of the traditional structures. Maenu'u in fact claims that "the gods, tribes and land of the indigenous triangular association have all disappeared, leaving the people exposed and vulnerable" (1984:8). However a dual system still remains and there are many traditionally oriented communities throughout the archipelago even if the dynamics of social change are impacting in different ways on those structures.

Tourism Development

Solomon Islands has substantial potential for tourism development because of its particular mix of hundreds of tiny islands and beaches, abundance of coral reefs and marine life, virgin tropical forests, rugged mountains, white water rivers, unique and varied bird population, friendly people, interesting cultures, as well as the added attraction of World War Two battlefields sites, sunken ships and aircraft which appeal to scuba divers.

Prior to independence in 1978, the British administration regarded tourism as an inappropriate form of development and concentrated its development efforts on agriculture and the provision of infrastructure for primary education, health and inter-island shipping. Following independence, twin concerns by successive governments about the possible domination of the tourism sector by foreign interests and a perception that adverse sociocultural impacts outweighed economic benefits contributed to lack of government enthusiasm for the industry. Slow growth in tourism reflects Solomon Islands as an undeveloped market where no clear profile has been created in visitor-generating countries.

Arrivals rose from 8000 in the year of independence to 10,000 in 1985, 12,000 in 1991 and 14,000 in 1995. Foreign exchange earnings generated by tourism in 1995 were estimated at just on $8.5 million (Central Bank of Solomon Islands 1996). Tourism plant on the ground saw little new development with two forty-year-old hotels in Honiara between them providing two thirds (180) of all rooms in the country until 1995 when four new hotels with a combined capacity of 140 beds were constructed in the city. Tourist numbers remained static between 1996 and 1999, when inter-tribal violence erupted and forced the evacuation of about 25,000 people from the main island of Guadalcanal back to their homeland provinces. Militants took over the capital city, and a hesitant peace was only brokered in the last months of 2000. Tensions and violence remain however, visitation has plummeted and resorts have remained closed ever since.

In the late 1980s, as national needs and population growth outstripped the capacity of resources to provide the income necessary to sustain economic growth, tourism began to gain a greater degree of political and social acceptability. For the first time, in December 1986, a government policy statement strongly supportive of tourism development was enunciated. The policy objectives set out in the Third National Development Plan were: to promote development of the tourism industry in an orderly and controlled manner to avoid social and cultural disruption and to minimize social and economic costs; to base the development of tourism on the inherent natural, cultural and historical attractions of the country and increase local participation in the industry; and to promote investment in tourism and related activities and decentralize such investment in tourist facilities to appropriate locations in the provinces (Solomon Islands Government 1986a:66).

The Third National Development Plan also gave high priority to environmental protection and stated that an objective of the government was to encourage and provide training to customary landowners to establish and manage protection zones such as national parks and wildlife sanctuaries to preserve species and habitats as well as provide scope for leisure and tourism activities.

Following the initial policy breakthrough in 1986, between 1987 and 1989 a national tourism strategy was developed, aimed at providing a structure for controlled tourism development. This was followed in 1989 with the first comprehensive foreign investment incentives package targeted specifically at tourism development; and in 1990 by the first Ten Year Tourism Development Plan 1990–2000. The policy (Solomon Islands Government 1989b) identified specific development strategies and principles to encourage both international and local investment. The subsequent Ten Year Plan was designed to "interpret and elaborate in operational terms the government's promulgated tourism policy" (Solomon Islands Ministry of Tourism and Aviation and Tourism Council of the South Pacific (1990:1).

While the government strategies and objectives enunciated in these documents provide an appropriate policy framework for indigenous tourism ventures, implementation is in some cases impeded by existing legislation and regulations. These may obstruct the very participation of local communities sought by government. They may prevent empowerment of village communities.

National Tourism Policy and Tourism Development Plan

Adopted by the Alebua government in November 1988 and refined by the subsequent Mamaloni government in 1989, the National Tourism Policy stated that:

- Development strategy number 1: Developments should include both international standard resorts and small-scale indigenous tourism businesses.
- Development strategy number 5: The National Government will support joint ventures [between foreign and local interests] in tourism development (Solomon Islands Government 1989b:1).

To assist Solomon Islanders wishing to venture into tourism, the policy stated that:

- Development strategy number 7: The National Government, through appropriate bodies and international agencies, will provide indigenous tourism small business entrepreneurs with counselling services relating to feasibility of proposals, potential sources of finance, marketing and training.
- Development Strategy number 8: Tourism attractions and strategies should be developed focussing on natural features, cultural/historical features, festivals and special events (Solomon Islands Government 1989b:2).

With reference to Strategy number 8, since "ownership" of cultural events is by definition vested in indigenous groups, the potential for local participation in tourism activities centered on such attractions is high. One example is the way in which the people of Laulasi Island, Langalanga Lagoon and Malaita have marketed the process of making traditional shell money as a tourism attraction.

In support of these strategies the national policy contained other elements sensitive to traditional Solomon Islands culture, the developing nature of the economy and the place of indigenous sociocultural and environmental factors in tourism. It contained a number of prescriptive clauses, including:

- Objective number 3: The development of tourism should be based on the inherent natural, cultural, and historical features of the country so as to achieve domestic cultural and environmental conservation and to facilitate international cross interaction.
- Objective number 8: Tourism marketing should highlight the country's unique cultural traditions and natural beauty (Solomon Islands Government 1989b:5).

The National Tourism Policy also had a section designed to facilitate the use of customary land for tourism purposes and as such to protect the rights of indigenous land owners. There were three pertinent guidelines:

- Land guideline number 1: The customary procedures for land acquisition as laid down in present legislation will be explained in a Development Information Brochure for prospective investors and land owners.
- Guideline number 2: The National Government, through the Ministry of Agriculture and Lands, will play a facilitating role between the potential investor and the Provincial Government, the Area Council and the land owners.
- Guideline number 3: To ensure an orderly and equitable system of compensation to landowners for tourist activities which infringe upon their traditional lands, reefs and fishing grounds, the Solomon Islands Tourist Authority will act to [*sic*] an intermediary role between landowners and operators to establish a collective system of payment based on a standard scale (Solomon Islands Government 1989b:7).

Another set of guidelines, on education and training, impinged upon indigenous participation in the tourism sector. These included:

- Education and Training Guideline number 1: The national government in conjunction with the Provincial Governments will institute a continuing public awareness program directed towards understanding the nature of the tourism industry, its advantages and disadvantages.

- Guideline number 2: Tourism studies will be introduced to Solomon Islands' schools, beginning at Standard Six.
- Guideline number 3: The National Government in conjunction with the Provincial Governments will undertake a full study of the manpower requirements needed to implement its tourism development plan and to specify the ongoing training needs to ensure that the maximum number of jobs in the tourism industry are filled by Solomon Islanders (Solomon Islands Government 1989b:10).

As these statements of intent were implemented so the government would expect a new generation of Islanders to grow up with an understanding of tourism. From that knowledge and training would come an enhanced capacity by those so inclined to take their part in the development of this industry. In sum, the National Tourism Policy contained diverse sets of strategies, principles and guidelines which combined to provide support and encouragement for a range of indigenous participation in the development of tourism in Solomon Islands. The tourism development plan was designed around the policy to provide a dynamic tool for implementing its objectives.

However, these two comprehensive documents are incapable of implementation in a number of their key elements. Externalities have led to Dunsire's (1978) implementation gap, because the policies and action plans exist in a legislative and regulatory environment which in effect negates much of their positive intent. It is useful to distinguish here between *non-implementation* and *unsuccessful implementation*. In the former case, a policy is not put into effect because those involved in its execution have not been able to overcome obstacles over which they had little or no control. Unsuccessful implementation on the other hand occurs when a policy is carried out in full but fails to have the desired result (Hogwood and Gunn 1986). Non-implementation is the current fate of much of Solomon Islands tourism development policy and lack of empowerment a major contributing factor. Ongoing social unrest and political instability since 1999 have exacerbated this situation.

Legislation and Regulations

While more than ten Solomon Islands Acts can impinge on tourism development and local participation, there are three important major areas which require elaboration: the Lands and Titles Act, the Town and Country Planning Act and the National Building Code.

The Lands and Titles Act (and Amendments)

This Act established three categories of land in Solomon Islands: customary land, alienated land, and leased land.

Customary land is clan/tribal land held since time immemorial in a form of group ownership based on ancestral settlement. Individuals or families may have usufructuary rights and these may be passed down the generations through a partriarchical or matriarchal lineage system (both systems are operative in different parts of the Solomon Islands).

Alienated land is land not governed by traditional customary land tenure and for which compensation has been paid to the original customary owners, the boundaries surveyed and the title registered with the Commissioner of Lands in accordance with the Act. The Government is the owner of significant alienated land, including land gazetted for towns, airfields and other government purposes. The holder of a title to alienated land is legally bound by the Lands and Titles Act and the regulations it incorporates. These regulations include the requirement that all construction on such land complies with the building code and standards, among other things. Development undertaken on alienated land must also comply with the Town and Country Planning Act, the Health Act, and, depending upon the type of development envisaged, other specific Acts.

Leased land is alienated land which may be made available to non-citizens for a maximum period of 75 years, after which time ownership reverts to the traditional owners. All former plantations which had been held under freehold title during the colonial period reverted to 75-year leases on independence in 1978. Solomon Island citizens may purchase alienated leased land and receive a "title in perpetuity" so that in such instances ownership does not revert to the original customary owners.

About 80 percent of all land in the Solomons is held under customary ownership. These owners have the freedom to register or not their land. Registration is often a lengthy process because frequently it provokes counter claims to the land. Those claims will be taken through a court process and the result is designed to be a definitive identification of the rightful owner(s). The court process has replaced the traditional mechanism of warfare and/or negotiations based on traditional systems of compensation for deciding land claims.

If customary owners choose not to register their land, they have relative freedom to "develop" the land as they wish. But they may run into problems.

If they need to raise funds for a tourism development, unregistered customary land will not be recognized by any lending institution in Solomon Islands as collateral since customary land cannot be bought and sold. If it is to be registered for commercial development, then the title must be vested in the Commissioner of Lands. The indigenous developer may find that to enter into a small-scale tourism venture, he must in a legal sense at least hand over control of his land to the Commissioner for Lands. The three guidelines of the national tourism policy on land are thus less than effective in assisting in the development process desired.

Fiji, Kiribati, Tuvalu, Vanuatu and Western Samoa, as former British colonies, all have echoes of the same legislation which vests trusteeship of customary-owned lands in the Commissioner of Lands (see Chapter 9 and the case study of Mana Island Resort, Fiji). It would seem that such paternalistic legislation was originally introduced to protect the villager against exploitation by land-hungry foreign settlers. It may indeed have fulfilled such a role in the early days of colonization, but it is perhaps surprising that the offending legislation was not amended upon independence. The failings of the system are recognized by the locals who ironically refer to problems of development on customary land as "the Solomon Islands disease." (Sir George Lepping, then Governor General of Solomon Islands, personal communication, 1991).

It must be acknowledged, however, that the whole issue of customary land tenure is one area where there was a concerted attempt over many years by the colonial power to devise a system which combined both traditional values and the contemporary development aspirations of its own settlers. Initially, the colonial power introduced its own freehold land system to pursue exploitation of the country by expatriate planters and businessmen. As part of its pacification policies, a court system was introduced to adjudicate conflicts between the local people, including land disputes. The present lands court system is cumbersome, but it is nevertheless a system which does take account, often comprehensively, of traditional values and customs at one level. The clause in the constitution, converting all alienated former freehold land in expatriate hands to leasehold for eventual return to the customary owners, is evidence of this approach.

Town and Country Planning Act

In Solomon Islands, the 1982 Town and Country Planning Act, is the legal instrument for the establishment of the Town and Country Planning Board which has responsibility for ensuring that development follows prescribed regulations. The Board polices the Act and determines that development occurs in appropriate locations or zones, especially on registered land. It shares with the Public Works Department responsibility for ensuring that any construction meets the national building code.

The national tourism policy acknowledges the importance of the Town and Country Planning Act by including three "development strategies" on zoning. However, these may inhibit a community from venturing into a tourism business. A community may find itself geographically outside areas designated for tourism development and thus unable to proceed because without zoning compliance it could be refused an operating licence. Therefore the policy has unwittingly reinforced a potential barrier to indigenous participation in tourism development.

The Public Works Act and the National Building Code

The National Building Code is based on a combination of New Zealand standards (for seismic stress since the Solomons lies in the earthquake belt of the Pacific) and north Australia for cyclones and tropical climatic conditions. This code was only introduced after independence in 1978, replacing a London code used by the British colonial government which contained only minor modifications for the Solomon Islands environment. The building code is complex and standards are high. Specialist training in architecture and engineering is necessary to interpret and implement it.

In the context of the building code, the tourism policy contains another impediment (not recognized at the time of formulation of the policy) to local participation in the tourism industry. In the section on Regulations and Controls it declares that:

> All tourism development will be subject to building regulations and all tourist operations will be required to operate under a tourist operating licence (Solomon Islands Government 1989b:12).

The Tourism Development Plan reinforces this policy and its chapter on "Model Facility Development" in which it sets out a range of models including for indigenously owned village resorts is predicated on strict observance of the relevant regulations (Solomon Islands Ministry of Tourism and Aviation and Tourism Council of the South Pacific 1990).

Compliance with the building regulations requires that formal plans be submitted, plans which under the legislation can only be drawn up by duly qualified and registered architects, engineers and draftsmen. To meet the code's standards for seismic stress, cyclone resistance and fire safety measures only non-traditional buildings, using imported components such as steel, bolts, plates and fasteners, installed by qualified engineers, plumbers and electricians can be constructed. Non-approved construction is ineligible for a habitation certificate and/or operating licences. Thus, the unforeseen but nevertheless practical effect of the policy guideline and the development plan's implementation proposals is to remove the skills and material resources of the indigenous community from the equation by insistence on unmodified application of the building code of a technologically advanced society. Therefore, indigenous villagers are disadvantaged once again despite the best intentions of the government.

The costs inherent in application of the building regulations also take even a small-scale tourism venture out of reach of most village communities in Solomon Islands. The Tourism Council of the South Pacific, for example, estimated in 1990 that a small village resort in the Solomons would cost a minimum of $100,000 (more later). However, a village-based resort in Western Samoa, consisting of six *fales* (traditional Samoan houses) modified to meet that country's building code, designed and constructed under the Council auspices in 1988/89, cost about $1 million (Tourism Council of the South Pacific 1990c), more than five times the estimated budget. These costs compare with the then average cost of a traditional *fale* built out of "bush" materials with a thatch roof, woven mat walls, and coconut rope binding (instead of bolts and nails) of about $8000 (Deputy Director, Western Samoa Visitors Bureau, personal correspondence, 1996).

The net result of the various Acts is to place outside approved or legal practice the establishment of a village guest house or resort constructed on customary land, built out of traditional materials available locally and utilizing traditional building skills. If the villagers register title to their customary land then control is taken out of their hands and vested in the Commissioner for Lands who by the Lands and Titles Act must comply with the constellation of Acts affecting any development proposed for that land. No matter how sympathetic he may be, no matter how closely the proposed development fits the policies enunciated in the National Tourism Plan, if any part of the venture fails to meet statutory and regulatory requirements, then the Commissioner cannot support an application for a tourism operator's licence; and without his support the application cannot succeed.

The Solomon Islands Tourism Development Plan 1991–2000 (Solomon Islands MTA and TCSP 1990) makes no mention of the problems confronting local communities wishing to set up a tourism venture. Indeed, the plan devotes

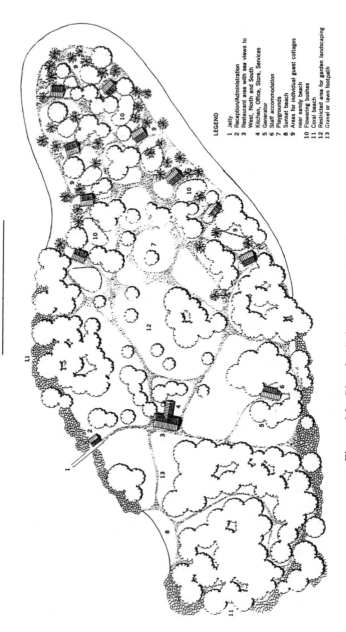

Figure 6.3: Plan for Solomon Islands Village Resort
Source: TCSP, 10-year Tourism Development Plan, 1990

considerable attention to developing and presenting a model for an "Indigenous Resort Project, specifically designed to assist indigenous entrepreneurs or landowning groups and communities who wish to develop and operate their own resort establishments" (Solomon Islands MTA and TCSP 1990:76). For the purpose of their model development they designed a modest ten-bungalow resort utilizing some local materials such as timber, sago palm and pandanus. This follows the "Bali model" of incorporating the style of traditional architecture but not the construction methods (see Figure 6.3).

This proposal, however, simply compounds the situation by insisting upon maintenance of what it terms *"minimum standards which are significantly higher than those attained* by the few small scale [indigenous] resort developments already in existence" (Solomon Islands MTA and TCSP 1990:76; italic added) and by failing to draw attention to the legislative impediments to local community initiatives. Total cost, as mentioned previously, is estimated at $100,000 (probably highly conservative if the Western Samoan experience is any guide). It is an amount well beyond the reach of virtually every village community in Solomon Islands and one which banks could not meet without some form of government guarantee or acceptance of responsibility for a loan, since customary land cannot be utilized for security.

In short the whole weight of the S.I. Government's definitive plan for tourism development actively disempowers its prospective clients and militates against the very principles and strategies identified in its own National Tourism Policy for greater indigenous participation in the industry.

Local Tourism Initiatives

Despite the negative effects of the formal, legislative structure there have been several efforts by local communities to establish small village-based guest houses. This is consistent with much of the development literature. For instance, Noronha (1979) posits that after an initial stage of "discovery" of a destination by a few tourists, local entrepreneurs in response will provide facilities to accommodate the growing numbers of visitors. As tourism expands, "institutionalization" or mass tourism follows, when the further development of tourism facilities tends to come under the control of agencies (public as well as private) located outside the local community and often outside the country.

One such example of Noronha's second stage may be found in North Malaita, initiated by villagers on an artificial island in the Lau Lagoon (Kuve 1989). In terms of government legislation it is illegal; and in terms of the Tourism Development Plan it should not have been established because it is located outside a designated zone for tourism development and is adjudged "inaccessible". On arrival in Honiara it is necessary to catch either a light aircraft or a small inter-island passenger/cargo boat for the 10-hour, 130-km journey to Auki, the administrative center for Malaita. Then travel will be by unsealed road (which has no bus service so one is entirely dependent upon itinerant traffic) fording innumerable streams without bridges for four to five hours. Finally travel will be by canoe for about one hour. No doubt Plog's alocentrics would enjoy the experience of journeying to Lau despite the development plan ruling it "off limits".

In 1988, the villagers decided to open their village to tourists. They set aside two huts for this purpose. The community placed limits on the numbers they felt they could handle: no more than six at a time and for only three weeks out of every month. The tariff was $50 per person per week. Activities were to be based around participation in normal day-to-day village activities, such as fishing; gardening on the mainland in the slash-and-burn plots on the hillsides; making thatch for roofs and bamboo panels for walls; canoe making; and so forth. Their marketing ignored the Solomon Islands Tourist Authority or any other local agency. Instead they wrote direct to a French Canadian anthropologist in Montreal who had spent some years with them in the 1970s, asking him to send them some tourists. He obliged and in 1988 four Canadians spent three weeks on the island in the village. They were followed at various intervals by a small number of "backpacker" tourists so that by the end of 1990 the village had grossed more than $4000, a large sum by village standards.

The tourism authority finally heard about the venture when several of the backpackers returned to Honiara from the Lau Lagoon to report what a wonderful experience they had enjoyed (Kuve 1989). When the authority looked into the venture, it discovered that the community had neither sought nor obtained approvals from anyone and was thus not licensed. It further discovered that, when a government minister had visited the province in 1989, he had officially opened this illegal operation. The community indicated in no uncertain terms that it was not about to apply for permits or licenses and was certainly not going to pay the Tourism Authority compulsory bed tax nor any other government charges.

On a field trip to Solomon Islands in 1992, it was a low-key operation entirely dependent upon word of mouth for tourists, and firmly under the control of the local community — because of its "illegality". By 1996 however it was barely operational. The original initiators had lost interest when it became necessary to rethatch the roof and community input to rebuild the "guest house" was not forthcoming.

Joint Ventures

Since the legislative and regulatory requirements demand a substantial injection of funds for any tourism project involving capital works, joint ventures would seem to offer a compromise solution. Indeed the Solomon Islands Government has itself promoted this concept, with local equity being derived from ownership of the land and the foreign investor obtaining his shareholding by providing the capital input and technical expertise required for a given project.

This is not a solution, however, if the joint venture project is basically a village product, that is, a guest house or several houses constructed traditionally to provide the tourist with an authentic village experience. As noted earlier, traditional dwellings do not comply with the building code, with fire regulations, nor with sanitation regulations. Traditional kitchen facilities, a thatched outhouse with a pit and stones, do not meet the requirements of the health regulations covering public preparation of food. Traditional toileting does not comply with the sanitation regulations. Storage of fuels and toxic substances, such as kerosene for refrigerators, diesel for outboard motors and bottled gas for lamps, would not meet with approval from the Safety Inspectorate if stored in a traditionally constructed building. The project would not be eligible for a Solomon Islands bank loan since customary land cannot be accepted as collateral. Nor would the buildings, since insurance would be unavailable because they would not comply with the set standards. Public risk insurance for the foreign investor would not be available because of the project's inherent "illegality".

Since foreign investors must agree to comply with all laws as an integral component of the process of approval by the Solomon Islands Foreign Investment Board, including those relating to construction and health standards, they would be participating in an unlawful project if they were to become a joint venture partner in traditional structures; and the property would be unable to obtain an operating license. The only way in which a joint venture could obtain an operating license would be to satisfy all necessary legislative and regulatory requirements. However, when minimum standards for buildings for commercial tourism purposes were met, the capacity of the indigenous investor(s) to retain a measure of control over a project would be severely retarded. An injection of capital, with lending institutions and insurance companies insisting on certain requirements, would "push" control into the hands of the foreign joint partner.

Additionally, the project would almost certainly require a form of management not available in a village community. Technical expertise to maintain the buildings and a power plant (such as a diesel generator, electrical and mechanical equipment, and the water and sewage systems) would also be required. The greater the degree of sophistication or "internationalization" of a village-based resort, the less capacity there would be for participation by traditional landowners, and the less the product would be able to satisfy market demand for an authentic village experience. Increasingly, alternative tourism which provides an experiential and educational holiday based on authentic traditional lifestyles is in global terms capturing an ever growing market. But the situation in Solomon Islands militates against such a product being legally developed.

The Tainiu Guest House provides an example of the pitfalls of the joint venture approach. This is a traditional Polynesian long-house built out over the waters of Lake Te Nggano near the village of Niupani in Rennell Island in 1989 (Rennell is a Polynesian "out-lyer" island: Figure 6.4). The Government, through the Ministry of Tourism, is developing a submission for Lake Te Nggano to be inscribed on the list of World Heritage Sites because of its unique biophysical features. Rennell Island has been identified by the Ministry as a priority region for nature-based indigenously owned and operated tourism development (Liligeto 1990).

With support from the Ministry of Tourism, a landowner obtained a grant of some $12,000 from the Provincial Development Fund in 1989. This source provided finance for community-based projects which had merit but could not meet the requirements, usually the need for collateral, of formal lending institutions. The long-house was constructed using a combination of undressed timbers, milled timber and glass louvre windows, with 18 beds in an open-plan style. There was no architectural or engineering input, the end result being a "pioneer" adaptation of traditional construction with some modern materials. The landowner was advised by the Development Officer of the Ministry that European-style toilets, showers and a kitchen were essential if he was to develop a sustainable product able to attract foreign tourists. The initial funding was insufficient for these additions, however, and there were no further funds available from the Provincial Development Fund, another $10,000 being necessary.

Having exhausted all possible avenues of local financing without success, the owner sought direct funding assistance from the Australian, New Zealand and British High Commissions in Honiara. However, all were bound by their own regulatory requirements and the venture fell outside "normal" guidelines for discretionary aid. Finally, on the advice of the Ministry, the owner sought a foreign partner for a joint venture, offering 30 percent equity in the project. A willing investor was located early in 1990. He was prepared to finance the upgrading of kitchen, toilet and shower facilities as well as to provide assistance for marketing and overseas promotions.

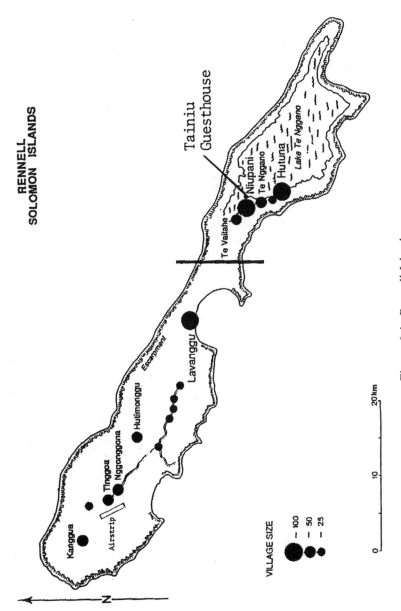

Figure 6.4: Rennell Island
Source: S.I. Ministry of Tourism

As details of the venture were pursued, however, the "illegality" of proceeding became obvious and prevented the foreign investor from taking up
equity. The long-house could not, for example, gain a "Certificate of Habitation" from the Public Works Department because it did not comply with the
building standards. Without that certificate, the building could not be insured.
It failed to meet the health and sanitation standards. Therefore, it could not be
registered as a commercial operation. On the one hand, the foreign investor was
faced with a government ministry threatening to cancel his approval for participation if he failed to comply with the legislative and regulatory requirements.
On the other hand he had the Ministry of Tourism impelling him towards participation. He found himself in a "catch 22" situation. The legislative requirements
again acted as disempowering agencies.

Thus, despite the active support of the Ministry of Tourism which promoted
the development (Tainiu Guest House) as a model for indigenous development,
and despite the fact that it "opened for business" in 1990 and hosted some 90
guests in its first six months (without the suggested European facilities) its
capacity to expand and operate as a legal indigenously owned tourism venture
is limited by restrictive legislative and regulatory requirements. The administrative and political systems of government failed to empower the community.
Yet as a tourism product providing an ethnic and nature-oriented experience, it
has outstanding qualities. It continues to operate with modest success outside
the formal economy and the formal legal system, but its long-term sustainability remains in doubt.

Breaking the "Circular Chain of Determination"

If the major factor leading to disempowerment and an implementation gap in
respect of policy for indigenous participation in tourism development policy is
to be found in government legislation and regulations, then by their current
ownership of the legislation, Solomon Islands planners cannot escape the
responsibility of deciding the future direction of their development, just as they
cannot avoid the systems and structures established by the colonialist. Colonial
residues are not unique and it is up to the independent state as to how cleverly
it uses the colonial heritage in the post-independence era.

This raises the issue of the degree to which a newly independent micro-state
is able to confront problems arising from that heritage and to identify ways
to change them which will "fit" indigenous values and empower indigenous
sociocultural systems. Bateson (1985) noted that it is very difficult for real
change or innovation to be expected to come from the indigenous people in

cross-cultural situations. This he averred was because, not being the architects of the non-traditional structures under which they live and work, they lack that in-depth understanding of the processes involved and the knowledge to begin demolishing before rebuilding. They may not possess the capacity to cross the sociocultural and technological barriers to break into Bateson's "circular chain of determination" by which the structures have been constructed.

As Francis Bugotu, a former Head of the Department of Solomon Islands' first Prime Minister, wrote:

> When and where do we start marrying village [tradition] and town life [modernity] if we think this is necessary for the survival of some of the things and attitudes we value? If our idea of "the civilized way of life" conforms to that set from outside by other cultures, the patterns that emerge will be patterns of those cultures. Is it any wonder that when we become awake to problems we immediately classify them into patterns as they have been seen and known elsewhere in the world (Harre and Knapman 1977:Prologue).

All of the micro-states of the South Pacific have relatively limited human resources. There is a lack of qualified nationals in many areas of western expertise with the training to develop an understanding of the impacts and implications of much of their colonial legislative legacy. In Solomon Islands, for example, there are fewer than five indigenous lawyers and only one of them has specialized in parliamentary drafting. There are only three qualified civil engineers. Less than 6 percent of the school-age population has access to the 12 secondary schools which make up the total complement in the country.

Furthermore, the few professionally trained locals have, without exception, received their tertiary education in western institutions. In many instances, they are the least likely of the indigenous people to challenge the technical foundations of their professions since the imported structures and models inculcated during their time at university and college provide the justification for their status as professionals, for their differentiation from the mass of their fellows as "educated" and therefore to underpin their status as "bigmen" in the Melanesian social system. Their western education is designed to support increased technological input, not less.

Saglio (1979) records how, during an attempt to establish village-based tourism in Senegal using mud houses and local skills, he was constantly criticized by Senegalese officials. Village houses were in their eyes "primitive".

They did not meet the standards of the building code. Accustomed to large-scale development projects they were:

> often suspicious or even hostile to our project. They criticized the small amount of the investment (about $10,000 per village), feared upheavals and problems in the villages, and doubted the desire of tourists to live in clay houses. There was also a deep-seated reluctance to show visitors some of the traditional ways of life, which many of the elite tend to hold in contempt. I was frequently reproached for not including glass windows, numbered doors, electricity and even air conditioning. Many highly placed individuals had to be convinced of the importance of preserving the integrity and quality of the traditional architecture. Even the villagers themselves would have preferred to build in cement blocks with sheet metal roofs because "it looks better and cleaner for tourists" (Saglio 1979:326–327).

An incident illustrating the complexities of this issue occurred in 1983 with the construction of 120 low-cost houses in Naha Valley, Honiara, funded under the Australian aid program. When the then Prime Minister, Solomon Mamaloni, educated in a missionary school in Solomon Islands run by New Zealanders, with subsequent higher education in New Zealand and the United Kingdom, inspected the project, he was incensed by what he perceived to be sub-standard dwellings. He went on national radio to lambast the Australian government and to demand the expulsion of the Australian construction firm. Australia, he declared might well build such "hovels" for its Aborigines, but independent Solomon Islands would not put up with "rubbish like that".

This outburst ignored the fact that it was his Government's own Public Works Department which had introduced a "conditional zone" for low-cost housing under which the normal building standards had been waived. Further, the government tender board which had approved the design and subsequent construction was composed of Public Works Department engineers and Solomon Islands nationals under the chairmanship of a Solomon Islander. The Australian construction company was simply the tool selected for implementing decisions made by the Solomon Islands Government and its agencies.

"Pioneer Space Empowerment"

If the policy of greater indigenous participation in tourism development is to be achieved, the creation of a new spatial system which will serve such interests first, combined with mechanisms for empowering local communities, is needed. In this context, a balanced equilibrium model which would permit planning for pervasive changes within a culture and the encouragement of values which enable adaptation to the changes that are inevitable, is proposed. Therefore, it is suggested that "pioneer space empowerment" needs to be created. This is an environment in which local people would be empowered and local (traditional) models could be accepted by the various formalized systems and brought at least partially "inside the system" (a form of cooptation).

The way this process is attempted at present often remains firmly under the control of "the experts", whose knowledge is privileged over the life experience of community members. But as noted in Chapter 2, ". . . as long as the processes [of development and change] are controlled by others who have access to the resources, then the process is actually disempowering" (Onyx and Benton 1995:51). Actually, several writers (including Craig and Mayo 1995) have emphasized the necessity for positive support from the public sector, working in partnership with communities, to engage the state and political processes at different levels if community participation and empowerment are to contribute to sustainable development.

"Pioneer" is used in the *Oxford Dictionary* sense of "initiator of enterprise, original settler" and "to act as a pioneer, to originate (course of action followed later by others)" (Turner 1961:828). This concept was first coined by the author in 1984 when overseeing Australia's development assistance program to Solomon Islands, and subsequently explored further by Kuve (1989) when he examined small-scale tourism ventures in Solomon Islands in a WTO-sponsored research project in 1989.

The central idea is to create conceptual space where a more "natural" evolution could take place, unrestricted to a degree by the existing legislative and other constraints. Empowerment would thus be extended to local communities despite the restrictions imposed by existing legislation and regulations. It borrows a little from the concept of "conditional zoning" in that it would "legalize" traditional buildings of otherwise unacceptable standards for commercial habitation and use. Empowerment would permit the transformation of traditional norms into legal norms: the Lau Lagoon initiative and the Tainiu Guest House could become "institutionalized norms".

It could also be utilized to deal with land disputes under a modified system of conflict resolution with greater community consultations and less recourse to the courts. Papua New Guinea has experimented with a "lease–lease back" scheme whereby the government assists in the registration of clan land, leases it from the customary landowners, and then leases it back to them for prescribed development. State tenure thus permits access to financing from commercial banks, a direct form of empowerment. A second scheme called "direct dealing" allows customary landowners to lease their land to other Papua New Guinea nationals in accordance with custom. The vital practical advantage of this scheme is that it can be accomplished without any registration (Asian Development Bank 1990). However, until codification of all land areas in Solomon Islands is accomplished, land issues will remain a problem which the concept of "pioneer space empowerment" could mitigate but not remove.

The concept also borrows a little from Woolard's (1977) "ecological approach" in which the then Solomon Islands Housing Authority architect argued for modified zoning to allow greater incorporation of traditional buildings in the urban situation. Noting that development usually meant "the imposition of alien standards", Woolard commented that low-cost housing too often used "design innovations and construction techniques to produce a cheap miniature version of an English house" (Woolard 1977:116) and ignored the success of the indigenous people in creating their own habitats by utilizing their own resources to the greatest potential, without architects and engineers. These structures were "highly successful" in dealing with the prevailing environment, climate, social organization and lifestyle (Woolard 1977:116). Since physical development was concerned primarily with environmental rather than human modifications, the ecological approach to planning was one which related humankind to the total environment.

Woolard advocated adapting the Solomon Islands standards and modifying them "only enough so as to produce satisfactory overall urban and rural environmental standards", but in a less codified way than that advocated by the Tourism Council of the South Pacific for its model indigenous resort (Woolard 1977:117). The term "empowerment" is absent from Woolard's paper but in effect this is what he was advocating.

Kuve (1989) suggested a three-stage "Pioneer Model" to facilitate indigenous participation in tourism ventures: an initial planning stage by the local community, with some input from the planning division of the Solomon Islands Tourist Authority after key decisions such as site selection had been made; a construction stage, with materials and construction methods utilizing traditional resources wherever possible; and an operations stage in which management would be entirely in local hands as the only way to ensure authenticity of experience.

Kuve saw his model as essential to ensure greater indigenous participation. Without it he considered that foreign investors could dominate the industry. In Fiji and the Cook Islands, for example, large capital-intensive resorts and hotels have resulted in high levels of foreign ownership, high levels of leakage, low levels of indigenous employment in skilled positions, a high degree of foreign influence on government and other institutions, and undesirable sociocultural and economic impacts (Britton 1987a). Kuve, however, does not confront the existing legislative and regulatory obstacles which impede indigenous participation. As demonstrated by the two examples outlined, Lau Lagoon and Lake Te Nggano, there is a need to precede his model and the Tourism Plan's $100,000 plan with the creation of a "pioneer space empowerment" environment which would allow Kuve's model to be applied.

The concept of "pioneer space empowerment" suggests that appropriate development would be small-scale, village-based tourism utilizing a limited range of intermediate technology. Such tourism by its nature would be "soft", culturally and environmentally oriented, with the emphasis on a traditional experience for the visitor. It would allow the development of a significant segment of the country's tourism industry by and under the control of Solomon Islanders.

Small numbers of tourists would allow village life to continue with minimum disruption from their presence. If they were accommodated in a traditional house either on the outskirts of the village or a little distance away the invasion of the private space of the villagers would be minimized. This is the case with Buna village, Oro Province, Papua New Guinea, which has four guest houses located one kilometer beyond the village (Iowa 1989) as well as the guest houses of Tufi (Ranck 1987). Tourist needs could be met from local resources in terms of food and labor. They could be absorbed into the daily routine of village activities without the necessity of the village community being diverted from everyday tasks, as with the example in Lau. There would be a possibility of Doxey's (1975) unidirectional measure of irritation levels not moving out of stage one where the visitor was perceived by the host as a welcomed guest. Farrell's (1977) "psychic exploitation", where the host community becomes saturated with tourists and feels manipulated and intruded upon, would also be avoided. Adverse tourist ratios could be controlled.

Intermediate technology might be designed to meet minimum requirements for sanitation. This can include the provision of passive sewage systems such as vented dry pit systems or composting toilet systems; the storage of food in a kerosene refrigerator; and the installation of solar power for hot water and also perhaps for lights. Basic food preparation practices such as the boiling of all water might be introduced. With such intermediate technology, the need for large capital inputs would be obviated and the skills needed to maintain equipment could for the most part be met by basic technical training of village residents. The White Plains Resort on the island of Tanna in Vanuatu, owned and operated by a local "bigman", follows this pattern (Bani 1989). Further, with the combined characteristics of smallness and limited technology, management of the venture would not require imported non-village skills; and the authenticity of the experience would be enhanced. Kuve (1989) emphasized the need for a venture to remain in control of and under management by local villagers if benefits were to be maximized for the host community.

Because the application of "pioneer space" short-circuits the expensive application of the building code in full, the opportunity might exist for some to take improper advantage of the proposed approach. An insistence on a community-based project would minimize such attempts since the Melanesian society of Solomon Islands' villages operates on the basis of consensus. Thus, many people (rather than one or two) would be involved in the decision-making process. Competing land claims by individuals and/or clans could be handled at this level. An assurance of wide community support for a venture would provide a measure of longer-term confidence that the project would be sustained. But since a village community lacks the resources to market its product, it would be appropriate for a national body to assist in marketing all approved projects. The Seychelles Government accepted a decade ago the need to undertake marketing of guest houses and other small ventures on a national basis. The success of this approach suggests that it is a model applicable to the Solomons.

In Vanuatu, the Government established "Tour Vanuatu Ltd" for this purpose, granting it a monopoly on marketing ethnic tourism and on arranging all internal travel (more later in Chapter 8). Tour Vanuatu has experienced significant success in its operations (Bani 1989). Kuve (1989) identified this need in his research into small-scale indigenous tourism development in the Solomons; and in Papua New Guinea, Iowa (1989) developed a model for linking village guest houses into established hotel chains to gain access to their marketing and promotional endeavours and thus to a visibility they could not otherwise attain. To succeed, the creation of pioneer space empowerment would need to incorporate amendments to existing legislation and regulations which would permit an indigenous project to proceed despite non-compliance with the technical and other standards included in the body of the legislation. Without this action empowerment would be less than complete.

All of these suggest that a government statutory authority with powers to approve projects and offer or deny operating licenses under restricted, specified conditions would be essential. A report to the Solomon Islands Government on legislative impediments to indigenous participation in tourism development suggested that the instrumentality to oversee this innovation might be called the "Community Tourism Development Board" (Sofield 1991c:17). In the context of licensing an operation, the Board could be empowered to carry out compulsory inspection prior to granting its approval. Periodic inspections could be undertaken to ensure continued compliance with the conditions specified for a particular project and the ultimate sanction would be cancellation of a license. Such inspections would assist in providing guarantees of minimum standards of buildings (including that foundations were not threatened by termites or central posts not weakened after cyclones or earthquakes). Just as some destinations are seasonal so village guest houses might be off limits during the annual cyclone season from November to April. Traditional structures usually cannot withstand winds stronger than 140 kph (Intertect 1984).

Considering these broad and specific points, then "pioneer space empowerment" would need to fulfil the following objectives:

- To create an environment in which village-based resources, both human and physical, could be utilized for indigenously owned and operated tourism development. In particular, the need for western technical expertise, and costs, would be kept to a minimum.
- To support the capacity of the local community to obtain and retain control over the venture.
- To maintain a high degree of authenticity to enhance the sociocultural experience of the visitor — *vide* MacCannell's (1976) front stage/backstage spectrum.
- To protect the host community from adverse tourist ratios which could undermine village stability.
- To provide tourists with the protection afforded by existing legislation and regulations; their accommodation should not fall down around their ears nor their health be threatened by unsanitary conditions.
- To protect the investor and establish a system of loan repayments appropriate to the situation where some capital is required. The small loans scheme initiated by the Solomon Islands Development Bank foundered in part on its inability to collect repayments.
- To introduce a system of checks and balances to prevent unscrupulous people from taking advantage of the non-application of normal legislative and regulatory requirements.

Conclusion

As already noted in Chapter 3, empowerment as a theoretical concept has been applied to explore the marginalization of indigenous communities following colonization. While most of the literature focuses on law and order issues, along the lines of the argument that colonization has caused the destruction of traditional social structures and thus the essential need is to restore indigenous autonomy as a necessary foundation and a vital ingredient of future justice strategies, many of the same arguments could equally be applied to the issue of development for such communities. In this context, the interconnectedness with dependency theory, center–periphery constructs, colonialism and also modernization is obvious. As noted in Chapter 3, development paths, patterns, and forms may be dictated by dominant outside authorities, often in terms of models imported from overseas with no regard for "fit" with the local community structures.

In addition to cultural "fit" genuine and enduring (sustainable) empowerment of communities requires that it be based on a constitutionally recognized right and sanctioned within an environment supported by the state. In traditional societies, before the advent of a state, empowerment could be achieved through "legitimate domination" which was endorsed by the social mores of the society in the absence of a formal legal foundation. The examination of the Solomon Islands situation in this chapter emphasizes the need for environmental reform to ensure that a community has the capacity to act upon its decisions.

The lack of empowerment and the implementation gap between Solomon Islands Government tourism policy and actual participation by its people in village-based tourism development results in large part from the colonial legacy which has imposed significant constraints. Policies which are biased toward the modern, formal sector need to be addressed. To overcome the obstacles, there is a need to create "pioneer space empowerment" which would give primacy to traditional structures and skills and allow them to be utilized for tourism in Solomon Islands in the 21st century. This would encourage the development of *Tings haemi fittim Solomon Aelans tumas*, pijin for "uniquely Solomon Islands ways of [doing] things".

It is suggested that this empowerment could be accomplished by proceeding with a double-pronged strategy of amending existing legislation to deregulate building and other standards in designated areas and by creating a national authority charged with defining specific conditions to oversee specific projects. Such a new spatial system would not obviate land disputes, arguably the single largest deterrent to many forms of development. But, once ownership of land was resolved, pioneer space empowerment would then allow legitimate village-based tourism development to proceed. This would be in marked contrast to the present situation where the unavoidable costs associated with existing laws and regulations put construction of even a small resort out of reach. It would empower the indigenous human and physical resources of a community with the end product under its control, managed and operated by its members to maximize the economic return to the community. However, if an appropriate path for village-based tourism cannot be found, then Solomon Islands faces the prospect of foreign domination, local elite control and/or government institutionalization of the tourism sector, as has occurred in many other small developing nations. The situation emphasizes the necessity of the state being involved in the transfer of power to local communities and conforms to the hypotheses enunciated in this treatise.

Chapter 7

Empowerment and Disempowerment at the Village Level: Anuha Island Resort, Soloman Islands*

In situations of pioneer tourism development (Miossec 1976), the foreign investor in a Third World country and the host community will both be entering uncharted waters. The reefs upon which the venture could founder are many. There is the reef of cross-cultural differences where lack of understanding, unwillingness to learn and unintended or deliberate breaking of traditional patterns of behavior could wreck the enterprise. There is the reef of inadequate government structures where insufficient guidelines and support are available to one or both parties. There is the reef of an imperfect legal structure operating in a dual system which may be unable to take full account of and resolve differences between contemporary commerce and traditional mores.

Politics may also constitute a dangerous reef: either group may be manipulated for ulterior, political motives or themselves seek to use the local political environment for other agendas. There is the reef of accelerated modernization which the tourism development introduces, and to which a traditional community may have great difficulty adapting. There is the reef of environmental impacts of a kind not experienced before. And there are those reefs outlined in the previous chapter where a colonial legacy and externally imposed standards from outside may prevent the vessel from making headway.

Because of the generally asymmetrical nature of the interaction between a foreign investor and a traditionally oriented community, the power imbalance between the two parties will tend to make navigation of the waters a complicated task. Both parties must ride in the same canoe and their different world-views (cf Chapter 4) will at times impel them to favor different courses. If they attempt to paddle in opposite directions, or paddle without coordinating their efforts, if an acceptable balance of benefits between the two cannot be

---

* This chapter is an adapted version of an earlier publication in *Tourism and Indigneous People*, Ch. 8, pp. 176–202.

achieved, and if conflict cannot be minimized, then the resultant tensions are likely to make the voyage short.

The case study which is examined here began with prospects for a long and fruitful journey as an Australian investor reached agreement for the 75-year lease of Anuha Island, Solomon Islands from its customary landowners for the construction of a four-star resort. Within five years, however, the canoe had run aground and it has now sunk without a trace. This chapter seeks to trace the processes of failure; identify and analyze the impacts of the resort development upon the host community, especially the nature of the relationship between the islanders and successive owners of the resort which eventually led to its closure; and analyze the nature of the "touristic transactions" in the context of empowerment/disempowerment and social exchange theory.

The author was Australian High Commissioner to Solomon Islands from 1982 to 1985 and was directly active in a minor way during the period of negotiations which resulted in agreement to establish the Anuha Island Resort. Subsequently, after retiring from the Australian Foreign Service, he "lent an ear" to all major players and stakeholders from prime ministers to villagers as the dispute intensified and became more complex. His former diplomatic status allowed him levels of access which would have been difficult in other circumstances. The information presented in this case study is grounded in participant observation over a 10-year period.

Anuha is a small uninhabited island of about 70 hectares lying just one kilometer off the north coast of Nggela (Florida Island) in Central Province, about 60 km by sea from Honiara (Figure 7.1). With a patchwork of virgin tropical rain forest and grassy knolls, 8 km of white sandy beaches, an encircling lagoon with two small palm-crowned islets on the fringing coral reef, and a small freshwater lake thrown in for good measure, it is the tropical island of tourists' dreams.

The island is owned under customary tenure by the 60 or so inhabitants of the small village of Rera, about 6 km away on the nearby main island of Nggela. There are four main clans on Nggela, Kakau (crab), Gaubata (cockatoo), Hogokiki (red parrot) and Hogokama (eagle), and they are closely related to people from the Bugotu district of Isabel, and from the north-central coast of Guadalcanal who share their clan system. Rera's acknowledged "bigman" in negotiations with outsiders was a retired Anglican priest, Father Robert Pule of the Kakau clan.

As outlined in Chapter 6, Melanesian society has a flat hierarchy of "bigmen" whose authority in pre-colonial times tended to be limited to specific areas of expertise in specific circumstances. However, "bigman" authority has often become broader since the introduction of central systems of governance because prominent individuals were mistaken as "chiefs" by the colonial power which

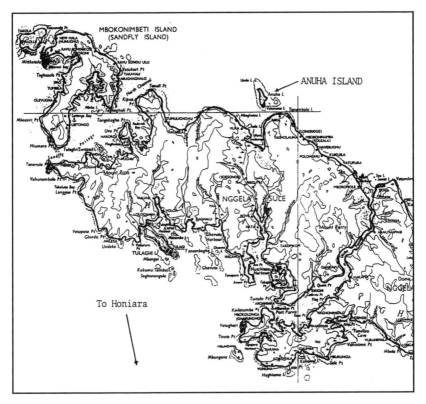

Figure 7.1: Location of Anuha Island, Solomon Islands

added legal elements to legitimate (traditional) forms of power and authority. Melanesian society, despite the introduction of western forms of governance and other institutions, at the village level is not inclined to draw distinctions among economics, politics, and religion. There is no oppositional distance constructed between society as governed by relative human laws on the one hand, and the cosmos as an intrinsic universal order represented by the figures of God or other deities, on the other hand (Josephides 1995). Rather society and cosmos are united in a hierarchical continuum, a certain wholeness since both society and the cosmos are of the same material — that is the ancestors and gods (de Coppet and Iteanu 1995). Thus, in traditional Melanesian society qualities of leadership were not separated into a secular/sacred dichotomy, although community members clearly distinguish between the different domains according to specific situations (Maenu'u 1984). Many communities in contemporary Solomon

Islands continue to uphold this integrated reality even when Christianity may have intruded on ancestor worship. Pule's status as a "bigman" illustrates this phenomenon.

Born in Koda village in about 1923 to a "bigman", Victor Vikino, reputedly the best canoe builder in Nggela, Robert Pule was educated in Anglican missionary schools, became headmaster of a primary school in 1946, and in 1953 studied at St John's Theological College in Auckland, New Zealand. He was ordained as an Anglican priest in 1954. He resigned from the Church in 1978 to devote his time to the development of his village in Nggela. But he remained active in church affairs, and in 1980 was elected to the Central Province General Assembly, his political role sitting easily with his clerical background. Indeed, analysis of politics in Solomon Islands suggest that after *wantok* affiliation, religious affiliation will be the main determinant for obtaining voter support and membership of the national and provincial legislatures (Alasia 1989; Allen 1984; Gegeo and Watson-Gegeo 1996; Larmour and Qalo 1985; Sofield 1993). The combination of church leader, Assembly member and educated man (specifically "man" not "person" in this male-dominated society) enhanced Pule's "bigman" status. During this time he developed a high public profile with his capacity to articulate village needs in the early years of independence and became something of a "character". In Melanesian terms this is identified as *mamana* or charisma, a common feature of many "bigmen" in Solomon Islands (Gegeo and Watson-Gegeo 1996). In Robert Pule's own words, his task was to assist his people integrate Christianity, development, and modernization with *kastom* (personal communications).

Pule's leadership was further substantiated when he coordinated the construction for the first time in many years of a *binabina* (a traditional Nggela war canoe) in 1982/83, and sailed it across to Honiara as "captain" of the canoe builders and crew (Pule 1983). The project, supported by the University of the South Pacific, incorporated a wide range of traditional activities during its construction (invocation of ancestors, a ritual feast, dances and songs), a Christian blessing on its launch, and more traditional songs and chants on its departure for the overnight voyage from north Nggela to Honiara. On its arrival in the capital it was welcomed by the Governor-General who shouted the traditional *Gau Hogugu!* ("Come ashore brothers — I am calling you!") and presented Father Pule and the crew with red shell money and other gifts while conch shells blared and warriors danced (Pule 1983). This activity, linking Pule to his father and a long ancestral line of Nggela canoe builders, reinforced the legitimate (traditional) elements of his "bigman" status. (The canoe has been on display in the National Museum's "Canoe House" ever since).

In Weberian terms, Pule's leadership thus had certain aspects of charisma, certain aspects of legitimate power since it rested on traditional grounds, and certain aspects of legal power and authority derived from both the church and the legislative assembly. The latter might be fleeting (in the case of Pule he served only one term), but the church remained as an institutional legal base for the continued exercise of power and authority in combination with the other two aspects. It may also be adduced that the Christian Church in a sense provided a modern alternative to the traditional normative of power residing in those with knowledge of secret ceremonies and sacred ritual, the source of authority for the most powerful "bigmen" in traditional society (Tonkinson 1982). The combination of these attributes gave Pule almost unchallenged leadership in his own community and extended his influence into the wider Nggela community. He was described as *"hevi"* (or "heavy", a solid leader).

In moving from priest to politician to established "bigman", Pule was following a path already worn by the likes of Father Momis in Papua New Guinea (Anglican, minister in the National Parliament), Father Walter Lini (Anglican, Prime Minister of Vanuatu at independence and for almost a decade thereafter), Sir Peter Kenilorea (Anglican priest, Prime Minister of Solomon Islands at independence and for several subsequent terms), Brother Ben Kinika (Catholic priest, Deputy Prime Minister of Solomon Islands at independence), and more than a dozen other Solomon Islanders who have been priests and members of Parliament. It is against this background of power and authority exercised at the local level that the discussion turns to the saga of Anuha Island Resort.

Resort Development

An Australian company decided to lease Anuha Island from its customary owners to build a small resort of about 20 bungalows. Negotiations began early in 1981 and a 75-year lease was signed with Father Pule and other landowners in April 1983. Most of the activity during this two-year period was taken up with counter-claims of ownership of the island by other Solomon Islands groups, which required adjudication by the Lands and Titles Court. The situation was not easy to resolve. Over the previous 400 years there had been a reasonably high level of integration between the people of the neighboring islands of Isobel, Buena Vista and Nggela. Father Pule had himself acknowledged this in a book about the building of the Nggela war canoe (Pule 1983). Although the current ownership of Anuha by the Nggela people of Rera village was not in dispute, antecedent claims as to original ownership were made.

One claim by a group of landowners from Isobel Island went all the way to the High Court on appeal. This group lodged a claim not as island owners but as the alleged owners of the fringing reef and its resources. Their claim was based on the undisputed fact that about 150 years earlier they had been granted refuge on Anuha Island by the people of Nggela, as they sought escape from the marauding head hunters of Marovo to the West. They had been given rights to live on the island, and use its land and its resources (but not own it) in accordance with Melanesian *kastom*. They claimed their ancestors had paid compensation for the surrounding reefs and marine resources.

For a period this case threatened access to the island, the right of the developers to moor their boats or even to swim in the lagoon, to snorkel over the coral, and their right to catch fish, lobsters, etc., until the Supreme Court rejected the claim in favor of Father Pule's village. Throughout the protracted negotiating period, relations between the Australian investors and Father Pule's village were characterized by cordiality.

The lease was registered with the Lands Department on 29 April 1983. Under the terms of the lease, yearly payments (negotiated in Australian dollars, which had been the Solomon Islands currency prior to independence) on a gradually increasing scale were agreed, so that up to three generations of customary owners would benefit monetarily over the 75-year period. A lump sum payment of $7500 was made on signing the lease and a $22,500 interest-free loan with no set repayment schedule (other than "within the 75-year period of the lease") was advanced to Father Pule and his villagers. Annual lease payments began from a low level during the first three years when site preparation and construction were to be undertaken — $1125 for the first year, $1500 for the second year, and $2250 for the third to fifth years; rising to $3750 for the sixth to fifteenth years; $5250 for the sixteenth to thirtieth years; $15,000 for the thirty-first to fiftieth years; and $45,000 for the final twenty-five years. Lease payments were to total $1.55 million. A supplementary agreement to construct an airstrip on an old coconut plantation on Anuha was negotiated in 1983, with the customary landowners being paid compensation for the coconut trees at standard rates set by the Government.

As the first resort of any size in Solomon Islands (there were only three other, much smaller ones, Uepi Island in New Georgia, Ngarando (Pigeon) Island in Santa Cruz and Tambea Beach, West Guadalcanal), the lease agreement was seen as a test case for foreign investment and a model for future tourism development. Construction commenced in 1983 and the Resort was officially opened by the Prime Minister of Solomon Islands in 1984. More than 1000 official guests were invited to the function, evidence of the perception of its key role in and importance to the development of a viable tourism industry in Solomon Islands. This function, and the agreement reached with Father Pule enhanced his "bigman" status even further, not only locally (where his ability to deliver "cargo" of such magnitude elevated him to a very high level) but also nationally (because the attendant publicity promoted him as a figure of some national importance). However, it should be noted that while he became a nationally recognized figure, his capacity to exert influence and exercise authority did not extend much beyond his Nggela community.

The original management of Anuha embraced a close working relationship with Father Pule and his community. A consultative management committee which included Father Pule and some of the other village elders and landowners was established to provide oversight of the development. All major proposals for the resort were put before this committee, which, although only advisory, was a key component of its operations: no major changes to the island took place until there was consensus agreement from the management committee. With the assistance of the management committee, care was taken to identify special sites and valuable resources such as "canoe" trees (a species which is easy to work, durable in water, and highly valued for the making of dug-out canoes) and fruit trees and to pay compensation when development needs necessitated the removal of such a tree. The original investors understood that the Islanders' concept of ownership extended beyond the land to include the jobs created by the resort. They made a point of training and employing local villagers and their kin. Several of Father Pule's nine sons and daughters and their wives and husbands were employed by the resort, Pule's eldest son being the most highly paid local. When specialist skills were not held by locals, the management consulted the customary owners to seek their approval before employing non-Nggela people. While there were occasional points of tension, for the most part Father Pule expressed himself happy with the development and management of the resort. The management committee proved an effective mechanism for devolving a real element of power to the traditional landowners of Anuha.

After two years of operations, and four years from the time of the first negotiations by the husband-and-wife management team, the original Australian shareholders were bought out by another Australian company. But the new owners had little sensitivity towards *kastom*. They considered that the lease gave them the legal right and thus the capacity to manage the island and its resources without recourse to informal practices or a need to take account of *kastom*. They saw the management committee as an unnecessary obstacle to their freedom to do what they wanted. They accused the original team of being "too close to the natives" and "too accepting of low standards of service" provided by the locals, hence running an inefficient and unacceptable operation. They also disagreed fundamentally with the "go-slow" policies of the original investors and management who considered it necessary (based on their experience) to consolidate and extend training of more locals before undertaking any expansion of the resort (personal correspondence). Accordingly, in their first few weeks the new management team dismissed the original one, disbanded the joint committee, and sacked many of the local workforce, replacing them with tribespeople from other islands. They also bulldozed a section of rain-forest to double the number of bungalows without consultation or compensation payments. This disturbed a sacred site and also caused seashore erosion as some of the new bungalows were built out over the water. In various other ways the new management insulted and demeaned the customary owners, isolating them from the operations of the resort and disempowering them. Some of their actions were unknowing because of their total ignorance of *kastom*, others were taken against strong objections from the Rera community.

Father Pule was incensed. He demanded to know why the new expatriate management team had been granted work and resident permits when there had been no negotiations with the customary owners. In fact, his objections revealed a serious flaw in Solomon Islands foreign investment policy. Although the original investor is subjected to stringent vetting, once a company is registered and approvals are in place, ownership through the sale of the company overseas can change but the new owners are not vetted in any way. Purchase of the company buys all its approvals and licenses. Father Pule claimed that since there had been no agreement with the new owners, the lease agreement was null and void. But because this position was not supported by law Pule began a campaign for a new lease, seeking the multiple payments as a single $2 million lump sum. Relations between the new expatriate management and the customary owners deteriorated rapidly and a period of increasing conflict began.

Overt hostility first gained national attention when Father Pule's villagers "invaded" their island and dug holes in the airstrip. Other incidents included a "raid" just before Christmas 1986 when Father Pule sent warriors in war paint to force guests off the island and close down operations. Threats were issued against non-Nggela employees, forcing them to flee the island. Strikes were instigated, equipment was damaged, and outboard motors sabotaged. Although the resort continued to operate, continuing incidents of vandalism and labor strife resulted in the owners placing the resort on the market. Father Pule subsequently confided privately that such actions were justified because of the recalcitrant attitude of the resort owners who refused to acknowledge the validity of customary rights.

The ownership of the resort changed hands twice in 1987, with an investment company Ariadne Ltd (Australia) owning it briefly before Queensland property developer Mike Gore paid $2 million for the resort in August 1987 (personal communication with Gore). It would probably be fair to say that the new owner was unaware of the legacy of distrust he inherited from his predecessors, because at that stage little news of the situation had reached the

Australian or international media. He very quickly discovered he had problems on his hands when confronted by a delegation of Rera landowners led by Father Pule on his first visit to Solomon Islands who demanded a new lease on terms which included the re-establishment of the joint management committee. Gore did not respond immediately but appointed an American lawyer (with no previous experience of Solomon Islands) from his Australian company to investigate the situation.

Tension escalated when the executive chef at the resort appointed by the second owners, Australian John Meint Smith, fell out with the Gore management in October 1987 and became influential with Father Pule. Smith had had a chequered career with several resorts in Australia where he had apparently attempted to oust management and assume control himself. In one such instance the resort had suffered a serious fire immediately after his dismissal (Australian Channel 7 television documentary film 1988). Under Smith's influence, the stance of Anuha's customary landowners changed: from demanding a new lease they now demanded compensation and the repossession of their island, with Smith as the resort's manager.

In December 1987 Father Pule's warriors again invaded Anuha, apparently at the exhortation of Smith, forced the expatriate management team off the island at spear point, and held about 40 guests and a construction crew hostage for several days. Some parts of the resort were damaged. Smith took control of the resort and the guests were entertained with *kastom* dancing. Finally, after three days the Royal Solomon Islands Police (RSIP) Field Force went to the rescue and detained a number of Father Pule's men. Smith was also forced to leave the island. The resort was closed until tension eased.

This incident escalated into a damaging conflict between the Australian and Solomon Islands Governments when the Australian High Commissioner took a prominent role in attempts to protect both Australian citizens (tourists and workers on the island at the time) and the Australian investors. He was instrumental in initiating the response from the Police and in arranging charter aircraft to fly the members of the Field Force into Anuha. While the High Commissioner's response was consistent with his consular responsibilities to work with the local authorities to safeguard Australian citizens against any unlawful activity, he apparently by-passed the official channel (the Solomon Islands Ministry of Foreign Affairs) and dealt directly with the police authorities. His actions also placed him in direct conflict with Father Pule and John Smith.

The Solomon Islands Cabinet had been considering what action it should take and was deeply divided between those wanting to uphold the rights of the customary landowners and those who were concerned about a breakdown in law and order. The High Commissioner's intervention pre-empted any decision by Cabinet. The Prime Minister considered the High Commissioner had interfered in the internal affairs of the country and in the Cabinet room asserted that his Government should demand the High Commissioner's withdrawal from the Solomons by the Australian Government. The Foreign Minister (who was also Deputy Prime Minister), concerned at the likely damage to the bilateral relationship with Australia, opposed the Prime Minister's demand. A serious rift within government ranks polarized around the two men.

Aggrieved by the prominent role of the Australian High Commissioner in his removal from Anuha Island, Smith made death threats against him and his staff. Since Smith claimed that he had his own band of Nggela warriors to do his bidding, these threats were taken seriously and resulted in Australian diplomatic residences being placed under 24-hour protection by the RSIP. No action was taken against Smith who had established protective links with Solomon Islands staff in the RSIP Special Branch through *wantok* connections with the people of Nggela.

Smith gained access to sympathetic Government Ministers, including the Prime Minister, and muddied the waters not only in respect of the Anuha resort owners but of a significant number of other Australian businessmen and interests in Solomon Islands. He leveled a whole series of allegations of corrupt business dealings and taxation evasion against them. Gold smuggling and drug running, with the active connivance of the Australian High Commission and its diplomatic bags being used to take the contraband in and out of Solomon Islands, were among some of his more sensational accusations. None of these was ever substantiated although two reached the courts, one of them drawing headlines of "Buggery by Australians" in the weekly *Solomon Star* (10 April 1988). This was after Smith alleged homosexual activity by the two Australian senior managers of the local airline. Even though no charges were proved a number of Australians had their residence and work permits canceled by the Solomon Islands authorities and they were forced to leave the country. Media reports at the time indicated that Smith had successfully "assisted" in the expulsion or premature departure of between six and 12 Australians (*Islands Business* 1988). Representations by the Australian High Commission against the deportation orders fell on deaf ears. Relations between the two governments deteriorated further.

The strains with Australia increased when Australian Broadcasting Corporation journalists were banned from Solomon Islands in April 1988 by the Solomon Islands Prime Minister following a Radio Australia report suggesting that he had allowed himself to be unwisely influenced by Smith. The Australian Government objected formally to what it termed an attack on the freedom of the press.

In May 1988 the resort's central complex burned down. Damage was estimated at about $1 million. Three Rera villagers who were arrested for arson claimed that Smith had instigated their action. The resort owners also alleged in an affidavit lodged with the authorities that Smith was responsible for the damage. He was formally summonsed to appear in Court to answer this allegation, but he departed for Australia prior to the due date. A prohibition order was filed against him in June 1988, giving police the power to detain him should he return to the Solomons. This order was renewed by the Minister for Police and Justice in June 1994, on advice from the Minister for Immigration who held that Smith remained an "undesirable person".

With the banning order in place against Smith, Father Pule terminated all attempts to negotiate a way out of the situation. He demanded restitution of Smith's right to visit Solomon Islands as a precondition to reopening talks. The Australian investor resorted to the courts to force Father Pule to recognize and respect the validity of the lease agreement. A court order against Father Pule and his supporters for damages and wrongful entry when they had raided the resort in December 1987 was obtained. They were forbidden to visit the island unless gainfully employed by the resort.

Father Pule retaliated with his own court action, contesting the lease. In a documentary aired on Australian television (Channel Seven: "Front Page — Behind the News", May 1988), Father Pule declared that he had not signed the original lease and that his signature must have been forged. This was despite witnesses who had co-signed the lease agreement such as the Central Islands Province senior police inspector and others who in the subsequent court case gave evidence against him. In a judgment at the end of August 1988, Chief Justice Gordon Ward rejected Father Pule's claims, ruling that the lease was a proper document. He stated that he found the former clergyman "to be totally unconcerned about the truth. He lied easily, frequently and unhesitatingly when it suited his case" (*Solomon Star*, 29 August 1988).

Following the court ruling, Anuha's lessees said they would withdraw the claims for damage and wrongful entry in the interests of resolving the deadlock, but Father Pule refused to re-enter negotiations. In mid-1989 the airstrip was replanted with coconut trees by customary owners, but the plants were uprooted by the resort's expatriate caretaker. Legal action was again contemplated but not pursued by the owner. With the constant threat posed by hostile villagers the resort remained closed.

There the matter rested for quite some time. Two new players then entered the scene. Under the normal rotation of ambassadors by the Australian Department of Foreign Affairs and Trade, a new Australian High Commissioner arrived in Honiara towards the end of 1988. He was under a ministerial directive to "use his good offices" to resolve as expeditiously as possible the Anuha affair and the impediment it presented to cordial relations between Australia and Solomon Islands.

Second, national elections in the Solomons in March 1989 resulted in the election of a new government under a former Prime Minister, Solomon Mamaloni. The incoming government desired to resolve the issue quickly. It was deeply concerned about the damage to its reputation as a sound repository for foreign investment (which had in fact virtually dried up from all sources for all sectors, not just tourism, with the exception of logging), and the negative impact on the country as a tourist destination. It also wished to ameliorate the adverse impact on its relations with Australia (which had undertaken a review of its aid program and restricted its development assistance to completing those projects already under way). Accordingly the Prime Minister himself directed ministers to defuse the situation and get the parties together.

In July 1989 pressure was placed on Father Pule through the Anglican Church (the Archbishop of Melanesia making a personal intervention) and a personal plea from the Solomon Islands Prime Minister to reach a settlement. Negotiations took place over the next 12 months involving the Prime Minister, the Minister for Finance, the Minister for Tourism, senior departmental officers from several government ministries, the American legal advisor to Gore, the new Australian High Commissioner, the Anglican Church, and Father Pule and his people. Agreement was finally reached and sealed with a ceremonial *kastom umu* (feast) in June 1990. The customary landowners led by Father Pule received "compensation" of $100,000 from the developer for damages caused to the island, the dismissal of village employees, and degradation of the sacred site, and a new lease similar in terms to the original lease was agreed.

In return for agreeing to meet the demand for compensation, Gore obtained approval from the Solomon Islands Government for a casino license. This was a concession which had been pursued actively by a number of other foreign investors (assisted by several Solomon Islands ministers) for several years. It had provoked — and continues to provoke — considerable opposition as being an unsuitable form of development for the country. Opposition to the concept of a casino was so strong that in May 1990 it was instrumental in forcing a Sydney development company to withdraw its proposal for a casino hotel just outside Honiara. To the extent that the Government was committed to finding a solution to the Anuha problem and accepting of the "Melanesian correctness" of a compensation payment, however, it found itself granting an approval it might have preferred to avoid.

The agreement, sealed with the ceremony in June, appeared to solve the Anuha affair. But one vital element was mismanaged. The national Government and the developer declined to provide the Premier of the Central Province with transport to the feast in a manner he considered befitting of his status. Consequently he boycotted it. His Central Province administration then refused to issue the business licence necessary to recommence operations on Anuha.

Despite the lack of a business license, the Australian developer attempted to obtain investment capital from Japan and other sources, using the lure of the casino license to attract potential investors. At the end of 15 months, having paid out the half a million dollars in compensation but only two of the agreed periodic payments, Gore was declared bankrupt in Australia. Father Pule, on behalf of the customary landowners, took out a Solomon Islands court order in March 1992 enjoining Gore to meet the terms of the agreement or forfeit his lease. When Gore had failed to respond within 90 days, the court declared the lease null and void. The lease was then transferred to Father Pule's clan.

This requires a brief word of explanation. Land once alienated and registered with the Lands Commissioner cannot revert to customary ownership. In this instance, the lease in the name of Gore was revoked but as a legal entity the lease remains in existence and it was ownership of the lease which was transferred. Non-Solomon Islands nationals may only obtain a lease for a maximum of 75 years. As noted previously, nationals may obtain a lease "in perpetuity" (Land and Titles Act, Solomon Islands Government 1984a), but legally the land remains alienated and the lease may be bought and sold.

With legal ownership of Anuha, Father Pule then attempted to find another developer to lease the island and restore the damaged resort. However, there were no "takers" and the lack of investor interest in Anuha led to Father Pule putting the resort up for auction in July 1992. Goods and chattels with a book value of around $1.5 million sold for a combined total of less than $50,000. Successful bidders were given 14 days to remove their new possessions from the island.

By July 31, 1992 Anuha Resort had ceased to exist. Father Pule died in 1997 and Gore in 1998. Despite repeated attempts by the Solomon Islands Government to find a new developer on behalf of the villagers, as the new millennium came and went Anuha Island remained deserted.

Conflict Analysis

This case study may be understood in terms of conflict and power plays at a number of levels, which then lead into an examination of empowerment in which social exchange theory (Cook 1987) is applied. Although the major areas have been separated into different categories in the following analysis, most are interdependent and interrelated and should not be viewed in isolation. Perhaps the most salient point to emerge from the following analysis is that, while the Land and Titles Court initially empowered the Rera villagers by transforming their traditional ownership of the land to legal ownership (Weber 1978), the act of signing an agreement with foreign investors effectively disempowered them by taking away control of that land. Although disempowered the villagers were not altogether powerless and much of the ensuing conflict arose from their attempts to reverse that state and resume a degree of control over the island and its development.

As noted in Chapter 3, a fundamental proposition of Jacobsen and Cohen (1986) is that all power relationships present themselves through contended issues. These are defined as issues which are important to both sides and on which there is disagreement. If there is no disagreement, power will not be evidenced; if the issue is unimportant to one side, there will be no exercise of power for the other party to achieve its end; and if both parties consider the issue unimportant, it is unlikely that either would resort to power. Where there is no consensus about power, there will be resistance which will impose some limits on power, and it is these limitations which allow resistance to contribute to the outcome of power relations. As noted in Chapter 3, resistance emphasizes the fact that power relations are characterized by both asymmetry and reciprocity. All relations of autonomy and dependence are reciprocal however wide the asymmetrical distribution of resources involved: all power relations express autonomy and dependence in both directions (Giddens 1976).

Resistance may be categorized as friction resistance and conflict resistance (Nadel 1963). In the former there could be an acknowledgment that friction could be reduced by a sharing of power, redistribution of responsibilities, and so forth. With directed opposition, its aggressive nature — conflict — could force a sharing or redistribution of power resulting in empowerment. When that resistance produces a transfer of some power, one may say that the process of empowerment has commenced; empowerment may be granted, it may be taken, or it may be a compromise between the two extremes.

Conflict Resistance

At least ten conflict resistance situations may be identified in the context of the attempts to establish a resort on Anuha Island. First, the desire of a foreign investor to develop Anuha Island as a resort provoked conflict and dissension among Solomon Islanders claiming customary ownership of the land. In the short term this was dysfunctional since it prevented negotiations with the investor and the development from proceeding. But in the longer term it proved functional because it resulted in a clear and unambiguous identification of the customary owners and their title to the land in dispute. The legal system through the Land and Titles Court effectively empowered the Rera villagers.

This created the situation where both sides had something of value desired by the other: the developer wanted access to the island and the Rera villagers wanted both cash income and employment. The relationship was not one of equals; it was particularly asymmetrical in the context of "useful knowledge" (van den Berghe 1994) where the developer had a far greater understanding of what a resort development entailed. But the capacity of each side to provide the other with the desired outcome led them into an agreement which initially provided satisfactory benefits to both sides. However, in signing the lease agreement, the traditional landowners ceded control of Anuha Island to outside agencies for the next 75 years. This effectively disempowered them and in terms of "legal domination" (Weber 1978) they lost formal ability to manage the development in any way. Although this was not recognized at the time it set the stage for the ensuing conflict.

Second, the changes of company ownership resulted in conflict between the customary owners and the resort lessees. This conflict was highly dysfunctional. It extended well beyond the confines of the small island of Anuha. It had far-reaching consequences on investor confidence in Solomon Islands, on the security of foreign businesses and residents in Solomon Islands, and on tourism to the country. At various times it pitted the government and its agencies against its own people, the customary landowners, in support of the foreign investor; at times against the latter in support of the customary owners; and against the Australian Government.

Third, the Anuha affair provoked significant domestic political tension. There were disputes within government between ministers and their departments and at times between ministers and the officials of their departments as different interpretations and assessments were made of the situation. There was conflict between some ministers and the police commissioner as the national police force sought to uphold the letter of the law in response to fairly straightforward breaches of that law while other ministers sought to interpret the situation in sociocultural terms.

It caused strain within the Solomon Islands Cabinet, between ministers concerned with the economic impact of the Anuha dispute and its effect on foreign investment and ministers who identified more closely with the customary landowners. It provoked serious strains between the Prime Minister and his deputy and Foreign Minister. It caused great personal difficulty for the Minister for Economic Planning who was also the local member for Nggela. Wearing his ministerial hat he was particularly well placed to appreciate the potential the situation held for economic damage, but wearing his constituency hat he was a *wantok* (same linguistic group) of Father Pule and his personal sympathies were with the customary landowners. This bifurcation of roles resulted in apparently inconsistent actions and statements by him. These conflicts emphasized the truism quoted from Chapter 3, that "politics is about control, and power governs the interplay of interested parties at all levels, whether local, regional, national or international, trying to influence the direction of policy, policy outcomes and the position of tourism in the political agenda" (Hall 1994; Lyden *et al.* 1969).

Fourth, the Anuha affair tested the legal system, an imported regime which in the view of many Solomon Islanders is inadequate to manage disputes involving *kastom* fairly and constructively (Campbell 1972; Saemala 1983). They consider that the law by its very nature favors the expatriate. For example, the expatriate has a better grasp of the concepts of the system (in this case, British) which are foreign to Melanesian customary law; of the need to use university trained lawyers to operate the system; of access to the financial resources needed to mount a challenge or a defence; of the use of English — and "legalese" at that — as the language of the courts; and of the formal protocol of the courts which is foreign to Melanesian *kastom*. A court appearance can be an intimidating experience to the Solomon Islander because of a combination of all of these factors (Hogbin 1970).

> You are familiar with the law, [a Malaitan man once said]. "It belongs to you: it comes from the place where you were born. For us the law is different. In olden days we behaved as our fathers did before us . . . It was the custom. Today it is changed. The whiteman has come and told us we must behave like his father. Our fathers? We must forget them. . . . In the olden days we always knew what was right. Now we have to say: "This thing I want to do, will the white man say that it is wrong and punish me? (Hogbin 1970:204).

As good an example as any of the different culturally determined attitudes to the legal system may be found in reactions to the Chief Justice's comment that the leader of the Anuha customary owners was an unmitigated liar. To the Australian owner's representatives (and, one suspects, the majority of the expatriate population of the Solomons), the Chief Justice's criticism and judgment was a vindication of their stance. It was interpreted as causing substantial loss of face to Father Pule and diminution of his "bigman" status. But so central to the cultural survival and identity of the clan and to the individual psychological well-being of the Melanesian is the maintenance of an unbroken link to ancestral lands that many of the words spoken and actions taken in pursuit of land rights which might be regarded as criminal before British law or immoral before Christianity, will be regarded by fellow Melanesians as justifiable. In Father Pule's case, there was at least understanding, if not complete acceptance, of his position. He received much sympathetic support from fellow Solomon Islanders: loss of face and "bigman" status was slight. His local power base was unaffected. The exercise of legal domination by the foreign investor did not diminish the legitimate (traditional) authority of the village leader. He remained a *hevi* leader — *haemi strong tumas* (*he is very strong*) was the pijin phrase Solomon Islanders used to describe Father Pule in the aftermath of the court case.

In examining the role of the legal system in the conflict between the parties to the Anuha (dis)agreement the affair could in a broad sense be deemed functional because of the educative impact of the court proceedings. Reports on the progress of the court case were broadcast regularly throughout Solomon Islands over the national radio news network and provoked considerable discussion in village communities (where more than 65 percent of the population has access to radio). The conflict could thus be held to have increased internal awareness about some of the implications of tourism-related development.

An etic interpretation, common to expatriates and foreign investors then resident in Solomon Islands, was that the affair was dysfunctional, in that a conclusion to be drawn by Solomon Islanders and investors alike was that a victory in the courts was not necessarily a victory out in the provinces. No matter what rulings were obtained through the courts and no matter what penalties were imposed, when it came to the final analysis the customary landowner was likely to achieve at least a "negative victory" — that is, he could prevent a venture proceeding because of his local control. No tourist operator can stay in business for very long if the resort must be ringed with barbed wire fences and armed guards employed to keep tourists in and local people out. From an emic viewpoint, the capacity of the local people (Chambers' "lowers") to achieve an outcome they desired despite court imposed penalties could be considered positive.

The court decision in favor of the resort developers may have empowered them theoretically; in practice, in the case of Anuha Island, it amounted to little. Powerlessness of Father Pule before the court system in Honiara did not translate into powerlessness on the ground in Anuha. If Conger and Kanungo's (1988) concept of location of the actor in the system is applied as a key determinant of power differentials between actors, then Father Pule and his villagers occupied an advantaged position because of their capacity to exercise the greater power by negative actions. By this is meant the capacity to exclude the developers from benefits of the Court outcome — the power to keep them out of exercising control over resources (in this case Anuha Island). As noted in Chapter 3, this capacity of exclusion is evidence of both empowerment (by those doing the excluding) and powerlessness (by those being excluded). In spite of a court ruling designed to reverse the illegal control exercised by Father Pule and his warriors following their invasion of the resort, the owners were unable to reopen it. Father Pule and his people of course did not see their entry into their own island as illegal. They exercised their right under *kastom* to attempt to re-assert ownership.

Fifth, in the context of foreign investment, the affair was highly dysfunctional. The Central Bank and others attributed the Anuha problems as a key factor in the lack of tourism investment in Solomon Islands from 1988 to 2000 (with the outbreak of inter-tribal violence after that date all investment in all sectors ceased completely). The apparent difficulty in gaining control of the Anuha situation by the Government, the lack of protection for expatriate residents in the country, and the shenanigans of Smith (who gained a degree of notoriety in Australia following the broadcasting of a television documentary in May 1988 dubbed "Cyclone Smith"), all combined to destroy investor confidence. With the exception of a $1 million remodeling of the capital's largest hotel (112 rooms) by its new Japanese owners in 1992, and two new hotel developments in Honiara valued at about $10 million, the tourism investment sought by successive governments for provinces failed to materialize.

Sixth, and paradoxically, however, the conflict between foreign investor and customary owner could be judged as functional because it precipitated a review of tourism policy and foreign investment procedures by two successive Solomon Islands Governments. New policies and regulations put in place which were designed to provide better protection for both foreign investor and customary landowner, owed their genesis directly to the Anuha imbroglio (the subject of Chapter 6).

Seventh, the Anuha affair resulted in conflict between the national government and the provincial government of Central Province. Since independence, significant authority has been devolved to the provinces and they thus have a capacity to frustrate national government objectives. In this instance, the national Minister of Tourism was powerless to direct the Central Province administration to issue a business license to the Australian developer of Anuha. The lessee may have had a license for a casino, but he could not take advantage of it until he had his operational license from the Province. A demarcation dispute over political and administrative responsibilities, with some parallels to the Australian and Canadian federal-states rights issue, was fueled in the Solomons by this ill-fated tourism venture.

Eighth, there was conflict between two neighboring countries which soured relations between them for a considerable period. Questions were raised in both the Australian and Solomon Islands parliaments and criticisms voiced on both sides. The incident impeded normal working relations. The Solomons Government was deeply concerned about the intrusion (in its view) of Australian diplomats and journalists into its internal affairs and the exploitation of Solomon Islanders by what it regarded as unscrupulous businessmen. For its part, Australia was highly concerned about an unjustified (in its view) Prime Ministerial demand (even if it remained informal) that its senior diplomatic representative be recalled, about the ban on the Australian Broadcasting Corporation and about the expulsion of Australian citizens for seemingly inconsequential reasons. The strain was sufficient to cause Australia to reconsider its aid program and its delivery of that assistance to Solomon Islands. A change of Australian High Commissioner in late 1988 and the election of a new government in Solomon Islands in March 1989 assisted in the recovery of the bilateral relationship but vexation over the Anuha affair lingered, albeit largely mitigated by the agreement in June 1990 which produced a new lease agreement. At the level of sovereign state relations, the conflict proved highly dysfunctional.

Ninth, the apparent resolution of the affair in June 1990 could be regarded as functional in that the terms of the agreement satisfied the economic objectives of the chief protagonists, justified Father Pules's antagonism towards the resort owners and increased his "bigman" status, removed tension between ministers and government departments, resulted in the first comprehensive tourism development policy and set of foreign investment incentives formulated for Solomon Islands (see Chapter 6), and deflated tension in the bilateral relationship between Solomon Islands and Australia. It proved dysfunctional in that the approval for a casino license contained the seeds for further domestic political confrontation, with the Anglican Church in particular annoyed by the deal. It thus set civil society on a collision course with government.

Tenth, the entire episode proved dysfunctional in that no investor, either local or foreign, came forward to continue the resort once the title reverted to Father Pule's clan. The final act, played out in 1992 with the auction of all the remaining goods and chattels, marked the end of Anuha Island Resort, but in 2000 when inter-tribal warfare broke out and brought all tourism activity to a halt, its impact had remained as a depressant to foreign investment in tourism in Solomon Islands.

Social Exchange Theory Analysis

An analysis of the Anuha Island Resort situation may also be considered in the context of power/dependence relations under the rubric of social exchange theory. Ap defined the latter as "a general sociological theory concerned with understanding the exchange of resources between individuals and groups in an interaction situation" (1992:688). The power relationship between parties is a central component of social exchange theory (Cook 1987; Friedman 1987; Madrigal 1992). Emerson (1972) proposed a power/dependence relations typology which leads to the development of social exchange; relative dependence between two parties determines relative power. As long as the pattern of exchange is perceived as equitable, both parties will continue with the exchange relationship. Balance between the relative power/dependence of the parties will produce cohesion leading to a more or less durable social exchange relationship. It should be noted that "balance" is not synonymous with "symmetry"; relations between the parties may be cohesive, but because a perfect balance of power or dependence rarely occurs, asymmetry is the norm. Provided the relationship tends toward balance, however, asymmetry may lead to a satisfactory exchange.

It should be noted that Emerson's concept of the exchange relation refers to social interaction not individual psychology or behavior. Thus, interaction between two parties in a balanced situation, either positive (high for party A and high for party B) or negative (low for party A and low for party B), is the focus of attention and subsequent comparisons between the possible states is the unit of analysis. In social exchange attention is centered "directly on the social process of give-and-take in people's relations" rather than on the psychological motivation of those involved in the process. [Exchange theory] "dissects the transaction process to explain the interdependent contingencies in which each response is dependent upon the other actor(s) prior action and is simultaneously the stimulus evoking the other's further reaction" (Blau 1987:85). It does not focus on egos' prior conditioning, experiences or attributes but rather on the alternating reciprocities underlying the social interaction, and the motivation of the participants is taken as given. In short, it ignores psychological reductionism to concentrate on the social processes of the exchange relationship. This point is important to a proper understanding of the nature of the exchange relation not as individual behavior of each party in an exchange *per se*.

Emerson's "balance" approach suggests that prediction of the actors' outcome is made by a comparison of an exchange relation where the actors are in a high balanced power situation with an exchange relation where actors are in a low balanced power situation. Thus, determination of perceived tourism

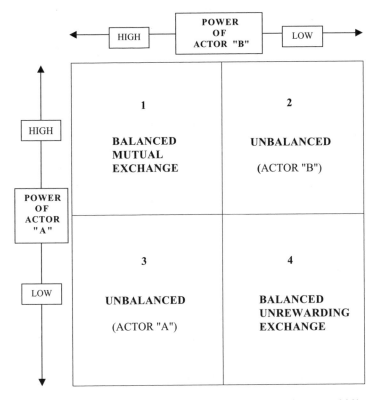

Figure 7.2: Social Exchange (Power) Outcome (After Ap 1992)

impacts, for example, would be made by comparing the nature of the exchange relation found in quadrants 1 and 4 of Figure 7.2 Power Outcome Matrix, that is, in situations of balanced mutual exchange and balanced unrewarding exchange, respectively.

Determination of the nature of the exchange relation, or the degree of balance between two actors, is obtained by examining the power discrepancy scores among the actors. A low discrepancy score would indicate a degree of balance in an exchange, while a high discrepancy score would indicate that there was an imbalance in an exchange. In calculating the discrepancy score, the magnitude of the discrepancy (that is the score calculated in absolute values) is of interest in accordance with the equation definition of Power Imbalance = Pab − Pba (Emerson 1962).

Examination of the outcome for the local villagers and resort owners can be analyzed in terms of asymmetric exchange. It should be noted that this constitutes a subgroup analysis where outcomes are examined for each individual group. There are three possible outcomes. One, where parties A and B have approximately equal levels of power, and there is mutual dependence, the resultant exchange relationship is described as balanced. Both are likely to get something of value out of the exchange and both will evaluate it as positive. In the case of Anuha, the Australian developer (party A) depended upon the Rera village landowners (party B) to achieve his identified goal of a tropical island resort. This entailed Father Pule's community agreeing to make available resources under their control, Anuha Island, which they themselves could not exploit for tourism because of lack of capital and expertise. The initial exchange, a 75-year lease of Anuha Island for more than $2 million, was perceived at the time as balanced with both parties receiving appropriate benefits.

Two, where one set of actors has control of resources and a high level of power, the other will be disadvantaged and the exchange relationship will be unbalanced. In this situation, the disadvantaged party will probably develop negative perceptions which will be detrimental to the continuation of the relationship.

Following the sale of Anuha Island Resort Ltd to the second Australian tourism operator, the power balance changed. The new operator lacked the experience and knowledge the first operator had obtained through the protracted negotiations to ascertain *kastom* ownership of Anuha Island and its reefs, and the resultant understanding of Solomon Islands culture. The consequent introduction of management techniques was defective in meeting the sociocultural imperatives of running a resort in a Melanesian environment.

The second owner embarked on a course which effectively destroyed the elements of mutual dependence and the relative sharing of power. The management strategy of the original owner which was sympathetic to traditional values was considered an encumbrance to cost-efficient management by the new owner. The indigenous landowners were excluded from the decision-making process, alienated from their island, and marginalized. Power rested with the new operator and the nature of the exchange relationship became unbalanced.

The hostile reaction of Father Pule's community may be understood in the context of the disregard by the new operator for the informal network of benefits flowing from the initial exchange. These benefits were additional to those set out in the legally sanctioned lease document. The key contribution these benefits made to an overall satisfactory exchange was neither understood nor accepted by the new management. The tension between the parties provided fertile ground for John Smith to influence the host community and to direct their hostility in ways which he considered would help him attain his goal of controlling the operation of the resort.

Three, where both parties have low levels of power *vis-à-vis* each other, their capacity to achieve significant gains from an exchange relationship will be commensurately low: negative perceptions by both will be the likely result. This accurately describes the situation following the closure of the resort after the 1987 arson incident and the subsequent court ruling in 1988. The then fourth operator (property developer Gore) was unable to reopen the resort despite the legal decision in his favor. Father Pule's community for its part was unable to obtain either a new lease arrangement or the return of the island to their control. A legal agreement between the two parties was extant, but neither had the power to force compliance by the other to its terms and conditions; it could not be implemented so that an exchange situation could hardly be held to exist.

In withholding approval of operations by the third and fourth owners (Ariadne Ltd and Gore, respectively) and by refusing to enter into new negotiations for a period of 12 months, Father Pule's community was instrumental in preventing the reopening of the resort. This reaffirmed that, despite a court ruling which would seem to have placed power in the hands of the resort operator, effective power resided with the host community. The balance of power had again changed and on this occasion it was the developer who was obliged to initiate an exchange transaction. The price he had to pay, $500,000 in "compensation" before a new lease agreement could be negotiated, was perceived by him to be worth the cost because of the millions of dollars tied up in the resort.

Drawing upon the social exchange theory writings of Levi-Strauss, Homans, Blau, Emerson, and others, Ap (1992) posed a model for analyzing residents' perceptions of tourism impacts (Figure 7.3). Fundamental components of his model are need satisfaction, exchange relations, consequences of exchange, and the no-exchange outcome. These are linked by a set of four processes: initiation of exchange, exchange formation, exchange transaction evaluation and evaluation of exchange consequences. For the latter, positive evaluation was likely to produce reinforcement of behavior and support for tourism. Negative evaluation of exchange consequences could manifest itself in a reduction of exchange behavior or possibly the withdrawal of exchange behavior, resulting in no-exchange. With minor modifications to encompass the perceptions of the tourism developer as well as those of the host community, and with resort development rather than tourism *per se* as the focus of the exchange relationship, Ap's model may be applied to the Anuha situation.

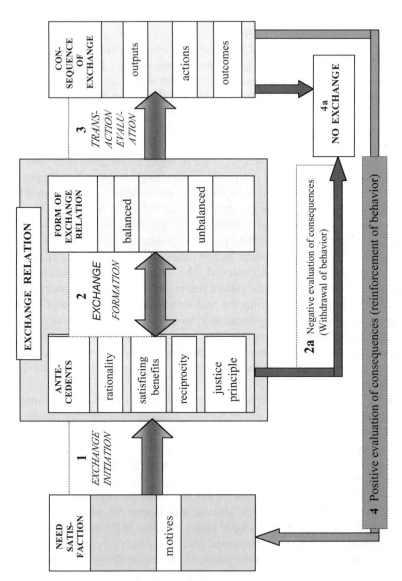

Figure 7.3: Model of the Social Exchange Process (After Ap 1992)

Initiation of Exchange

Expression of need leads to this first process. According to Ap "An actor will initiate an exchange relationship when there is a need to satisfy" (1992:672). Thus, the Australian resort developer initiated an exchange relationship with Father Pule because of the need for land controlled by the village community. The nature of this exchange relationship is determined by two subcomponents, antecedents and the form of the relation.

The antecedents represent the opportunities or conditions for an exchange to occur. Searle (1991) identifies four opportunities (antecedent conditions) perceived by at least one of the parties prior to the exchange developing: rationality of behaviour, "satisficing" of benefits, reciprocity, and the justice principle. In his examination of each of these antecedents, Ap then posits several propositions:

> *Rationality of behavior* refers to the behavior of participants in an exchange being based upon the seeking of rewards. Without rewards, material or psychological, an actor has no motivation for engaging in exchange (Ap 1992:673). Applying the concept of rationality to a tourism setting, residents (hosts) will develop expectations that their involvement in tourism will reap rewards by way of improvements in their social and economic well-being. Thus, the greater the perceived rewards from tourism, the more positive are host actors' perceptions of tourism . . . [and] the greater the perceived costs of tourism, the more negative are host actors' perceptions of tourism (Ap 1992:674).

When applied to Anuha, the initial Australian proposal to develop a resort on Anuha Island created expectations of economic and social benefits for the indigenous landowners; the incipient host responses were positive. At that time, with no previous experience of tourism development, the indigenous landowners had only vague notions about costs to them associated with tourism and these were restricted to some concerns about its potential to undermine traditional values. However, the isolation of the proposed resort as an enclave on an offshore island led Father Pule to believe that adverse social impacts of tourism could be contained.

Only subsequently, when the second operator engaged in activities which decreased rewards and increased costs, both material and social, for the resident community did they become strongly negative about the form of the development. When the fourth owner, Gore, offered to meet the basic demands of the landowners, the pendulum swung back towards acceptance of a revised agreement to allow the resort to continue.

> *Satisficing of benefits* refers to the situation where the actors accept a satisfactory level of benefits that may be less than optimal. Since ideal maximized benefits (of tourism) are not always possible, a trade-off or 'satisficing' result is often acceptable and continued engagement in the exchange relationship is likely to be maintained. Despite negative effects of tourism, the benefits (financial, economic, social or environmental) may be perceived by resident actors to outweigh the costs and support for tourism is likely to continue (Ap 1992:675). Thus a resident actor will assign a positive value or attitude towards tourism if the benefits meet an acceptable level of satisfaction determined by the actor . . . [and] a resident actor will assign a negative value or attitude towards tourism if the benefits do not meet an acceptable level of satisfaction determined by the actor (Ap 1992:675).

The original terms of the lease of Anuha Island, supported by the flow of additional informal benefits, while falling short at times of the desires of the indigenous landowners proved generally acceptable to them. When the level of benefits was reduced by the second developer, however, support for the development by Father Pule's community was withdrawn. The prospect of those benefits being reinstated by Gore led Father Pule's community to react positively.

> *Reciprocity* is a key element of social exchange theory and refers to a mutually gratifying pattern of exchanging goods and services (Gouldner 1960). It signifies that in an exchange each actor will provide benefits to the other equitably and with units of exchange that are important to the actors (Ap 1992:675). Where reciprocal obligations exist but one actor feels disadvantaged the exchange transaction will experience problems. Thus, when the exchange of resources between residents and tourism actors is reciprocated (i.e. balanced), the effects of tourism are perceived positively by the respective actors. . . . When the exchange of resources between resident and tourism actors is not reciprocated (i.e. unbalanced), the effects of tourism are perceived negatively by the respective actors (Ap 1992:676).

In examining these propositions, it can be seen that the management strategy of the original Australian company was based on reciprocity which was mutually beneficial and so the host/developer relation was perceived positively. However, the second management regime failed to meet the expectations of the resident community; the landowners considered themselves disadvantaged *vis-à-vis* the original arrangement and adopted a negative attitude towards the project. The acceptance by Gore of a more equitable arrangement resulted in the villagers responding positively.

> *The principle of justice* extends the notion of reciprocity. The exchange must be viewed as fair in the context of each actor's social environment (Ap 1992:676). Violating the norms of fair exchange can lead to conflict and retaliation against violators and the breakdown of the exchange. However, the relationship may be continued in circumstances of power dependence where the disadvantaged actor may have little capacity to influence the exchange. The result may be an unbalanced exchange relationship in which tension militates against an amicable partnership. Thus, when the value of resources exchanged between the host resident and tourism actors is approximately equal, the exchange transaction is likely to be perceived as fair . . . When the value of resources exchanged between the host resident and tourism actors is greater for one than for the other, the exchange transaction is likely to be perceived as unfair by the disadvantaged actor . . . When the value of resources exchanged between the host and guest actors is perceived as fair, the host actor is likely to have positive perceptions of tourism . . . When the value of resources exchanged between the host and guest actors is perceived as unfair by the host actor, the latter is likely to have negative perceptions of tourism (Ap 1992:677).

To these the following can be added:

> When the exchange transaction is perceived as fair and the host actor has positive perceptions of tourism the relationship is likely to endure. A sustainable operation is the likely outcome. When the exchange transaction is perceived as unfair and the host actor has negative perceptions of tourism the relationship is unlikely to endure. A sustainable operation will not be achieved (Sofield 1997).

The range of responses by the indigenous community over time to the Anuha development supports these propositions of justice as prerequisites for the establishment and continuation of an amicable social exchange relationship and alternatively, where they are not met, breakdown of the social exchange relationship and the collapse of a sustainable operation.

Exchange Formation

When the antecedents are viewed positively, an environment will have been created conducive to this second process. This "involves a two-way directional linking of the antecedents to the forms of exchange relation" where the actors consider that a mutually rewarding transaction can be finalized. "Alternatively, if either actor anticipates or perceives that the consequences of exchange will be unworthwhile or unrewarding, then withdrawal of exchange behavior will result and no exchange between the actors will occur" (Ap 1992:677).

Because each transaction has both a past (history) and a future for the participants, an exchange relation implies a more or less durable social relationship between them, which is modifiable across time (Emerson 1972:46). This leads to two more propositions by Ap:

> The antecedents of the exchange relation should be met favorably for the exchange relation to form. . . . Where one or more of the antecedents of the exchange relation are abused, the exchange relation will not form (1992:678).

In the case of the first developer of Anuha Island, the antecedents were met, transactions took place and a social exchange relationship was formed. In the case of the second developer, the exchange relationship broke down. In the case of Gore, antecedents were again met, an agreement was negotiated, but an exchange relationship was not sustained because Gore failed to deliver the agreed benefits.

Consequences of Exchange

Upon establishment of an exchange transaction, an *evaluation of its consequences* takes place. The consequences depend upon what resources are valued and exchanged by the respective actors and the evaluation will be multi-faceted covering outputs, actions and outcomes (Ap 1992). *Outputs* from the exchange will be examined, the *actions* of the participants in response to the outputs obtained will be determined, and the psychological *outcomes* of the consequences will be evaluated.

Where the consequences of an exchange transaction/relationship meet the needs of the parties, their behavior will be reinforced. Attitudes towards the tourism development will be positive and the exchange relationship will endure. Where those needs are only partially met and/or are accompanied by negative outputs, the evaluation may be negative. Thus, access of Rera villagers to the cash economy (through lease monies, compensation payments and employment), access by Father Pule's community to an anti-malarial clinic run for the resort, and the accrual of profits for the developer, were perceived as positive outputs of the Anuha resort development. But when that access was reduced to the local villagers, for example, when the second owner dismissed a considerable number of local employees, resources were destroyed without compensation (such as the bulldozing of a stand of rainforest), services of the anti-malarial clinic were withdrawn, and traditional values were disregarded, the indigenous residents assessed that, on balance, the negative outweighed the positive outputs and they withdrew their approval of the exchange relationship.

Their actions (behavior) became negative in response to the tourism development. They no longer treated tourists with courtesy and friendliness; they withheld their labor from the employer; they engaged in various small acts of sabotage such as damaging outboard motors and cutting water pipes, and more dramatic acts of displeasure such as digging up the resort airstrip and "invading" the resort. For his part, the developer's actions became increasingly hostile toward the residents, for example, a court injunction was taken out to prevent the landowners from setting foot on the island.

In terms of psychological outcomes, the resident community was not only physically alienated from its land but from the ancestors associated with Anuha. The continuum of interaction with them was interrupted. The trauma of this and the resultant depth of resentment toward the developer was never fully understood by him. It was the psychological aspects which John Smith was able to exploit so deftly and which led to the demand by the local community that the lease be terminated and the island returned to them.

The eventual removal of the resort and the total cessation of all income and other benefits from the development might appear as irrational in the eyes of Western economists; but to the islanders, the sociocultural and psychological values associated with control of their ancestral lands was of greater value than material outputs. Ap's final proposition is valid for the saga of Anuha:

> A host actor will perceive tourism negatively when the consequences of exchange provide an unrewarding or unfavorable exchange experience (1992:685).

Conclusion

This resort development highlights the dynamic nature of exchange and exposes the fluctuating condition of the Rera community as they moved from a position of empowerment to disempowerment and back again. It effectively illustrates the fallacy of the "capacity-outcome" approach which assumes that the outcome of a struggle can be determined by identifying the comparative financial and material resources available to both sides (Hindness 1982). It also substantiates the need to draw a clear distinction between power resources and power potential to explain why potential power is translated into action in some situations but not in others; and why groups with relatively poor power resources can at times impose their will on others who are much more richly endowed (Jacobsen and Cohen 1986).

The Anuha situation also suggests elements of Braithwaite's (1992) concept of "weak power" where if battles were fought purely in economic terms, the powerless would invariably be beaten because the stronger interests would always prevail. But the weaker party may be able to broker a shift in political support in their favor by seizing high moral ground and by linking that to a perception that their cause is also in the national interest. The powerless may then be able to unsettle the powerful as in the case of Anuha, where a strong degree of general and political disapproval against the powerful was mobilized and articulated.

The objectives of national development may see a multimillion-dollar resort deserving of government support because of its contribution to the tourism industry, its generation of foreign exchange earnings, creation of employment, and provision of basic infrastructure. But if that development dislocates traditional landowners, alienates their lands, and degrades traditional practices and values, then the national identity that "we are a country which values village life and traditions and we do not want that happening in our village" may also have wide support. The action of the dispossessed landowners in invading Anuha forced powerful actors — the Cabinet members — to make a choice: *either* support a foreign investor and economic (growth model) development *or* support their own citizens, Melanesian values and the ideals of national identity in opposing that development.

As noted in Chapter 3 it is not simply a case of power equated to resources and conversely powerlessness/lack of resources which constitutes the determinant of outcomes. Even without resources, the powerless can move through a process of empowerment which allows them to redress the original power imbalance and achieve an outcome favorable to their objectives. This can be explored further with reference to the findings of Molm (1989a), Lawler and

Bacharach (1986), and others that power/dependence relations may "structure control over both positive outcomes (rewards) and negative outcomes (punishments)" (Molm 1989a:1393). Also relevant is Molm's (1989b) demonstration that in an unequal power relationship punishment was the most likely power strategy the weaker actor would resort to where expected rewards were not forthcoming and where the disadvantaged party lacked the capacity to substantially increase its rewards to the dominant party to improve reciprocal benefits. Molm suggested that a punishment power strategy by a weaker party would only be effective where it increased the other actor's reward exchange and shifted the asymmetry of reward exchange in favor of the weaker actor. If in fact it brought punitive retaliation rather than reward, then it would serve to consolidate and reinforce the domination of the stronger actor. In the Anuha affair, the illegal actions of the Rera villagers in sabotage and "invasion" appeared in the short term to reap punitive action as they were taken to court and penalized; but in the longer term that demonstration of capacity to disrupt the resort prevented it from reopening and shifted the balance of power back to the landowners.

This aptly illustrates Conger and Kanungo's (1988) concept of structural location (as outlined above in conflict situation number four) and reinforces the notion of Jacobsen and Cohen (1986) that an ability to use resources effectively will depend not only upon the amount and type of those resources but also the position of one party relative to the other to bring more or less of its resources to bear on the issue at hand. As noted in Chapter 3 there will be both a temporal and a spatial dimension to position: one must be in the right place at the right time to convert resources into effective action and thereby achieve control to ensure the desired outcome. But by themselves neither position nor resources are sufficient to conceptualize power. As stated earlier: "Resources which cannot be applied to contended issues leave their owner impotent, while a position of strength without adequate resources to hold it under pressure is a temporary illusion of power, not its reality" (Jacobsen and Cohen 1986:110).

The developer of Anuha, seemingly empowered by the 1988 court decision, in fact could not apply the court decision effectively (to reopen the resort), so that his position of strength was illusory. It could be said that he had mastered technicity but not indeterminacy in the redefinition of the Atkinson and Delamont (1990) concepts, technicity in this case being the explicit, rule-governed, codified part of the lease agreement and foreign investment project approval, and indeterminacy being the hidden agenda of Melanesian social values and behavior.

Conversely, the apparent powerlessness of the Rera community was more apparent than real. They had not mastered technicity but they used the power

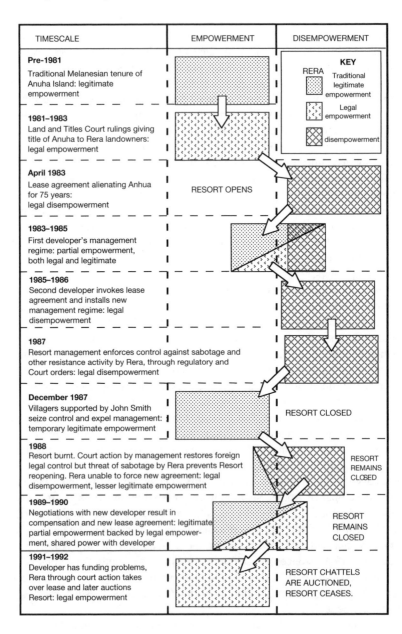

TIMESCALE	EMPOWERMENT	DISEMPOWERMENT
Pre-1981 Traditional Melanesian tenure of Anuha Island: legitimate empowerment		**KEY** RERA Traditional legitimate empowerment Legal empowerment disempowerment
1981–1983 Land and Titles Court rulings giving title of Anuha to Rera landowners: legal empowerment		
April 1983 Lease agreement alienating Anhua for 75 years: legal disempowerment	RESORT OPENS	
1983–1985 First developer's management regime: partial empowerment, both legal and legitimate		
1985–1986 Second developer invokes lease agreement and installs new management regime: legal disempowerment		
1987 Resort management enforces control against sabotage and other resistance activity by Rera, through regulatory and Court orders: legal disempowerment		
December 1987 Villagers supported by John Smith seize control and expel management: temporary legitimate empowerment	RESORT CLOSED	
1988 Resort burnt. Court action by management restores foreign legal control but threat of sabotage by Rera prevents Resort reopening. Rera unable to force new agreement: legal disempowerment, lesser legitimate empowerment		RESORT REMAINS CLOSED
1989–1990 Negotiations with new developer result in compensation and new lease agreement: legitimate partial empowerment backed by legal empowerment, shared power with developer		RESORT REMAINS CLOSED
1991–1992 Developer has funding problems, Rera through court action takes over lease and later auctions Resort: legal empowerment		RESORT CHATTELS ARE AUCTIONED, RESORT CEASES.

Figure 7.4: Rera Community — Empowerment/Disempowerment

inherent in the "habitus" (social space) in a negative way to prevent the resort from being reopened. Their control of habitus provided the base from which they were eventually able to launch a renegotiated lease agreement and compensation claim that met their requirements. Subsequently their utilization of technicity — seeking a court ruling to declare Gore's lease invalid — allowed them to obtain legal control over the island. Figure 7.4 charts the path between the empowerment and disempowerment of Rera community between 1981 and 1992.

To summarize, in examining the conflict inherent in the Anuha situation, the Parsonian modernization perspective and its concept of functionalism is elbowed aside in favor of what developmental theorists such as Smandych, Lincoln and Wilson (1995) have termed the Marxist world perspective. Parsons (1937, 1966) considered that society functioned through consensus and agreement, as though it were perfectly integrated, a harmonious whole. However, Marxian and Weberian concepts of conflict and power conceived of struggle as more essential to social organization than the consensus/agreement compacts advocated by Parsons. Functionalist doctrines were criticized for not giving much significance to classes and class conflict so were targeted by Marxists for overestimating agreement in society and failing to appreciate class differences. They also considered that functionalism failed to recognize the extent to which social relations are rooted in economic and political considerations. Consequently, according to Weber, social relations are permeated with differences of interest.

Both approaches share important concepts: system needs, the relationship of parts of the system, the way systems "pressure" or "structure" individual actions. Therefore, both can be characterized as "structuralist". But the differences in the basic starting point, that society functions through conflict or consensus, leads to markedly different descriptions of society. Merton (1963) combined elements of both perspectives by adding functional/dysfunctional, manifest/latent functions in exploring tension and conflict and, at a methodological level, the analysis of the Anuha situation draws to some extent upon this "middle path" by incorporating social exchange theory with conflict theory to provide a frame of reference for understanding the interaction between the parties to the dispute.

The definition of empowerment as a multidimensional process can suggest that in the final analysis the Rera community participated in a consultative process as a more-or-less equal party to the discussions. The whole affair provided the community members with exposure to tourism development, court processes and other forms outside the normal experience of isolated, traditionally oriented Solomon Island communities (the opportunity to learn). They were in the end able to exercise choice and make decisions acceptable to them. The undoubted power and authority of Father Pule locally, which extended to a national profile, contributed significantly to this outcome.

A key component of the definition used here — that a community to be empowered must both have the choice to make its own decisions and then have the capacity to implement or apply them and accept responsibility for them — was met through the utilization of the legal system which returned the lease of Anuha to the Rera landowners. This was the outcome they sought and it directly benefited the community and its members.

Finally it is argued that an understanding of the complexities of the failure of Anuha Island Resort supports the central propositions that without the element of empowerment tourism development at the level of community will have difficulty achieving sustainability; that the exercise of traditional or legitimate empowerment by traditionally oriented communities by itself will be an ineffectual mechanism for attempting sustainable tourism development; that such traditional empowerment must be transformed into legal empowerment if sustainable tourism development is to be achieved; that empowerment for such communities will usually require environmental or institutional change to allow a genuine reallocation of power to ensure appropriate changes in the asymmetrical relationship of the community to the wider society; and conversely, empowerment of indigenous communities cannot be "taken" by the communities concerned drawing only upon their own traditional resources but will require support and sanction by the state, if it is to avoid being short-lived.

Chapter 8

Empowerment and Sustainability Through Village Ownership: The *Ghol*, Vanuatu*

Ethnic Tourism in Vanuatu

In examining the role of empowerment in sustainable ethnic tourism in the South Pacific it is proposed to examine a traditional event in Vanuatu which has been "opened" to tourism. This is the annual *ghol* (land diving) ceremony carried out by the Sa people of Pentecost Island. The research of Jolly (1982, 1994), Bani (1989) and de Burlo (1996), supported by the earlier work of Tonkinson (1982), is fundamental in reaching an understanding of the many-faceted aspects of this ceremony in its "touristized landscape".

Vanuatu (previously called New Hebrides) is one of the smaller of the island states in the South Pacific, having a total population of less than 200,000. It gained independence in 1980, having been a Condominium under joint colonial powers, Britain and France. Independence was won after overcoming an armed insurrection. It was the only state in the South Pacific to have faced such a trauma.

One direct consequence of this politico/military struggle was a strengthening of *kastom* which, in a Melanesian society with more than 90 tribes and where fragmentation was normative, was part of a deliberate strategy to forge a new national identity divorced from the prior imposition of colonial, western values (Tonkinson 1982). Land rights, integrally bound up in wider *kastom* through the doctrine of "first appearance", was one of the major issues confronting the Islanders in the 1970s and as such it constituted a strong unifying cultural and political force. Indeed, the words *kastom* and land have the same connotations for many ni-Vanuatu (Bonnemaison 1975:59).

In central and southern Vanuatu, identity and power are derived from the root-place where the founding ancestors first appeared and each clan, lineage and each custom name borne by men refers back to their *stamba* (Tonkinson, 1982)

* This chapter is an adapted version of an earlier publication in *Journal of Tourism Studies*, Vol. 2, No. 1, pp. 56–72.

(a Bislama (pijin) word meaning "place of first appearance", the derivative of which is the English word "stump" or "stock"). Its reference point back to the first ancestors integrates sacrality into power (Durkheim 1961). The strength, both political and traditional, of clans and individuals mirrors the power associated with their *stamba*, and the doctrine of first appearance is the basis for land rights and space where control and authority are exercised (Bonnemaison 1975). When conflicts over land or authority arise, the first step "is to trace the spatial chain of successive authority to determine which person has the right to settle the matter" (Bonnemaison 1975:41). The elders or "bigmen" of a clan are the keepers of the powers of the *stamba* and will hold mastery over the ceremonies and other aspects of *kastom* required to maintain the integrity of the relationship between man and land.

In 1971, three prominent ni-Vanuatu formed the New Hebridean Culture Association, the aim of which was:

> To promote, to preserve, to revive and to encourage New Hebridean culture. To seek the advancement of the New Hebrideans socially, educationally, economically and politically in relation with New Hebridean culture and western civilization (Plant 1977:24).

These three were Walter Lini, who was subsequently elected Prime Minister for the first decade of independence after 1980, Donald Kalpokas, a cabinet minister since independence, and Peter Taurakoto, a former schoolteacher and subsequently General Manager of the National Tourism Office until his retirement in 1990.

Overt political parties were banned at the time by the colonial powers and the Culture Association provided both a cover and a forum for ni-Vanuatu to advance their interests. Developing cultural policies and attempting to educate the indigenous residents about issues such as land alienation and tourism and their impact on ni-Vanuatu and their customs was "safe" as culture not politics, but also central to the emerging identity of ni-Vanuatu. Because the Association advocated Melanesian culture and the welfare of the ni-Vanuatu it initially attracted only Melanesian membership and was subsequently branded as a racist organization by the colonial powers.

In a short space of time, however, the Culture Association became a political party, changing its name to the New Hebrides National Party and then localizing that to the *Vanuaku Pati* when the colonial powers decided to permit the formation of indigenous political parties (Kele-Kele 1977; Lini 1980). Its thrust moved more directly toward activist politics and the struggle for independence, yet it retained a strong cultural identity, a feature which has persisted throughout the past two decades to the present, with Lini and subsequent prime ministers and governments taking a direct interest in cultural affairs. The independence of Vanuatu was achieved in the name of *kastom* and land, and "the very word *kastom* [was] brandished as a rallying cry by the Government and all political parties" (Bonnemaison 1975:59) and even by Christian leaders who in the past had been energetic in suppressing it as pagan (Tonkinson 1982). Many ni-Vanuatu understood the end of colonial rule to mean that parallel to achieving political sovereignty would be the reclaiming of their traditional lands and return to their traditional places of origin incorporating the wider aspect of the so-called "doctrine of first appearance".

In the year before independence, the Vanuaku Party organized the first National Arts Festival (December 1979) as a means of reinforcing national identity (Ligo 1980). The festival has become a major event and is now integrated into the annual independence celebrations. It is against this background of rather more activist support for and maintenance of traditional culture by successive Vanuatu governments than some other governments of South Pacific countries that this chapter examines empowerment arising from ethnic tourism in Vanuatu.

The "Ghol" (Pentecost Land Dive)

Pentecost Island is about 200 km north of Port Vila (Figure 8.1). Its isolation has been a factor in the retention by a group of eight villages of the Sa people around Bunlap and Lonorore of a non-Christian, non-western way of life. So-called *kastom* groups such as the Kwaio of Malaita in Solomon Islands (Keesing and Corris 1980) and the "John Frum Movement" of Tanna in southern Vanuatu (Rice 1974; Steinbauer 1979) which have consciously resisted modernization are not uncommon in Melanesia. The traditionally oriented villages of South Pentecost Island are no exception.

These villages celebrate a particular ceremony each year in April/May in which specially selected initiates leap headfirst to the ground from a platform about 25 meters high, with vines lashed to their ankles so that their foreheads just brush the earth. Called the *ghol*, the ceremony is deeply rooted in legend and occupies the thoughts of those involved year-round. It is central to "an ensemble of indigenous ritual" performed in association with the yam harvest (Jolly 1982:352). It is believed that the quality of the current yam harvest will determine the safety and efficacy of the *ghol* and that a good yam harvest the next year is dependent on a successful *ghol*. Jolly states that "there is a metaphysical identity of men and yams and the ritual is a spectacle that is seen as a powerful statement of the strength and sanctity of men" (1982:353).

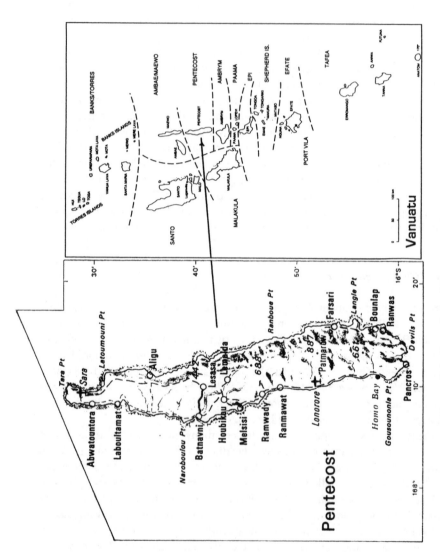

Figure 8.1: Location of Pentecost Island, Vanuatu
Source: Vanuatu National Tourism Office

The ceremonies are performed at the time of the year when the vines have the correct tensile strength to withstand the strain, with up to 30 "divers" participating in each jump.

The *ghol* is based on the legend of a woman who to avoid constant mistreatment by her husband, Tamalie, kept on running away but was always caught and forced back. On the last occasion she climbed to the top of a tall coconut palm tree to escape. As Tamalie climbed up after her, she jumped to the ground, got to her feet unharmed and dared her husband to follow her. Tamalie did so and plunged to his death, not realizing that his wife had tied jungle vines around her ankles before her leap which had broken her fall. Since that time the jump has been performed by males only from specially constructed towers.

The tower is an intricate piece of traditional engineering. While steel knives and axes have replaced stone tools to fell the trees, no modern materials such as nails, nylon rope or wire are used in the construction. The tower may be 12 meters wide at the base, tapering to about two meters wide at the top. The major "stress columns" are vertically positioned trunks braced horizontally around a central tree trunk, with branches stripped of their foliage and lashed together with vines. "Guy ropes" of liana vine take the strain, being fastened to nearby trees. Tower sections represent the human anatomy, each named after a part of the body beginning with the feet at the base to the crown of the head at the top. The whole tower is termed *tare be ghol* or the body, the internal struts and braces *lon te ghol*, the inside organs of the body. The central strut of each jutting platform is termed *utsin* or penis, and the side supports are *bwelan kenen* or labia. Each platform is supported by a branch designed to collapse when the vines are fully extended by the jumper's weight, thus helping to cushion his fall (personal communications, Kurt Huffman, Director, New Hebrides Cultural Center, 1980).

Each jumper must select his own vines with careful attention to his weight and size so that no other person may be held responsible for any mishap, or "spoil" the materials by invoking evil spirits. The supervisor of the construction of the tower has the supreme privilege of performing the last jump from the highest platform, or of granting the privilege to a brother or clan member.

When Jolly studied the Pentecost communities in 1981/82, the *ghol* ceremony was in danger of being taken over by European interests intent on exploiting its touristic appeal. This process had been in train for several years and it was the experience of this author when resident in Vanuatu in 1979 that arrangements for seeing the event were handled by two French entrepreneurs in Port Vila. Jolly considered that the Sa were being placed under pressure from tourism "whose great allure masks the risk of a rise of *kastom* (Bislama: "custom", traditional ways) as a commodity packaged for sale, and of the erosion of *kastom's* centrality as living practice" (1982:338). The traditionalist villagers were then "very ambivalent" about external interest in the rite: "They had also often been angered by the intrusive behavior of some European spectators." Jolly observed that there was evidence that some outside entrepreneurs intervened to ensure that the rite cosmetically conformed to their notions of *kastom*. She expressed concern that the villagers would not be able to make the final decision on tourism themselves, and that "tourism might prove a test case for the problem of reconciling the meanings of *kastom* as political symbol and as lived practice" (1982:353).

The Pentecost villagers would appear to have been affected at that time by what has been termed "psychic exploitation": within their limited spatial environment and among their small populations tourists become highly visible and often demanding. They may be perceived as intruders intent on manipulation (Farrell 1979:124). As Britton (1987a:175) noted, this problem is exacerbated in remote communities (such as those of South Pentecost) which have evolved a special cultural coherence with minimal western modernization since they can be more susceptible to outside change. Alienation between tourist and local will be more acute the greater the social and cultural distance between them. By 1980 the problems of Pentecost suggest the Sa communities had reached a level of social disruption where the perceived benefits of tourism were outweighed by the social costs (Murphy 1985).

In the early 1980s the people of Bunlap asserted their cultural ownership of the *ghol*, removing all elements of expatriate control (Bani 1989:7). For a short time they considered banning all outside observers. However, the monetary rewards of opening up the *ghol* and the concomitant access to consumer goods had exposed the traditional villagers to new forms of life, new standards of enjoyment and new possibilities of satisfaction (manifestations of the demonstration effect or Hoogvelt's (1986) new-want formation and social mobilization). As Jolly had noted in 1982, although the villagers appeared to be conscious of the cultural risks involved in the tourist industry, they were keen to make money in this way rather than by cash-cropping or wage labor (1982: 345). Further, de Burlo observed that the villagers recognized the dangers of tourism but continued "to embrace it as political capital in opposition to local Christian groups and as a symbol of their cultural identity as a community with traditional world view and practice" (1996:257). As inland people living away from the coast and its coconut plantations, the Sa people also had limited access to the cash economy, and tourism enabled men to stay at home and earn some cash while supporting *kastom* at the same time. These experiences modified the cognitive and attitudinal barriers of the traditional culture and promoted new levels of aspirations and wants.

In response to these tensions, discussions arose among the villagers as to how they might themselves be able to harness the proven attraction of their ceremony to produce an income for those needs requiring cash. The result was the formalization by the local "bigmen" of a group which Bani (1989) identified as "The South Pentecost Tourism Council" to manage the event in cooperation with tour operators in Port Vila. This title appears to have been bestowed by indigenous bureaucrats in Port Vila on the group of "bigmen" who historically have held responsibility for the event, because of the need of government to have an "official" point of contact. It appeared to have been accepted quite readily by the Sa people. The "bigmen's" primary responsibility is to safeguard the cultural integrity of the event. Their consequential task is to harness the appeal of the ceremony for community projects requiring cash inputs (Bani 1989).

Maintaining the cultural integrity of the event involves, *inter alia*, supervising preparatory rituals undertaken by the participants and *tabus* such as sexual abstinence and fasting, for the villagers believe that unless the ancestors are correctly propitiated the jumpers may be harmed and famine befall their communities. The spirit of Namalie is believed to reside in the tower until the ritual is complete, and other spirits invest the jump area. For these reasons the presence of women within about 20 meters of the tower is *tabu* (prohibited) at all times.

The "bigmen" have responsibility for consulting the ancestors to select the sites for the jumps. They determine how many there will be, who the participants will be, and on what days they will jump. Thus, in 1988 for example eight jumps were decreed by the ancestors, 15 men "dived" from each tower, and the *ghol* was performed for eight consecutive weeks from April through to May (Sofield 1991a).

In the context of earning income for the communities, the council of "bigmen" must consult the villagers to identify what facilities, equipment or other requirements are wanted. Having determined their cost, they can then decide how many tourists will be permitted to see the event and what "entrance fee" they will be charged to finance the approved community project(s). This fee also covers cameras and videos, which were initially banned.

This was so because, according to de Burlo (1996), the Sa had been exploited by journalists and film makers in the past who had sold the videos and photographs for profit without passing any of the proceeds back to the people. Bani (1989) suggested that the ban was imposed on grounds that potential customers might be lost by seeing the event beforehand and having no need to see the real thing. However, he also considered that this appeared to be a rationalization to a degree of a long-standing distaste by the villagers of past filming experiences where they considered they were made to perform "like animals" for the camera. Subsequently, cameras and videos were permitted but at a price: a camera may cost the tourist an additional $50, a video an additional $350.

The number of tourists to each "jump" is determined by the "bigmen's" views on how many people in a single group can be adequately educated about the event. Importance is placed on ensuring that they will understand and have sensitivity for the symbolic importance of the rite. This is an important change from the time when tourism for the event was controlled by non-Sa. Both Jolly and de Burlo indicated that in the early 1980s many tourists were unaware of the place of the ritual in the Sa culture and its links to the yam cycle, often thinking it was a male initiation ceremony.

In this context the council has two objectives to meet. First, tourists' actions must not be allowed to disrupt the *ghol* in any way: its cultural integrity must be maintained. Second, through understanding of the event the tourist will feel satisfied at the end of his trip: "quality of service" will have been provided (Bani 1989:12). This last may be interpreted as a manifestation of the traditional Melanesian contract of reciprocity in an exchange agreement; if the villager takes the tourists' money s/he has a responsibility to pay back something of equal value. The tourists' education in fact begins before leaving Port Vila, with a briefing provided by the Vanuatu Cultural Center. This not only provides information on the *ghol* but introduces the outsider to village protocol.

Concern about the absorptive capacity of the small village societies of South Pentecost to handle large numbers is very real, according to Bani (1989:12). In 1988, as noted, only 40 tourists were permitted to witness each jump. In 1989 there were four jumps and only 50 tourists per jump were admitted. In 1990 also only 50 tourists per jump were allowed. Fifty appears to have been accepted as the maximum number of tourists per ceremony although there are variations on occasions (Sofield 1991a).

Marketing, which is acknowledged by the Sa "bigmen" to be outside their area of expertise, has been subcontracted to the partly government-owned, fully indigenized agency, Tour Vanuatu. In 1983, as one of a series of measures designed to ensure a degree of control over the development of tourism and an element of local participation in the industry, the Vanuatu Government passed the Business Licence Act No. 25 which declared categories of businesses closed to non-citizens. Included were road transport operators (taxis and bus services) and tour agents and tour operators for domestic tours. The Government has a controlling 51 percent share holding in Tour Vanuatu with the remaining 49 percent being held by its ni-Vanuatu employees and members of the public. The company has its headquarters in Port Vila with about 30 staff and three branches on the outer islands of Tanna, Santo and Pentecost.

Each year, immediately after the meeting of the council which has decided on details of the forthcoming *ghol*, Tour Vanuatu is notified and a standing agreement for 3 percent commission is initialled. Tour Vanuatu then works with the National Tourism Office of Vanuatu to promote the event internationally (this was first carried out in 1988 and Gabriel Bani had responsibility for this task). Tour Vanuatu sells 50 percent of the tickets to overseas wholesalers. It packages groups of up to 50 tourists at a time, arranging air transport from Port Vila and lunch (overnight stays are not permitted except in very rare circumstances). The structure of the organization of the *ghol* is set out in Figure 8.2.

The financial success of the venture may be gauged by the fact that, since the Sa themselves took control of the touristic exploitation of the *ghol*, direct annual income for the villagers has exceeded $20,000. This is far in excess of previous earnings from the *ghol* and far more than was ever earned through sporadic copra cutting. Thus, in 1988 the 40 tourists to each of the eight jumps paid about $340 each for the privilege. Of this amount, $85 was the per person fee for entrance and photography and a total of $27,200 was paid direct to the Council. The rest of the package covered air fares, lunch and the 3 percent commission for Tour Vanuatu. In 1989 when 50 persons for four jumps were "admitted", the per capita entrance fee was $106, raising a total of $21,200 for community disbursement (Tour Vanuatu). The success of the *ghol* as an ethnic cultural attraction is indicated by the fact that all ceremonies to date have been fully subscribed and Tour Vanuatu holds bookings up to four years in advance.

Monetary rewards to most individuals of the Sa community are not great (social rewards are examined later). This is because traditionally their society demands a wide distribution of resources according to status, gender and the actual role of the individual in preparing for and participating in an event. Thus, virtually everybody except small children will receive a share of the tourist revenue. De Burlo (1987) recorded that women received $2–5, men $10–20, with larger sums for those who played specialist roles such as the man who "worked" the magic to ensure a successful *ghol*. According to Bani (1989), most of the money is put towards a community project or item, such as a cultural house.

In marketing terminology, the "unique selling proposition" of the *ghol* is the authenticity of the event which can only be guaranteed by control remaining in the hands of the Sa villagers of South Pentecost. Authenticity in this context is not to be equated with an absence of change or something that is preserved, rock-hard, by tradition. Innovation, adaptation and reinterpretation of cultural elements are constantly occurring even in those societies where tradition and heritage seem unchanging.

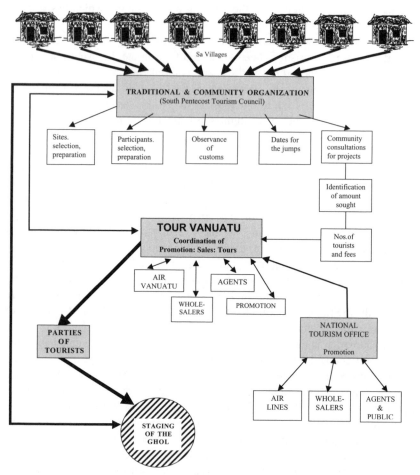

Figure 8.2: Organizational Structure of the *Ghol* (After Sofield 1991a)

The *ghol* is an example where the objectives of viable tourism, traditional culture and social values on the one hand and commercial gain on the other are not mutually exclusive. The villagers depend upon the tourists as their single greatest source of income, and the tourists depend upon the villagers to maintain the cultural integrity of the event. The conflict which Jolly perceived developing between the two groups more than a decade ago has been replaced by an alliance of common interest, a symbiotic relationship where both parties rely upon their ability to meet the needs of the other (Figure 8.3). In the context

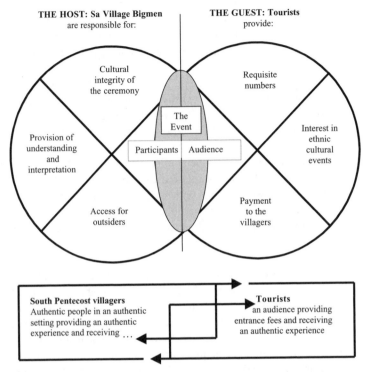

THE HOST: Sa Village Bigmen
are responsible for:

THE GUEST: Tourists
provide:

Cultural integrity of the ceremony

Requisite numbers

The Event

Participants | Audience

Provision of understanding and interpretation

Interest in ethnic cultural events

Access for outsiders

Payment to the villagers

South Pentecost villagers
Authentic people in an authentic setting providing an authentic experience and receiving ...

Tourists
an audience providing entrance fees and receiving an authentic experience

Figure 8.3: Symbiosis in Ethnic Tourism: the *Ghol* (after Sofield 1991a)

of the *ghol*, Budowski's (1977) concepts of conflict, coexistence and symbiosis can be seen not as distinctive circumstances but as a dynamic process in which the *ghol* as tourism has moved from the first to the third in a progression from disempowerment to empowerment. In the context of Ap's social exchange theory as applied to tourism, both hosts and guests receive "high" benefits and reciprocity is achieved in a situation of mutually balanced exchange. Emically the Sa actors perceive tourism in a positive light because of the perceived high level of rewards.

The Issue of Authenticity

In examining the sustainability of the *ghol* as ethnic tourism the issue of authenticity must be considered since it is argued that authenticity is a major determinant in the ability of the ceremony to endure as successful tourism. This concept, especially its relationship to tradition and cultural heritage, cannot be divorced from Sa concepts of power because so much of their capacity to dominate surrounding Christian communities is bound up in the *ghol.* It is the basis of their empowerment.

Authenticity is a problematic concept. MacCannell (1976) contends that all tourists seek authenticity: genuine, worthwhile and spontaneous experiences, even if they do not always find it. Urry (1990) challenges this and Pearce (1988) suggests that provided tourists placed a low value on authenticity they could still enjoy a cultural experience that was staged. Not all tourists would be upset and dissatisfied because of a perception that they had been manipulated to some extent. Indeed Boorstin suggested that mass tourism had spawned a new type of tourist who was satisfied with superficial and contrived experiences ("pseudo-events"), that authenticity had been compromised by commercialism to such an extent that the tourist seldom saw a living culture "but usually specimens collected and embalmed especially for him, or attractions especially staged for him" (1964:102).

Three particular aspects of authenticity — spatial, the actor, and behavior — may be considered as more relevant than others in looking at the *ghol.* The first is spatial: the dichotomy of "back" and "front" regions to explain guest/host social interaction as suggested by Goffman (1951). The front is the meeting place for guests and hosts characterized by a not-normal formality and artificiality. The back, by contrast, is the place not penetrated by the outsiders, where the residents relax and do "their own thing" away from prying eyes, where their behavior is "natural", and where they perform activities for reasons unassociated with and unaffected by an outside audience.

MacCannell (1976), expanding on the work of Goffman, constructed a continuum of six distinct physical stages for tourist settings, starting from the front and ending at the back, to analyze whether a tourist experience is indeed culturally authentic. It is always possible that what the tourist believes is entry into a back region is in fact entry into a front region which has been set up in advance to duplicate aspects of backstage reality especially for touristic visitation. Given the increasing sophistication of the contemporary tourist and the desire of many to avoid a plastic or artificial or commercialized experience, MacCannell considered that many tourists strove to get behind Goffman's front region because they knew that there they could not find authenticity. He identified "the artificial backstage" created specifically to deal with this eventuality; in reality a front region which has been totally organized to look like a back region and which provides simulations of "real" back region life or aspects of it.

A difficulty with MacCannell's schemata is that it is not always possible to distinguish clearly between his four intermediary stages and they tend to concentrate more on place-related environments rather than on the actors in the scene. Accordingly, Cohen (1979) reduced MacCannell's six stages to two, one "real" (analogous to Goffman's back region and MacCannell's three backstages) and one "staged" (analogous to Goffman's front region and MacCannell's three front stages) and looked at them from the tourist's point of view. He used the terms "overt tourist space" to describe the staging of an event in which the tourist was aware that it was being staged for his benefit; and "covert tourist space" when the fact that an event was made to appear real but was in actuality a packaged or artificial creation was disguised (1979:26).

Both MacCannell and Cohen emphasized the place more than the actor, so Pearce (1988) devised four authenticity "scenes" to put the emphasis equally on the actors, ranging from "authentic people in authentic environment, defined as backstage people in a backstage region" to "inauthentic people in authentic environment, defined as front stage people in a backstage region" (1988:180). This formulation still omitted the issue of whether behavior was authentic, so Pearce's spectrum was extended by Sofield to incorporate "authentic people in authentic environment carrying out authentic behavior, defined as backstage people in a backstage region engaged in backstage behavior" (Sofield 1991a:63–64).

As the *ghol* is staged at present, there is scant room to cast aspersions on its authenticity. It is unquestionably in Goffman's and MacCannell's back region, in Pearce's first scene and in Sofield's extension of Pearce's first scene. Arrangements especially and specifically for the small number of tourists permitted to enter the vicinity of a jumping tower are minimalist — a designated space is cleared for them (but it is part of the same cleared area used to accommodate the normal audience of villagers). Special arrangements are made for their lunch which is provided by the Tour Vanuatu agent, they are given a short guided tour of the immediate area and elders provide them with an explanation of the ceremony they are there to witness. No accommodation is provided. Tourists are admitted into the social space of the *ghol* where once there were only the villagers-as-participants. But this alien presence does not seem to have changed the ceremonial, behavior or activities of the people in any significant way. To all intents and purposes the *ghol* is performed as it always has been. Indeed it could be argued that the touristic element of the *ghol* is used both to bolster a traditional practice and traditional power structures in a contemporary setting and to challenge contemporary alternative authorities. The state plays a part in the maintenance of this traditional behavior through support for its touristic aspects.

Increasingly the Sa cannot maintain the isolation of past times. The regular influx of tourists, even though small in numbers, represents a new and systematic contextual, processural and comparative point of contact which inevitably influences the present. Out-migration for work, sickness and other reasons exposes individuals to other values, other ways of approaching issues and doing things. Change over time may be anticipated: but outside economic forces and values have not yet eroded the central significance of the yam and its harvest. The *ghol* is likely to continue for quite some time yet because in its present form it vests the Sa with a very real power. The social significance of that power cannot be lightly dismissed.

An Exercise in Power and Empowerment

For Sa traditionalists *kastom* is enduring and powerful, tying them to their place of origin. They describe themselves and their *kastom* as being imbued with power (Bani 1989; de Burlo 1996; Jolly 1982, 1994). The *ghol* is both a source of power for Sa traditionalists generically and it may bestow power on those individuals participating, especially men. Its characteristic of empowerment is derived from two main intertwining elements: its association with secret and sacred knowledge and its association with place (the doctrine of first appearance). As Tonkinson (1982) observed, secret or unshared knowledge is at the heart of Melanesian concepts of power. "Such esoteric knowledge separates groups and individuals and becomes the basis for political competition. Traditionally, Melanesian 'bigmen' are leaders who are able to convince others of their power by successfully staging rituals which depend upon knowing and correctly using powerful knowledge" (de Burlo 1996:269). In South Pentecost men who know how to construct and perform the *ghol* are regarded as "hot" with the power of sacred *kastom* knowledge (de Burlo 1996; Sofield 1991a).

This knowledge is bound up in their myths and legends which contain an element of ideology. It is "a social charter that ensures the existing form of society with its system of distributing power, privilege and property" (Malinowski 1948:61). It has "a justificatory function that the guardians of tradition and the controllers of political apparatus know how to exploit" (Balandier 1970a:33). Ritual may play a similar role, "when for example the rituals are exclusively (in the case of cults and procedures concerning kingship) or inclusively [in the case of ancestor worship] the sacred instruments of power" (Balandier 1970a:34). In other words, power emanating from and through the *ghol* combines both the sacred (religious through ancestor worship) and the political in the Durkheimian sense: power is sacrality because the maintenance of order within Sa society rests on the dual basis and the one cannot be divorced or viewed in isolation from the other (de Burlo 1996). This power is not isolated around the *ghol* but extends to all areas of tradition with sacred connotations such as yam cultivation and pig-killing "grade" ceremonies. The latter are common throughout much of central and northern Vanuatu and involve men gaining entry to a higher status or grade "by the performance of ritual based on the sacrifice of pigs, the transfer of payments for insignia and services, and the performances of elaborate dances" (Allen 1981:24). As individuals move up the grade ladder they achieve higher degrees of supernatural power which can then be translated into secular power over other men. In the same way, Jolly (1994) suggested, the *ghol* uses height as a metaphor of the power of men.

The Sa people have used the power of *kastom* to resist the European colonization which began in the 18th century and dispossessed people of their lands for plantations in the 19th century, Christian missions, the colonial regime, and other externally-directed agents of change (modernization). As a community they have demonstrated an ideological commitment to *kastom* as a way of life and source of identity in an increasingly diverse cultural landscape inhabited by a range of disparate and competing ideologies. They have used the *kastom* of the *ghol* as tourism to assert their power and independence from all of these forces.

The Catholic Church was the first to establish a mission station in the area in 1906 and the Church of Christ followed with an aggressive dogma of strong opposition to all traditional beliefs and practices. At times the churches and the colonial administration combined to combat perceptions of a resurgence in traditional practices. In 1952, for example, the Catholic Church in South Pentecost persuaded the colonial government that an indigenous social movement was being fomented and five Sa leaders were arrested (Tonkinson 1982). Jolly (1994) noted that Court records revealed that the five were released on the intervention of the French Resident Commissioner on condition that they would organize a performance of the *ghol* (presumably so that the authorities could see for themselves that it was not in any way an uprising).

Jolly (1994) recorded that the Sa people used the occasion to compose a new song for the jump in their own language, ridiculing the French Resident Commissioner who thought he was powerful but lacked the power of the *ghol*. According to Jolly, for the Sa people the episode reinforced for them their view of the power of *kastom* to challenge both the Christian churches (whose original allegations were proved false), and the power of the colonial regime (since it was specifically the *ghol* which had led to the release of their leaders).

This story is often told in conjunction with another relating to the injury of a jumper whose liana vines broke at a *ghol* performed by the Point Cross

Melanesian Mission for a visit by Queen Elizabeth II in 1972. In the retelling and mythologizing of the incident the man is now recorded as having died with a broken neck. *Kastom* people assert that the accident happened because the Christians did everything the wrong way, having lost the skills and the magic powers necessary for a successful performance of the *ghol*. These stories are still repeated today and have become symbols of the active power of *kastom* over outside entities (Kalpokas, personal communication). In the words of de Burlo the *ghol* "acts as an arena for contesting ideological truths in the political landscape" (1996:266).

Independence in 1980 bestowed a new legitimacy on *kastom* and the *ghol*. As a matter of pre-eminent public policy *kastom* as a unifying force for the nation suddenly attained positive values that had been denied by the colonial regime and opposed by the churches. The author experienced this negativism towards *kastom* in 1979 when the colonial powers would not underwrite costs associated with the Vanuatu Cultural Center. The Vanuaku Pati, leading the struggle for independence, used the Center to promote its cultural policies. It was the only indigenous institution operating in cultural affairs, and it often found itself competing against the combined efforts of the Alliance Française and the British Council, both of which were promoting their own cultures and which, together with the Christian missions, controlled the school curricula. As then Australian Consul to Vanuatu, the author persuaded the Australian Government to provide the necessary funding under the (Australian) South Pacific Cultures Fund to keep the Center operating prior to independence. This was achieved against protests from several of the churches and the French Resident Commissioner (the British Resident Commissioner took no sides in the issue).

For the Sa people, the politicization of culture was particularly important (de Burlo 1996). After independence their sustained maintenance of tradition became a matter of increased pride and gave them additional power over the neighboring Christian communities because the *ghol* served as a national marker of traditional culture both internally in Vanuatu and externally ("marker" as defined by MacCannell 1976).

The use of the *ghol* for tourism also exemplified traditional Sa community empowerment in several contexts. At one level it reinforced their sense of superiority (and therefore power) over tourists. All Europeans were regarded as "weak" because they lacked an attachment to place and its sacred powers: they were *aisalsaliri*, "the floating ones". But tourists, *aituristiri*, "by being even more rootless wanderers adrift from the power of place" were the weakest of all (Jolly 1994:133). For the Sa, the superior power of the *ghol* is evidenced by its capacity to attract tourists from all over the world to come to far-distant Pentecost and part with thousands of dollars just to get a glimpse of *kastom* in operation.

At another level, the *ghol* as tourism is used to demonstrate superiority over the nearby Christian communities whose loss of *kastom* knowledge and inability to perform the *ghol* is derided by the traditionalist Sa people (Bani 1989; de Burlo 1996). When the Christian communities in South Pentecost do mount a *ghol* (as occurs from time to time when they decide they would also like to benefit from the cash flow generated by ethnic tourism) they can only do so with the assistance of the experts in *kastom*. This aspect transforms *kastom* into a political resource (Greenwood 1989) and provides political power and economic advantage to the traditionalist Sa over the Christian settlements. "Tourism has become a stage for the *kastom* people to define and uphold tradition" (de Burlo 1996:273) as the keepers of the authentic, and thus a symbol of their resistance to the Christian missions and the forces of modernization.

At yet another level, the fact that the *ghol* has become an ethnic and political marker for the nation as a whole has gained esteem for the Sa people which translates into power for the men in charge of the *ghol*. This is because the ability to organize successful rituals with large numbers of participants and spectators is an accepted pathway to "bigman" status in Melanesia. Therefore, it is a symbol of the superiority of their *kastom* and a derivative of perceived superiority over other linguistic groups within Vanuatu.

Finally, for the Sa people, "tourism that relies on *kastom* provides a new strategy to sustain the active resistance to outside influences the *kastom* people have chosen for themselves" (de Burlo 1996:271). Rather than erecting an impervious barrier to keep unwanted influences out, the Sa traditionalists, like the Amish of North's 1992 study, have actively sought to bring tourists into their spatial environment, thus empowering the Sa in a variety of ways and reinforcing the values they consider necessary to counter the "false" ways of modernization.

This author has called this "cultural durability", a term to incorporate a concept about the sustainability of natural environments from Koslowski (1985), which has then been applied to ethnic tourism. Koslowski developed his "Ultimate Environmental Threshold Model" with key indicators to evaluate biophysical areas to be targeted or avoided for tourism development. One of his key elements is *fragility*, that is, an ability to resist destructive effects and to self-generate to a relatively unchanged state. This has much in common with the concept of *irreversibility*, a situation where events are set in train which result in the loss of aspects of an environment (Hare 1990).

A set of sensitive social indicators to replace Koslowski's biophysical indicators could be adapted for application to ethnic tourism, a key one of which would be the capacity to maintain ownership over traditional activities and prevent their exploitation and modification for commercial or other ends by outside agents. In a model for sustainable ethnic tourism, the ability to preserve authenticity and to resist negative influences such as acculturation (including the demonstration effect), modernization, and commoditization would be of fundamental importance. *Stamba* where control and authority are exercised might constitute the social and physical space upon which this cultural durability could be constructed. Hence, cultural durability is applied to describe the way in which the Sa have been able to withstand unwanted western values and practices (Sofield 1991a).

Empowerment and Sustainable Ethnic Tourism

The sharp edges around the ownership, organization and marketing of the *ghol* provide an opportunity to examine principles of empowerment underlying the sustainability of this example of ethnic tourism. Two major elements immediately present themselves; the role of indigenous ownership and control in the cultural authenticity of an event, and a government with policies and other structures (such as legislation) in place which will support and maintain the phenomenon. As noted, the notion of "bottom-up" (community) input and "top-down" (government) input are essential in sustainable development.

Indigenous ownership and control is absolutely fundamental to empowerment in terms of cultural or ethnic tourism. However, it needs to be said that indigenous ownership will not necessarily or automatically ensure the maintenance of historical or traditional forms of cultural expression (often synonymous in the literature with authenticity: but as argued, change does not necessarily lead to inauthenticity). In other countries the desire to maximize financial returns has sometimes led to the indigenous people themselves taking the lead in making changes to their traditional practices and performances, responding to what they perceive the tourist might prefer.

For example, in the Cook Islands, where traditionally women's dances were much more sedate than those of the menfolk (in many dances they sat rather than stood, and only the upper parts of their bodies were involved together with graceful arm and hand movements), they now gyrate with as much if not more vigor than the men. Troupe leaders were quick to notice that they attracted greater audiences to their floor shows when their female dancers complied with the South Seas stereotype of vigorously swaying hula hips (see Syme 1980 for a satirical cameo by a Cook Islander on tourism in Rarotonga).

If indigenous ownership and control might not ensure traditional expression it may nevertheless contribute to the survival of a traditional practice albeit in a new form. Thus, fire-walking in Fiji, once exclusively magico-religious and sacred in nature, has been effectively secularized. It is tourism that has provided a reason for the skills of fire-walking to be reconstituted after its banning by missionaries more than 100 years ago, even if the presentational context of those skills has changed (Sofield 1992, 1996). The touristic element of *vilavilairevo* (fire-walking) has been condemned by some Fiji commentators as crass commoditization with tourism as the perpetrator of the crime (Prasad 1987). Yet while the magico-religious elements of former times may be absent, "jumping into the oven" remains "an act of solidarity with one's community and an exhibition of loyalty and obedience to one's chief", thus reinforcing fundamental aspects of Fijian society (Stymeist 1996:16). An emic approach to fire-walking, focusing on actor-oriented, culture-specific values will reveal that the Fijian participants regard fire-walking in a positive way. Contemporary Fijian fire-walking may be regarded as "reconstructed ethnicity" which is the maintenance and preservation of ethnic forms for the entertainment of ethnically different others (MacCannell 1994). Such reconstructed ethnicity is not necessarily less authentic than "natural" ethnicity.

Papson (1981) might argue that such staging was spurious. One would suggest that because it retains a degree of authenticity, it is not spurious reality but "new reality" (which would classify it as a modified example of Sofield's (1991a) second tourist scene — that is, authentic people in an inauthentic environment engaged in a derived authentic activity). The original reason and magico-religious validity for the ceremony being performed may have disappeared; the motivation of the participants has certainly changed; and the form which the ceremony takes in contemporary Fiji may be different from the historical original; but it remains undeniably Fijian (and thus "authentic") and a vivid example of the fact that culture is not static but dynamic and changing (Sofield 1992).

There are also instances where authenticity in terms of place may not be necessary to sustain ethnic tourism. Brigham University's "Polynesian Cultural Center" at Laie, Hawaii, is often quoted as a successful reconstruction of traditional architecture and lifestyles displayed for tourism. It is the second most visited attraction in Hawaii. It is owned and operated by the University, providing employment for some of its Pacific Islander students (van Haarsel 1988:243). The Center itself is artificial, consisting of several reconstructed Polynesian village houses, each depicting the indigenous culture of a different people. There one may see indigenous Samoans, dressed traditionally, making tapa cloth by traditional methods using traditional materials outside a traditional Samoan *fale* (house) — but constructed on foreign (Hawaiian) soil, their authentic behavior occurring in a front stage environment.

As a tourist product, the Polynesian Cultural Center successfully meets the criteria for cultural and financial sustainability even if its American management is sometimes culturally insensitive and it falls short of authenticity. In the words of Pere, the Center originally commercialized culture but is now "quietly culturizing commerce" (1980:145). If authenticity as demonstrated by the *ghol* is to be sustained, however, then indigenous ownership and control is fundamental.

The second major element, government support, will also be crucial as to whether ethnic tourism is sustainable: without it empowerment is unlikely to be achieved in an enduring way. Middleton has noted that while it was "theoretically possible that the commercial sectors of the tourist industries . . . could contribute to enhancing cultural provision through the adoption of altruistic objectives and strategies in tune with the long term cultural benefit of host communities, in practice this was unlikely to happen" (1990:5). Commercial objectives and profit in most instances would not be in tune with the spirit of long-term commitments to the preservation and development of living national cultures for their own sake and as a source of national identity and pride. He suggested that it was even more unlikely that individual commercial decisions, presumably even if empathetic towards cultural integrity, would have any significant impact unless coordinated nationally. His conclusion was that the Tourism Council of the South Pacific and member governments had "an inescapable" policy role in this context (Middleton 1990:5).

Harnessing the tourist potential of culture for financial reward is not suggested as a major justification for mounting efforts to maintain and preserve traditional culture in the South Pacific (or indeed anywhere else). The primary justification for that rests in the fundamental contribution that traditional practices make to the social fabric and community structures of the peoples in each country. However, throughout most of the South Pacific region where many elements of traditional culture remain strong and vibrant, the potential exists to access tourist revenue both to promote and support community values and culture as well as to assist in attaining national economic objectives. In the case of the Sa villages, the pursuit of power over adjacent Christian communities and power to withstand pressures of modernization and externally directed change have played a significant role in utilizing the *ghol* for tourism. Economic exploitation is only one motive albeit an important one in the presentation of the ceremony for tourists.

As Middleton observed, provision for residents and tourists for cultural experiences may exist side by side and

> no major economic activity other than tourism can provide this community-wide synergy of interests. Indeed, the opportunity

for visitors to share in the experience of cultural provision with residents is especially attractive to growing numbers of potential visitors who will not be satisfied with artificial or bogus experiences put together solely as commercial products for their entertainment (1990:9).

In Vanuatu, the government's role has been crucial for the Pentecost *ghol*, in two main areas. The first is by its public policies of support for *kastom*. These have been supported with legislation, specifically the 1982 National Tourism Office Act (which provided a mandate for the office to promote and assist in the development of ethnic tourism) and the 1983 Business Licence Act. The second area is in direct assistance with the marketing of the *ghol*, and illustrates one of the most difficult problems for village-based tourism in the South Pacific — the lack of visibility. Villagers may have the product but usually lack the means, both technical and financial, to establish a presence in the market place. To distribute just one color brochure to the 6000 travel agencies in Australia and New Zealand would cost $10,000, for example.

The willingness of both the Vanuatu National Tourism Office and Tour Vanuatu to assist in marketing, advertising, promotions and sales, the former as part of its free services to indigenous tourism ventures and the latter for a non-commercial commission well below the going rates of between 20 and 30 percent, are critical to the success of the *ghol* in attracting customers and providing access to tourists. The Vanuatu Government is able to get back a little through its ownership of Air Melanesie (access to Pentecost is by air from Bauerfield in Vila to the grass strip at Lonorore) but it receives no taxes or other income from its support for the event except its 51 percent share of the 3 percent commission paid to Tour Vanuatu. In effect there is a disguised subsidy to the Sa people.

The enactment of the localization legislation of 1983 reinforced the ability of the South Pentecost villagers to control the *ghol* for tourism purposes and indirectly encouraged the establishment of the South Pentecost Tourism Council by creating a climate for greater indigenous participation in Vanuatu's tourism industry. It is now no longer possible for non-nationals to take control of the performance as a touristic event. Rival Pentecost groups could however attempt to utilise the *ghol* for their own advantage, as has already occurred.

In summary, the Vanuatu Government has made a critical contribution to the sustainability of the *ghol* as an ethnic tourist experience by a series of empowering actions: public policies of support for *kastom*; enabling legislation in support of those policies; direct assistance through government agencies such as the National Tourism Office and Tour Vanuatu, such as in marketing and promotion of the *ghol*, the sale of tours in Port Vila and through Air Vanuatu; and generalized assistance in creating a climate of support for ni-Vanuatu culture and localized ownership of tourism ventures.

The "top-down" process of government legislative action and policies created the necessary environment of active support for the maintenance of tradition and *kastom* which allowed the South Pentecost venture to flourish from the "bottom-up" (see Figure 8.4). It is this combination which, it is argued, is an imperative if empowerment is to be achieved by village communities in their attempts to establish viable tourism ventures.

The South Pentecost example of "top down–bottom up" integration is not to be confused with the "top-down" planning which may involve "bottom-up" consultations as espoused by the WTO and others referred to in Chapter 3 because it has moved beyond rhetoric and consultations of rationalization to implementation. It should also to be noted that, unlike the situation in Solomon Islands, there has been a concerted effort by the Vanuatu Government to ensure that the rhetoric of policy is matched by effective action. The implementation gap, so much a feature of the Solomon Islands situation, has been countered. Empowerment has been real rather than illusory.

The organization of the *ghol* points to a number of other principles for empowerment in sustaining ethnic tourism that may have application beyond the specificity of South Pentecost. They are not "stand-alone" generators but are linked in a complex network of mutually reinforcing relationships. They include, first, indigenous ownership and, second, indigenous control through an appropriate structure. Both provide the greatest assurance of maintaining cultural authenticity by *inter alia* supporting traditional leadership roles. Both are based on the third principle, community support, which supplies acceptable consultative and decision making processes, without which the venture as a tourism attraction would wither.

A fourth principle is that within the community there will be mechanisms for ensuring that younger generations learn the skills to perform in the future. This is necessary to address the concept of inter-generational equity that is central to sustainability. The village communities of South Pentecost contain such culturally-directed measures not only for the *ghol* but for the totality of ritual of which the *ghol* is but one ceremony. Fifth, priority is accorded to cultural integrity over commercialism by the owners of the cultural property so that commercial considerations are woven into and around traditional requirements, rather than becoming imperatives which could dominate and thus change elements of authenticity. Sixth, in South Pentecost this approach finds expression in pride in one's own culture, which reinforces "doing things the right (or traditional) way". It manifests itself in a willingness to share the value

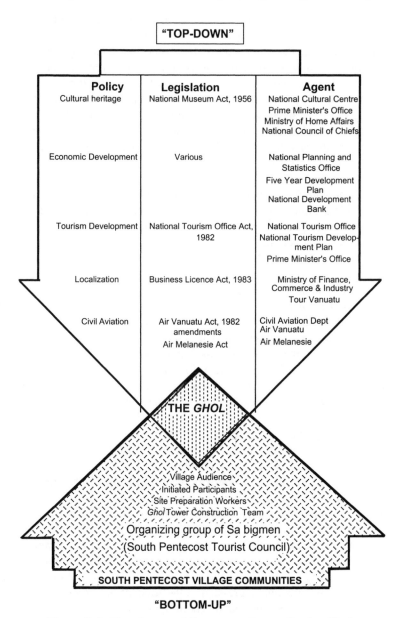

Figure 8.4: Top-down and Bottom-up Inputs for the *Ghol*
(After Sofield 1991a)

of the cultural entity concerned with sensitive outsiders, or the educative element, demonstrating its worth in the eyes of both the owners and the onlookers. Seventh, the other side of the "educative coin" encompasses the responsibility of the tourist to be informed about the event so that s/he will know how to behave in the cross-cultural contact situation and not break *tabus*.

Another (eighth) principle concerns carrying capacity, that is, tight control over the size of the audience (smallness) and the time spent at the site assists the community's absorptive capacity in managing tourism and the influx of strangers into the private space of their tribal territory. This results in a degree of exclusivity. This latter characteristic although not essential enhances the appeal of an event and hence its marketability.

Cultural durability is a ninth principle necessary to sustain ethnic tourism. It is evident in the *ghol* as it contributes to maintaining authenticity and resisting negative influences such as acculturation (including the demonstration effect), modernization, and commoditization.

A tenth principle is that there needs to be government policies and structures of support, as noted above. Eleventh, an ethnic cultural performance must be an intrinsically interesting or spectacular event. Cultural gaps can be so wide in some instances that the event may be incomprehensible or boring or both, and thus difficult to stage successfully to touristic outsiders. If interesting, it will have marketable qualities essential to the twelfth principle, the capacity to attract a financial return. Without some remuneration, the rationale for continuation of a *commercial* ethnic tourism venture is lost and the participants are likely to lose interest. While the *ghol* has been exploited for tourism it is fundamentally a *cultural* phenomenon whose continued existence is not of course predicated on tourism.

A thirteenth principle is that there needs to be an equitable/acceptable system for distribution of rewards among the community. Such a system is necessary to minimize internal conflict which could disrupt the continued staging of the event for tourism purposes. A final (fourteenth) principle is that through the staging of an event there should be the reinforcement of cultural values which bring social rewards. This is particularly important in the Melanesian-oriented world-view of the Sa people.

To briefly return to the four fundamentals of sustainable development, one finds that the *ghol*-as-tourism reflects all of them in a quadripartite integration. Economic benefits are generated through the commercialization of the ceremony. Social elements find expression in the solidarity of community and the participation of all community members in the staging of the *ghol*. The traditional heritage of the Sa people that is manifested in the *ghol* contributes to cultural sustainability. As a major component of a world-view of cyclical regeneration of nature and man, the *ghol* is also a manifestation of environmental values and sustainability.

Conclusion

The fieldwork of Jolly (1982, 1994), Bani (1989) and de Burlo (1996), supported by the earlier work of Tonkinson (1982), constitutes an excellent basis for understanding emic traditional manifestations of power in the Melanesian society of the Sa people. As an example of an ethnic tourism venture in Vanuatu, the *ghol* of South Pentecost has provided a window through which the notion of empowerment leading to sustainable ethnic tourism may be examined. It is an instance of a traditionally oriented community located in the social and political space of a modern state where empowerment embedded in Weber's traditional or legitimate base has been transformed into legally sanctioned empowerment by the state. Legal empowerment has not replaced legitimate empowerment: rather the two forms of empowerment coexist in a symbiotic relationship in which they are mutually supportive and reinforcing. The conditions for the "environmental change" deemed necessary for enduring empowerment by Wallerstein and Bernstein (1988) occurred with the attainment of independence in 1980.

It is necessary to distinguish between empowerment in the traditional milieu which the people of the *ghol* have been able to attain, and which provided them with the capacity to stand against the directions of change that the missions and the colonial regimes wished to impose, and the empowerment which the *ghol* as tourism has brought. The latter has been possible largely because of the involvement of the state in the context of the suggestion quoted earlier by Craig and Mayo that "Without engaging with the state and with political processes at different levels, localized community actions risk remaining marginalized, if occasionally incorporated" (1995:9–10).

The *ghol* exhibits the necessary qualities of community consensus and support (bottom-up input) working within an environment provided by the government which reinforces and encourages that community effort (top-down input). An outcome of empowerment of and by the dual system is that of ownership and control remaining in the hands of the local community. This ensures maintenance of the cultural integrity of the event and the power-and-sacrality that is derived from those traditional links with place and ancestors. It is also crucial to the establishment of a symbiotic relationship between host and guest, since the tourist is dependent upon the villager for ensuring authenticity of the event and the villager is dependent upon the tourist for ensuring a cash income for the community.

It is suggested that the case study of the *ghol* of South Pentecost supports all five propositions about empowerment, with particular emphasis on the third and fourth propositions; the third, that traditional empowerment must be transformed into legal empowerment if sustainable tourism development is to be achieved; and the fourth, that empowerment for such communities will usually require environmental or institutional change to allow a genuine reallocation of power to ensure appropriate changes in the asymmetrical relationship of the community to the wider society.

Chapter 9

Sustainability Through Empowerment and an Adaptive Response: Mana Island Resort, Fiji

This chapter examines a resort development in Fiji, Mana Island Resort, which was leased from its traditional Fijian landowners from the village of Yaro on adjacent Malolo Island, opened in 1972 and entered an expansionary phase in the 1990s. The sustainability of this resort is explored in the context of two particular elements: traditional land rights and the role of the Fiji Government in empowering customary landowners, and the actions of the landowners themselves in pursuing their own rights. To set the scene, details of Fiji's traditional land tenure system, its social structure, chiefly system and relationship to the land are probed. Further, contemporary institutions with responsibility for adjudication over transactions involving customary owned land, the Native Lands Commission and the Native Lands Trust Board are outlined. The development of Mana Island Resort is described and issues of empowerment through adaptation are analyzed. Finally, comparisons and contrasts are drawn with the case of Anuha Island Resort in Solomon Islands (Chapter 7) which collapsed within six years.

Customary Land Tenure in Fiji

In Fiji all land was originally owned under the descent group structure of the traditional tribal hierarchy (Larmour, Crocombe, and Taungenga 1981). There are presently three categories of land ownership: Freehold Land, Crown Land and Native Land. The first is owned by individuals and can be bought and sold at will. Freehold Lands comprise 8.3 percent of Fiji's total land area of 1.8335 million hectares and include some of the most productive agricultural land in the country. Much of it was alienated prior to cession in 1874 for European settler plantations. Crown Land comprises 8.7 percent of the total land area and is owned by the government. It includes traditionally owned lands which have reverted to the government *ultimus haeres* due to the extinction of the original landowning clan or *mataqali* (Ward 1982). Native Land comprises 82.9 percent of the total land area and belongs to the Fijian people at the clan level.

The family unit in Fiji is termed *tokatoka*. A number of *i-tokatoka* (families) linked through kinship ties will constitute a *mataqali* (clan). Individuals will often be referred to by their *mataqali* membership rather than their *tokotoka*. *Mataqali* will be grouped together to form a larger unit called the *yavusa* which was traditionally composed of six *mataqali* tracing lineage to a common ancestor, and spatially forming a village. On top of the basic social structure a higher order of grouping occurs. A number of *yavusa* occupying a recognized territory will form a communal political unit called a *vanua* (Figure 9.1). Several *yavusa* might combine to recognize the chief of the largest or most significant of their number as head of a *vanua*. This latter is thus a political association as distinct from the smaller units that are based on kinship ties (Routledge 1985). To the Fijian, the word *vanua* has physical, social, religious and cultural connotations. It is an all-encompassing term signifying "the people, their land, their sea and their culture" and thus emphasizes the integrity of the whole (Sawailau 1989:3).

All of these groupings will occupy land, but it is the *mataqali* category of land ownership that is enshrined in contemporary law. In 1877, three years after signing the deed by which the Great Council of Chiefs ceded Fiji to the United Kingdom, the Council advised the Crown that the *mataqali* be nominated as the legally recognized land owning unit. In the more isolated parts of rural Fiji individual forms of ownership, known as *kovukovu*, *ketekete* and *kawa* are recognized socially and informally. These "have no legal standing however and have become an ever increasing cause of land disputes and misunderstandings" (Eaton 1988:47).

It is debatable whether the *mataqali* held such a pivotal position over individual ownership rights or wider *yavusa* rights in pre-contact times. This was because traditionally the *yavusa* was accorded the role of the basic social unit, all members of which claimed descent from a common legendary founder. Ideally the *yavusa* was coextensive with the village and consisted of six *mataqali* organized in two sets of three and functioning in two distinct ways. In the first instance the *mataqali* were concerned with aspects of everyday living such as owning and cultivating land and using its family units, *i-tokatoka*, to organize activities on a cooperative basis. The second role of the *mataqali* concerned their responsibility for ritual and ceremonial functions within the village and for those extending beyond the village associated with such activities as war (such as food-bearing or weapon-bearing), where they represented the *yavusa* (Nayacakolou 1975; Seemann 1862; Williams 1858).

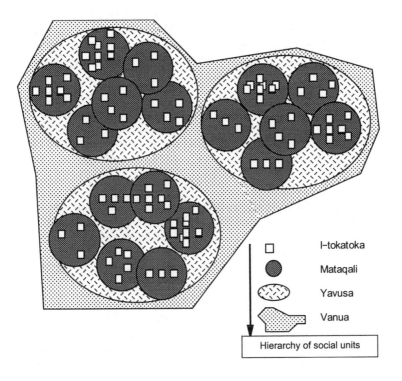

Key
i-tokatoka	=	the basic family units
mataqali	=	the basic land owning group or clan composed of numbers of *itokatoka* linked through kinship ties
yavusa	=	traditionally composed of six *mataqali* tracing lineage to a common ancestor, spatially forming a village
vanua	=	a political grouping of several *yavusa* occupying a recognized territory

Figure 9.1: Idealized Socio-political Structure of Traditional Fijian Society

As Routledge noted, this model is rarely seen in Fiji today:

The "perfect" arrangement of one *yavusa* to one village is a non-existent ideal. Simple fluctuations in population necessitated the occupation of new villages or the abandonment of old, with corresponding effect upon *yavusa*, *mataqali* and *i-tokatoka* alike. Quarrels among *mataqali*, particularly over ceremonial matters, resulted in the break-up of *yavusa* and the fortunes of war (in pre-contact times) caused them to be conquered and dismembered. . . . *Yavusa*, like larger scale units, existed within the context of political processes. They were power constructs articulated by the continual exercise of force (1985:28–29).

In fact the *mataqali* was only one of several Fijian social institutions with formal responsibilities over land. Reshaping society in Fiji, like many societies elsewhere, was often a matter of political processes and power plays. Routledge, citing Nation (1978) and Quain (1948) noted that not only are *yavusa* and *mataqali*

not universally occurring groups having the same purpose but that the nature of their existence differs widely from one part of Fiji to another. Even the reality of blood relationship was unnecessary, as an ideology of common descent could be constructed in order to define a link between different peoples (1985:29).

Traditional power in contemporary Fiji derives in a large part from land ownership, which is asserted through ancestral settlement (which had often been achieved by conquest) and through which chiefly lineages seek to bolster their legitimacy and their status. Competing claims over the generations have led to a certain dynamism in the land tenure system which is reflected in changes recorded by the Native Lands Commission over the past 100 years.

This dynamism continues in a new form into current times. As land which once held little commercial value has become of value in the monetized economy of the 21st century, especially those lands which have become tourism sites or have the potential for development, so some indigenous claims have been pursued vigorously against other Fijians. While "traditional rights" might be the catch-cry for action, it has been land as a tourism resource leading to potential wealth which has been the underlying impetus for a number of land claims (for example, over the now defunct Korolevu airfield which used to service the resorts along the Coral Coast of Viti Levu; or the west coast beach of Lomawai).

Even land over which title may have been extinguished many years ago through alienation or sale and validated through the legal system and the constitution of Fiji, has been subject to resurrected claims against the current owners. This has been especially so of any such lands for which title is held by non-Fijians, as with foreign investment in islands and resorts. Prior to the military coup of 1987 indigenous Fijian rights were pursued through civil unrest led by the Taukei Movement (literally, "Original Landowners" Movement) which feared that an Indo-Fijian dominated government might erode its traditional land rights. The whole issue of Fijian land rights was one of a number of key elements leading to that coup. With the most recent coup in May 2000, also against an Indo-Fijian dominated government, fear of loss of traditional land rights was again a motivating factor. As part of the unrest associated with this coup, at least four island resorts (two of them owned by US investors, one of them the famous Turtle Island Resort) were invaded in July 2000 by groups of Fijians attempting to reassert ownership. In each case the rule of law upheld the title rights of non-Fijian owners, but the contemporary invasions of 2000 may at one level be likened to the traditional method of expanding land holdings by conquest. In short, land rights remain a very live issue in contemporary Fiji.

The Chiefly Structure of Malolo

The village of Yaro is comprised of three *i-tokatoka*: Nacavacola (previously called Nacavamate), Nabukelevu, and Bua. They comprise the *mataqali* Ketenamasi of Yaro which together with the adjacent village of Solevu make up the *yavusa* Lawa. The *yavusa* Lawa, and three other *yavusa* from Malolo make up the *Vanua* of Malolo (Figure 9.2).

In the Mamanucas, the *i-tokatoka* will have their own *ratu* (a senior chief and minor chiefs) and the *mataqali* will have a *turanga* (head chief) chosen by the *ratu i-tokatoka*. The *yavusa* has a *Tui* (paramount chief) as its leader. In 1994 the position of *Tui Lawa* (paramount chief of the *Vanua* of Malolo) was drawn from the chiefs of Yaro. Each person occupying a chiefly position will carry the generic title of *Ratu* preceding his/her name, with the specific title added as a descriptor.

In 1995 the *turanga mataqali* of Yaro was Ratu Jeremiah Matai. The three senior chiefs of the three *i-tokatoka* of Yaro Village were:

I-tokatoka	Chief
Nacavacola	Ratu Ponipate (the most senior of all Yaro *ratu*)
Bua	Ratu Jonah Naivalu
Nabukelevu	Ratu Akuila Koroi

There are also minor chiefs in each *tokatoka*, and playing a pivotal role in the development of Mana Island was a minor chief from the *tokatoka* Nabukelevu, Ratu Kiniboko.

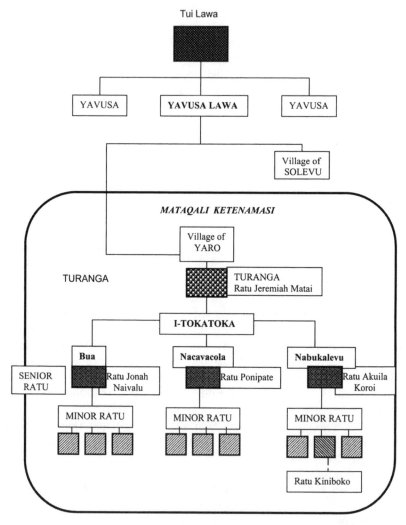

Figure 9.2: Schematic Representation of the Chiefly System of Malolo, 1996

The Native Lands Commission

The colonial Administration established the Native Lands Commission in 1878. It was tasked with the identification of all the landowner members of each *mataqali* and the demarcation of the physical boundaries of the 6000 or more *mataqali* land holdings. As in the case of Solomon Islands Lands Commission, the Fiji Native Lands Commission was in part a protective measure to prevent wholesale alienation of indigenous lands by non-Fijians, predominantly European settlers, who by 1874 had obtained ownership of a significant proportion of the country's most fertile land. By the mid-1960s after a sustained effort over 90 years the task of registering owners through the *mataqali* and delineating land holding boundaries was virtually complete. Some *mataqali* numbered in the hundreds, some numbered a handful; their lands ranged from one or two hectares to several thousand (Ward 1965). The Register of Native Lands records the membership of each *yavusa*, *mataqali* and *tokatoka*, which is kept up-to-date through the births and deaths recorded by the Registrar-General (Nayacakolou 1972).

Eaton has conjectured that the elevation of the *mataqali* to a position of centrality in land tenure may have been

> an expedient move by the chiefs and colonial administration to circumvent individual ownership rights. Clearly it would have been far more complex to ascertain the true ownership of smaller parcels of land such as the *i-tokatoka* (family units) and individual cultivators or *galala*, creating a climate for widespread disputes and counterclaims throughout the entire rural society, which was then entirely dependent upon subsistence agriculture (1988:54).

This view reinforces that of France who noted that Maxwell, a colonial official of the Native Lands Commission in the early 1900s, "was officially discouraged" from "highlighting individual land ownership rights" among Fijians because of difficulties in formalizing such a system (1969:173). Routledge suggested that "the fundamental heterogeneity of Fijian society was subsumed" under the customs and social norms of Polynesian communities in eastern Viti Levu whose leaders dominated the Council of Chiefs, which was itself a hierarchical pyramid composed of a paramount chief, senior chiefs and lesser chiefs (1985:219). Chapelle (1977) suggested that "old truths" about traditional land tenure were sometimes only "middle-aged myths" and the view of this author is that many "traditions" which contemporary Fijians hold to come "from time immemorial" in fact date back only to the formation of the Great Council of Chiefs which met for the first time in 1876 just after Cession.

The Great Council itself is one such myth: it did not exist prior to 1873, its most senior chiefs are of Tongan origin and it is modelled on the Tongan hierarchy of noble families (Lawson 1990), but many Fijians believe that it is ethnically Fijian and has existed for hundreds of years. This is not to deny that there existed a strong chiefly system in Fiji prior to colonial administration, at least in eastern Fiji. This had come under Tongan control following an invasion by the warrior prince from Tonga, Ma'afu, in 1849 (Routledge 1985). There, the chiefly system was "relatively authoritarian and highly stratified sociopolitically . . . essentially Polynesian in character . . . (in contrast to) the smaller, less stratified and more Melanesian structures of western and central Viti Levu" (Lawson 1990:6). The incorporation by the British colonial administration of many eastern chiefly leaders into the new order resulted in the adoption of eastern norms and values, and its sociopolitical structure, as the standard model. Thus, as Kaplan pointed out "customary practices in other regions [of Fiji] were necessarily viewed as illegitimate and disorderly" (1989:358). The Great Council of Chiefs was constructed as the main local instrument through which the British colonial administration extended *pax Britannica* throughout Fiji. With independence in 1970 the Council was relegated to a minor role in the new democratic system of an elected parliament, but in both the 1987 and 2000 coups the coup leaders brought the Great Council of Chiefs back into a leadership position over the elected parliament. Within the Great Council of Chiefs both coups also witnessed a subsequent power struggle between the eastern (Polynesian) and western (largely Melanesian) factions to determine who would take control from the Indo-Fijian governments which were deposed.

The codification of land tenure by the Native Lands Commission, which commenced more than a century ago, has helped to create a major distortion which still continues: that *mataqali* have an "immemorial" relationship with particular localities (Chapelle 1978; France 1969). In fact, prior to the advent of European land acquisitions and a more sedentary way of life following the cessation of persistent warfare, groups were constantly moving about in a way which emphasized their kinship relationships rather than their relationship to a particular locality (Larmour, Crocombe and Taungenga 1981). According to Nayacakolou (cited in Eaton 1988):

> One serious defect in the Commission's interpretation of Fiji custom is that it froze the land owning units at a particular time by tying them to particular pieces of land. But over the years

these social groups have grown or decayed, moved to new locations or reconstituted themselves in response to pressures of population, conflict, rivalry, or jealousy, competition for power or women, and nowadays in response to employment and other quite novel factors. The outcome of this process is a new social scene that bears little relation to the Commission's records. The recorded units often embrace new members unknown to the record; some have grown and split, others have declined and amalgamated with others so that new groups emerge with a new name (1975:213).

A press article (*Fiji Times*, 14 February 1986) reported that some 19,000 Fijians were not registered on the Native Lands Commission's official records (meaning that officially they had no rights to land title). Ignorance of their *yavusa*, *mataqali*, and *tokatoka* relationships was considered the main reason. In addition, Nayacakolou (1975) estimated that as many as 30 percent of rural Fijians were *vulagi* (migrants from other districts). Many of these will have migrated to the urban centers (by 2000, the estimated population of the combined urban area of the capital Suva and its satellite city, Nausori, was more than 250,000 or about 30 percent of the total population). According to Eaton:

> *vulagi* commonly lose the advantage of local domicile on their own hereditary land which is often occupied by other *mataqali* members, and trying to repossess birthright to land by physical occupation is difficult (1988:56).

Regardless of historical reality, the entities of *mataqali* and *yavusa* have been formalized through the contemporary legal system and form the basis for all dealings with customary land in Fiji. These social units are also important in terms of land tenure and the ceremonial context of the formation, structure and inheritance of the great chiefdoms of Fiji.

The Native Lands Trust Board (NLTB)

By the 1930s it was apparent that some measure of control was necessary to oversee the process of native land leasing. On the one hand individual *mataqali* were being exploited by unscrupulous expatriates and on the other, when disputes arose between the landowners and the tenants, security of tenure was sometimes difficult to maintain. A Lands Trust to protect and further the interests of both parties was proposed and in 1936 at a meeting of the Great Council of Chiefs the prominent Fijian statesman and high chief, Ratu Sir Lala Sukuna, gave his unequivocal support to the concept:

> It is the only way in which native lands can be made of general use and benefit — and all without storing up troubles for ourselves. It is in the best interests of the native race that all lands not required for maintenance of the Fijian owners be opened for settlement . . . and that all land including leases not so required be handed over to the Government to lease on behalf of the Fijians. . . . As the leasing will be under better control we shall receive more rent, for there will be no more waste land (Fiji Government: NLTB Supplement 1986: np).

Sukuna's advocacy for the Board was considered crucial to its establishment: without the weight of his personal stature behind it commentators have doubted whether the Great Council of Chiefs would have agreed to its formation. In the event, World War Two (1939–1945) delayed its implementation. However, in 1946 the Colonial Government established the Native Lands Trust Board (NLTB) to manage indigenous lands and act as an agency for indigenous landowners. It was designed to advance the general policy of national economic development (the growth model) while taking into account the wishes of the customary landowners and the desires of developers by addressing two major objectives: to ensure that Fijians gained due recompense for use of their land, with set schedules providing for levels of annual payments deemed commercially fair and reasonable; and to provide lessees with security of tenure for long-term development.

Five main categories of leases were identified: agricultural, commercial, industrial, residential, and special, each with its own particular lease arrangements. In October 1969, the growth of tourism prompted the NLTB to formulate new regulations for tourism leases. They became effective in January 1971 and provided for a maximum lease period of 99 years. They required that the landowners should be given the right to acquire a minimum of 10 percent of shares in the developer company, completely or partly free in lieu of a premium on the land; at least one seat on the Board of Directors of the developer company; and that the unimproved capital value of the land (on which the annual lease rate is based) would be reassessed every 10 years. In addition, the NLTB assumed responsibility for supervising the negotiations between the land owners and the developer. It plays a direct and active rather than a passive role in formulating the agreement, overseeing its implementation according to the terms and conditions which have been set, and then collects fees on behalf of the landowners for distribution to them (NLTB Information Paper 1971). These regulations were designed not only to secure higher lease payments for landowners (until the advent of tourism which increased the capital value of unimproved land dramatically the cost of securing agricultural leases was relatively low) but also to secure participation by Fijians in the tourism industry (Nayacakalou 1972).

An initial step is to obtain an independent valuation of the land to be leased. The NLTB then sets specific fees to be applied in each case according to scheduled formulae. Lessees will be charged a designated percentage per annum on the unimproved value of the land (for example, 6 percent in the case of agricultural land), royalties (for example, in the case of utilization of resources such as timber, minerals, fisheries), and a fixed percentage of the annual turnover of a development venture. The NLTB will collect the monies due on behalf of the *mataqali* from the lessee, retain 25 percent of leased monies and 10 percent of any royalties or turnover fee, and forward the balance to the designated account of the *mataqali* where distribution to members of the group will be for the group's determination (the NLTB deals with only one point of contact representing the *mataqali* and exercises no control over intra-group distribution).

In the case of a major dispute between the lessee and the *mataqali*, there is an appeals process and the NLTB may exercise its right to intervene and chair meetings of the two parties to resolve any differences. In the case of any major new development on the leased lands (such as the expansion of a resort) the NLTB has the responsibility to ensure that plans are submitted to it, that both environmental and social impact assessments will be carried out by approved independent experts before any implementation (under Fiji's Town and Country Planning Act 1946 and Amendments, including provision for environmental impact assessments, 1982), and that the plans meet with approval in due course by the *mataqali*. Only then will the NLTB, on behalf of the landowners, give permission for the proposal to be implemented.

Mana Island Resort

Mana Island is situated in the Mamanuca Islands Group about 35 kilometers due west of Viti Levu, the main island of Fiji, in the central South Pacific (Figure 9.3). Australia lies 2000 km to the west of Fiji and New Zealand lies about 2500 kilometers to the south. The Island is 130 hectares in extent, and is 3.5 kilometers east-to-west by half a kilometer north-to-south.

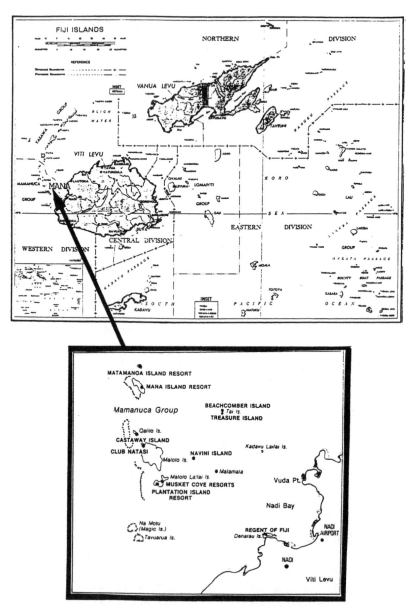

Figure 9.3: Location of Mana Island, Fiji
Source: Fiji Visitors Bureau

The region's hub airport of Nadi is located adjacent to the Mamanucas Group on the central west coast of Viti Levu. It provides international entry to Fiji and the disembarkation point for the ferry to Mana Island. This is a large motorized catamaran with a capacity of 200 passengers, which visits five or six other island resorts on the way. The voyage to Mana takes about two hours and is made twice daily, with Mana Island as the terminal. Alternatively, a four-passenger seaplane may be chartered for a journey of about 20 minutes.

The traditional Fijian land owners of Mana Island, members of the clan or *mataqali* Ketenamasi, originally all resided at Yaro Village on nearby Malolo Island. Mana was uninhabited when the original lease from the *mataqali* by an Australian company for the development of a resort was negotiated in 1971–1972. At that time about one third of the island was clothed in secondary forest (most of the valuable timber had been cut before the turn of the 20th century) and some fruit was gathered (including mangoes, paw-paws, and bananas) by members of the *mataqali*. There were two small coconut holdings, one in the central part of the island and the other at the eastern end (Nabubu) covering less than 50 acres combined; and sporadic copra cutting was carried out. Most of the slopes of the low hills were grasslands with patches of woodland in the gullies. Prior to 1972 there seems to have been only intermittent swidden agriculture (gardening) on these areas and Mana was used mainly by fishing parties for several days at a time. The lack of surface water was a major constraint to permanent settlement.

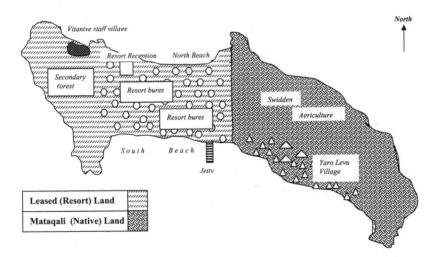

Figure 9.4: Mana Island Land Tenure Features

Only the western half of the island was leased and the resort was constructed in the central coconut plantation (Figure 9.4). With 132 *bures* (bungalows) constituting 600-bed capacity it was, and remains, the largest island resort in Fiji. (*Bure* literally means "house" and is the Fijian term for a family's dwelling, but throughout Fiji all resort bungalows and many other units, including a thatched players' shelter beside a tennis court or a gardening tool shed, are referred to as *bures*). Staff quarters were erected, originally for 120 persons, out of sight around a headland about 200 meters from the resort, at a small northern beach called Vitanive. Accommodation consisted of male and female dormitories for a combined total of 66 single staff and 30 small *bures* for married staff. The resort provided Vitanive with electricity and water, two central ablution blocks, and a soccer/rugby field. The latter became a focus of identity and local pride in the first decade of the resort with successful soccer and rugby teams composed of staff.

Over a period of time a new village grew on the eastern boundary of the resort's lease, which the landowners called Yaro Levu (New Yaro). This settlement is now almost as large as Yaro village itself. It consists of residents drawn from many parts of Fiji and represents a major adaptation to the tourism environment. It has become a primary vehicle for Fijian empowerment, as well as a source of considerable tension between the resort management and the traditional chiefly system of the *mataqali*. Yaro Levu is discounted as a separate entity in the context of being a third village to make up the *yavusa* Lawa largely because the majority of its population is not *mataqali* Ketenamasi even if it occupies *yavusa* territory. Vitanive is not considered a village at all: it is simply an extension of Yaro. While Yaro Levu at this point in time does not "fit" comfortably into the *mataqali* Ketenamasi (or any other *mataqali* for that matter) even though it occupies *mataqali* Ketenamasi land, it is a physical entity accountable to the government and to be accounted for in population censuses. Since a village in Fiji must have an authority to respond to the government, it has a *Turanga ni koro* (loosely translated as "mayor"). This position is filled by the person acknowledged to be the most senior chiefly person resident in the village by both the community and the government. Ratu Kiniboko, a minor chief from the *tokatoka* Nabukelevu of the *mataqali* Ketenamasi, occupies this position. Yaro Levu is an example of Nayacakolou's (1975) new social/spatial units that are distanced from *mataqali* and that have appeared as a response to a novel situation (in this instance a tourist resort).

In 1988 the Australian company sold its interests in Mana Island to a Japanese enterprise, AOI Resorts Ltd, and in 1991 the new owners decided to upgrade and expand the resort to 600 accommodation units with a total capacity of 2600 beds. With the approval of the landowners, based on minor revisions of the lease agreement, some new works were carried out by the resort (upgrading of the power house and sewage system, construction of a 40-bed double story deluxe accommodation unit, and replacement of several existing *bures* with six luxury bungalows). However, the major redevelopment proposals are still under consideration and have involved lengthy consultations with the traditional landowners. The sustainability of the resort for more than 30 years presents a marked contrast to the ill-fated Anuha Island Resort in Solomon Islands.

Village Demographics

The three residential areas associated with Mana Island Resort — Yaro village, Vitanive staff quarters, and Yaro Levu — demonstrate the fluid and fluctuating nature of residence which is becoming increasingly common in Fiji. Vitanive of course did not exist prior to the development of Mana Island Resort. Yaro Levu only appeared subsequently.

At the time of the 1976 census, Yaro village had a recorded population of 114 persons living in 19 households. At the 1986 census, as employment on Mana Island had attracted many former residents back to Malolo from the mainland and other islands where they had migrated, it had grown to 194 while Vitanive staff quarters held another 163 Yaro-based residents. At the time of the second field trip by this author in October 1992, the population of Yaro had increased to 291 persons in 44 households and Vitanive had increased to 195 of whom 175 were *mataqali* Ketenamasi from Yaro. Yaro Levu then had a population of 216. By October 1994, however, both Yaro and Vitanive had lost small numbers to Yaro Levu. Yaro had decreased to 278 and Vitanive to 189 (170 from Yaro). Yaro Levu, however, had 61 households and a total population of 263 (Table 9.1).

The first house at Yaro Levu appeared around 1975 and the village slowly grew to a population of 104 at the time of the 1986 census. After that time it

Table 9.1: Mana Island Village Demographics (October 1994)

Category	Yaro Village	Vitanive	Yaro Levu
Adult male	42	84	87
Adult female	63	81	97
Children (under 20 yrs)	173	24	79
Total	278	189	263

grew rapidly to its 1994 total of 263. The trend was for Yaro Levu to increase, drawing most of its additional residents from other parts of Fiji. The great majority were not *mataqali* Ketenamasi. Where Yaro and Vitanive are mono-lithically (almost) Methodist, most residents of Yaro Levu are Seventh Day Adventists. The situation of preferred migration to Yaro Levu might seem para-doxical at first sight, since the settlement has few of the amenities of the first two: but it exerts a centripetal attraction for reasons other than basic infra-structure, as will be outlined.

The Mana Island Lease Agreement

The NLTB utilizes a standard lease agreement that can be modified to suit specific circumstances. The Mana Island lease agreement follows the standard with figures negotiated in Fijian dollars, but quoted below in US dollar equiv-alents. Its clauses cover a survey of the boundaries of the land to be leased, a range of conditions governing its use and others relating to the operations of the resort. The developers were required to take out an Option to Lease for six months at $700. Upon acceptance of their plans, rental was fixed at $6000 per annum for the first four years, and at 2½ percent of gross receipts subject to a minimum of $10,000 and a maximum of $25,000 per annum thereafter, according to the success of the venture (Nayacakalou 1972). The annual rental was to be reviewed every 10 years.

Under the terms and conditions of the lease the resort operators must employ members of the *mataqali* Ketenamasi before recruiting others. As a result about 165 of the 180 local staff on Mana are from the *mataqali* Ketenamasi. This condition of the lease agreement is a standard one imposed by the NLTB and is a major source of empowerment for the landowners. The largest source of income for the residents consists of wages of staff employed at the resort. Since 1972 the resort has paid out more than $7.3 million in wages to its local staff (more than $0.5 million in 1998) and because of the system of obligations which extends throughout the *yavusa*, all members benefit and the wants of all will be met to a certain degree.

In association with employment of landowners, there is also another stan-dard clause in any agreement which is designed to advance landowner rights and this relates to appropriate training. Under the terms of the lease of Mana Island the lessee is required to use his "best endeavors to promote training of members of the *mataqali* Ketenamasi in all aspects of the resort's operations." It has been applied since the opening of the resort and in discussions concerning the proposed expansion of it and the need for approximately three times as many staff, the *mataqali* Ketenamasi invoked this clause in order to maximize employment opportunities for their members.

Under the standard Fiji lease any expansion of a resort from the original specifications requires NLTB intervention to ensure the rights of the landowners are protected. The 1991 proposal by AOI Resort Ltd to expand the number of *bures* on Mana Island five-fold to 600 acted as the trigger for NLTB supervision of the process of consultation between the landowners and the company, and the initiation of compulsory environmental and social impact assessments. Consultants were engaged to carry out the social impact assessment and were also requested by the NLTB to participate in meetings between the residents and the company to discuss implications of the proposed expansion. The Fiji Government's authorized agent, backed by legislation, thus provides a capacity to protect indigenous rights and empowers customary landowners in situations of resort expansion. It provides a basis for sustainable resort development.

Another standard clause under NLTB lease agreements provides for public access to beaches below the high tide mark. Since customary ownership extends to marine resources, this lease condition is predicated on ensuring that the *mataqali* retains unhindered access to the resources of beach, sand and reef flats. In Fiji these are rich in a wide variety of shellfish, crabs and other crustaceae, edible seaweeds and worms, small fish and other inter-tidal products. They are gathered often on a daily basis, some in season, by the women and children of the villages, and form an important part of staple diets. Specifically in the case of Mana Island Resort, the agreement states that "The lessee will at all times allow free access of the public to all beaches on Mana Island."

In addition to its utilitarian functions, this provision empowers the landowners in a legal sense in several different ways: the landowners retain a degree of control over possible foreshore developments such as jetties and sewage ocean outlets, which cannot be constructed without their agreement and for which they are able to claim compensation; and developers may not "privatize" beaches as in the Solomons and other Pacific island states, landowners are as free to exercise the right of access as any others. This legal empowerment as an outcome of the provision relating to beach access was probably unforeseen at the time of its formulation but it is nevertheless an effective mechanism for extending a degree of additional power to the landowners in adapting to tourism development within the boundaries of *mataqali* lands.

In its form and functions the NLTB thus constitutes a vehicle for empowerment of the landowners in a variety of ways which contributes to the immediate and future interests of the landowners and assists in sustaining a resort development over the longer term. The Board's considerable longevity means that it has had a significant period of years to define and refine its operations. It has moved from the "first beginnings stage" with a pioneer development like Mana Island Resort in which all parties are on a steep learning curve, to the point where it is now a mature instrumentality. Its provisions have been tested in law many times. It now has a capable body of resident expertise comprising officials who have participated in the negotiation of agreements, their implementation and their subsequent operations over many years, gaining the respect of both landowners and lessees.

The NLTB is not without its critics, and the process of registering both *mataqali* and their landholdings is defective in not taking full account of the dynamic processes of social change. But in a case such as Mana Island, the Board's success underlines a central tenet of this analysis of empowerment: that if local communities are to achieve a modicum of control over the tourism environment particularly in the context of "development" (however defined), then it is essential that the central authority, which is the government, devolves power to them through legally sanctioned means.

Material Benefits Accruing from Mana Island Resort

As an outcome of the successful application of the NLTB-brokered lease agreement between the *mataqali* Ketenamasi and the resort developers, the villagers have received significant material benefits. The relatively high levels of personal incomes have resulted in improved health, educational and living standards generally for the members of the *mataqali* Ketenamasi. All villagers are comparatively well dressed, their houses are furnished with western furniture (lounge suites, dining tables and chairs, and some with refrigerators, video sets and TV monitors powered by individual generators), and their boats are new with outboard engines. Other forms of conspicuous consumption include frequent visits to the mainland cities of Nadi and Suva. Not one single household in Yaro lives in poverty.

The second major source of funds for the *mataqali* is the actual lease of one third of Mana Island for the resort. Under the terms of the lease agreement the *mataqali* Ketenamasi receives between about $24,000 to $27,000 each year after standard deductions have been made by the NLTB. The land lease fee is set but the amount varies each year according to the turnover generated by resort activities and its occupancy rate. Since 1972, the *mataqali* has received more than $1.7 million from the resort through the NLTB. Again in contrast to the Solomon Islands situation, the NLTB plays an active role in determining a fair and reasonable annual payment by the resort to the landowners and there are formal channels for any revision of the lease or appeal regarding the amount received. The rights of both parties are protected and the agency of the NLTB thus ensures a stability in the situation which is conducive to sustaining a long-term operation.

Funds received collectively by the *mataqali* have been used for a range of purposes. For example, all of the 44 houses in Yaro village have been upgraded and constructed of "permanent" materials. This is the word the locals themselves use to describe buildings made of cement blocks, bricks and corrugated iron roofs, presumably because they do not need replacing on a regular basis. A thatch roof by comparison must be replaced about every 10 years. The village has no electricity but water is piped to some houses and 20 of them have septic tank toilet systems.

A large (Methodist) church, built of concrete blocks out of funds from the same source as the houses, is the largest building in the village. With a capacity of about 100 it is already too small, and future funds are to be utilized for an extension. At the opposite end of the *rara* (grassy village square, a common feature of all traditional villages in Fiji around which the houses are grouped) is the imposing *bure* of the *Tui Lawa*. Built in traditional style on a raised mound about 1.5 meters high, its thatch roof reaches to about 15 meters. While this is constructed of traditional materials, its cost was covered in part by the annual lease monies and in part by contributions from *mataqali* members. There is a small craft and shell shop built as a community project with funds from the lease of Mana Island, and this also doubles as a clinic for visiting medical staff. A four meter-wide channel about 150 m long was blasted through the reef flat in front of the village some 12 years ago to allow the village boats to be drawn up on the beach even at low tide. The affluence of the village is immediately apparent from the standard of housing.

At Yaro Levu, three "permanent" houses have been constructed from lease monies due to the *mataqali*, together with a small "mini-mart", an arts and craft shop, and a large church (Seventh Day Adventist). A particular point of contention is that the small Methodist church in Yaro Levu, which is constructed with tin walls and a tin roof and is about a quarter the size of the other church, was built without assistance from the resort.

One of the houses, owned by the self-proclaimed chief of the village, Ratu Kiniboko, is larger than any in Yaro village. Indeed it is about three times the size of the house of the manager of the resort, with five toilets/showers, and is supplied with electricity and water from the resort. It was built with its many bathrooms at Kiniboko's request so that he could let rooms for additional income independent of his job with the resort. The other two houses built from lease monies (for Kiniboko's brothers) are also larger than those constructed at Yaro Village on Malolo Island. There are three other houses constructed from permanent materials in the village but apparently they have not been built from lease monies (at least they are not acknowledged to have been so funded). A Seventh Day Adventist school is currently being built in the village (although it is not clear whether any lease monies have been used for this purpose). The resort has agreed to provide it with water and electricity free of charge.

The diversion of *mataqali* funds to projects within Yaro Levu is a cause of tension between the two villages and will be examined further. A characteristic of the Mana Island Resort situation is that there are probably more disputes *within* the *mataqali* over disbursement of lease monies than between the landowners and the lessee over dues.

Informal Empowerment

If the NLTB legislation has provided a vehicle for formal empowerment for members of the *mataqali* Ketenamasi, the establishment of a resort on Mana Island has accommodated another, informal, avenue for community empowerment and adaptation to tourism development through the establishment of the new village of Yaro Levu. The resort has been a catalyst for this empowerment.

No one is quite sure exactly when the village of Yaro Levu appeared, other than "several years after the resort became operational" (Pfeiffer, personal communications). Until February 1985 it was quite small. Since then it has tripled in size. It consists of about 90 buildings in all. In addition to the church, mini-market, craft shop, new school and the three houses mentioned above, there are five more houses built of "permanent" materials. There are six *bures* constructed traditionally with thatch roofs. The remaining buildings (about 70) are of "shanty-town" style, built out of salvaged roofing iron, packing cases, etc. They have no water, electricity, or sewage system. About 30 of the buildings are outhouses for cooking and consist of three-sided tin sheds with dirt floors and a stone *lovo* (pit oven). Many of them belong to *vulagi* (immigrants) from outside the Malolo *mataqali* structure.

While the village is generally clean, there are some free ranging chickens and dogs (but no pigs) and Yaro Levu in general presents a picture of a shanty town. As such is out of keeping with the image of Mana Island as a luxury resort on a pristine island. Because many of the huts of Yaro Levu extend along the beach front at the edge of Mana Island Lagoon they are immediately visible to all incoming tourists (by contrast Vitanive staff village is out of sight) and in the view of the resort management it represents an eyesore. However, as the landowners are exercising their rights of residence on *mataqali* land, the resort lacks control over the settlement and its inhabitants.

The Role of Ratu Kiniboko

It is necessary at this stage to examine the role of Ratu Kiniboko in developments on Mana Island over the past 28 years. When the original lease of the western half of Mana Island was agreed in 1971–1972, the chiefs of Yaro appointed Kiniboko as their representative. He was relatively well educated and spoke the best English of all of the chiefs. He was charged with three major tasks: to ensure that the Australian developers kept to the conditions of the lease and did not encroach on *mataqali* land nor take resources (sand, rocks, timber, etc.) from *mataqali* land for the construction of the resort without authorisation and payment of compensation; to maintain an accurate record of the trees, especially coconut palms, which were cut down for the construction of the resort. Each coconut tree, for example, was worth $2 compensation; and to ensure that the developers employed *mataqali* Ketenamasi whenever possible. As noted, a key feature of the lease agreement is that preference must be given to *mataqali* Ketenamasi for employment in the resort.

Kiniboko carried out these functions well and the *mataqali* chiefs acknowledge his energy in the formative years of the resort. He also became indispensable in the eyes of the original developers for his ability to solve problems between the resort, the *mataqali* and its staff so that he became entrenched as "their" key figure in *mataqali* Ketenamasi affairs. There appears to have been a misunderstanding by the original developers about his real position — that of just a minor chief — within the hierarchy of Yaro chiefs. His success in persuading the resort management to accept him as in effect the paramount chief may be gauged by the following comment from one of the original Australian developers: Kiniboko, he said, was "Number One", and the old chiefs in the village were "just a bunch of troublemakers who could not speak proper English, who got around in scraggy clothing and who sat around the grog (kava) bowl all day thinking up ways to cause problems".

As a result Kiniboko was able to use the management support to bypass the authority of his own chiefs. His appointment to an executive position (that of "Local Director", responsible for hiring and firing Fijian staff) allowed Kiniboko to embed himself. Over 18 years he controlled more than 150 staff at a time. He held this position until 1990, during which time he became the most influential individual Fijian on Mana Island.

It is probable that Kiniboko's rise to prominence was also aided by the lingering attributes of Melanesian society with its power structure vested in "bigmen" rather than hereditary chiefs. In Western Fiji the chiefly system is more fluid than in the eastern islands where the "Tongan" Polynesian power structure is dominant. Chiefs are challenged in the Mamanuca Islands in ways which are alien to the Polynesian tradition (and indeed, one comment from a Polynesian official of the NLTB about the Mana Island chiefly rivalry was to the effect that it was only to be expected among lesser people).

Kiniboko's influence was so great with the previous management of the resort that he persuaded them to spend thousand of dollars in his "own" village community, money which should have been distributed among the entire *mataqali* Ketenamasi, with the Yaro chiefs (not Kiniboko) controlling its distribution. Thousands of dollars, for example, went into Kiniboko's house and two houses for his brothers, the craft shop and the Seventh Day Adventist Church instead of into the village of Yaro. The resort management discounted these disbursements against the distribution of lease funds to the *mataqali* and the NLTB acquiesced because at the time Kiniboko was the appointed representative of the *mataqali*. The breakdown in distribution and the diversion of funds to Yaro Levu was at the point of Kiniboko rather than the NLTB. The management could be held to have contributed to the situation by its preference for dealing with Kiniboko, thus marginalizing the Yaro chiefs to an extent. Attempts by the chiefs to have Kiniboko removed and replaced were to no avail until the new Japanese management took over the resort.

It was then recognized that Kiniboko was a problem for the resort's relationship with the *mataqali*. There was also a perception by the new Japanese owners that Kiniboko was too influential with local staff and that they could not exert management control to the extent desired. Systematic pilfering of resort food and beverage supplies and drunkenness among staff was also a problem sheeted home to Kiniboko (his drinking prowess is legendary). With the approval of the chiefs of Yaro, Kiniboko was replaced as Local Director by Moses Soqeto, the grand nephew of the *Turanga Mataqali*, Ratu Jerry Matai. The latter was nominated as the *mataqali* representative for receiving lease monies.

Although Kiniboko was thus forced outside the formal structure of the resort and no longer accepted as the *mataqali* representative by the NLTB, he was the person responsible for hiring most of the present resort staff in the first instance; and as the *turanga ni koro* of Yaro Levu where some of them reside, he continues to hold a degree of influence among many of them. He retains a capacity to impact negatively upon resort operations in given circumstances.

It is necessary at this stage to delve further into sociocultural aspects of the situation to explain how Kiniboko gained power to the point where he could defy his own chiefs and continue to interact with the resort as a principal player. While some of his actions have been interpreted as detrimental to the interests of the *mataqali* Ketenamasi by its own chiefs, it is suggested that Kiniboko has played a pivotal role in the adaptive response of his original village and his new village to tourism development.

It seems that around mid-1984, when the chiefs of Yaro considered that Kiniboko was exceeding his role and their attempts to impose their authority on him had failed, they requested the Yaro village pastor to call upon the greater power of the Methodist Church to bring him to heel. The authority of the church in rural Fiji is not to be lightly dismissed (*vide* its leading role in the build-up to, and the aftermath of, the military coups in Fiji in 1987) and the pressure on Kiniboko to bow to the direction of his chiefs would have been considerable. Kiniboko was able to deflect that pressure, however, with a "spiritual experience" in the midst of Cyclone Hina which swept over Mana Island in February 1985 and which persuaded him to become a Seventh Day Adventist. Whether Kiniboko had a genuine religious vision is a moot point for the date coincides with the attempt by Yaro village to invoke the authority of the Methodist Church to control him. As a Seventh Day Adventist, however, Kiniboko was able to disavow the dictums of his erstwhile church. In classical Durkheimian terms, he was able to imbue power with sacrality.

The expansion of Yaro Levu, the diversion of *mataqali* lease monies to the village, and the settlement on Mana Island of non-*mataqali* Ketenamasi from other parts of Fiji also date from this time. As a chief of the *tokatoka* Nabukelevu, Kiniboko has undisputed rights to reside on Mana Island and he has used his position as a *ratu* for *oga* ceremonies to authorize the settlement of *vulagi* (immigrants) on *mataqali* Ketenamasi land. An *oga* is the ceremony whereby a form of compensation is accepted for settlement rights, usually of *tabua* (a gift with symbolic connotations of great value traditionally, such as whales' teeth) or some other form of gift/offering/ payment.

But the chiefs from Yaro dispute that Kiniboko has the authority to allow outsiders to settle on *mataqali* Ketenamasi land. It is now difficult to determine which non-*mataqali* Ketenamasi in fact have rights to settle in Yaro Levu because there has been a degree of intermarriage between *mataqali* Ketenamasi and outsiders over the years. The situation is further complicated because some of the settlers come from nearby islands in the Mamanucas where the lineages are claimed to go back to a single common ancestral line from Malolo. There is thus a relationship of sorts between many of them and the *mataqali* Ketenamasi, even if that relationship is not formally recognized by the Native Lands Commission or the NLTB. It is estimated that perhaps two thirds of the households in Yaro Levu do not have *mataqali* Ketenamasi rights and reside there without the sanction of the chiefs from Yaro. This is a cause of major friction between the two villages, with the chiefs of Yaro being united in the view that outsiders should be sent from Mana Island.

Kiniboko's empowerment in standing out against his chiefs has its roots in five main sources (not ranked in any particular order): his support from the resort management of the time; as *turanga ni koro*, which formalized his leadership of Yaro Levu in terms of some government agencies and which dates back to the 1986 census at least when he was so recognized; his new-found relationship with the Seventh Day Adventist Church which has been active in its support, especially with the strategic construction of a primary school in Yaro Levu; the non-*mataqali* Ketenamasi *vulagi*, who owe their residence on Mana Island to Kiniboko; and some of the 40 resort staff members of the *mataqali* Ketenamasi who at the time of this research had moved out of Vitanive into Yaro Levu, particularly 13 who with their families subsequently converted to Seventh Day Adventism, and whose loyalties are now split. In October 1992, the resort staff and their dependents living in Yaro Levu totalled 129 persons; 82 adults and 47 children in 26 households. Of the 47 children, 26 were attending the Seventh Day Adventist school and the other 21 were pre-school age.

The support of the church post-1990 was as important as the former resort management in bolstering Kiniboko's position. Most of the *vulagi* are in fact Seventh Day Adventists. A survey in October 1992 revealed that 160 (74 percent) of the then population of 216 were adherents. They originated from as far afield as Lau, Vanua Levu, Levuka, and Viti Levu (such as the village of Viseisei, south of Lautoka). The school together with three schoolteachers and a pastor were crucial in the context of attracting resort staff to reside in the village (see below). Anthropologists, historians and political scientists have all commented on the closeness of the attributes of power and religion and the links that exist between them, and Kiniboko's empowerment is derived to some extent from invoking that relationship.

The support for Ratu Kiniboko by some of the resort staff and other settlers from Yaro (who by definition are members of the *mataqali* Ketenamasi) is also important. Interviews with a number of the staff indicated that some had relocated from Vitanive to demonstrate solidarity with Kiniboko. Others had exercised their own usufructuary rights to set up house with their families on *mataqali* land because of dissatisfaction with conditions at Vitanive. Others wanted their families with them.

This latter covers a somewhat contentious issue. It is not possible to have children other than infants in Vitanive because when Mana Island Resort was first established the *mataqali* Ketenamasi leadership proposed that the staff quarters not provide family accommodation. The community did not want its children growing up in a resort environment and it was considered that by compelling the children to remain in the home village they would be protected from adverse influences, would retain their Fijian traditions and culture, and not be "spoiled" by the alien morals and hedonistic lifestyles of foreign tourists (interviews, senior chief Ratu Ponipate and Mana resort developer, Errol Pfeiffer). As other resorts were later developed in Fiji's islands, the separation of children from parents became the accepted pattern for staff quarters in most of them.

This explains the atypical demographic structure of Yaro village which lacks substantial numbers of residents in the mid-level age groups (20 to 49 years). In 1992 some 155 (53 percent) were children under the age of 15 years. Another 30 were aged 16–19 years giving a total of 64 percent of the village population under the age of 20 years. Sixty-seven of the children attended the government primary school at the adjacent village of Solevu about two kilometers away and 20 attended high schools on Viti Levu (the mainland) since there is no high school in the Mamanucas. Of the 106 adults residing permanently in the village, 61 (58 percent) were aged 50 or above; the younger adults were employed by Mana Island and other resorts.

Interestingly, in the 1990s the resorts were being criticized for imposing conditions of service which break up families (interview, N. Plange, University of the South Pacific, October 1992). Some Mana Island staff members also questioned the situation, and the enforced separation from their children was a major cause of complaint at the time of the 1992 social impact survey, even though Yaro Village is only 30 minutes away by boat and many of the staff take advantage of their weekly day off to return there. During school holidays, many of the children travel to Mana and live temporarily with relatives at Yaro Levu where their parents can then see them daily.

As already mentioned, several staff moved out of Vitanive and into Yaro Levu in order to have their school-age children with them. Until the advent of the church school it was necessary for their children to stay on Malolo to attend the government primary school at Solevu. But the school on Mana changed that situation and numbers of staff established a household in Yaro Levu because it permitted them to live together as a family unit.

By 1992 the church had raised $30,000 in Australia and Fiji to construct a new four-classroom school and 40 Australian volunteers had been organized to build it (interview, Ratu Kiniboko and Mereama Nadola, principal teacher, Yaro Levu primary school, October 1992). It could not be ascertained whether lease monies were also being accessed although the evasiveness of responses from Kiniboko to this question suggested that it was a possibility. A ten-acre plot located behind the present church at Yaro Levu, which the church had arranged to lease from Kiniboko for the school, was surveyed on 5 October 1992. Under the draft agreement Kiniboko was specified as the sole recipient of lease monies ($300 per year).

It is suggested that the Seventh Day Adventist Church perceived in the school an opportunity for proselytizing among Vitanive staff, while Kiniboko saw an additional means of extending his community's standing and his personal income. A new school with greatly expanded capacity would be likely to attract even more of Vitanive's staff to establish a household in Yaro Levu, a number of whom would probably become adherents in the process. With more people under his control, Kiniboko's influence and authority would then expand while the authority of the chiefs on Yaro would be commensurably diminished. Subsequently, however, the NLTB refused to allow the church to lease the land without the approval of the Yaro *mataqali* chiefs, who continue to oppose Kiniboko.

Kiniboko's response was to go ahead with the building of the new school anyway, sanctioning its presence on *mataqali* land under an *oga* ceremony, thus utilizing traditional means to achieve his ends instead of the contemporary legal mechanism of a formal lease. Because the two systems exist contemporaneously and much tradition has been incorporated into the legal system of the state (*vide* the traditional chiefly structure and the question of land ownership, both of which have been enshrined in the national constitution) Kiniboko found in the situation another lever for empowerment. This is consistent with this author's contention that empowerment of indigenous communities cannot be "taken" by the communities concerned drawing only upon their own traditional resources but will require support and sanction by the state, if it is to avoid being ephemeral. In this instance, a church registered with the state also lent its authority to Kiniboko's actions.

The Relationship between Yaro and Yaro Levu

Yaro Levu is an example of the breakdown of the coextension of *mataqali* and locality noted by Nayacakolou (1975), Routledge (1985), Eaton (1988) and others which is becoming a more frequent occurrence in contemporary Fiji. As indicated previously the structure of "traditional" Fijian village society is based upon a common heritage of one or more ancestors acknowledged by all. It is lineage, a commonality of kinship ties, which forms the foundations, the floor, the walls and the roof of the Fijian village (Sawailau 1989). There are a number of doors by which outsiders may enter and become part of a village, usually through marriage and occasionally by adoption. In these cases, social kinship ties are created which integrate new members into the community and the bonds of biological kinship. In the case of Yaro Levu, the linkage binding most members of the village is achieved by common ties to a church and there

Figure 9.5: *Oga* Ceremony

is no traditional kinship structure supporting the "brothers and sisters" who form the "family" of the church. The end result is a village without the normative lineage structure to bind all of its members into a single cohesive unit.

When relationships between Fijians are in a state of "disorder" or are "not right" they are said to be *duka*. In the case of Yaro Levu, the relationship with the Yaro Village community was disrupted and the senior chiefs of the *mataqali* Ketenamasi considered that bonds had to be repaired. Things were "wrong" and must be "put right": relationships "spoiled" must be returned to relationships "correct". The negative state of *duka* must be transformed to the positive state of *sava sava*. Only through traditional ceremony — *oga* (cleansing) — can this transition from the negative to the positive be made (Figure 9.5). Until *oga* is performed tensions between Yaro and Yaro Levu will continue, exacerbated by the religious split which developed between members of the *mataqali* Ketenamasi, monolithically Methodist until nine years ago, with the Seventh Day Adventist Church providing Kiniboko with substantial support.

This situation was further complicated because Kiniboko, by his actions, was held by the leadership of Yaro to be in a personal state of social debt or *dinau* to others which required *bulubulu* (atonement, reconciliation or compensation). The problem for the *mataqali* Ketenamasi was that Kiniboko refused to recognize or accept that any action on his part was required. Kiniboko had in his view the authority to formalize the right of the outsiders to settle on *mataqali* Ketenamasi land through traditional rituals. From his position of power in Yaro Levu he could ignore the attempts at social sanctions by his chiefly peers.

In this context it is important to reiterate that the chiefly system of Western Fiji retains some Melanesian characteristics which can result in instability in leadership. Because the Great Council of Chiefs and much of the legislation of Fiji as it relates to traditional social structure is based on the Polynesian model of a rigid hierarchy, the impression is projected of a stable society in which the status of chiefs is unquestioned. Leadership in Polynesian societies was ascribed, as a birthright, and restricted to noble families. By contrast, Melanesian society rarely had hereditary chiefs, no "noble" family lines as in Polynesia and no distinction between royalty and commoners. As noted in Chapters 6 and 7, Melanesian leadership was based on a series of "bigmen" who earned their status through achievement and any individual could by merit aspire to and attain leadership (Maenu'u 1984). Leadership constantly fluctuated between a number of "bigmen" in each village; persistent, often robust, rivalry and a strong sense of egalitarianism pervaded the society. In eastern Fiji, challenges to the established chiefs are rare but in the west in the Mamanucas shifting allegiances and temporary alliances of convenience are constantly being forged as individuals vie for status, wealth, and power. The aberrant existence of Yaro Levu simply adds a further ingredient of instability to the social fabric of the *mataqali* Ketenamasi which can at any time complicate community affairs and spill over into the operations of Mana Island Resort.

Community Empowerment

The adaptive response of Yaro Levu to tourism development under Kiniboko's leadership has resulted in further empowerment of the community. This finds expression in a number of different ways. One is that in any matters related to the Mana Island Resort lease (the proposed expansion of the resort, for example) the Yaro Levu community is consulted more or less as an equal with the Yaro community. Yaro Levu, with Kiniboko as its head, cannot be disregarded. It was notable, for example, that in the public meetings called by the NLTB in 1992 to discuss the plans for expanding the size of the resort half of the audiences were from Yaro Levu (although the village does not represent more than about 25 percent of the *mataqali* Ketenamasi). In these meetings Kiniboko was more vocal than the other chiefs in raising questions and suggesting the need for various compensation payments, although this was probably as much a function of his understanding of the greater impacts on his village of the proposed expansion than on Yaro, and his greater familiarity with leasing negotiations and arrangements than with any perception of himself as a pre-eminent spokesman for the entire *mataqali*.

Another form of empowerment arises from membership of the Seventh Day Adventist Church. It provides resort staff who join the sect with a small element of control over the management in the context of removing from the jurisdiction of the resort the ability to determine when they will and will not work. This relates to the *dictum absolut* of the church that its members shall undertake no paid employment on their Sabbath from 6 p.m. on Fridays to 6 p.m. on Saturdays. Thus, the adherents are able to dictate to their employers that they will not be available for duty on their sabbath. Even though the management may need specific skills held only by staff members (such as the electrical engineer to run the resort's power house), it is powerless in the face of the inflexible religiously sanctioned ban. This empowerment encompasses not only those staff with high status or essential skills but to workers with few rights and low status who have no management responsibilities and must take orders, like gardeners and cleaners.

As Local Director, Kiniboko was able to accustom the former resort management to the religious practices from 1985 until his dismissal in 1990. When the new Japanese management attempted to take a different approach by rostering staff without due regard to their religious affiliation, it immediately faced strike action engineered by Kiniboko. This was successful and the exclusion of Adventist staff from Saturday rosters was reinstated. The Japanese management disliked what it viewed as a restriction on the freedom of management to manage; but it now guards against any perception of discrimination against the Adventist staff to pre-empt future strike action, so that this empowerment is real. Even in the immediate aftermath of the 1987 coups when the Methodist Church was able to impose a "no-work-on-Sundays" diktat on all of Fiji, workers in the tourism industry were exempt and Methodists and other religious denominations could not use the situation in the way that Adventist followers do. To the extent that the resort must roster its staff according to Adventist members' religious proclivities, that part of the Yaro Levu community may be said to have been effectively empowered.

The community of Yaro Levu by its proximity to the resort is also able to interpose itself and exert a degree of negative control through disruption when issue is taken with resort actions. Thus, in May 1992 the community was able to prevent a boatload of tourists from disembarking at Mana wharf because of a dispute over alleged non-payment of compensation by the resort for rocks taken for landscaping from "Yaro Levu land". The resort is well aware of the capacity of Yaro Levu community to interdict its operations; and, therefore the Japanese management maintains close relations with its members and Kiniboko. Its management, for example, expressed readiness to allow resort water and electricity to be used by the new school. It also entered into an agreement with Kiniboko to provide lodgings for 10 of its staff in his house at $7 per person per week and initially provided the house with electricity and water free of charge.

Empowerment Through an Adaptive Response

The literature emphasizes that "one of the most common factors underlying a host of social impacts of tourism is the restriction of the local peoples' opportunities" in different areas such as recreation, personal privacy, living style, and so forth (Pearce, Moscardo, and Ross 1991:6). Much tourism development in Third World countries exhibits this restrictive approach and the small island countries of the South Pacific have been no exception (Britton 1987a; Crocombe 1987; Finney and Watson 1975; Fletcher 1987; Milne 1992; Pearce 1989; Sathiendrakumar and Tisdell 1988; Sofield 1990a). As a result negative perceptions of tourism by the host community are formed. The corollary is that tourism development which enhances opportunities for resident communities will tend to be viewed positively.

In the context of Mana Island, it is suggested that when a resident community takes the initiative to turn opportunities arising from resort development into economic activity of benefit to individuals and the community as a whole, then it has empowered itself. It has broken out of the dependency imposed when its relationship is determined predominantly by employment in mainly subservient positions in that resort. This empowerment is particularly evident when the resort management hinders or opposes indigenous entrepreneurial effort which draws upon resort resources, but proves unable to prevent it.

Yaro Levu has a thriving informal economy (by contrast with Yaro and many other rural villages throughout Fiji) consisting of several small businesses which operate without licenses. All of them are further examples of an adaptive response to tourism development and while dependent upon it nevertheless provide a degree of economic independence from the resort for the Yaro Levu community. To that extent they may be regarded as empowerment taking the form of economic exploitation of various opportunities created by the resort. Several of these opportunities are partly detailed below.

Fishing

About one third of Yaro Levu's fleet of 20 motorized boats will be actively engaged in fishing for resort consumption in any week. The resort purchases fresh fish every day from Yaro Levu and itinerant fishermen from surrounding villages in the Mamanucas region and the Yasawa Islands a little further north. On average it spends $250 per day. When occupancy rates are high it may spend up to $450 per day. Over 1993/1994 the resort spent an average of $6500 per month ($78,000 per year) on purchases from local fishermen and a further $150 per day ($4500 per month, or $54,000 per year) for fish bought from the mainland. Total fish purchases per year are thus more than $132,000. Of this, Yaro Levu fishermen earn about $2000 per month or about $24,000 per year. An income of this magnitude is far in excess of most coastal villages in Fiji. In terms of the environmental impact on fish stocks, no assessment of the sustainable annual yield has been carried out. Anecdotally, the expatriate game fishing operator at Mana Islands believed that stocks were holding up.

Agricultural Produce

Limited use is made of the *mataqali* land around Yaro Levu for swidden agriculture, a little of it for cash crops. A total of about seven hectares was under cultivation in October 1994, most of it cassava, with several small plots of beans, pumpkins, spring onions, and sweetcorn also evident. There are the remnants of a small coconut plantation (about 5 hectares) on the eastern end of the island at Nabubu and a small banana plantation of about half a hectare in a small valley on the northern side of the island, directly over the ridge from Yaro Levu. Mango trees, paw-paws, coconut trees and bananas are interspersed among the houses of the village. Limited amounts of agricultural produce (cassava, bananas, pumpkins and fruit in season) are sold to the resort, mainly for staff consumption. This totals less than $100 per month. One Yaro Levu resident began growing spring onions for the resort and payments have totaled more than $500 per year since he began the project in early 1992. The generally dry climate and the absence of surface water, however, limits more systematic agricultural activity on Mana Island. Investigations revealed that the market garden entrepreneurs were all *vulagi* who were not employed by the resort and as non *mataqali*-Ketenamasi members had no direct access to royalties and other lease payments.

The Yaro Levu Backpacker Resort

There is a backpacker operation run by Ratu Kiniboko and one of his brothers on Mana. In 1992 Kiniboko placed posters in several shops in Nadi which proclaimed that a stay in the village of Yaro Levu would cost only $12 per person per day with all resort facilities "free of charge" (Figure 9.6). He had no agreement with the resort for this and its management threatened legal action to prevent such advertising. Kiniboko, however, continued to pursue his course and the resort did not act upon its threat. In 1995, in addition to the two traditional bures and the camping ground, Kiniboko's brother set up the Mereani Vata Backpackers' Inn in Yaro Levu, with dormitory accommodation for about 40 guests.

One of the problems for Mana Island Resort was that with no physical barrier between Yaro Levu and the resort and with staff unable to distinguish between resident guests and day trippers (of whom there may be up to 150 per day) backpackers from Yaro Levu may freely wander around the resort utilizing its facilities, including swimming pools, tennis courts, showers, TV/video room, table tennis tables and games room facilities, etc. In any case, the lease agreement provides access for all persons to the beaches of Mana, as already noted, so the presence of Kiniboko's backpackers under beach umbrellas erected by the resort is legitimate.

In an effort to control unwanted backpacker access, in April 1996 the resort constructed a wire fence two meters high across the island on the boundary of the leased land, with security boxes and guards at both ends. The construction of the fence angered Kiniboko and his brothers and led to increased tensions between the village and the resort. Kiniboko's view was that since the land of the resort belonged to the landowners they had the right to allow their own tourists access to that land, and as such they should also be accorded the right to utilize resort facilities. Further the fence should not have been erected at all since the land belonged to the people (Harrison 1997b). Some of the resort staff who resided in Yaro Levu were also annoyed because they had to walk around the fence to go to and from home.

For its part the resort maintained that they had the right to enforce a "no-go" area for backpackers and that "the fence and guards were a necessary defence of Hotel interests" (Harrison 1997b:175). While the resort and the backpacker operations were not in competition for guests, the resort considered that the "invasion" of backpackers into its exclusive preserve constituted an illegal infringement on its lease rights, and an affront to its image.

It is not surprising that the fence should have engendered strong feelings given the circumstances of its construction. It sharpened the age-old concerns of some Fijians with *vanua*, the Fijian concept of the indivisibility of "people-and-land". As Ratu Ponipate noted, however, barriers are not unknown in Fiji: indeed until the advent of British colonization every community in Fiji had its fortified village. One of the most elaborate is on the island of Naigani where two concentric walls of rocks more than six meters high and each one kilometer in length completely encircled a hilltop village. There is a fortified village near Sigatoka, about 60 kilometers from Mana Island, which has been transformed into a major tourism attraction under local ownership with assistance from UNESCO. Thus, while the fence on Mana Island may be symbolized as a delineation of different spaces (physical, cultural and socio-economic) it has a certain cultural "fit" with Fijian tradition. After several years the fence has reluctantly been accepted as a fact of life, although it retains the capacity to be a trigger for indigenous sentiment against the resort.

No accounts of the backpacker businesses were kept by Kiniboko or his brother. They estimated that "about 20 to 30" backpackers per week stayed in

INTER-OFFICE MEMO

TO: .... MR NISHIDA ....   FROM   RESORT MANAGER

TITLE: ....   TITLE

DEPARTMENT: ....   DEPARTMENT

DATE: 16JUL92

SUBJECT: "BACK-PACKERS" ACCOMMODATION YARO LEVU VILLAGE

Further to my confidential memo of 14th July, regarding Mataqali matters, please find attached a photograph taken by Mr Mike Pettitt of Sia's Travel Agency Nadi, boldly displaying our Mana Island Resort Brochure in connection with an *GOVT* for budget accommodation. The Fiji Visitors Bureau have asked for clarification.

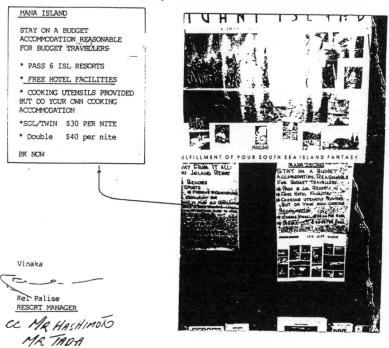

MANA ISLAND

STAY ON A BUDGET
ACCOMMODATION REASONABLE
FOR BUDGET TRAVELLERS

* PASS 6 ISL RESORTS

* FREE HOTEL FACILITIES

* COOKING UTENSILS PROVIDED
BUT DO YOUR OWN COOKING
ACCOMMODATION

*SGL/TWIN $30 PER NITE

* Double $40 per nite

BK NOW

Vinaka

Ke Palise
RESORT MANAGER

cc *MR HASHIMOTO*
MR TADA

Figure 9.6: Mana Island Resort and Kiniboko's Backpacker Advertising the two traditional *bures* and the hostel and "about six to 10 people" pitched their tents in the designated camping ground adjacent to the church. If the lower figures are accepted then in 1998 the operations were earning about $5000 per year with further income generated through backpacker expenditure on food, beverages and craft items purchased in the village, all of which were at prices cheaper than those offered in the resort outlets.

Fishing Boat Hire

Another operation is the hire of village boats for fishing. A concession for deep sea game fishing was granted by the resort to an expatriate-owned company, Pleasure Marine, which charged $40 per hour. Resort guests were made aware by Fijian staff that an opportunity existed for cheaper fishing trips by hiring village boats. The charge was $8 per hour. The village fishermen would also take guests to the nearby resort on Matamanoa for $8 as against $40 charged by Pleasure Marine. Anecdotal evidence suggested that about two hirings per day were made, for an annual income of more than $3500.

At one level, the village fishing boats offered a better service than Pleasure Marine: the guest was taken out by Fijians with an intimate knowledge of the reefs, waters and habits of the fish at different seasons; when the hour was up instead of: "Time to return to base" they said: "You have not yet caught enough fish", or "You have caught only a small fish, so let's try a little longer for a big one", and the guest received an extension not possible on the "hi-tec" costly boat run by Pleasure Marine; and the guest obtained a "Fijian experience" and was immersed in a Fijian cultural experience not possible in the large game fishing boat of Pleasure Marine.

In short, for one fifth of the price the guest received a quality Fijian experience. However, at another level the guest received a lesser service. The village boats are not licensed, do not have expensive game fishing equipment, do not carry life-saving equipment nor two-way radios and do not register the absence from the island of guests availing themselves of their services. If an accident were to occur it is unlikely that there would be a timely search and rescue.

Craft Shop and Mini-mart

Both shops operated on a cooperative basis, the first providing a service to tourists, while the second provided a service to villagers and a small number of tourists (the backpackers). The craft shop in fact has difficulty maintaining sufficient output for demand and more than half of its stock consists of tee shirts and printed *sulu* (wrap around cloths). Other handicrafts include fans made from pandanus palm, Fijian war clubs, small carved wooden bowls, and shell necklaces. While some of the stock originates in Yaro, most of the handicrafts are made in Yaro Levu. Turnover exceeds $10,000 per year and is an important source of income for those households without resort employment.

Water

Another business under the informal economy was the supply of water to households in Yaro Levu. The resort must ship water in from the mainland every day at a cost of 1 cent per liter. For the month of September 1992 the resort, with an occupancy rate averaging more than 80 percent, shipped in some 3.6 million litres at a cost of $36,000. Through the pipeline into Yaro Levu, water was supplied free of charge to the house of Kiniboko and several other buildings. Kiniboko supplied water through his taps to all those in his village who wanted it at a charge of 20 cents per day. This theoretically provided Kiniboko with a daily income of about $12, or an annual income of about $4300.

A water meter installed on Kiniboko's house in mid-1992 indicated that he was consuming more than 350,000 litres per annum ($3500 worth). The resort took steps to control this loss by limiting Kiniboko to a set volume and introducing a fee for any excess. The result was that Kiniboko removed his outside taps and exercised strict control and payment over use where previously he had been lax. Some villagers now walk several hundred meters to the resort with their buckets to obtain free water from garden taps and ablution blocks. There are increasingly strong demands from the Yaro Levu community for the resort to accept that it has a social responsibility to provide water to the village as it does for Vitanive, especially as more of its staff relocate there.

Board and Lodgings

As Mana Island Resort has expanded and the accommodation at Vitanive has deteriorated (only basic maintenance has been carried out over the past 20 years), alternative staff accommodation became necessary. In 1991, the management entered into an agreement with Kiniboko to board 10 of their staff in his house, as mentioned previously. The resort, not the staff, pays the weekly rent. This is of course known to all members of the Fijian communities associated with Mana Island and is regarded by them as evidence of Kiniboko's continued leverage with the resort.

Some of the entrepreneurial vigour of Yaro Levu is in fact consistent with Fiji Government policy, which in 1989 established the Secondary Tourism Advisory Service (STAS) unit in the Ministry of Tourism in Suva to advise and provide support to indigenous Fijians wishing to establish tourism businesses (Sawailau 1989). The backpacker ventures, the fishing boat service, the boarding house, and the crafts outlet fall squarely within the kind of activities desired by the Fiji Government for its nationals. However, the fact that these businesses are not licensed and therefore strictly speaking not legal, cuts across the Government's approach.

Yaro Village

In contrast to Yaro Levu, backward linkages into fishing and agriculture by Yaro village for resort requirements are weak. Yaro also has about 20 boats, individually owned, most with outboard motors, and fishing is a daily occurrence undertaken for domestic consumption. However, commercial fishing for sale to nearby resorts, while a prominent activity 10 years ago, is now only pursued opportunistically. Interviews with Yaro residents suggest that the combination of wages and lease monies act as a disincentive to engage in fishing as an alternative form of income generation. In addition, about 70 percent of all *mataqali* Ketenamasi adult males aged between 20 and 49 years are already employed either by Mana Island or other resorts so that there are relatively few of them available for fishing. There is a gender-based labor differentiation and while women gather shellfish and may catch reef fish they do not fish from boats.

Malolo also has the same climatic restrictions imposed on swidden agriculture as Mana Island, and Yaro village has no produce sales to the resort. It is no longer self-supporting and much of its basic food requirements, including rice and tinned fish, are now imported from the mainland. This may have adverse dietary implications but more positive effects environmentally. The length of fallow between burning and cultivation of garden plots has increased from every two to three years 20 years ago to five to six years and even longer currently. The overworked soil and the bush cover is slowly regenerating, although many fires are allowed to burn across the Malolo hills out of control.

With reference to the craft and shell shop in Yaro, in the past the village used to receive regular visits from tourists holidaying at three resorts on Malolo Lailai (Dick's Place, Musket Cove and Plantation Island, about five kilometers to the east) and from Mana. Such visits are now infrequent, although Mana Island

and Dick's Place still offer the opportunity for those interested. In 1998 visitation from Mana Island Resort constituted only two visits per week averaging five tourists each. Pleasure Marine Company, which operated the tours from Mana Island, paid the village 35 cents per tourist, and average expenditure per tourist on village handicrafts and shells was around $4. Average weekly income was about $45. Active interaction between Yaro villagers and tourists was thus slight.

Host Community Attitudes

The degree of empowerment enjoyed by the three Fijian communities associated with Mana Island Resort is reflected in their generally positive attitude about the impacts of tourism and their support for it. In a survey by questionnaire of 69 residents from Yaro, 62 from Vitanive and 66 from Yaro Levu ($n = 197$) in 1992 more than half of the respondents — 52.3 percent (103) — were very supportive of increased tourism development, selecting the highest score of 10 on a 10-point Likert scale. A further 94 respondents (47.7 percent) recorded degrees of support ranging from values of 7 to 9. All respondents identified a range of personal and community benefits to be gained from tourism, only 26 percent expressed concerns about negative impacts, and some 84 percent indicated that they and/or their dependents were strongly desirous of working in the tourism industry (Figure 9.7).

The findings from the social impact survey are consistent with those studies on social impacts of tourism which indicate that "the overall favorability of tourism impact perceptions increases" with individual and community benefits (Perdue, Long, and Allen 1990:71), and that those who benefit economically from tourism perceive fewer social and environmental impacts than those who do not benefit (Milman and Pizam 1988; Murphy 1985). Pearce *et al.* (1996) have added social representations to the equity function. Their research indicated that in the case of certain north Queensland communities the residents' responses to tourism were based on a combination of personal benefits they had received plus the image(s) of the particular tourism industry that they were using or working with. Interestingly, they also record that expressed attitudes do not always influence behavior, but "when an individual is highly involved with a topic or object (for example if it forms part of their work or daily life) then they are more likely to hold detailed attitudes towards it" and may express negative feelings equally with positive feelings (1996:24–25).

The Mana findings are inconsistent with those studies which suggest that where the tourist presence is much larger than the local community "the greater

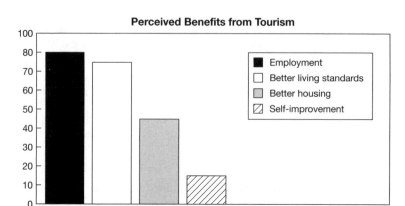

Figure 9.7: Mana Island Social Impacts Survey. Source: Sofield (1992). Columns are Expressed in Percentages: *n* = 197

the amount of intrusion on both social and physical dimensions the greater the negative reaction to tourists and tourism" (Cohen 1978, cited in Pearce 1988:4); and that negative effects on host communities will be greater when the cultural and technological gap between guests and hosts is large (Cater 1987, cited in Pearce 1988:4). Nor does the Mana Island Resort situation comply with Doxey's "irritation index" or "Irridex" (1975). The Irridex is a model which postulates that host/guest relations move in a unilinear direction through four stages from an initial warmth and friendliness toward tourists to eventual antagonism by the resident community. As Pearce states, Doxey's one-dimensional approach does not take into account the fact that "direct and indirect effects are on different time scales", that different aspects of the receiving society "may ameliorate or exacerbate the impacts", and that while "tourism developments and impacts . . . may follow some common rules, they also produce unorthodox and unique impacts according to situationally specific factors" (1988:4–5). In the case where a tourism development is imposed on a community without any consultations, located on land they have traditionally regarded as theirs, and which has been alienated without their consent, the community reaction to tourism may be outright hostility from the very start, rather than a third stage reached only after an initial welcome that slides into indifference, as postulated by Doxey (1975).

The Mana Island situation suggests that there has been an adaptive response to tourism, adaptive in the sense of a process whereby the Fijian community of the *mataqali* Ketenemasi has adjusted to the new environment of tourism in its midst. It is a process where empowerment taken and/or granted has been sufficiently effective to transform the receiving community into stakeholders with a capacity to control to some extent the development of tourism and their future in that development. It is not only that the economic and consequential social benefits accruing to the receiving community outweigh perceived negative impacts but that empowerment is a crucial factor which would incline the community to regard tourism in a positive way even when some disbenefits exist. Empowerment would seem likely to have a positive influence in turn on the social representation of tourism as a "good" industry even if previously its image was poor or negative, since empowerment confers a degree of ownership of the industry by the host community and its own identity becomes integrated with that of the tourism development.

The adaptive response has changed Yaro from a "traditional Fijian coastal village" into a "tourism-involved village" in Fiji which is in transition. Yaro Levu as an offshoot from the original landowners' village may be seen as a logical (and perhaps inevitable) outcome of that adaptation to tourism. The empowerment entailed in this adaptation, however dysfunctional it may seem to the established chiefly hierarchy of the *mataqali* Ketenamasi, paradoxically may be considered essential to the sustainability of Mana Island's tourism because of the additional options provided for a stake in its tourism activity, and the options it has provided for the resort staff families to be together. For any system to survive it must be both sustainable and adaptable, "incorporating elements of continuity and elements of change" (Harrison 1996) and the Mana Island situation reflects this vital combination in the dynamics of the processes of empowerment.

Anuha Island and Mana Island Compared

It is germane to examine Mana Island as an example of empowerment which has underpinned its sustainability and Anuha Island Resort which at the other end of the continuum proved completely unsustainable. The two resort developments bear many similarities. Both islands are under traditional land tenure; were uninhabited prior to the resort development; had their landowners living on an adjacent island within 10 kilometers; have communities which had not experienced direct resort development on their lands prior to their agreement to lease the islands; were developed initially by Australian interests; have communities which are strongly Christian-oriented (Anuha was affiliated with the Anglican Church, Yaro village with the Methodist Church, and Yaro Levu village with the Seventh Day Adventist Church); manifested strong local leadership and community structures; had a government institution to oversee the process of development (the Solomon Islands Commissioner of Lands in the case of Anuha, and the Fiji Native Lands Trust Board in the case of Mana); and were pioneer developments of a scale not previously experienced in either country before.

In trying to understand the reasons for the different outcomes, it is suggested that there are three key distinctions: the role of the Fiji Native Lands Commission and the Fiji Native Lands Trust Board, which evolved quite differently from the Solomon Islands Lands Commission although their objectives are similar; the requirement under law to have *mataqali* representation on a resort's board of directors, and to employ and train members of the landowning *mataqali* for the resort's labor needs; and the fact that only half of Mana Island was leased to the developers so that the Fijian landowners were not excluded from the island and were able to establish co-residency with the resort. All three factors empowered the traditional landowners of Mana Island and it is argued that this capacity to exert a degree of control over and to protect and further their own interests created the situation where the Mana Island Resort, and its proposed expansion, achieved overwhelming support among them.

The role of the NLTB differs significantly from the Lands Commission in Solomon Islands in that it has been accorded legal responsibility for supervising negotiations between landowners and developers. As outlined above, the Board plays a leading role in pursuing the interests of its constituents, whereas the SI Lands Commission is a much more passive observer. The NLTB is able to guarantee that the landowners will receive benefits accruing to them under any agreement negotiated with a developer company. Its role does not cease with the negotiation of a start-up agreement but with any proposed expansion or redevelopment of a resort. The uncontrolled expansion of Anuha Island Resort, where the local landowners were disempowered and ejected from the island, a sacred site violated, rainforest destroyed and seashore erosion resulted, stands in marked contrast to the Fiji situation where the government's authorized body, the NLTB, and its supporting legislation has empowered Fijian landowners and provided a basis for sustainable resort development. Yet again in contrast to the Solomon Islands situation, the NLTB plays an active role in determining a fair and reasonable annual payment by the resort developer to the landowners and there are formal channels for any revision of the lease or appeal regarding the amount received. The rights of both parties are protected and the NLTB thus ensures a stability in the situation which is conducive to sustaining a long-term operation. There was no such appeal mechanism in the case of Anuha Island.

As outlined above, the standard clause under NLTB lease agreements which provides for public access to beaches below the high tide mark is also an empowering agent. It ensures continuing access to marine resources of the shoreline by locals; it provides them with the power of veto over jetties, sewage outlets, and any other contrivances which project beyond the designated terrestrial boundaries of a resort, or alternatively the right to compensation where they permit such developments; and it prevents the sort of "lock-out" of landowners experienced by Anuha Island at least in respect of foreshore areas below the high water mark of lease boundaries. It has assisted the villagers of Yaro Levu to continue their backpacker operations with access for their tourists guaranteed to the best beaches on the island, despite the construction of a fence between the resort and the village. In Fiji, in contrast to Solomon Islands, the NLTB provision confers additional *legal rights* upon landowners and is thus an effective mechanism of empowerment. In this context, the NLTB has progressed over many years to a respected institution where its provisions and decisions have been tested, defined and refined in the Fijian legal system many times; its capacity to act in the interests of the Fijian landowners and to provide a fair environment for investment and tourism development is accepted. By contrast, the Solomon Islands still has a long road to travel.

In Fiji the legally supported conditions of participation by the *mataqali* in a resort's board of directors and their employment and training constitute a robust medium for empowerment: the *mataqali* cannot be legally excluded from the operations and decision-making process of the resort. It was this empowerment which Kiniboko was able to so adroitly exploit, and which the landowners invoked to maximize their employment opportunities under the proposed expansion of the resort. The Fijian landowners have not been marginalized and alienated, as was the case with Anuha, but incorporated into the *habitus* of Mana Island Resort. In Solomon Islands there are no such mandatory requirements placed on resort developer lessees and it was the dismissal of many of the landowners from resort employment that precipitated the eventual demise of Anuha Island Resort. It is an empowering mechanism in Fiji that is absent in the Solomons.

Finally, the fact that only one third of Mana Island was leased whereas all of Anuha Island came under developer control created a situation in Fiji where the Mana Island principals could not exclude a range of *mataqali* factors from impinging on their capacity to determine courses of action and outcomes based on their own etic values and interests. They were compelled to take into account *mataqali* desires and actions and were often placed in a reactive position where the initiative lay with the landowners. Empowerment in this context was very real in Mana Island. However, to the extent that the villagers of Rera were able to impose control on the ground over events affecting Anuha through extra-legal activities they were able to create a situation where the resort owners were disempowered (negative rather than positive power). The fact that employees of Mana resort may also live in their own village/accommodation outside the resort control has allowed families to re-amalgamate as a unit seven days a week. This is an added factor in creating improved work and family conditions for those staff who have exercised this option. Additionally, the entrepreneurial activity of Yaro Levu residents has contributed to the adaptation of the local community to tourism.

In the final analysis, the "whole-of-environment" for tourism development in Fiji, which includes fundamental underpinning by the legal system, has provided structures, mechanisms and support services for the empowerment of local landowners which is conducive to sustainable tourism development. In Solomon Islands an immature system lacks the capacity to provide such support and Anuha Island's disintegration may be seen as evidence of that inadequacy.

Conclusion

In analyzing the Mana Island situation, it can be seen that empowerment of the traditional landowners has been both formal and informal. Formal through the agency of the NLTB, and informal through the traditional land tenure system which has permitted co-residency with the resort and provided some of the local landowners with opportunities to exploit the resort/tourism situation adroitly. Empowerment has also moved the traditional landowners beyond coexistence to a symbiotic relationship where both parties now depend upon each other. It is different from the symbiotic relationship of the Pentecost villagers and their tourists in that this relationship is one between expatriate resort owners and local landowners rather than hosts and guests.

It is also one where, despite the symbiosis, strain — manifested through disputes — exists. Resort objectives and local community desires do not always coincide. There are also significant inter- and intra-community disputes affecting the two communities of Yaro and Yaro Levu created by the resort development in their midst. Nevertheless, the landowners have adapted to tourism and it is argued that their empowerment, in its different forms, has been part of a dynamic process that has carried them from passive acceptance of tourism to strong support of the resort and active involvement in several consequential activities.

The continuation of overt antagonism by host communities toward tourism postulated by Doxey (1975) in his Irridex as the final stage in the relationship between hosts and guests — and which the Anuha case would appear to support

— is not openly evident in the current Mana Island situation. In the late 1980s there was considerable friction between the resort management and the leadership of the landowners. But the relationship then moved beyond that negative state of affairs to adaptancy as the nature of the relationship changed through a process of empowerment.

Tensions remain (generated for example by the construction of the dividing fence). But rather than ownership of the resort being actively or generally sought by the residents, their efforts tend toward maximizing economic gain and material benefits (such as improved housing, "pirating" resort tourists for their fishing trips, or getting access to the resort's own facilities for its backpackers). One could argue that this relationship is based on a dependency that has become entrenched over the years. But such an argument would deny on the one hand the very real element of power which the resident communities of both Yaro and Yaro Levu villages have ("old" power retained and reasserted, not destroyed or replaced, plus "new" power that has been acquired), and on the other hand, the fact that the resort is dependent upon the goodwill of the two Fijian communities for its continuation. Hence, despite ongoing tensions, a certain symbiosis is considered a more accurate portrayal of the power balance between the parties.

In this context it is suggested that Doxey's Irridex is incomplete and that in many instances the reality of tourism within the social space of a community will result in adaptancy over time with a degree of power sharing denied by Doxey's original hypothesis. The parties may reach this point without necessarily proceeding in a unilinear fashion through Doxey's chronology of stages. In the case of Mana Island the situation may be validly described as one in which the residents have put tourism to work for them rather than simply working for tourism. Since "stages" carries the clear connotation of a chronological series of progressive change (as in stage 1, stage 2, stage 3) Doxey's label is discarded in favour of a more neutral term: "state of affairs", to describe the varied responses of communities to tourism development in their midst. However Doxey's four responses are retained as valid states of affairs. Because of the emphasis on a continual process of adaptancy, we have reworked this model as the "Adaptindex".

In the case of Mana Island and the community of Yaro one could plot a state of affairs and responses which, after the initial euphoria of welcome, moved steadily through a series of adaptations to the new change agent in their midst — the resort — which has led to sustained acceptance. This has been achieved without experiencing indifference or irritation (except in minor ways and not by a majority of the community), or antagonism and hostility. Rather a partnership has developed which has resulted in the sustainability of the resort through empowerment of the community. A similar path could be charted for Yaro Levu,

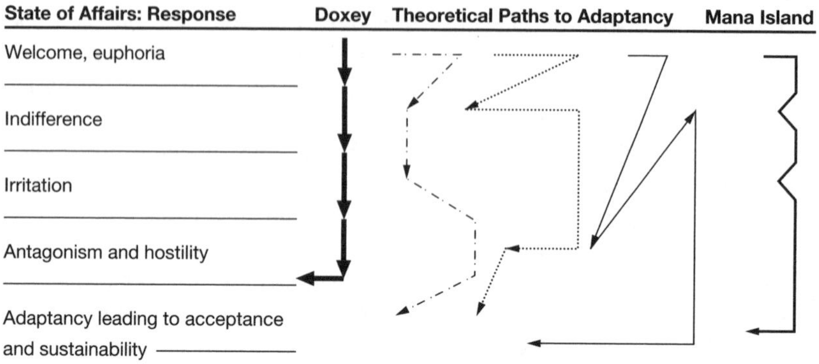

Figure 9.8: The Adaptindex: a Modified Irridex (Sofield After Doxey)

although after initial adaptancy leading to high levels of acceptance and satis-faction for more than 15 years there has been a degree of marginalization and the ingress of some antagonism following the removal of Kiniboko from his position of responsibility with the resort. But that hostility is not unremitting and indeed the community of Yaro Levu and Kiniboko rely to a considerable extent on maintaining a working relationship with the resort management. In short, the Adaptindex (Figure 9.8) provides a tool for longitudinal analysis which underlines the dynamic processes of response to a powerful change agent within a community's social, cultural, political and physical space. The findings of Friedman (1988:8) writing about tourism in the case of St Lucia (West Indies), as quoted previously in Chapter 2, are pertinent: there is no single uniform response by a community to conditions imposed or introduced by an external agent of change; rather there is a variety of responses.

Exploring the resort/host-community relationship further, it is also necessary to distinguish between two different situational demonstrations of empower-ment. The first is that of the landowners of Mana Island, the *mataqali* Ketenamasi, and the second is that involving Ratu Kiniboko and the community of Yaro Levu village. The traditional power of the former as exercised by its chiefs is derived from patrimonial descent and accords with Weber's patri-monialism referred to in Chapter 3. Its norm is custom, regarded as inviolable in pre-contact times. Its mode of authority is essentially personal and its organization entails no administration in the modern sense, although both are now supported by the legal and bureaucratic structures of the modern state of Fiji, specifically the NLTB and its enabling legislation. Through traditional land rights, sanctioned by the state, the chiefs of the *mataqali* Ketenamasi have been able to encompass tourism development in which there is an acceptable symmetry of the power relationship between the old (the tribe) and the new (the foreign developers). However, there is less symmetry between the old (Yaro) and the new (Yaro Levu) in that adaptive response to tourism.

If the six-point concept of empowerment is applied, then the Mana Island situation fits neatly. It is a multidimensional process which has provided the *mataqali* with a consultative process with input of outside expertise (in this case the NLTB) to counter "unconscious incompetence" and the power imbalance; the opportunity to learn and to choose (the consultations on the expansion of the resort were lively and well-informed); the ability to make decisions (granted to them under the provisions of the NLTB); the capacity to implement/apply those decisions (supported by the provisions of the NLTB legislation); acceptance of responsibility for those decisions and actions and their consequences (very strong in the case of Kiniboko); and outcomes directly benefiting the community and its members (highly visible in the standard of housing and other facilities in both Yaro and Yaro Levu, and evident in their overall living standard).

The second demonstration of empowerment by Kiniboko and the Yaro Levu community may be considered an amalgamation of several aspects of power. It can be likened to Weber's concept of "charismatic domination". As noted in Chapter 3 this is extra-legitimate, an exceptional type of power which can operate against regimes of traditional or legal character. It is an apt description of Kiniboko's initial power play when he moved himself outside the jurisdiction of his own chiefs and the Methodist Church and diverted *mataqali* funds to Yaro Levu.

It is also an example of the *reputational* model where power in a given social context will reflect the way it is distributed among those with a reputation for power and influence. This tendency will be an important resource and Kiniboko enjoyed unrivalled influence on Mana Island for many years, an attribute he exploited skilfully. Associated with this model is the *positional* approach (referred to in Chapter 3) in which "powerholders are defined as those who occupy formal positions of leadership and management" (Jacobsen and Cohen 1986:107). Kiniboko is the holder of two formal titles, *ratu* of the *tokatoka* Nabukelevu and *turanga ni koro* of Yaro Levu. In the context of Yaro Levu, these positions translate into acceptance of his power and authority to make decisions and take actions on behalf of the community.

This capacity to act as leader then points to the *decision-making* model. As defined in Chapter 3 this is "the ability to make decisions and have them implemented, irrespective of other people's wishes": it is an operational view of power, in that "it compares outcomes with prior decisions of the actors: the powerful are those whose decisions constantly match the outcomes" (Jacobsen and Cohen 1986:107). Its basic idea is sound: power is only as effective as its application and without a capacity to implement decisions, there cannot be empowerment. That Kiniboko's empowerment is not illusory is evidenced by his ability to control events within Yaro Levu regardless of the contrary views of his chiefs and/or the resort management (the so-called "control model" of power). His diversion of funds to Yaro Levu, the establishment of the Seventh Day Adventist Church school, the initiative of the backpacker business, and the conferring of settler rights upon non-*mataqali vulagi* demonstrate this. The entrepreneurial efforts of community members are also a reflection of this empowerment, lessening their dependence upon decisions of the resort management and bringing considerable benefits to the community both individually and cooperatively.

Supported by the Seventh Day Adventist Church, by members of Yaro Levu village (both *mataqali* and non-*mataqali*), and by government agencies and deriving power from both traditional and contemporary sources, Kiniboko and the Yaro Levu community have attained a degree of empowerment which, as an outcome of the social processes of social exchange, has resulted in a shift of the power balance between the actors. This could change of course. If Kiniboko were disempowered, marginalized, and unable to obtain sufficient benefits for himself and the Yaro Levu community from the adjacent resort, destructive discord could ensue. However, while a degree of marginalization occurred with Kiniboko's dismissal from employment with the resort, and occasional "flashpoints" of antagonism may erupt into anti-resort activity, the kind of conflict which destroyed Anuha Island is considered unlikely. Kiniboko continues to enjoy substantial benefits from the resort. He is entrenched in his own village and is supported by powerful outside agencies (the government and the Seventh Day Adventist Church). In social traditional terms, his status cannot match those of his senior chiefs: his bloodline is simply not of the same pedigree. But in effective, practical terms, he remains an influential player and this is acknowledged by both the chiefs of Yaro and the Japanese resort management. In specific community issues, for example, one or other of the Yaro chiefs may actively solicit Kiniboko's support, again further evidence of Fijian perceptions of his power.

However, as always with Fijian society, especially those Western Fijian villages with significant Melanesian characteristics, power and authority are fluid, social tensions are a constant, and conflict is never far below the surface: minor irritants could develop into substantial power plays (Nayacakolou 1978). These are likely between the chiefs as they vie for greater standing and influence. Aspects of the communities' relationship with the resort could from time to time become embroiled in village politics. Nevertheless, it is considered unlikely that such tensions would attain a magnitude where they would threaten the existence of the resort.

In short, the Mana Island Resort case study is supportive of the contention that empowerment for and of traditional communities requires institutional change to allow a genuine reallocation of power, and that traditional power must be transformed into legal empowerment if sustainable tourism development is to be achieved. This was not the case in Solomon Islands, and Anuha Island Resort no longer exists. Mana Island Resort, however, is now 30 years old. The empowerment of the local landowning communities is held to be a defining characteristic of its sustainability.

Chapter 10

Tourism Development, Sustainability, and Empowerment

Development, sustainability and empowerment are all problematic concepts and sustainable tourism development is but a subset of sustainable development. "Community" is also an ambiguous term. This study has set out to address the question of how to realize the potential of communities to participate in a meaningful way in deciding options for tourism as sustainable development, taking as its point of departure the concept of community empowerment. In constructing this framework it has been necessary to explore in some depth the literature of development theory and aspects of power, so that economics, political science, sociology, and ethnographic research have all contributed to the discourse. An expanded notion of empowerment has been produced by synthesizing different elements from these theoretical and conceptual areas and in this context the study has gone beyond a focus on the impacts of tourism to explore the relevance of a body of political and sociological theory. It is argued that this expanded concept of empowerment constitutes a useful standpoint from which to consider the community/tourism development relationship.

The approach which has been adopted combines the emic paradigm with the etic, and an emphasis on process-based analysis linked to longitudinal studies. The methods and conclusions of previous research have been critically assessed. Chapter 2 journeyed into the literature of the relationship between the state, development and tourism, and development theory. Chapter 3 considered the concept of empowerment, related existing literature to tourism's fairly recent "discovery" of the need to consult host communities about development of this industry, but noted that most involvement fell short of valid empowerment. A synthesized construct of empowerment, taking key elements from different approaches, was formulated, and that provided the focus for assessing the role of empowerment in achieving sustainable tourism development, drawing on five case studies taken from the South Pacific.

In Chapter 4, the role of tourism in the development of South Pacific Island countries was outlined to provide necessary background for the case studies which followed in Chapters 5 to 9. The use of tourism as a tool for economic development by governments is now well established, although the focus of much of the early tourism development literature on the promise of this industry as an economic panacea has been tempered by more accurate analysis of real benefits and costs, a better understanding of the leakage factor, social costs and opportunity cost (e.g. Bryden 1973; Jenkins 1980; Sofield 1993; Tisdell *et al.* 1988). However, in the South Pacific there remains an often major imbalance between resources devoted to tourism in comparison with other less-well performing sectors, a legacy of inertia in the political and bureaucratic structures of both the Island countries themselves and their development assistance benefactors. They have been unable to adapt to the fast changing scenario of this new industry, tourism, now playing such a dominant role in their economies.

A range of case studies from the South Pacific were then presented to assist in developing an understanding of the contextual factors and complexity of the situational elements which need to be taken into account. The five case studies covered the macro, meta, and micro levels: a region-wide attempt at coordination of tourism development and marketing through the establishment of the Tourism Council of the South Pacific (the macro level); formulation of a national policy and 10-year plan for tourism development by the Solomon Islands Government (the meta level); and three communities involved in tourism development, Anuha Island in Solomon Islands, the Sa people of Pentecost Island in Vanuatu, and Mana Island in Fiji (the micro level). The empirical research underlines the importance of environmental change in achieving empowerment which in turn may lead to tourism as sustainable development.

Contextualizing Culture and Power

Much of the research and debate on tourism development in Third World countries "has focused on whether its effects are beneficial or negative and whether they are developmental or anti-developmental" (Hitchcock *et al.* 1993:5). Increasingly a number of analysts of tourism development are querying the simplistic assertions of those from Jafari's cautionary platform that tourism is destructive of culture. Such critics of tourism attribute passivity to the host community, thus denying that community the capacity to respond creatively to the presence of tourism within its social space. The critics suggest that change is a process of destruction of pre-existing social structures and they assert that the causal factors lie with the impacts of tourism. Yet, as noted previously, sociocultural change is difficult to interpret objectively, and concepts such as cultural degradation, cultural corruption, loss of tradition, and ethnicity may defy rational measurement (MacCannell 1994).

When culture is conceived of as a static entity lacking the dynamics of change, the actions, motivations, and values of local community members are ignored. What such an etic approach overlooks is the fact that tourism cannot be isolated from many other aspects of culture, that in treating tourism as an exogenous force analysts run the risk of ignoring how tourism may become part of the local reality (Picard 1993; Hitchcock *et al.* 1993:9). But as the understanding of the complexities of community responses to tourism develops, increasingly one finds that many societies are in fact resilient and have exhibited a capacity to avert the dominance of the outside force; they have put tourism to work for them rather than working for tourism, and so have incorporated it into their social space. Empowerment is the key to this resilience, determining the path of their adaptive response. The case studies of the Sa of Pentecost and the *mataqali* Ketenamasi of Mana Island both illustrate this point.

A crucial factor to emerge from the case studies presented in Chapters 6 to 9 is that to be sustainable a system must be adaptable, incorporating elements of both continuity and change (Harrison 1996). Adaptation may be described more or less objectively but when the impacts of adaptation to tourism are examined and said to be "positive" or "negative" the argument often becomes subjective, related "more to ideology than logic" (Harrison 1996:76). The argument can be applied in both directions to the case studies presented in this book.

In the case of Mana Island, the adaptive response of the community of Yaro Levu to tourism development could be interpreted as "destructive" since it created disequilibrium by challenging the existing chiefly system and traditional power structure and may be contributing to their demise over the longer term. Equally, however, it could be argued that many of the changes deriving from tourism could be viewed as functional because of their contribution to the sustained continuation of the wider whole and to the alleviation of poverty.

In the case of the Sa villagers of Pentecost, the inclusion of a touristic aspect in their traditional organization of the *ghol* may also be interpreted as a positive adaptation to tourism rather than as a negative or destructive impact of tourism on their culture. In both cases it is suggested that empowerment is the key determinant impelling the communities toward adaptive responses which have contributed to sustainability because of their ownership of and degree of control over the direction of change. Conversely, the problems encountered with community tourism development in Solomon Islands can be located in a lack of empowerment. Consideration of the issue of adaptancy has also led to the modification of Doxey's "Irridex" with the Adaptindex by suggesting that host community responses to tourism will not always follow the linear route that he charted, and that a fifth element — adaptancy — will be the outcome in many instances.

The case studies in Chapters 6 to 9 also raise the question, particularly in considering sociocultural factors related to sustainable development, of just what is to be sustained. In this context, the concepts of "culture" and "authenticity" are key elements. Dictionary definitions of heritage emphasize the notion of inheritance: what is or may be transmitted from ancestors. Tourism usage often classifies it as *cultural* or *natural* heritage. The World Heritage Convention (UNESCO 1982) also enjoins signatory nations to ensure the identification, protection, conservation, presentation, and transmission to future generations of the world's cultural and natural heritage.

Cultural heritage may be broadly defined to encompass the history and ideas of a people and/or a country, values and beliefs, buildings and monuments, sites of important past events, the arts (literature, music, dance, sculpture, art), traditional events and festivals, and traditional lifestyles. Natural heritage refers to landscapes in which pristine wilderness (unlogged forests, undammed rivers, and unfarmed mountains) predominate. Landscapes modified by human endeavor are regarded as part of the cultural estate.

It is to a certain extent artificial to separate heritage into cultural and natural divides, because the values associated with landscapes are cultural. For many indigenous peoples their cosmology is based on the indivisibility of humankind and nature. The two cannot be bisected. Their past is linked with the present into the future and heritage is a lived experience. The Anuha Island episode constitutes a graphic illustration of the dangers of attempting to divorce the two using imported concepts (the land classification and judicial system of Britain) and attempting to apply them in a legalistic way with insufficient regard to the indigenous social structure and value system.

These issues underline the difficulty of defining heritage because, ultimately, it can be virtually anything that anybody wants it to be. This becomes apparent when the social and political significance of heritage is considered. Its social significance lies in its association with identity. It is fundamental in helping individuals, communities and nations define who they are, both to themselves and to outsiders. It may provide a sense of belonging in a cultural sense and in terms of place. It can be personal past or impersonal tradition.

In this context, ownership of heritage is linked to ideology and its symbolism takes on strong political overtones. The constant affirmation of legitimate and exclusive ownership of the "true" *ghol* by the Sa people when confronted with its attempted exploitation by neighboring Christian communities, is a manifestation of this. Similarly, the conflict between Ratu Kiniboko and his senior chiefs with respect to the right to control the *mataqali's* relationship with and accompanying benefits from Mana Island Resort, rests in contested heritage. Interpretation of heritage may change to suit or satisfy particular needs because heritage, its ownership, and its utilization will involve considerations of changing values, power structures, and politics. Heritage is thus not a "thing", static in time, but through continuous interpretation may be viewed as a process, as is the concept "traditional".

Perhaps the most striking example of the "imposed etic" (Berry 1990) in interpreting the impacts of tourism may be found with reference to Bali where numerous analyses have criticized tourism as a destructive agent of change (Boon 1977; Francillon 1979; Hanna 1972; Maurer and Zeigler 1988; Turnbull 1982). However, the research of Picard (1993, 1997) and McKean (1982) (who have both spent 25 years studying tourism in Bali) and Sanger (1988) demonstrates that by using a more actor-oriented (emic) approach the interrelationship between tourism change and culture change cannot be viewed as a "one-way street". Host communities adapt to and in turn modify the tourism which takes place within their social space. Tourism is also spatially compartmentalized: most of the population is not directly impacted, especially by the more unseemly elements of visitation (D. King, personal communication, 1997). Berno (1996), writing about tourism in the Cook Islands, also examines the emic/etic perspective in cross-cultural analysis of content/context.

Picard has termed this "touristic culture": through tourism, culture has been transformed into the main economic resource of Bali and by the same token Balinese culture has become a major bargaining point with the central Indonesian government, tourism authorities and operators (Picard 1993:86). Since Balinese tourism relies upon their culture, if this industry were to destroy the culture it would destroy Balinese tourism (McKean 1982).

The result is one in which the Balinese have been compelled to define their "Balinese-ness" and in the process they have put tourism to work for Bali and Balinese society. This process includes their "ongoing symbolic construction of tradition and authenticity" (Wood 1993:60). The terrorist bombing of tourist-frequented nightclubs in Bali and the deaths of more that 180 tourists in October 2002 may have destroyed tourism to this destination in the short term, but those acts of terrorism have not destroyed Balinese culture which remains as vibrant as ever. It is probable that, just as Egyptian tourism recovered from the terrorist-initiated massacre of a group of European tourists in the Valley of the Kings in 1995 within four years, so visitation to Bali may recover within a similar time-frame if security of tourists is achieved.

An interesting range of emic views about the Bali bombings began to emerge in the weeks immediately after the event. One of Bali's foremost academics and cultural leaders, Dr Ketut Suryani, said in an interview with *The Australian* (22 October 2002) that the Kuta bombings should be seen as "an act of cleansing by God", an event "that would cleanse Bali of unwanted foreign influence", that it was divine punishment because Bali "has not developed cultural tourism but brought in many things outside Balinese culture", such as "prostitution, gambling, paedophilia, drugs, casinos – things that are not Balinese". She asserted that Bali would benefit by the cessation of mass tourism for a year or more because "my people could go back to the land, to their paddy". An opposite Balinese view was expressed by rural *losman* (Balinese guest house) owners who refuted Dr Suryani's animosity towards tourism and said that they welcomed especially backpackers because they were sensitive to Balinese culture (*The Australian*, 23 October 2002). Yet another emic view, diametrically opposed to Dr Suryani's stance, was evidenced in the decision of the Hindu priests of Kuta to hold a cleansing ceremony one month after the event on the site of the nightclub that had been destroyed. They believed that evil spirits had assumed control of the site; rather than being cleansed by the bombing the site had in their view been demonized and polluted. The Hindu religious ceremony was intended to restore the principle of *Tri Hita Karana*, the guiding force that creates harmony between God, humans and the environment. Animals, including buffaloes and turtles, were sacrificed as part of the ritual, which was attended by more than 5000 people, including 28 foreign ambassadors and almost the entire Indonesian Cabinet. The Balinese Minister for Tourism, Gede Pitana, said that, after the bombing, the harmony of the island had become unbalanced and that with the ceremony the balance was restored. For many Balinese, that balance was not only spiritual but economic and they prayed that the cleansing ritual would wash away the economic ills that struck the island after the bombing on 12 October (*The Australian*, 14 November 2002).

The key difference in the analyses lies in the emic approach of Picard, McKean, and Sanger, as distinct from the etic approach of most. This conclusion recalls Wilson's insistence that tourism analyses will benefit by "a thoroughly empirical research strategy which seeks hermeneutic understanding in terms of the knowledge possessed by the participants themselves: their definitions, goals, strategies, decisions, and the perceived consequences of their actions" (1981:477).

This debate points to the interrelationship between development and culture: "development itself cannot really be conceptualized outside of culture; it is above all a form of discourse which has welded an enormous range of phenomena into a single concept and provided the framework for the exercise of a wide range of forms of power" (Wood 1993:68). It is in scrutinizing power in the context of development that one focuses on empowerment of communities as a necessary element for tourism ventures to achieve sustainability.

The Role of the State

Any discussion of tourism, sustainable development, and empowerment of necessity requires an examination of the role of the state and often politics and their relationship to the many facets of the tourism system. Governments are intrinsically political and concerned with maintaining and exercising power. From the perspective of political science, "the organization of power around tourism policy issues, the political motivations surrounding decisions affecting tourism, and the decisions regarding who will be the political constituencies for tourism policy are particularly germane" (Richter 1993:180).

In scanning much of the literature, the relationship of the state to tourism development is generally absent or subsumed under economic or sociological constructions. The writings of Richter (1980, 1982, 1984, 1985, 1989, 1991, 1993), and most recently Hall (1994, 1996) are conspicuous exceptions. The general dearth of such research is unfortunate because, although tourism as an industry is generally regarded as a private sector activity where market forces predominate, in fact the involvement of the state is comprehensive. The degree of that involvement varies from country to country, but invariably there is some role for government in tourism. The question is not whether government should have a role at all, rather an acceptance that it does have a role. In examining the nature of that role, it is more often than not one that works with a top-down approach to planning for development, rather than one that involves communities in a proactive way.

This situation emphasizes the asymmetrical relationship of power and dependence between government and community. Power/dependence relations may determine control over both rewards and punishments and dictate the responses of the two parties in an adversarial situation. Jamal and Getz (1995) attempt to overcome unequal power balances in their application of collaboration theory by suggesting that local government authorities act as an impartial instrument for redressing the imbalance. However, this approach is flawed to the extent that such authorities will have their own agendas for development, may be comprised of a collection of vested interests, are often exercising control and/or influence to ensure a desired outcome, and cannot be regarded as neutral arbiters seeking to manage conflict and draw opposing parties for a freely attained optimal solution.

Nevertheless, it should not be assumed that local communities, governments and tourism developers will always be positioned in opposition to each other. The tripartite cooperation among Mana Island's traditional landowners, the Fiji Government, and the foreign investors when the development of the resort on Mana Island was welcomed and successfully negotiated, is an indication of this. Jamal and Getz (1995) would probably suggest that this is an example of successful collaboration. The dissonance, uncertainties and hostilities that were generated by the Anuha Island development stand in stark contrast.

The term "development" has been used to describe both a process and a state. When referring to social and economic change, it is defined as a process. When it refers to a condition (a "developed" or "undeveloped" or "less developed" country) it is used to describe a state of being. The later theories broadened its meaning from an initial narrow emphasis on development as economic growth to encompass qualitative measures and principles of equity: a more even distribution of the benefits of progress, wider accessibility to education, health and welfare facilities, in short "a general improvement in the material and social well-being of the society as a whole" (Mehmet 1978:175). Modernization and the processes of globalization have taken the whole discussion of development down a different path, with tourism identified as paradoxically an agent for both globalization and localization. In this context, tourism as a force for globalization has played a key role in modernization (Harrison 1997b). Sustainable development takes the concept further by projecting the ethical considerations beyond the present generation to future generations for intergenerational equity.

Craik suggests that "sustainable tourism must be managed [by governments]" (1991:131); and de Kadt argues that only states can provide the conditions for movement toward greater sustainability (1990). Richter's many studies of tourism policy direction in different Asian countries highlight the need for governments to become more actively involved in the "neglected" area of tourism's sustainability (1993:196). In some cases this has led to "a realization that tourism issues need to be coordinated at a government level" because the complex interdependence of the issues are too great for "either the industry or the local political jurisdictions to cope with them", although Richter suggests that too few governments perceive the issues as urgent (1993:196). These authors support the contention of Craig and Mayo that the state and political processes at different levels must engage with communities for development to be sustained: "If community participation and empowerment are to contribute to (national development) goals, then strategies need to be formulated . . . to engage wider political processes and to be set within a framework of economic, social and political structures" (1995:10). Harrison (1988) also notes the importance of analyzing political structures to gain an understanding of the decision-making processes in development.

The examination of the case study material presented in this study emphasizes the central role of the state as a necessary ingredient for underpinning both sustainable development and empowerment. The case studies demonstrate in various ways the fact that empowerment of communities for tourism development requires a political framework that is either supportive or at least neutral, not obstructionist. In situations of dual systems (traditionally oriented communities located in the social and political space of a modern state) there must be effective means whereby empowerment embedded in Weber's traditional or legitimate base can be transformed into legally sanctioned empowerment if it is to be a vehicle for sustainable development. A shared willingness by community, individuals, and external entities is basic to initiate and undertake the processes leading to "environmental change" (Wallerstein and Bernstein 1988).

In Solomon Islands, the rhetoric of tourism policy suggested one thing but the reality is another. The necessary support is not forthcoming in terms of policies which can actually be implemented or transformed into legal practical activity, and hence local communities struggle to become involved in tourism development. In Vanuatu and Fiji, by contrast, the social forces of local communities (legitimate power) have combined with the political forces of the state (legal power) to arrive at a situation of empowerment: sustainable community-based tourism development has occurred.

These examples support the contention that on the one hand empowerment must include as an essential characteristic the involvement of the state in setting conditions that will provide the environment for assigning real power to communities. On the other hand, it is essential that the community should have the capacity to set the agenda for consideration of tourism development, have access to appropriate resources, and a concomitant ability to implement its decisions. Empowerment requires a genuine sharing of power. If a community cannot/does not have that capacity for choice and decision implementation, then it can not counter dependency and cannot be defined as being empowered.

Empowerment

While sustainable development features four integrated elements, ecological, economic, social and cultural sustainability, in this study the role of the local community in tourism development in particular is highlighted. It is consistent with the principle of the need for local communities to be involved in decision-making for development. This is not meant to indicate that the social and cultural dimensions are more important than the ecological and economic dimensions: they are all important and integral to each other. Rather, it is designed to place the concept of empowerment in the development process under the microscope.

As the definition of development has expanded, there has been some movement toward concepts such as community consultations, community participation, self-determination, and self-management which reach out toward empowerment. But for the most part empowerment which involves a meaningful transfer of power and resources to communities has yet to be implemented as a fundamental component of development. The ideology of consultations and participation is often hollow, a form of manipulation and management of community, tokenism without enabling power. Chambers (1983, 1997) has clearly delineated the limitations of much endeavor which masquerades as participatory community development.

References in the tourism planning literature to empowerment which moves beyond rhetoric have been found in only a few instances such as Brass (1994), Macbeth (1996), and Sofield and Birtles (1996). Few texts advocate a real devolution of power to communities, to set the agenda in a situation where proactive forward planning accompanied by power to implement decisions of real choice is vested in them. Rather, the community is restricted to a reactive response to an external agenda. The tourism development and planning literature tends to be dominated by the top-down approach with agendas for community consideration set by outside professionals, politicians, planners, investors and other stakeholders.

Macbeth has described this deficiency as "dissonance and paradox in tourism planning" (1996:2). The dissonance arises from commitments to development by those in control who are often in conflict with community. Paradoxically, tourism planning models allow the "public" or "local community" a participatory role, but this "participation" is "in effect public relations rhetoric that permits the local community to do little more than *react* to plans, proposals and developments that will be implemented" (Macbeth 1996:3; italic in the original).

As with sustainable development, so empowerment as a concept rests on a philosophical base: the acceptance of equity principles and social justice. The presence of these elements in empowerment thus introduces ethical considerations: what is "right", what is "wrong", what is "good", what is "bad". Empowerment is also about political power just as development is about political power: who gets what, where, how and why. It is at these points that empowerment and development coincide, hence the contention that empowerment needs to be incorporated into the definition of development if implementation of policies and plans are to be effective and if sustainability is to be achieved.

As noted in Chapter 3, the concept developed in this text of empowerment by and of communities is at once both a process and an outcome. It is an amalgamation of several different emphases, derived in part not only from political science but also from the social exchange theory literature, especially Emerson (1962, 1972, 1987); Blau (1964, 1977, 1987); and Molm (1981, 1986, 1988, 1989a, 1989b) who, among other things, deal with prestige and power in social exchange and link structure and the use or non-use of power.

It is important that the working definition of empowerment formulated in this research be perceived in political and structural sociological terms (Emerson's power/dependence relationships) rather than in individual behavioral psychological terms (Keiffer's self-development model). This is seen as essential in the context of communities being enabled to exercise effective decision-making and undertake consequential action for tourism development. Social exchange theory assists in emphasizing that it is the social as distinct from the psychological framework which is the nub of the construct as applied to communities. It focuses on the social process of alternating reciprocities underlying this interaction (Blau 1987) and is particularly relevant for Melanesian communities where reciprocity and exchange is a major determinant of power. The exercise of the latter moves the concept of empowerment directly into the political arena.

A key component in this consideration of empowerment is the decision-making model which incorporates application or implementation of decisions. As noted in Chapter 3, this is an operational view of power because it compares outcomes with prior decisions of those involved in a particular situation. The powerful are those whose outcomes match the decisions. A community which is "participating" in consultations cannot be said to be empowered if its decisions are ignored or incapable of implementation.

This is only part of the story, however. Even if a community's decisions are accepted and implemented, if those decisions are in respect of an agenda for tourism development set by powerful outsiders so that the community's response is only its reaction to that agenda, the lack of choice in the first instance about the direction of any development would suggest that there is imperfect empowerment. If, however, there is a real capacity to reject a development proposal, rather than simply have it shaped or amended to fit with the community's preferences, then a degree of real power could be said to reside with the host community. This raises the question which much of the discussion on empowerment leaves ambiguous: the degree of self-reliance or self-sufficiency necessary for empowerment to have occurred. At one end of the spectrum are those writers who consider that it is essential for self-help to be total, with minimal outside intervention or assistance. At the other end are those who consider that involvement in decision-making is sufficient (McArdle 1989).

Both extreme viewpoints have weaknesses. An immediate problem with the purist's approach is that often it is those most in need who have the least resources and capacity to help themselves (and may witness "unconscious incompetence"). The difficulty with the other extreme view is that, other than involvement in consultations, everything else is left to the experts and the professionals. This can be validly criticized as tokenism, particularly because it fails to recognize the fundamental proposition that as long as the process is controlled by others who have access to the resources then the process is actually one of disempowerment (Rose and Black 1985). While Macbeth (1996) does not use the term "disempowerment" nor focus on control of resources, his concern with "outside" control of the agenda amounts to the same thing. In his approach a community is disempowered before it starts the consultation process because it is limited to a reactionary stance. The community is "backgrounded": the state, professional planners and investors are "foregrounded".

Where a community is deprived of any real say over its future, that powerlessness may result in the community being alienated and marginalized from the development process (Reed 1997). In many cases where powerlessness is not accepted such negative positioning will result in resistance (Barbalet 1985). If the resistance results in resolution of tension without conflict, it will move to Nadel's (1963) condition of "consociation" because of the interdependency of the disputants. In extreme circumstances resistance may, however, lead to either or both parties resorting to physical force. In the case of Anuha, the disempowerment of the Rera community led to the use of physical force by both adversaries: the villagers who invaded the resort, and the government whose police force restored law and order. It is an example of conflict resistance arising from disempowerment (Giddens 1976) and in terms of the community's status in the asymmetrical relationship with the state it failed to achieve a redistribution of responsibility and power. But the community's actions limited the capacity of the resort's owners to continue operating it, and it was this limitation which allowed resistance to contribute to the eventual outcome in which effective power over the future of the island reverted back to the traditional landowners.

In contrast to the negative actions of the Rera community in seeking control over tourism development within its social and economic space, the cases of the Sa in Vanuatu and Mana Island demonstrate positive action, in which the environment for empowerment in the context of tourism development has government underpinning. A combination of social and political structures facilitates the capacity of the communities to exert a degree of control over the direction of their involvement in tourism.

In the context of tourism development it is proposed that empowerment be regarded as a multi-dimensional process which provides communities with a consultative process often characterized by the input of outside expertise; the opportunity to learn and to choose; the ability to make decisions; the capacity to implement and apply those decisions; acceptance of responsibility for those decisions and actions and their consequences; and outcomes directly benefiting the community and its members, not diverted or channeled to others. The case studies raise the question of temporality since empowerment is a process which takes place over time: a snapshot of a particular situation may lead to conclusions which would likely be amended were a series of snapshots to be taken over a period of years.

In the case of Anuha Island, while in the final analysis there was a capacity to undertake decisions, implement them and derive a modicum of benefits for the community, in fact the resort itself had failed. It could be said that there was empowerment in the context of the return of the island to its traditional landowners but there was not empowerment for tourism development. However, it is conceivable that at some time in the future a new investor could appear in the Solomons who would negotiate a new lease of Anuha Island which could be very favorable to the traditional landowners; and the long-drawn-out conflict which eventually returned the island to them could be construed as a highly positive outcome of empowerment. Scenarios of change could be drawn for the other case studies which, should they eventuate, would then also require reassessment.

Based on the expanded construct of empowerment proposed in the first chapter, five propositions were formulated and then applied to the case studies to test their validity. The first was *that without the element of empowerment tourism development at the level of community will have difficulty achieving sustainability*. The two case studies from Solomon Islands illustrate the difficulties in attaining sustainability of tourism development and specific ventures by communities when there is no empowerment. At the national level, the impediments caused by legislation and regulations designed in the first instance for the spatial system of urban centres have resulted in an inability to implement tourism development policies designed to facilitate the entry of indigenous communities into that development process. The structures of government have tended to disempower rather than empower local communities. The example of the Tainiu Guest House highlights the obstacles which exist. They have kept this development, highly desired by government policy, out of the formal economy and operating illegally because of its inability to comply with a range of regulatory requirements without which it cannot be licensed.

The now-defunct Anuha Island Resort provides a graphic example of the drastic consequences which may occur when the host community is disempowered, alienated, and marginalized from the development process. The inability of the Rera community to have a proactive role in the shape and form of tourism within its social space, its exclusion from the decision-making ambit of the resort's operations and expansion, and its frustration with the imported legal system, pushed its members in the direction of illegality and violence as they attempted to redress perceived grievances. The village attempted both legal and legitimate means to assert its rights as it viewed them. In the final analysis, the failure of the environment (sociocultural, legal, and governmental) to provide durable empowerment, coupled with the community's disempowerment at key points in time, generated centrifugal forces which literally destroyed the resort.

Social exchange theory (Ap 1992) has proved an incisive tool for analyzing the dynamics of the relationship between the local Melanesian community of Rera village and the developers of Anuha Island Resort. It is suggested that social exchange theory could be applied to a wide range of situations in Melanesian society where exchange based on reciprocity is a central feature and where power is a constantly shifting and dynamic characteristic. For example, social exchange theory could be utilized to analyze both the host/guest relationship of the *ghol* of Pentecost and the local/investor relationship of Mana Island Resort.

The second proposition states that *the exercise of traditional or legitimate empowerment by traditionally oriented communities will of itself be an ineffectual mechanism for attempting sustainable tourism development.* Returning to the two case studies from Solomon Islands, the deficiencies of traditional structures and mechanisms to empower communities in the contemporary state indicate that sustainable development will not be achieved. Anuha stands as mute testimony to the validity of this proposition.

At first sight, the case study from Vanuatu would seem to contradict the second proposition because it demonstrates that legitimate empowerment can be achieved by a community drawing only upon its traditional resources. Over a long period of time, the Sa people of South Pentecost *were* able to exercise traditional (legitimate) power in the face of attempts by legally constituted authorities (the colonial powers and the Christian churches) to suppress their traditional ceremonial activities (Bani 1989; de Burlo 1996; Jolly 1982, 1994; Sofield 1991a; Tonkinson 1982). However, when that ceremony was commoditized by external entrepreneurs the local owners of the *ghol* lost such a degree of control that they finally reacted by "closing" it to outsiders. In other words, legitimate domination was insufficient in the face of the forces of contemporary development to sustain local control. It required that element of state intervention and support to add legal empowerment to legitimate empowerment.

This introduces the third proposition *that traditional empowerment must be transformed into legal empowerment if sustainable tourism development is to be achieved*; and the fourth proposition *that empowerment for such communities will usually require environmental or institutional change to allow a genuine reallocation of power to ensure appropriate changes in the asymmetrical relationship of the community to the wider society.* The successful touristic presentation of the *ghol* by the Sa people required the power of the state (legal domination) being added to legitimate domination to ensure that sole owner-ship and exploitation of the *ghol*-as-tourism rested with the local community. That ownership is seen as essential to the retention and maintenance of authen-ticity, a problematic concept but one which is fundamental to the capacity of the *ghol* to attract outside visitation and command relatively high prices for those admitted to the ceremony. The result is a symbiotic relationship between the Sa and tourists in which the local community depends upon tourism as its major source of income and the visitors depend upon the local community for that elusive characteristic, authenticity.

If the application of the third and fourth propositions to Solomon Islands is examined it can be argued that the country's development path, patterns, and forms have to a large extent been dictated by outside authorities. Models have been imported from overseas with little regard for "fit" with the indigenous structures. This forms a significant contrast with the situation in Vanuatu. In addition to cultural "fit", genuine and enduring (sustainable) empowerment of communities requires that it be based on constitutionally recognized rights and sanctioned within an environment supported by the state. As noted in Chapter 9, Vanuatu had to fight both politically and militarily for its independence and this appears to have been a salient aspect in the declaration of the centrality of indigenous culture and identity which finds expression in its constitution and its development policies. The *ghol* is an expression of these values as well as an example of a sustainable community-based tourism venture.

In Fiji, one finds that an indigenous political structure, the Great Council of Chiefs, was able to negotiate a legal format for the registration of native land with the colonial power. Fiji uses a combination of legitimate (traditional) and legal (state sanctioned) rights dating back more than one hundred years which provided a base for post-independence legislation to produce a relatively stable environment for the empowerment of communities. The development of Mana Island Resort and its continued operations over an unbroken period of more than 25 years is an outcome of the successful integration of the dual state where traditional and "modern" values coexist. Ratu Kiniboko has been able to move adroitly between both worlds, utilizing elements from both in his quest for power and the empowerment of his community of Yaro Levu.

In Solomon Islands, however, the lack of empowerment by communities and the implementation gap between the government tourism policy and actual participation by its people in village-based tourism development requires that the bias toward the modern, formal sector be countered. The concept of "pioneer space empowerment" has been advanced to achieve the necessary transformation of the development environment. A double-pronged strategy of amending existing legislation to deregulate legal constraints in designated areas and the establishment of a national authority charged with defining specific conditions to oversee specific projects is suggested. Such a new spatial system would not obviate land disputes but, once ownership of land was resolved, pioneer space empowerment would then allow legal village-based tourism development to proceed. This is in marked contrast to the present situation where existing laws and regulations put construction of even a small resort out of economic and legal reach. "Pioneer space empowerment", it is argued, would facilitate the use of human and physical resources of a community for tourism development, with the end product under its control, managed and operated by its members maximizing the resulting economic return. The concept is designed as an enabling mechanism to regularize and legalize community-based ventures which do not meet the formal requirements of various government Acts and to overcome the obstacles identified in the analysis of Solomon Islands' tourism policies and plans.

The fifth proposition of the empowerment construct states that *conversely, empowerment of indigenous communities cannot be "taken" by the communities concerned drawing only upon their own traditional resources but will require support and sanction by the state if it is to avoid being short-lived.*

The Anuha Island Resort case study supports this proposition in both the negative and the positive. Rera village's attempts to draw upon its traditional resources without the backing of constitutional or other state structures to assert a degree of control over its island resulted in the power of the state through the court system imposing penalties upon the community; and in the process the resort was destroyed. However, when the community utilized that court system to have the lease transferred from the foreign investor to the community, it was successful in regaining control over the island (even if there was no longer a viable resort to operate).

In the case of the *ghol*, it may be argued that without the support of legal power the attempt by the Sa people to reassert control over the utilization of their traditional resource for tourism would not have succeeded. The village required the assistance of the government to translate into actuality its desire to reopen the *ghol* for outside visitation, with its ownership of the staging of the ceremony sanctioned and protected by the state.

With reference to Mana Island, Ratu Kiniboko has authority within Yaro Levu and a capacity to influence operations and events related to the resort because of support by powerful external actors, the Fiji Government and the Seventh Day Adventist Church. Without those external elements of support, it is very doubtful that Kiniboko, as a minor chief drawing upon traditional authority, would have been able to sustain his position of relative dominance and power.

All three country situations — Solomon Islands, Vanuatu and Fiji — emphasize the necessity of the state being involved in environmental transformation to ensure real power is passed to local communities, for without such empowerment there is unlikely to be tourism as sustainable development. Even sustainable development, narrowly defined as tourism which is economically viable over the longer term, may be jeopardized if it must contend with host community hostility. This is not to suggest that local control should be all powerful: the *caveat* is that there are obviously important national interests which in certain circumstances must take priority over local community desires (national environmental concerns). The overriding conclusion, however, is that the case studies point to the validity of the five propositions embedded in the expanded construct of empowerment explored in this research.

Directions for Future Research

It has been posited that empowerment is a crucial determinant in the sustainability of community-based tourism development and in exploring this contention the need for more detailed research in several areas has become obvious. These include (a) an examination of empowerment and disempowerment in communities involved with tourism both in First and Third World countries where equity issues are increasingly being incorporated as a matter of course in political discourse about and action concerning the welfare of society at large; (b) operationalizing empowerment in planning, that is, developing ways in which the process of community empowerment may be fully incorporated into the planning process to achieve the objective of a stronger role for communities in sustainable tourism development, foregrounding community rather than professional planners and external agencies; (c) probing linkages with other theories, such as social representations theory, which could be explored in the context of contributing to an understanding of empowerment of community and tourism development; (d) developing a detailed set of criteria with which to measure sustainability and relating that to a community-based tourism venture or a community's involvement in tourism and the effectiveness of empowerment; and (e) in this context (and in a reinforcement of the need for more longitudinal studies) monitoring the communities involved in the case studies presented in this study and undertaking field trips to revisit them in another five years' time to reassess the sustainability of their involvement in tourism development. Research into these questions may assist researchers to find some answers to key issues confronting tourism policy, and specifically the need to better understand sustainable development, the role of empowerment in that process, and residents' perceptions, values, and priorities regarding tourism's place in their community and its ability to alleviate poverty.

Following the events of 11 September 2001, a sharper focus has fallen upon the need to alleviate poverty, since a conclusion drawn by various analysts and policy makers was that endemic poverty underlies instability in many parts of the world and may motivate desperate people to resort to acts of terrorism. The Bali bombings of 2002 reinforced this inference. In drawing this conclusion it was also accepted that development assistance programs were in many cases failing to reach those most in need and that more research was required to define how tourism development might contribute to a more directed approach to ensure that benefits flowed to the poorest, marginalized and oppressed sections of populations.

Tourism has only very recently been recognized by some aid donors and some international funding agencies as an effective tool for poverty reduction. The United Kingdom has played a leading role in this activity over the past five years and has termed the intervention "Pro-Poor Tourism" (PPT). Other agencies such as the World Tourism Organization and UNCTAD have used the term "Sustainable Tourism for Eliminating Poverty" (STEP). The CRC Sustainable Tourism (Australia) has utilized the term "Sustainable Tourism Actively Reducing Poverty" (STARP). In the aftermath of the Twin Towers atrocity, the World Bank (December 2001) and the Asian Development Bank (May 2002) reassessed their policies and revised their funding of tourism activities by directing it into areas where they considered that tourism has the potential to make a significant contribution to poverty reduction (Sofield, DeLacy, Bauer, Moore, and Daugherty 2002). For more than 50 of the world's poorest countries tourism is ranked first, second or third in terms of their economies and tourism is the only service industry to show a positive balance of trade, with flows from first world countries to developing countries exceeding those in the opposite direction by $US66 million (World Tourism Organization 2000). In the South Pacific, tourism is the single largest industry for a number of the micro-states, yet development assistance to the South Pacific has paid almost no attention to the tourism sector. A reduction in world poverty is an internationally agreed priority and targets have been set to halve poverty by the year 2015. Achieving poverty reduction requires actions on a variety of complementary fronts and scales, but a prerequisite of significant progress is pro-poor growth (growth that benefits the poor). As an industry that is clearly important in many poor countries, can tourism be one source of such growth?

PPT/STEP/STARP is not a new form of tourism, nor a new kind of tourism product. It is an approach to tourism in which the tourism "cake" is tilted so that benefits are specifically directed towards the poor. As a new field of endeavor for development assistance bureaux and international funding agencies, there is no established track record on which they can draw to implement appropriate programs and hence the need for more research. Case studies in the field of PPT/STEP/STARP are rare because of its innovative recency. However, the UK has produced a small booklet on six case studies (Ashley, Roe, and Goodwin 2001), and Australia has collated a similar number of cases (Sofield *et al.* 2002). One area to emerge from these few studies is that the so-called "trickle-down effect" (a passive approach which holds that economic development will, through backward linkages, eventually impact upon all segments of society) is inadequate in ensuring that the benefits of tourism reach those most in need and that a proactive interventionist approach is needed. In association with this, it is also recognized that a directed approach is dependent upon institutional change: to construct a multifaceted institutional framework. This framework should extend vertically and horizontally through the encompassing environment of Society (attitudes) and Government (public policy formulation), which "control" how (or indeed if) poverty is addressed formally and informally. Prevailing attitudes and policies shape the environment in which poverty exists, creating a situation where there is often little remedial action. Education is required to attempt to change attitudes and society's values, and devolution of power is required for effective intervention. In short, the poorest segments of populations need to be empowered if alleviation of their plight through tourism is to be sustainable. The WTO (Lipman 2002) has recognized the necessity to understand how the dynamics of this empowerment might function and in May 2002, at the World Ecotourism Summit in Quebec, it announced a new program designed to mobilize the research community to explore key linkages between sustainable tourism and the elimination of poverty.

References

Adelman, I. and Morris, C.T.
  1973   Economic Growth and Social Equity in Developing Countries. Stanford: Stanford University Press.
Agarwala, A.N. and Singh, S.P., eds
  1963   The Economics of Underdevelopment. New York: Oxford University Press.
Alasia, Sam
  1989   Politics. *In* Ples Blong Iumi: Solomon Islands: The Past Four Hundred Years, H. Laracy, ed., pp. 112–120. Suva: University of the South Pacific.
Allen, M., ed.
  1981   Vanuatu: Politics, Economics and Ritual in Island Melanesia. Sydney: Academic Press.
Allen, M.
  1984   Elders, Chiefs and Big Men: Authority Legitimation and Political Evolution in Melanesia. American Ethnologist 11: 20–41.
Altman, Jon C.
  1989   Tourism Dilemmas for Aboriginal Australians. Annals of Tourism Research 16: 456–476.
Amarshi, A., Good, K., and Mortimer, R.
  1979   Development and Dependency. The Political Economy of Papua New Guinea. Melbourne: Oxford University Press.
Amin, S.
  1974   Accumulation on a World Scale: A Critique of the Theory of Under-Development. New York: Monthly Review Press.
Anderson, J.
  1990   Home Care Management in Chronic Illness and the Self-care Movement: An Analysis of Ideologies and Economic Processes Influencing Policy Decisions. Advances in Nursing Science 12(2): 71–83.
Annals of Tourism Research
  1990   Special Issue on Tourism in Socialist Countries. London: Elsevier Science.
Ap, J.
  1992   Residents' Perceptions on Tourism Impacts. Annals of Tourism Research 19: 655–690.
Apple, M.W.
  1995   Education and Power. New York: Routledge.
Apter, D.
  1972   The Political Kingdom in Uganda. Princeton: Princeton University Press.

1987   Rethinking Development: Modernization, Dependency and Postmodern Politics. Newbury Park: Sage Publications.
Archer, Brian
1996   Sustainable Tourism: An Economist's Viewpoint. *In* Sustainable Tourism in Islands and Small States: Issues and Policies. L. Briguglio, B. Archer, J. Jafari and G. Wall, eds, pp. 6–17. London: Pinter.
Arndell, R.
1989   Tourism as a Development Concept in the South Pacific. The Courier (July–August): 83.
Arnstein, S.R.
1971   A Ladder of Citizen Participation in the USA. Journal of the Town Planning Institute 57: 176–182.
Asad, Talal, ed.
1973   Anthropology and the Colonial Encounter. London: Ithaca Press.
Ashley, Caroline, Roe, Dilys, and Goodwin, Harold
2001   Pro Poor Tourism Strategies: Making Tourism Work for the Poor. A Review of Experience. London: UK Government Overseas Development Institute.
Asian Development Bank
1990   Papua New Guinea Urban Sector Profile. Manila: Asian Development Bank.
ASMAL
1991   Pacific Report. First Quarter. Auckland.
Atkinson, B.
1988   UNDP/WTO and International Tourism Organisations: The Need for Leadership and Global Thinking. Lecture presentation for the First South Pacific Tourism Fellowship, James Cook University. Suva: UNDP/WTO.
Atkinson, P. and Delamont, S.
1990   Professions and Powerlessness: Female Marginality in the Learned Occupations. The Sociological Review 38(1): 90–110.
The Australian
2002   "Bombing Was Good: Bali Academic", 22 October, p. 5.
2002   "Tourism Good for Bali", 23 October, p. 5.
2002   Cleansing to Ward Off Evil", 14 November, p. 6.
Australian Agency for International Development (AusAID)
1995–2001   Annual Report. Canberra: AGPS.
1998   Papua New Guinea Agricultural Cluster Evaluation. Evaluation no. 5. Canberra; AusAID.
Australian Department of Foreign Affairs and Trade.
1995   Outline on Solomon Islands. Canberra: DFAT.
Australian International Development Assistance Bureau (AIDAB)
1987–1994   Annual Report. Canberra: AGPS.
1991a   Australian Development Cooperation in the Agricultural and Rural Development Sector. Report 1990–91. Canberra: AGPS.
1991b   Environmental Assessment for International Development Cooperation. Canberra: AGPS.
Australian National Centre for Development Studies
1988   Import Content of Tourist Hotel Food and Beverage Purchases in the South Pacific. Islands/Australia Working paper No. 88/1. Canberra: ANU.

Bacharach, S. and Lawler, E.J.
1980　Power and Politics in Organization. San Francisco: Jossey-Bass.
1981　Bargaining: Power, Tactics and Outcomes. San Francisco: Jossey-Bass.
Baines, G.B.K.
1987　Manipulation of Islands and Men. *In* Ambiguous Alternative: Tourism in Small Developing Countries. Stephen Britton and William C. Clarke, eds, pp. 16–24. Suva: University of the South Pacific.
Balandier, G.
1965　Traditional Social Structures and Economic Changes. *In* Africa: Social Problems of Change and Conflict, P. L. van den Berghe, ed., pp. 81–96. New York: John Wiley.
1970a　Political Anthropology. Translated by A.M. Sheridan Smith. London: Allen Lane.
1970b　Sociocultural Unbalance and Modernization in the Underdeveloped Countries. *In* Readings in Social Evolution and Development, S.N. Eisenstadt, ed., pp. 361–378. Oxford: Pergamon Press.
Bani, G.
1989　An Examination of Small Scale Tourism and Hospitality Sector Business Enterprises in Vanuatu. Unpublished SPFP Research Paper. Townsville, Australia: James Cook University.
Banks, D.J., ed.
1976　Changing Identities in Modern Southeast Asia. The Hague, Paris: Mouton Publishers.
Barbalet, J.M.
1985　Power and Resistance. British Journal of Sociology 36: 521–548.
Bateson, G.
1985　Mind and Nature. A Necessary Unity. London: Fontana Publications.
Bauer, P.T.
1972　Economic Analysis and Policy in Underdeveloped Countries (2nd edn). Durham: Duke University Press.
Beals, R.L., Hoijer, H., and Beals, A.R.
1977　An Introduction to Anthropology (5th edn). New York: Macmillan Publishing.
Beaud, Michel
1984　A History of Capitalism 1500–1980. Tanslated by Tom Dickman and Anny Lefebvre. London: Macmillan.
Beckford, G.L.
1973　The Economics of Agricultural Resource Use and Development in Plantation Economies. *In* Underdevelopment and Development: The Third World Today, H. Bernstein, ed., pp. 115–151. Harmondsworth: Penguin Books.
Bergerot, J.
1982　Tourism Promotion Project, South Pacific. Submission Prepared for the EEC on Behalf of the South Pacific Bureau for Economic Cooperation. Paris: SEDES.
Berno, Tracey
1996　Cross-cultural Research Methods: Content or Context? A Cook Islands Example. *In* Tourism and Indigenous Peoples, R.W. Butler and T. Hinch, eds, pp. 376–395. London: International Thomson Publishing Company.
Bernstein, H., ed.
1973　Underdevelopment and Development. The Third World Today. Harmondsworth: Penguin Books.

Berry, J.W.
1990   Psychology of Acculturation: Understanding Individuals Moving between Cultures. *In* Applied Cross Cultural Psychology, R. Brislin, ed., pp. 232–253. Newbury Park: Sage.

Bertram, I.G.
1999   The MIRAB Model Twelve Years On. The Contemporary Pacific: A Journal of Island Affairs 11: 105–137.

Bertram, I.G. and Watters, R.F.
1985   The MIRAB Economy in South Pacific Microstates. Pacific Viewpoint 26: 497–519.

Bettelheim, C.
1961   Studies in the Theory of Planning. New York: Asia Publishing House.

Bhabha, Homi
1994   The Location of Culture. London: Routledge.

Bhatnagar, B., and Williams, A.C., eds
1992   Participatory Development and the World Bank. World Bank Discussion Paper No. 183. Washington: World Bank.

Bierstedt, Robert
1950   An Analysis of Social Power. American Sociological Review 39: 427–443.

Blank, U.
1989   The Community Tourism Imperative: The Necessity, the Opportunities, its Potential. State College, TX: Venture Publishing.

Blau, P.
1964   Exchange and Power in Social Life. New York: John Wiley.
1977   Inequality and Heterogeneity: A Primitive Theory of Social Structure. New York: Free Press.
1987   Microprocess and Macrostructure. *In* Social Exchange Theory, K. Cook, ed. pp. 83–100. London: Sage Publications.

Boldt, M.
1993   Surviving as Indians: The Challenge of Self-Government. Toronto: University of Toronto Press.

Bonnemaison, J.
1975   New Hebrides. Tahiti: Les Editions du Pacifique.

Boon, J.A.
1977   The Anthropological Romance of Bali, 1597–1972. Cambridge: Cambridge University Press.

Boorstin, D.J.
1964   The Image: A Guide to Pseudo-events in America. New York: Harper and Row.

Braithwaite, J.
1992   A Sociology of Modelling and the Politics of Empowerment. American Sociological Review 57: 458–479.

Bramham, P., Henry, I., Mommaas, H., and van der Poel, H., eds
1989   Leisure and Urban Processes: Critical Studies of Leisure Policies in Western European Cities. London: Routledge.

Brass, J.L., ed.
1994   Community Tourism Assessment Handbook. Corvallis: Oregon State University.

Briguglio, L., Archer, B., Jafari, J., and Wall, G., eds
1996   Sustainable Tourism in Islands and Small States: Issues and Policies. London: Pinter.

Briguglio, L., Butler, R., Harrison, D., and Filho, W.L., eds
1996   Sustainable Tourism in Islands and Small States: Case Studies. London: Pinter.
Britton, Stephen
1977   Making Tourism More Supportive of Small State Development: The Case of St Vincent. Annals of Tourism Research 4: 268–278.
1980   A Conceptual Model of Tourism in a Periphery. *In* Tourism in the South Pacific: The Contribution of Research to Development and Planning. UNESCO Man and the Biosophere Report No. 6, Douglas Pearce, ed., pp. 1–17. Christchurch: UNESCO.
1982   The Political Economy of Tourism in the Third World. Annals of Tourism Research 9: 331–358.
1984   Tourism and Underdevelopment in Fiji. Canberra: Australian National University.
1987a Tourism in Pacific Island States: Constraints and Opportunities. *In* Ambiguous Alternative: Tourism in Small Developing Countries, Stephen Britton and William C. Clarke, eds, pp. 113–139. Suva: University of the South Pacific.
1987b Tourism in Small Developing Countries: Development Issues and Research Needs. *In* Ambiguous Alternative: Tourism in Small Developing Countries. Stephen Britton and William C. Clarke, eds, pp. 167–194. Suva: University of the South Pacific.
1991   Tourism, Capital and Place: Towards a Critical Geography of Tourism. Environment and Planning D: Society and Space 9: 451–478.
1996   Tourism Dependency and Development: A Mode of Analysis. *In* The Sociology of Tourism: Theoretical and Empirical Investigations, Y. Apostolopoulos, S. Leivade and A. Yiannakis, eds, pp. 155–172. London: Routledge.
Britton, Stephen, and Clarke, William C., eds
1987   Ambiguous Alternative: Tourism in Small Developing Countries. Suva: University of the South Pacific.
Brown, D.
1991   Human Universals. Philadelphia: Temple University Press.
Brown, H.
1974   The Impact of the Tourist Industries on the Agriculture Sectors. The Competition for Resources and the Market for Food Provided by Tourism. Kingston, Jamaica: National Planning Agency.
Bryden, J.M.
1973   Tourism and Development. A Case Study of the Commonwealth Caribbean. London: Cambridge University Press.
Buck, R.C.
1978a Boundary Maintenance Revisited: Tourist Experience in an Old Order Amish Community. Rural Sociology 43(2): 221–234.
1978b Towards a Synthesis in Tourism Theory. Annals of Tourism Research 5: 110–111.
Budowski, G.
1977   Tourism and Conservation: Conflict, Coexistence and Symbiosis. Parks 1(4): 3–6.
Bugotu, F.
1977   Prologue. *In* Living in Town. Problems and Priorities in Urban Planning in the South Pacific. J. Harre and C. Knapman, eds, p. *x*. Suva: University of the South Pacific.

Butler, Richard W.
1980 The Concept of a Tourist Area Cycle of Evolution: Implications for Management of Resources. Canadian Geographer 24(1): 5–12.
1990 Alternative Tourism: Pious Hope or Trojan Horse? Journal of Travel Research 20: 40–45.
1992 Alternative Tourism: The Thin Edge of the Wedge. *In* Tourism Alternatives, V.L. Smith and W. Eadington, eds, pp. 31–46. Philadelphia: University of Pennsylvania Press.
1993 Tourism — An Evolutionary Perspective. *In* Tourism and Sustainable Development: Monitoring, Planning, Management, J.G. Nelson, R.W. Butler and G. Wall, eds, pp. 27–43. Waterloo: University of Waterloo Press.
Butler, Richard W., and Hinch, Tom, eds
1996 Tourism and Indigenous Peoples. London: International Thomson Business Press.
Butterfield, P.
1990 Thinking Upstream: Nurturing a Conceptual Understanding of the Societal Context of Health Behaviour. Advances in Nursing Science 12(2): 1–8.
Cameron, C.
1989 Cultural Tourism and Urban Revitalization. Tourism Recreation Research 14(1): 23–32.
Campbell, D
1972 Solomon Islands Law Courts System. *In* The Sixth Waigani Seminar, Ron G. May, ed., pp. 131–135. Canberra: Australian National University and the University of PNG.
Cater, E.
1987 Tourism in the Least Developed Countries. Annals of Tourism Research 14: 202–226.
Central Bank of Samoa
1989, 1990, 1991 Annual Report. Apia: Government Printer.
Central Bank of Solomon Islands
1989–1996 Quarterly Reviews. Honiara: CBSI.
1990–1995 Annual Report. Honiara: CBSI.
Chambers, Robert
1983 Rural Development: Putting the Last First. New York: Longman Scientific and Technical.
1997 Whose Reality Counts? Putting the First Last. London: Intermediate Technology Publications.
Chapelle, Tony
1978 Customary Land Tenure in Fiji: Old Truths and Middle-aged Myths. Journal of the Polynesian Society 78(2): 71–88.
Clarke, William C.
1987 Introduction. *In* Ambiguous Alternative: Tourism in Small Developing Countries, Stephen Britton and William C. Clarke, eds, pp. 1–7. Suva: University of the South Pacific.
Cler, J.M.
1987 We are New Caledonians. Noumea: Imprimerie des Editions Nouvelles-ducos.
Clifford, J.
1988 The Predicament of Culture: Twentieth Century Ethnography, Literature and Art. Cambridge: Harvard University Press.

Cohen, Erik
1972   Towards a Sociology of International Tourism. Social Research 39: 164–182.
1978   The Impact of Tourism on the Physical Environment. Annals of Tourism Research 5: 215–237.
1979   Rethinking the Sociology of Tourism. Annals of Tourism Research 6: 18–35.
1983   Hill Tribe Tourism. *In* Highlanders of Thailand, J. McKinnon and Wanat Bhruksasri, eds, pp. 307–352. Kuala Lumpur: Oxford University Press.
1987   "Alternative tourism" — a Critique. Tourism Recreation Research 12: 11–18.
1988a Authenticity and Commoditization in Tourism. Annals of Tourism Research 15: 371–386.
1988b Traditions in the Qualitative Sociology of Tourism. Annals of Tourism Research 15: 29–46.
Cohen, Y.A.
1983   A Theory and a Model of Social Change and Evolution. Journal of Anthropological Archaeology 2: 2–12.
Collinson, M.
1981   A Low-cost Approach to Understanding Small Farmers. Agricultural Administration 8(6): 433–50.
Commonwealth Government of Australia
1992   Task Force on Ecologically Sustainable Development. Final Report. Canberra: AGPS.
1994   National Strategy for Aboriginal Tourism. Canberra: AGPS.
Commonwealth Secretariat
1984   South Pacific Colloquium on the Special Needs of Small States. Summary Record. Wellington, 13–14 August, 1984.
Conger, J.A., and Kanungo, R.N.
1988   The Empowerment Process: Integrating Theory and Practice. Academy of Management Review 13: 471–482.
Connell, John
1984   Islands Under Pressure — Population Growth and Urbanisation in the South Pacific. Ambio 13 (5–6): 306–312.
Constantino-David, K.
1995   Community Organizing in the Philippines: The Experience of Development NGOs. *In* Community Empowerment. A Reader in Participation and Development, G. Craig and M. Mayo, eds, pp. 154–167. London: Zed Books.
Cook, K.S., ed.
1987   Social Exchange Theory. Newbury Park: Sage Publications.
Cornwall, A. and Fleming, Sue
1995   Context and Complexity: Anthropological Reflections on PRA. PRA Notes 24: 8–12.
Craig, G. and Mayo, M., eds
1995   Community Empowerment. A Reader in Participation and Development. London: Zed Books.
Craik, J.
1991   Resorting to Tourism: Cultural Policies for Tourist Development in Australia. Sydney: Allen and Unwin.
Crick, M.
1989   Representations of International Tourism in the Social Sciences: Sun, Sex, Sights, Savings, and Servility. Annual Review of Anthropology 18, 307–344.

Crocombe, R.
1983 Regional Cooperation: Overcoming the Counter-pulls. *In* Foreign Forces in Pacific Politics, R. Crocombe and Ahmed Ali, eds, pp. 178–212. Suva: University of the South Pacific.
1987 The South Pacific: An Introduction. Auckland: Longman Paul.
Crocombe, R., and Rajotte, F., eds
1980 Pacific Tourism as Islanders See It. Suva: University of the South Pacific.
Cuneen, C.
1990 A Study of Aboriginal Juveniles and Police Violence. Sydney: Human Rights and Equal Opportunity Commission.
Cuneen, C., ed.
1992 Aboriginal Perspectives on Criminal Justice. Sydney: Institute of Criminology, Dag Hammarskjöld Foundation
1975 What Now? Upsala: Dag Hammarskjöld Foundation.
Dahrendorf, Ralf.
1968 Essays in the Theory of Society. Stanford: Stanford University Press.
D'Amore, L.J.
1983 Guidelines to Planning in Harmony with the Host Community. *In* Tourism in Canada: Selected Issues and Options, Peter Murphy, ed., pp. 135–157. Ottawa: Western Geographical Series 21.
Dann, Graham
1996 The Language of Tourism: A Sociolinguistic Perspective. Wallingford: CAB International.
Davis, G., Wanna, J., Warhurst, J., and Weller, P.
1993 Public Policy in Australia (2nd edn). Sydney: Allen and Unwin.
Davis, W.
1987 Religion and Development: Weber and the East African Experience. *In* Understanding Political Development. M. Weiner and S.P. Huntington, eds, pp. 101–124. Boston: Little, Brown.
de Burlo, C.
1987 Neglected Social Factors in Tourism Project Design: The Case of Vanuatu. Tourism Recreation Research 12(2): 25–30.
1996 Cultural Resistance and Ethnic Tourism on South Pentecost, Vanuatu. *In* Tourism and Indigenous Peoples, Richard W. Butler and Tom Hinch, eds, pp. 255–277. London: International Thomson Publishing Company.
de Coppett, Daniel, and Iteanu, Andre, eds
1995 Cosmos and Society in Oceania. Oxford: Berg Publishers.
de Kadt, E., ed.
1979 Tourism, Passport to Development? New York: Oxford University Press.
1990 Making the Alternative Sustainable: Lessons from Development for Tourism. *In* Environment, Tourism and Development: An Agenda for Action? A Workshop to Consider Strategies for Sustainable Tourism Development. Centre for Environmental Management and Planning. Valetta, Malta, 4–10 March 1990.
Deloria, V., and Lytle, C.
1983 American Indians, American Justice. Austin: University of Texas Press.
Dos Santos, T.
1972 Dependence and the International System. *In* Dependence and Under-development, J.O. Cockroft and A. Gunder-Franks, eds, pp. 71–72. New York: Anchor.

1973 The Crisis of Development Theory and the Problem of Dependence in Latin America. *In* Underdevelopment and Development: The Third World Today, H. Bernstein, ed., pp. 57–79. Harmondsworth: Penguin Books.

Douglas, Ngaire
1996 They Came for Savages: 100 Years of Tourism in Melanesia. Lismore: Southern Cross University Press.

Dowse, M.
1995 Tourism Studies at the USP. Discussion Paper by the Pacific ACP, EC Bureau for the Tourism Council of the South Pacific and the University of the South Pacific, Suva.

Doxey, G.V.
1975 A Causation Theory of Visitor-Resident Irritants, Methodology and Research Inferences. The Impact of Tourism. Sixth Annual Conference Proceedings, pp. 195–198. San Diego: Travel Research Association.

Dunsire, A.
1978 Implementation in a Bureaucracy. Oxford: Martin Robertson.

Dunst, C., Thrived, C., Davis, M., and Cornwell, J.
1988 Enabling and Empowering Families of Children with Health Impairments. Children's Health Care 17(2): 71–81.

Durkheim, E.
1933 Division of Labour in Society. New York: Macmillan.
1961 The Elementary Forms of the Religious Life. Translated from the French by Joseph Ward Swain, originally published in Paris, 1912. New York: Collier Books.

Dyck, N., ed.
1985 Indigenous Peoples and the Nation State: Fourth World Politics in Canada, Australia and Norway. St John's: Memorial University Press.

Eaton, Charles
1988 Directed Smallholder Farmers in Fiji: A Case Study of Virginia Tobacco Production. Unpublished M.Phil. thesis. Suva: University of the South Pacific.

Eisenstadt, S.N.
1966 Modernization: Protest and Change. Englewood Cliffs: Prentice-Hall.
1970 Readings in Social Evolution and Development. Oxford: Pergamon Press.

Ellsworth, R.R.
1989 Leadership and the Quest for Integrity. Boston: Harvard Business School Press.

El-Shakhs, S., and Obudho, R., eds
1975 Urbanization, National Development, and Regional Planning in Africa. New York: Praeger Publishers.

Emerson, R.
1962 Power-Dependence Relations. American Sociological Review 27(1): 31–34.
1972 Exchange Theory. *In* Sociological Theories in Progress, J. Berger, M. Zelditch and B. Anderson, eds, pp. 32–60. New York: Houghton-Mifflin.
1976 Social Exchange Theory. Annual Review of Sociology 2: 335–362.
1981 Social Exchange Theory. *In* Social Psychology: Sociological Perspectives, M. Rosenberg and R.H. Turner, eds, pp. 30–65. New York: Basic Books.
1987 Towards a Theory of Value in Social Exchange. *In* Social Exchange Theory. K.S. Cook, ed., pp. 11–46. Newbury Park: Sage Publications.

Epstein, C.F., and Coser, R.L., eds
 1981   Access to Power: Cross-National Studies of Women and Elites. Sydney, Boston: Allen and Unwin.

Erisman, M.
 1983   Tourism and Cultural Dependency in the West Indies. Annals of Tourism Research 10: 337–361.

European Community
 1982   Tourism for the European Community. Brussels: EC.
 1988   Financing Agreement, document VIII/11167/88-DN. Suva: TCSP.

European Community and the South Pacific Bureau for Economic Cooperation
 1981   Financial Agreement for the South Pacific Regional Tourism Development Program. Suva: SPEC.

Evans, P.B., and Stephens, J.
 1988   Studying Development Since the Sixties. Theory and Society 17(5): 713–745.

Fagan, W.
 1989   Empowered Students, Empowered Teachers. The Reading Teacher 42(8): 572–578.

Fairbairn, Te'o I.J.
 1985   Island Economies: Studies from the South Pacific. Suva: University of the South Pacific.

Farr, R.M., and Moscovici, S. eds
 1984   Social Representations. Cambridge: Cambridge University Press.

Farrell, B., ed.
 1977   The Social and Economic Impact of Tourism on Pacific Communities. Santa Cruz: University of California.
 1979   Tourism's Human Conflicts: Cases from the Pacific. Annals of Tourism Research 6(2): 122–136.

Favell, J.
 1986   Disaster Preparedness in the South Pacific. Unpublished report, South Pacific Bureau for Economic Cooperation. Suva: SPEC.

Featherstone, Mike
 1995a Undoing Culture: Globalization, Postmodernism and Identity. London: Sage Publications.
 1995b Nationalism, Globalization and Modernity. London: Sage Publications.

Feinberg, R., and Watson-Gegeo, K.A., eds
 1996   Leadership and Change in the Western Pacific. London: The Athlone Press.

Fiji Government
 1946   Town and Country Planning Act. Suva: Government Printer.
 1971   Native Lands Trust Board: Information Paper. Suva: NLTB.
 1982   Town and Country Planning Act: Amendment. Suva: Government Printer.
 1985   Eighth Five Year Development Plan, 1986–1990. Suva: Government Printer.
 1986   Native Lands Trust Board: Supplement. Suva: NLTB.
 1990   Ninth Five Year Development Plan, 1991–1996. Suva: Government Printer.

Fiji Hotels Association
 1990, 1995 Accommodation Guide. Suva: Fiji Times.

Fiji Times
 1990   "Sina Devastates Sugar Crop", 6 November, p. 1.

Finney, B. and Watson, K. eds
1975   A New Kind of Sugar: Tourism in the Pacific. Honolulu: East West Center.
Fletcher, J.E.
1987   The Impact of Tourism on the National Economy of the Solomon Islands. Madrid: UNDP/WTO RAS/83/002.
Forgas, J.P. ed.
1981   Social Cognition: Perspectives on Everyday Understanding. London: Academic Press.
Foster-Carter, Aidan
1994   From Rostow to Gunder Frank. London: Macmillan.
Foucault, Michel
1980   Power-Knowledge: Selected Interviews and Other Writings, 1972–1977. Edited by Colin Gordon. Brighton: Harvester Press.
France, Peter
1969   The Charter of the Land: Custom and Colonization in Fiji. Melbourne: Melbourne University Press.
Francillon, G.
1979   Bali: Tourism, Culture, Environment. Paris: UNESCO.
Frank, A.G.
1966   The Development of Underdevelopment. Monthly Review 18(4): 17–31.
Freire, P.
1970   Cultural Action for Freedom. Ringwood, Victoria: Penguin Education.
Friedman, D.
1987   Notes on "Towards a Theory of Value in Social Exchange". *In* Social Exchange Theory, K.S. Cook, ed., pp. 47–58. Newbury Park: Sage Publications.
Friedman, J.A.
1988   From Plantation to resort: Tourism and Dependency in a West Indian Island. Ann Arbor: UMI Dissertation Information Service.
Friedmann, J.
1980   An Alternative Development and Communalistic Society: Some Principles for a Possible Future. *In* Development Strategies in the Eighties, J. Friedmann, E. Wheelwright and J. Connell, eds, pp. 12–42. Sydney: Development Studies Colloquium, Monograph No. 1.
Friedmann, J., Wheelwright, E., and Connell, J. eds
1980   Development Strategies in the Eighties. Sydney: Development Studies Colloquium, Monograph No. 1.
Furtado, C.
1973   Elements of a Theory of Underdevelopment — the Underdeveloped Structures. *In* Underdevelopment and Development: The Third World Today, H. Bernstein, ed., pp. 33–43. Harmondsworth: Penguin Books.
Galjart, B.
1995   Counter-development: Possibilities and Constraints. *In* Community Empowerment. A Reader in Participation and Development, G. Craig, and M. Mayo, eds, pp. 12–23. London: Zed Books.
Geertz, C., ed.
1963   Old Societies and New States. New York: Free Press.
1973   Java and Japan Compared. *In* Underdevelopment and Development: The Third World Today. H. Bernstein, ed., pp. 44–56. Harmondsworth: Penguin Books.

Gegeo, D.W., and Watson-Gegeo, K.A.
1996   Priest and Prince: Integrating *Kastom*, Christianity and Modernization in Kwara'ae Leadership. *In* Leadership and Change in the Western Pacific. R. Feinberg and K.A. Watson-Gegeo, eds, pp. 298–342. London: The Athlone Press.

George, V.
1987   Tourism on Jamaica's North Coast: A Geographer's View. *In* Ambiguous Alternative: Tourism in Small Developing Countries, Stephen Britton and William C. Clarke, eds, pp. 61–77. Suva: University of the South Pacific.

Gerth, H.H., and Mills, C.W. (translators)
1948   From Max Weber: Essays in Sociology. New York: Oxford University Press.

Getz, Donald.
1991   Festivals, Special Events and Tourism. New York: Van Nostrand.

Ghai, Y.
1983   The Making of the Independence Constitution. *In* Solomon Islands — Politics and Government, P. Larmour and S. Tarua, eds, pp. 9–52. Suva: Institute of Pacific Studies, University of the South Pacific.

Gibson, C.H.
1991   A Concept Analysis of Empowerment. Journal of Advanced Nursing 16: 354–361.

Giddens, A.
1976   New Rules of Sociological Method. London: Hutchinson.

Gilg, Andrew W.
1978   Countryside Planning. North Pomfret, VT: David and Charles.

Gluckman, M.
1958   Custom and Conflict in Africa. Oxford: Blackwell.
1961   Politics, Law and Ritual in Tribal Society. Chicago: Aldine.

Goffman, E.
1951   The Presentation of Self in Everyday Life. New York: Doubleday.

Gouldner, A.W.
1960   The Norm of Reciprocity: A Preliminary Statement. American Sociological Review 25: 161–178.

Goulet, D.
1968   On the Goals of Development. Cross Currents 18: 387–405.

Graburn, N.H., ed.
1976   Ethnic and Tourist Arts: Cultural Expressions from the Fourth World. Los Angeles: University of California Press.

Graburn, N.H.
1983   The Anthropology of Tourism. Annals of Tourism Research 10: 9–33.

Green, L.
1995   Internal Minorities and Their Rights. *In* The Rights of Minority Cultures, W. Kymlicka, ed., pp. 256–274. Oxford: Oxford University Press.

Greenwood, D.
1977   Culture by the Pound: An Anthropological Perspective on Tourism as Cultural Commoditization. *In* Hosts and Guests: The Anthropology of Tourism, Valene L. Smith, ed., pp. 129–138. Philadelphia: University of Pennsylvania Press.
1989   Epilogue to "Culture by the Pound". *In* Hosts and Guests: The Anthropology of Tourism (2nd edn), Valene L. Smith, ed., pp. 171–186. Philadelphia: University of Pennsylvania Press.

Guam Economic Research Center
1990   Annual Economic Review and Statistical Abstract. Guam: Department of Commerce.
Gunn, C.A.
1993   Tourism Planning (3rd edn). New York: Taylor and Francis.
Gupta, Akhil and Ferguson, James, eds
1997   Culture, Power, Place: Explorations in Critical Anthropology. Durham and London: Duke University Press.
Gusfield, J.R.
1967   Tradition and Modernity: Misplaced Polarities in the Study of Social Change. American Journal of Sociology 72(4): 351–362.
Hall, C.M.
1994   Tourism and Politics: Policy, Power and Place. London: Belhaven Press.
1995   Introduction to Tourism in Australia (2nd edn). Melbourne: Longman.
1996   Tourism and the Maori of Aotearoa, New Zealand. *In* Tourism and Indigenous Peoples, Richard W. Butler and Tom Hinch, eds, pp. 155–175. London: International Thomson Business Press.
1998   Making the Pacific: Globalization, Modernity and Myth. *In* Destinations: Cultural Landscapes of Tourism, Greg Ringer, ed., pp. 140–153. London: Routledge.
Hall, C. Michael, and Page, Stephen, eds
1997   Tourism in the Pacific: Issues and Cases. London: International Thomson Business Press.
2000   Tourism in South and South East Asia: Issues and Cases. London: Butterworth-Heinemann.
Hall, S., and Jaques, M.
1991   New Times: The Changing Face of Politics in the 1990s. London: Lawrence and Wishart.
Haney, P.
1988   Providing Empowerment to the Person with AIDS. Social Work 33(3): 251–256.
Hanna, W.A.
1972   Bali in the Seventies. Part I: Cultural Tourism. American Universities Field Staff Reports, Southeast Asia Series 20(2): 1–7.
Hapgood, D., and Bennet, M.
1968   Agents of Change: A Close Look at the American Peace Corps. Boston: Little, Brown.
Hare, W.L., ed.
1990   Ecologically Sustainable Development. Sydney: Australian Conservation Foundation, Greenpeace (Australia), The Wilderness Society, World Wide Fund For Nature — Australia.
Harkin, Michael
1995   Modernist Anthropology and Tourism of the Authentic. Annals of Tourism Research 22: 650–670.
Harre, J., and Knapman, C., eds
1977   Living in Town. Problems and Priorities in Urban Planning in the South Pacific. Suva: University of the South Pacific.

Harrison, D.
1988 The Sociology of Modernization and Development. London: Unwin Hyman.
1996 Sustainability and Tourism: Reflections from a Muddy Pool. *In* Sustainable Tourism in Islands and Small States: Issues and Policies, L. Briguglio, B. Archer, Jafari and G. Wall, eds, pp. 69–89. London: Pinter.
1997a Aid, Government and Tourism Studies in a Less Developed Country: The Route from Muddle to Cooperation in Fiji. Paper. Suva: University of the South Pacific.
1997b Globalization and Tourism: Some Themes from Fiji. *In* Pacific Rim Tourism, Martin Opperman, ed., pp. 167–183. Wallingford: CAB International.
Havemann, Paul
1988 The Indigenization of Social Control in Canada. *In* Indigenous Law and the State, B.W. Morse and G.R. Woodman, eds pp. 55–74. Dordrecht: Floris Publications.
Hawkes, D.C., ed.
1987 Aboriginal Peoples and Government Responsibility. Exploring Federal and Provincial Roles. Ottawa: Carleton University Press.
Hawkins, D.E.
1993 Global Assessment of Tourism Policy: A Process Model. *In* Tourism Research: Critiques and Challenges, D.G. Pearce and R.W. Butler, eds, pp. 175–200. London: Routledge.
Hayes, Geoffrey
1991 Migration, Metascience and Development Policy in Island Polynesia. The Contemporary Pacific 3(1), 1: 58.
Haywood, K.M.
1988 Responsible and Responsive Tourism Planning in the Community. Tourism Management 9: 105–118.
Hazlehurst, K.M.
1993 Political Expression and Ethnicity: Statecraft and Mobilisation in the Maori World. New York: Praeger Publishers.
Hazlehurst, K.M., ed.
1987 Ivory Scales: Black Australia and the Law. Kensington: New South Wales University Press.
1995 Perceptions of Justice. Issues in Indigenous and Community Empowerment. Sydney: Avebury.
Hegar, R., and Hunzeker, J.
1988 Moving Towards Empowerment-based Practice in Public Child Welfare. Social Work 33(6): 499–502.
Herr, R.A.
1980 Institutional Sources of Stress in Pacific Regionalism. Working Paper Series, Pacific Islands Studies. Honolulu: University of Hawaii.
1985a Alignment and Alliance: Security in the South Pacific. Paper presented at the National Defence University Pacific Symposium on "Regional Balances of Security in the Pacific Basin", Honolulu, 21–22 February 1985.
1985b Regional Cooperation in the Pacific Islands. Hobart: University of Tasmania.
1985c The Future of South Pacific Regionalism. Paper presented in "The Pacific Islands in the Year 2000" Seminar Series. Honolulu: University of Hawaii.

1986   Regionalism, Strategic Denial and South Pacific Security. Journal of Pacific History, March 1986.

Hess, R.
1984   Thoughts on Empowerment. Prevention in Human Services 3: 227–230.

Hettne, Bjorn
1995   Development Theory and the Three Worlds: Towards an International Political Economy of Development (2nd edn). Essex: Longman Scientific and Technical.

Hildebrand, P.E.
1981   Combining Disciplines in Rapid Appraisal. Agricultural Administration 8(6): 423–432.

Hindness, B.
1982   Power, Interests and the Outcomes of Struggles. Sociology 16: 498–511.
1987   Politics and Class Analysis. Oxford: Blackwell.

Hirschman, A.O.
1959   The Strategy of Economic Development. New Haven: Yale University Press.
1975   Policy-making and Policy Analysis in Latin America: A Return Journey. Policy Sciences 6: 385–402.

Hitchcock, M., King, V.T., and Parnwell, M.J.G., eds
1993   Tourism in South-East Asia. London: Routledge.

Hobbes, T.
1991   Leviathan. Translated by Richard Tuck. Cambridge: Cambridge University Press.

Hogbin, Ian
1970   Social Change. Melbourne: Melbourne University Press.

Hogwood, B., and Gunn, L.A.
1986   Policy Analysis for the Real World. New York: Oxford University Press.

Hokansen Hawks, J.
1992   Empowerment in Nursing Education: Concept Analysis and Application to Philosophy, Learning and Instruction. Journal of Advanced Nursing 17: 609–618.

Holden, Peter, ed.
1984   Alternative Tourism, with a Focus on Asia. Bangkok: Ecumenical Coalition on Third World Tourism.

Hollinshead, Keith
1990   The Powers Behind Play: The Political Environments for Recreation and Tourism in Australia. Journal of Park and Recreation Administration 8: 35–50.
1992   The Play of Politics in Tourism: Powerscapes for Fiji. Unpublished manuscript. College Station: Texas A and M University.
1998   Tourism and the Restless People. Tourism, Culture and Communication 1(1): 49–78.

Hoogvelt, A.M.H.
1986   The Sociology of Developing Societies. London: Macmillan Education.
1990   Rethinking Development Theory. Sociological Review 38(2): 352–361.

Hudson, B.
1987   Tourism and Landscape in Jamaica and Grenada. *In* Ambiguous Alternative: Tourism in Small Developing Countries. Stephen Britton and William C. Clarke, eds, pp. 46–60. Suva: University of the South Pacific.

Huntington, P.
1968   Political Order in Changing Societies. New Haven: Yale University Press.

Huyton, J. and Baker, S.
1992   Empowerment: A Way to Increase Productivity and Morale. *In* Direction 2000: Education and Human Resource Development for the Hospitality and Tourism Industry. PATA/WTO Education Forum Proceedings, Hong Kong, pp. 511–518. Hong Kong: Hong Kong Polytechnic.

Hyden, G.
1983   No Shortcuts to Progress: African Development Management in Perspective. London: Heinemann.

Imai, M.
1986   Kaizen: The Key to Japan's Competitive Success. New York: Random House.

Inskeep, E.L.
1991   Tourism Planning: An Integrated and Sustainable Development Approach. New York: Van Nostrand Reinhold.

Institute of Pacific Studies
1980   Pacific Tourism as Islanders See It. Suva: University of the South Pacific.

International Labour Organization (ILO).
1976   Declaration on Employment Growth and Basic Needs. Geneva: World Employment Program of ILO.

International Union for the Conservation of Nature (IUCN)
1980   World Conservation Strategy. Paris: IUCN.

Intertect
1984   Minimum Structural Standards for Low Cost Cyclone Resistant Housing in Solomon Islands. Honolulu: PIDP, University of Hawaii.

Iowa, B.
1989   An Examination of Low Cost Tourism Accommodation Development. Papua New Guinea's Indigenous Village Based Guest House Industry. Unpublished SPFP Research Paper. Townsville: James Cook University.

Islands Business
1985–2000. Islands Business Suva: Fiji.

Jacobsen, C., and Cohen, A.
1986   The Power of Social Collectivities: Towards An Integrative Conceptualization and Operationalization. British Journal of Sociology 37(1): 106–121.

Jaensch, D.
1992   The Politics of Australia. Melbourne: Macmillan.

Jafari, J.
1990   Research and Scholarship: The Basis of Tourism Education. Journal of Tourism Studies 1(1): 33–41.

Jamal, T.B., and Getz, D.
1995   Collaboration Theory and Community Tourism Planning. Annals of Tourism Research 22: 186–204.

James, C.
1992   New Territory: The Transformation of New Zealand. Wellington: Bridget Williams Books.

Jenkins, C.L.
1980   Tourism Policies in Developing Countries: A Critique. International Journal of Tourism Management, March: 17–24.

Johnson, H.T.
1992   Relevance Regained. From Top-down Control to Bottom-up Empowerment. New York: The Free Press/Macmillan.

Jolly, M.
  1982   Birds and Banyans of South Pentecost: Kastom in Anti-colonial Struggle. Mankind 13(4): 338–353.
  1992   Specters of Inauthenticity. The Contemporary Pacific 4(1): 49–72.
  1994   Kastom as Commodity: The Land Divers as an Indigenous Rite and Tourist Spectacle in Vanuatu. *In* Culture, Kastom, Tradition: Developing Cultural Policy in Melanesia, L. Lindstrom and G.M. White, eds, Suva: University of the South Pacific.
Jones, P., and Davies, A.
  1991   Empowerment: A Study of General Managers of Four Star Hotel Properties in the UK. International Journal of Hospitality Management 10(3): 211–217.
Josephides, Lisette
  1995   Replacing Cultural Markers: Symbolic Analysis and Political Action in Melanesia. *In* Cosmos and Society in Oceania, Daniel de Coppett and Andre Iteanu, eds, pp. 189–212. Oxford: Berg Publishers.
Kanter, R.M.
  1977   Men and Women of the Corporation. New York: Basic Books.
Kaplan, M.
  1989   *Luve ni Wai* as the British Saw It: Construction of Custom and Disorder in Colonial Fiji. Ethnohistory 36(4): 353–363.
Katz, R.
  1984   Empowerment and Synergy: Expanding the Community's Healing Resources. Prevention in Human Services 3: 201–226.
Keesing, Roger, and Corris, Peter
  1980   Lightning Meets the West Wind: The Malaita Massacre. Melbourne: Oxford University Press.
Keesing, Roger, and Strathern, Andrew
  1998   Cultural Anthropology: A Contemporary Perspective. Fort Worth: Harcourt Brace College Publishers.
Kele Kele, and Kalkot Matas
  1977   The Emergence of Political Parties. *In* New Hebrides: The Road to Independence, C. Plant, ed., pp. 17–34. Suva: University of the South Pacific.
Kent, N.
  1975   A New Kind of Sugar. *In* A New Kind of Sugar: Tourism in the Pacific. B. Finney and K. Watson, eds. Honolulu: East West Center.
Kieffer, C.
  1984   Citizen Empowerment: A Developmental Perspective. Prevention in Human Services 3: 9–36.
King, Anthony D., ed.
  1991   Culture, Globalization and the World System: Contemporary Conditions for the Representation of Identity. Basingstoke: Macmillan Education.
King, D.
  1992   Routes to Urban Primacy and Economic Development: Physical and Economic Planning in the South Pacific. Unpublished manuscript. Townsville: James Cook University.
Koslowski, J.
  1985   Threshold Approach in Environmental Planning. Ekistics 311: 146–153.

Kotze, D.
1987   Contradictions and Assumptions in Community Development. Community Development Journal 22(1): 31–35.

Krippendorf, J.
1987   The Holiday Makers: Understanding the Impact of Leisure and Travel. London: William Heinemann.

Kuilamu, Marika
1995   Village-based Ecotourism Ventures in Fiji. Unpublished Honours thesis. Townsville: James Cook University, Australia.

Kuve, P.R.
1989   An Analysis of the Development of Small Scale Indigenously Owned Tourism Businesses in Solomon Islands. Unpublished SPFP Research Paper. Townsville: James Cook University.

Kymlicka, W.
1995   The Rights of Minority Cultures. Oxford: Oxford University Press.

Labonte, R.
1989   Community and Professional Empowerment. The Canadian Nurse 85(3): 23–28.

Lal, D.
1984   Distribution and Development: A Review Article. World Development 4: 9.

Lanfant, Marie-Francoise, Allcock, John, and Brunner, E.M., eds
1995   International Tourism: Identity and Change. London: Sage Publications.

Lansing, J.S.
1974   Evil in the Morning of the World: Phenomenological Approaches to a Balinese Community. Ann Arbor: University of Michigan Press.

Larmour, P.
1981   Solomon Islands: Compulsory Acquisition. *In* Land, People and Government. Public Lands Policy in the South Pacific, P. Larmour, R. Crocombe and A. Taungenga, eds, pp. 31–34. Suva: University of the South Pacific.

Larmour, P., Crocombe, R., and Taungenga, A., eds
1981   Land, People and Government: Public Lands Policy in the South Pacific. Suva: University of the South Pacific.

Larmour, P., and Qalo, Ropate, eds
1985   Decentralisation in the South Pacific: Local, Provincial and State Governments in Twenty Countries. Suva: University of the South Pacific.

Lattimer, H.
1985   Developing Island Economies — Tourism v. Agriculture. Tourism Management 6(1): 32–42.

Lawler, E.J., and Bacharach, S.B.
1986   Power Dependence in Collective Bargaining. Advances in Industrial and Labour Relations 3: 191–212.

Lawler, E.J., and Markovsky, B., eds
1987   Advances in Group Processes. Greenwich: JAI.

Lawson, S.
1990   The Ideology of Constitutional Change in Fiji. Paper presented at the Annual Conference of the Australasian Political Studies Association, University of Tasmania, 23–26 September 1990.
1991   The Politics of Tradition: Problems for Political Legitimacy and Democracy in the South Pacific. Paper presented to the Third Annual Conference of the Pacific

Islands Political Studies Association, Monash University, Melbourne, 16–18 December 1991.

Leontidou, Lila
  1988 The Mediterranean City in Transition: Social Change and Urban Development. Cambridge, New York: Cambridge University Press.

Lerner, D.
  1958 The Passing of Traditional Society: Modernizing the Middle East. New York: Free Press.

Levy, M.
  1966 Modernization and the Structure of Societies. Princeton: Princeton University Press.

Lew, Alan
  2000 China: A Growth Engine for Asian Tourism. *In* Tourism in South and South East Asia: Issues and Cases, C. Michael Hall and Stephen Page, eds, pp. 268–285. London: Butterworth-Heinemann.

Li, Fung Mei Sarah, and Sofield, T.H.B.
  1994 Tourism and Socio-cultural Change in Rural China. *In* Tourism: The State of the Art, A.V. Seaton et al., eds, pp. 854–867. Chichester: John Wiley.

Ligo, G.
  1980 Custom and Culture. *In* Vanuatu, Institute of Pacific Studies, pp. 55–65. Suva: University of the South Pacific.

Lijpmart, A.
  1995 Self-determination Versus Pre-determination of Ethnic Minorities in Power-Sharing Systems. *In* The Rights of Minority Cultures, W. Kymlicka, ed., pp. 275–287. Oxford: Oxford University Press.

Liligeto, W.
  1990 Implementation of Government Policy to Inscribe Solomon Islands Sites in the World Heritage Site Listings. *In* Education for Tourism in the South Pacific, T.H.B. Sofield, ed., pp. 3–34. Townsville: James Cook University.

Lini, Walter Hayde
  1980 The Future. *In* Vanuatu, Institute of Pacific Studies, pp. 282–291. Suva: University of the South Pacific.

Lipman, Geoffrey
  2002 STEP: Sustainable Tourism Eliminating Poverty. Statement by Geoffrey H . Lipman, Special Advisor to Secretary General WTO for Trade in Tourism Services, World EcoTourism Summit, Quebec, 22 May.

Lockhart, D., and Drakakis-Smith, D., eds
  1996 Island Tourism. Trends and Prospects. London: Pinter.

Long, V.
  1991 Government-Industry-Community Interaction in Tourism Development in Mexico. *In* The Tourism Industry: An International Analysis, M.T. Sinclair and M.J. Stabler, eds, pp. 205–222. Wallingford: CAB International.

Lukes, S.
  1974 Power: A Radical View. London: Macmillan.

Lyden, F.J., Shipman, G.A., and Kroll, M., eds
  1969 Policies, Decisions and Organisations. New York: Appleton-Century-Crofts.

Mabogunje, Akin L.
  1980 The Development Process: A Spatial Perspective. London: Hutchinson.

McArdle, J.
1989   Community Development Tools of Trade. Community Quarterly 16: 47–54.
MacArthur, Robert H., and Wilson, Edward O.
1967   The Theory of Island Biogeography. Princeton: Princeton University Press.
Macbeth, J.
1996   Dissonance and Paradox in Tourism Planning — People First? ANZALS Research Series 3: 2–18.
MacCannell, D.
1976   The Tourist: A New Theory of the Leisure Class. New York: Shocken.
1994   Tradition's Next Step. *In* Discovered Country: Tourism and Survival in the American West, Scott Norris, ed. Albuquerque: Stone Ladder Press.
McConnochie, K., Hollinsworth, D., and Pettman, J.
1988   Race and Racism in Australia. Wentworth Falls: Social Science Press.
McIntosh, R.W., and Goeldner, C.R.
1986   Tourism: Principles, Practices, Philosophies (5th edn). Colombus: Grid Publishing.
McKean, P.F.
1976   Tourism, Culture Change, and Culture Conservation in Bali. *In* Changing Identities in Modern Southeast Asia, D.J. Banks, ed. The Hague, Paris: Mouton Publishers.
1977   Towards a Theoretical Analysis of Tourism: Economic Dualism and Cultural Innovation in Bali. *In* Hosts and Guests: The Anthropology of Tourism, Valene L. Smith, ed., pp. 129–138. Philadelphia: University of Pennsylvania Press.
1982   Tourists and Balinese. Cultural Survival Quarterly 6(3): 32–33.
McMaster, James
1993   Strategies to Stimulate Private Sector Development in the Pacific Island Economies. *In* The Future of Asia-Pacific Economies: Pacific Islands at the Crossroads, Rodney V. Cole and Somak Tambunlertchai, eds, pp. 275–313. Canberra: National Centre for Development Studies, ANU.
McMullen, S., and Jayawardene, C.H.S.
1995   Systemic Discrimination, Aboriginal People, and the Miscarriage of Justice in Canada. *In* Perceptions of Justice: Issues in Indigenous and Community Empowerment, K.M. Hazlehurst, ed., pp. 27–50. Sydney: Avebury.
MacNamara, L.
1995   Aboriginal Justice Reform in Canada: Alternatives to State Control. *In* Perceptions of Justice: Issues in Indigenous and Community Empowerment, K.M. Hazlehurst, ed., pp 1–26. Sydney: Avebury.
MacNaught, T.J.
1982   Mass Tourism and Dilemmas of Modernisation in Pacific Islands Communication. Annals of Tourism Research 9 (3): 359–382.
Madrigal, R.
1992   Residents' Perceptions and the Role of Government. Annals of Tourism Research 22: 86–102.
Maenu'u, L.
1984   Land Within Traditional Societies of Solomon Islands. *In* Land and Investments in the Solomon Islands, Solomon Islands Government, pp. 7–11. Honiara: Government Printer.

Maeroff, G.
1988   The Empowerment of Teachers: Overcoming the Crisis of Confidence. New York: Teachers College Press.
Mair, L.
1970   Primitive Government. Harmondsworth: Penguin Books.
Malinowski, Bronislaw
1948   Magic, Science and Religion. Glencoe: The Free Press.
Marsden, P.V.
1987   Elements of Interactor Dependence. *In* Social Exchange Theory. K.S. Cook, ed., pp. 83–100. Newbury Park: Sage Publications.
Martin, W.G., ed.
1991   Semi-peripheral States in the World Economy. New York: Greenwood Press.
Marx, Karl
1995   Capital: An Abridged Edition. With an Introduction by David McLellan. Oxford: Oxford University Press.
Matthews, H.G.
1977   Radicals and Third World Tourism: A Caribbean Focus. Annals of Tourism Research 5: 20–29.
Matthews, H.G., and Richter, L.K.
1991   Political Science and Tourism. Annals of Tourism Research 18: 120–135.
Maurer, Jean-Luc, and Zeigler, H.
1988   Tourism and Indonesian Cultural Minorities. *In* Tourism: Manufacturing the Exotic, Pierre Rossel, ed., pp. 65–92. Copenhagen: IGWIA.
May, Ron G., ed.
1972   The Sixth Waigani Seminar. Canberra: Australian National University and the University of PNG.
Meade, J.E.
1961   A Neo-classical Theory of Growth. New York: Allen and Unwin.
Mehmet, O.
1978   Economic Planning and Social Justice in Developing Countries. London: Croom Helm.
Merton, Robert K.
1963   Social Theory and Social Structure. Glencoe: The Free Press.
Middleton, V.T.C.
1990   Review of Museums and Cultural Centres in the South Pacific. Suva: Tourism Council of the South Pacific.
Milman, A., and Pizam, A.
1988   Social Impacts of Tourism on Central Florida. Annals of Tourism Research 15(2): 191–204.
Milne, S.
1988   South Pacific Regional Tourism Project. Madrid: UNDP/WTO RAS/86/134.
1992   Tourism and Development in South Pacific Micro-States. Annals of Tourism Research 19: 191–212.
1996   Tourism, Dependency and South Pacific Micro-states: Beyond the Vicious Cycle? *In* Island Tourism: Trends and Prospects, D. Lockhart and D. Drakakis-Smith, eds, pp. 281–301. London: Pinter.
Minkler, M.
1989   Health Education, Health Promotion and the Open Society: An Historical Perspective. Health Education Quarterly 16(1): 17–30.

Minkler, M., and Cox, K.
1980 Creating Critical Consciousness in Health Applications of Freire's Philosophy and Methods to the Local Care Setting. International Journal of Health Services 10(2): 311–322.
Miossec, J.M.
1976 Elements pour une Theorie de l'Espace Touristique. Les Cahiers du Tourisme C-36, Aix-en-Provence, CHET. Cited in Pearce, D. (1989) Tourist Development. Harlow: Longman Scientific and Technical.
Mishra, R.
1990 The Welfare State in Capitalist Society. Brighton: Harvester Wheatsheaf.
Mitchell, L.S.
1984 Tourism Research in the United States: A Geographic Perspective. GeoJournal 9(1): 5–15.
Molm, Linda D.
1981 The Conversion of Power Imbalance to Power Use. Social Psychology Quarterly 44: 151–163.
1986 Gender, Power and Legitimation: A Test of Three Theories. American Journal of Sociology 91: 1356–1386.
1987a Extending Power-Dependence Theory: Power Processes and Negative Outcomes. In Advances in Group Processes. E.J. Lawler and B. Markovsky, eds, Vol. 4, pp. 171–198. Greenwich: JAI.
1987b Linking Power Structure and Power Use. In Social Exchange Theory. K.S. Cook, ed., pp. 101–129. Newbury Park: Sage Publications.
1988 The Structure and Use of Power: A Comparison of Reward and Punishment Power. Social Psychology Quarterly 51: 108–122.
1989a Punishment Power: A Balancing Process in Power-Dependence Relations. American Journal of Sociology 94 (6): 1392–1418.
1989b An Experimental Analysis of Imbalance in Punishment Power. Social Forces 10: 123–132.
Mommaas, H., and van der Poel, H.
1989 Changes in Economy, Politics and Lifestyles: An Essay on the Restructuring of Urban Leisure. In Leisure and Urban Processes: Critical Studies of Leisure Policy in Western European Cities, P. Bramham, I. Henry, H. Mommaas and H. van der Poel, eds, pp. 254–276. London: Routledge.
Moore, Wilbert E.
1979 World Modernization: The Limits of Convergence. New York: Elsevier.
Morawetz, D.
1974 Employment Implications of Industrialisation in Developing Countries: A Survey. The Economic Journal 84, September Special issue.
Morgan, D.
1992 The Efficacy of International Aid for Tourism Projects — A Case Study of Four Tourism Projects in Tonga, B. Administration Tourism Honours thesis. Townsville: James Cook University.
Moscovici, S.
1981 On Social Representations. In Social Cognition: Perspectives on Everyday Understanding, J.P. Forgas, ed., pp. 181–209. London: Academic Press.
1984 The Phenomenon of Social Representations. In Social Representations, R.M. Farr and S. Moscovici, eds, pp. 3–69. Cambridge: Cambridge University Press.

Moser, Claus Adolf
1988   Survey Methods in Social Investigation. Aldershot: Gower Publishing.
Mowforth, M., and Munt, I.
1998   Tourism and Sustainability: New Tourism in the Third World. London: Routledge.
Muqbil, Imtiaz
2002   "Asian Development Bank Singals Funding Pull and Visa Puch," Travel Impact Newswire, New Edition 15, 10 April.
Murphy, P.
1985   Tourism: A Community Approach. New York: Methuen.
Murphy, P., ed.
1983   Tourism in Canada: Selected Issues and Options. Ottawa: Western Geographical Series 21.
Murrell, K.L., and Vogt, J.F.
1990   Empowerment in Organizations. Amsterdam: Pfeiffer.
Myrdal, G.
1957   Economic Theory and Underdeveloped Regions. New York: Duckworth.
1965   Rich Land and Poor Land. New York: Harper.
Nadel, S.F.
1963   The Foundations of Social Anthropology. London: Cohen and West.
Nash, D.
1977   Tourism as a Form of Imperialism. In Hosts and Guests: The Anthropology of Tourism, Valene L. Smith, ed., pp. 149–156. Philadelphia: University of Pennsylvania Press.
1981   Tourism as an Anthropological Subject. Current Anthropology 22(5): 461–481.
1984   The Ritualisation of Tourism. Annals of Tourism Research 11: 503–507.
Nation, John
1978   Customs of Respect: The Traditional Basis of Fijian Communal Politics. Development Studies Centre, Monograph No. 14. Canberra: ANU.
National Reserve Bank of Tonga
1989, 1990   Annual Report. Nuku'alofa: NRBT.
Nayacakolou, R.R.
1972   The Leasing of Native Land for Tourist Plant Development in Fiji. In The Sixth Waigani Seminar, Ron G. May, ed. pp. 151–158. Canberra: Australian National University and the University of PNG.
1975   Leadership in Fiji. Melbourne: University of Melbourne.
1978   Tradition and Change in the Fijian Village. Suva: South Pacific Social Sciences Association.
Neemia, U.F.
1986   Cooperation and Conflict. Costs, Benefits, and National Interests in Pacific Regional Cooperation. Suva: University of the South Pacific.
Nelson, J.G., Butler, R.W., and Wall, G., eds
1993   Tourism and Sustainable Development: Monitoring, Planning, Management. Waterloo: University of Waterloo Press.
Nerfin, M., ed.
1977   Another Development: Approaches and Strategies. Uppsala: Dag Hammarskjöld Foundation.

New International Economic Order (NIEO), United Nations
1975   Seventh Special Session of the United Nations General Assembly. New York: United Nations.
Nisbet, Robert, ed.
1972   Social Change. New York: Harper and Row.
Noronha, R.
1979   Paradise Reviewed: Tourism in Bali. *In* Tourism. Passport to Development? E. de Kadt, ed., pp. 177–204. New York: Oxford University Press.
Northern Territory Tourist Commission
1980–1996   Annual Report. Darwin: NTTC.
Nunez, Theron
1977   Touristic Studies in Anthropological Perspective. *In* Hosts and Guests: The Anthropology of Tourism, Valene L. Smith, ed., pp. 207–216. Philadelphia: University of Pennsylvania Press.
Nwe, Daw Kyin
1993   Tourism Planning and Development in Myanmar. Myanmar, Ministry of Hotels and Tourism. Paper presented at the Asian Productivity Organisation Seminar on Tourism Planning and Development, Jakarta, 23 August–3 September 1993.
Nye, J.S.
1968   Central American Regional Integration. *In* International Regionalism: Readings, Joseph S. Nye, ed., pp. 377–379. Boston: Little Brown and Co.
O'Dowd, G.
1967   Some Issues of Economic Development and of Development Economics. Journal of Economic Issues 1(3): 153.
OECD
1968   Perspectives of Planning: Proceedings of the OECD Working Symposium on Long-Range Forecasting and Planning, November 1968, Bellagio, Italy ("The Bellagio Declaration on Planning"). Paris: OECD.
O'Gorman, F.
1995   Brazilian Community Development: Changes and Challenges. *In* Community Empowerment. A Reader in Participation and Development, G. Craig and M. Mayo, eds, pp. 206–217. London: Zed Books.
Onyx, J., and Benton, P.
1995   Empowerment and Ageing: Towards Honoured Places for Crones and Sages. *In* Community Empowerment. A Reader in Participation and Development, G. Craig and M. Mayo, eds, pp. 46–58. London: Zed Books.
Opperman, Martin, ed.
1997   Pacific Rim Tourism. Wallingford: CAB International.
Owen, R., and Sutcliffe, R., eds
1971   Studies in the Theory of Imperialism. London: Longman.
Oxaal, I., Barnett, T., and Booth, D., eds
1975   Beyond the Sociology of Development. London: Routledge and Kegan Paul.
Pacific Magazine with Islands Business
2001   January, February issues.
Painter, M.
1992   Participation in Power. *In* Participation in Government, M. Munro-Clark, ed., pp. 21–37. Sydney: Hale and Iremonger.

Papson, S.
1981   Spuriousness and Tourism: Politics of Two Canadian Provincial Governments. Annals of Tourism Research 8: 220–235.
Park, Robert Ezra
1952   Introduction to the Science of Sociology. Chicago: University of Chicago Press.
Parsons, Talcott
1937   The Structure of Social Action, Vols I and II. New York: Free Press.
1966   Societies. Englewood Cliffs: Prentice-Hall.
Pateman, C.
1970   Participation and Democratic Theory. Cambridge: Cambridge University Press.
Peacock, J.L.
1986   The Creativity of Tradition in Indonesian Religion. History of Religions 25: 341–351.
Pearce, Douglas G.
1980   Tourism in the South Pacific: The Contribution of Research to Development and Planning. UNESCO Man and the Biosophere Report No. 6. Christchurch: UNESCO.
1989   Tourist Development. London: Longman
1992   Tourist Organization. London: Longman
Pearce, Douglas G., and Butler, R.W., eds
1993   Tourism Research: Critiques and Challenges. London: Routledge.
Pearce, Philip L.
1988   The Ulysses Factor: Evaluating Visitors in Tourist Settings. New York: Springer Verlag.
Pearce, Philip L., Moscardo, Gianna, and Ross, Glenn F.
1991   Tourism Impact and Community Perception: An Equity-Social Representational Perspective. Australian Psychologist 26: 147–152.
1996   Tourism Community Relationships. Oxford: Pergamon.
Perdue, R.R., Long, P.T., and Allen, L.
1990   Resident Support for Tourism. Annals of Tourism Research 17: 586–599.
Pere, B.
1980   Commercializing Culture or Culturizing Commerce? *In* Pacific Tourism as Islanders See It, Institute of Pacific Studies, pp. 139–145. Suva: University of the South Pacific.
Pettman, J.
1992   Living in the Margins. Sydney: Allen and Unwin.
Picard, Michel
1987a   Du Tourisme Culturel a la Culture Touristique. Problems of Tourism 10(2): 38–52. Cited in Tourism in South-East Asia, M. Hitchcock, V.T. King and M.J.G. Parnwell, eds. London: Routledge.
1987b   Cultural Tourism in Bali: Cultural Performances as Tourist Attraction. Indonesia 49: 37–74.
1993   Cultural Tourism in Bali: National Integration and Regional Differentiation. *In* Tourism in South-East Asia, M. Hitchcock, V.T. King and M.J.G. Parnwell, eds, pp. 71–98. London: Routledge.
1996   Bali: Cultural Tourism and Touristic Culture. English translation by Diana Darling. Singapore: Archipelago.

Picard, Michel, and Wood, Robert E., eds
1997 Tourism, Ethnicity and the State in Asian and Pacific Societies. Honolulu: University of Hawaii Press.
Piddington, Ken
1986 South Pacific Forum: The First 15 years. Suva: South Pacific Bureau for Economic Cooperation.
Pi-Sunyer, O.
1977 Through Native Eyes: Tourists and Tourism in a Catalan Maritime Community. *In* Hosts and Guests: The Anthropology of Tourism, Valene L. Smith, ed., pp. 149–156. Philadelphia: University of Pennsylvania Press.
Plant, C., ed.
1977 New Hebrides. The Road to Independence. Suva: University of the South Pacific.
Pollard, S.J.
1987 The Viability and Vulnerability of a Small Island State: The Case of Kiribati. Islands. Australia Working Paper No. 87/19. Canberra: ANU.
Poon, A.
1992 Tourism, Technology and Competitive Strategies. Wallingford: CAB International.
Portes, A.
1976 On the Sociology of National Development: Theories and Issues. American Journal of Sociology 82(1): 55–85.
Prasad, P.C.
1987 The Impact of Tourism on Small Developing Countries. *In* Ambiguous Alternative: Tourism in Small Developing Countries. Stephen Britton and William C. Clarke, eds, pp. 9–15. Suva: University of the South Pacific.
Pule, Robert
1983 Binabina: The Story of a War Canoe. Honiara: University of the South Pacific.
Quain, Buell
1948 Fijian Village. Chicago: University of Chicago Press.
Queensland Government
1979 The Queensland Tourism and Travel Corporation Act. Brisbane: Queensland Government Printer.
Queensland Tourism and Travel Corporation (QTTC)
1985–1998 Annual Reports. Brisbane: QTTC.
Rahman, Muhammad Anisur
1995 Participatory Development. Towards Liberation or Co-optation? *In* Community Empowerment. A Reader in Participation and Development. G. Craig and M. Mayo, eds, pp. 24–32. London: Zed Books.
Rajotte, F.
1977 The Impact of Tourism on the Culture of Fiji. Institute of Applied Social and Economic Research Paper No. 33. Port Moresby: IASER.
1987 Safari and Beach-resort Tourism: The Costs to Kenya. *In* Ambiguous Alternative: Tourism in Small Developing Countries. Stephen Britton and William C. Clarke, eds, pp. 78–90. Suva: University of the South Pacific.
Rajotte, F., ed.
1982 The Impact of Tourism Development in the Pacific. Ontario: Trent University.

Ranck, S.
1987   An Attempt at Autonomous Development. The Case of the Tufi Guest Houses, Papua New Guinea. *In* Ambiguous Alternative: Tourism in Small Developing Countries. Stephen Britton and William C. Clarke, eds, pp. 154–166. Suva: University of the South Pacific.

Ranis, G., ed.
1972   The Gap between Rich and Poor Nations. London: Macmillan.

Rappaport. J.
1984   Studies in Empowerment: Introduction to the Issues. Prevention in Human Services 3: 1–7.
1987   Terms of Empowerment/Exemplars of Prevention: Towards a Theory for Community Psychology. American Journal of Community Psychology 15(2): 121–148.

Rayner, A.C.
1970   The Use of Multivariate Analysis in Development Theory: A Critique of the Approach Adopted by Adelman and Morris. Quarterly Journal of Economics 84: 638–647.

Reed, M.
1997   Power Relations and Community Based Tourism Planning. Annals of Tourism Research 24: 566–591.

Rhoades, R.
1982   The Coming Revolution in Methods for Rural Development Research. *In* RAP: Rapid Assessment Procedures: Qualitative Methodologies for Planning and Evaluation of Health Related Programmes, N. Scrimshaw and G.R. Gleason, eds, pp. 61–78. Boston: International Nutrition Foundation for Developing Countries.

Rice, E.
1974   John Frum He Come. New York: Doubleday.

Richter, Linda K.
1980   The Political Uses of Tourism: A Philippine Case Study. Journal of Developing Areas 14: 234–257.
1982   Land Reform and Tourism Development: Policy-making in the Philippines. Cambridge: Schenkmen.
1983   Tourism Politics and Political Science — A Case of Not So Benign Neglect. Annals of Tourism Research 10(3): 313–335.
1984   The Political and Legal Dimensions of Tourism. *In* Alternative Tourism, With a Focus on Asia, Peter Holden, ed., pp. 1–21. Bangkok: Ecumenical Coalition on Third World Tourism.
1985   The Fragmented Politics of US Tourism. Tourism Management 6(3): 162–173.
1989   The Politics of Tourism in Asia. Honolulu: University of Hawaii Press.
1991   Political Issues in Tourism Policy: A Forecast. *In* World Travel and Tourism Review, Donald E. Hawkins and Brent Ritchie, eds, pp. 189–194. London: CAB International.
1993   Tourism Policy-making in South-East Asia. *In* Tourism in South-East Asia, M. Hitchcock, V.T. King and M.J.G. Parnwell, eds, pp. 179–199. London: Routledge.

Ringer, Greg, ed.
1998   Destinations: Cultural Landscapes of Tourism, pp. 140–153. London: Routledge.

Ritchie, J.R. Brent
1993   Tourism Research: Policy and Managerial Priorities for the 1990s and Beyond. *In* Tourism Research: Critiques and Challenges, D.G. Pearce and R.W. Butler, eds, pp. 201–216. London: Routledge.
Ritchie, J.R. Brent, and Zins, M.
1978   Culture as a Determinant of the Attractiveness of a Tourist Region. Annals of Tourism Research 5: 252–267.
Robertson, R.
1972   Non-European Foundations of European Imperialism: Sketch of a Treaty of Collaboration. *In* Studies in the Theory of Imperialism, R. Owen and R. Sutcliffe, eds, pp. 33–56. London: Longman.
Robertson, Roland
1991   Social Theory, Cultural Relativity and the Problem of Globality. *In* Culture, Globalization and the World-System: Contemporary Conditions for the Representation of Identity, Anthony King, ed., pp. 69–90. London: Macmillan Press.
Roche, M.
1991   Mega-events and Micro-modernisation: On the Sociology of the New Urban Tourism. British Journal of Sociology 43(4): 563–600.
Roe, Dilys and Urquhart, Penny
2001   Pro Poor Tourism: Harnessing the World's Largest Industry for the World's Poor. London: UK Government Overseas Development Institute.
Romm, C., and Taylor, W.
2000   Explaining Community Informatics Success Prospects: The Autonomy/ Harmony Model. *In* Cultural Attitudes Towards Technology and Communication. Proceedings of the Second International Conference on Cultural Attitudes Towards Technology and Communication, Perth, Australia, 12–15 July 2000, Fay Sudweeks and Charles Ess, eds, pp. 275–289. Perth: Murdoch University.
Rose, S., and Black, B.
1985   Advocacy and Empowerment: Mental Health Care in the Community. New York: Routledge and Kegan Paul.
Rosenberg, M., and Turner, R.H., eds
1981   Social Psychology: Sociological Perspectives. New York: Basic Books.
Rosenstein-Rodan, P.N.
1963   Plantation Economies. *In* The Economics of Underdevelopment. A.N. Agarwala and S.P. Singh, eds, pp. 112–129. New York: Oxford University Press.
Ross, R.
1992   Dancing with a Ghost: Exploring Indian Reality. Markham: Octopus Publishing.
Rostow, W.W.
1952   The Stages of Economic Growth. New York: Nortono.
1960   The Stages of Economic Growth (2nd edn). Cambridge: Cambridge University Press.
Routledge, D.
1985   Matanitu. The Struggle for Power in Early Fiji. Suva: University of the South Pacific.
Rudolph, L., and Rudolph, S.
1967   The Modernity of Tradition: Political Development in India. Chicago: Chicago University Press.

Sa'aga, F.S.
1989 Foreign Investment for Tourism in Western Samoa. An Examination and Evaluation of Policy Options. Unpublished SPFP Research Paper. Townsville: James Cook University.

Sabatier, P.A., and Mazmanian, D.A.
1983 Implementation and Public Policy. Glenview: Scott Foresman.

Saemala, F.
1983 Constitutional Development. *In* Solomon Islands — Politics and Government, Peter Larmour and S. Tarua, eds, pp. 1–5. Suva: University of the South Pacific.

Saglio, C.
1979 Tourism for Discovery: A Project in Lower Casamance, Senegal. *In* Tourism — Passport to Development? E. de Kadt, ed., pp. 321–335. New York: Oxford University Press.

Sanger, A.
1988 Blessing or Blight? The Effects of Touristic Dance Drama on Village Life in Singapadu, Bali. The Impact of Tourism on Traditional Music. Kingston: Jamaica Memory Bank. Cited *in* Tourism in South-East Asia. M. Hitchcock, V.T. King and M.J.G. Parnwell, eds, pp. 179–199. London: Routledge.

Sathiendrakumar, R., and Tisdell, Clem
1988 Economic Importance of Tourism for Small Indian Ocean and Pacific Island States. *In* Economics of Tourism: Case Study and Analysis, Clem Tisdell, C.J. Aislabie, and P.J. Stanton, eds, pp. 205–228. Newcastle, Australia: University of Newcastle.

Sawailau, S.T.
1989 Secondary Tourism in Fiji: The Indigenous Participation. Unpublished SPFP Research Paper. Townsville: James Cook University.

School of Travel Industry Management, University of Hawaii
1987 The Impact of Tourism on the Commonwealth of the Northern Mariana Islands. Manoa: University of Hawaii.

Scrimshaw, N., and Gleason, G.R., eds
1982 RAP: Rapid Assessment Procedures: Qualitative Methodologies for Planning and Evaluation of Health Related Programmes. Boston: International Nutrition Foundation for Developing Countries.

Searle, M.S.
1991 Propositions for Testing Social Exchange Theory in the Context of Ceasing Leisure Participation. Leisure Studies 13: 279–294.

Seemann, B.
1862 Viti: An Account of a Government Mission. Cambridge [reprinted by the Fiji National Museum, *c*.1992].

Seers, D.
1969 The Meaning of Development. International Development Review 11(4): 2–6.
1977 The New Meaning of Development. International Development Review 19(3): 2–7.

Selins, S., and Beason, K.
1991 Interorganizational Relations in Tourism. Annals of Tourism Research 18: 639–652.

Selwyn, Tom
  1996   Atmospheric Notes from the Field: Reflections on Myth-Collecting Tours.
         In The Tourist Image: Myths and Myth Making in Tourism, Tom Selwyn, ed.,
         pp. 147–162. Chichester: John Wiley.
Selwyn, Tom, ed.
  1966   The Tourist Image: Myths and Myth Making in Tourism. Chichester: John
         Wiley.
Senghaas, D.
  1985   The European Experience: A Historical Critique of Development Theory.
         Translated from the German by K.H. Kimmig. Dover, NH: Berg Publishers.
Shipman, M.D.
  1969   Participation and Staff–Student Relations: A Seven Year Study of Social
         Changes in an Expanding College of Education. London: Society for Research into
         Higher Education.
Simmons, C., and Parsons, R.
  1983   Empowerment for Role Alternatives in Adolescence. Adolescence 18(69):
         193–200.
Sinclair, M.T., and Stabler, M.J., eds
  1991   The Tourism Industry: An International Analysis. Wallingford: CAB Inter-
         national.
Singer, M.
  1972   When a Great Tradition Modernizes. New York: Praeger.
Smandych, R., Lincoln, R., and Wilson, P.
  1995   Towards a Cross-cultural Theory of Aboriginal Criminality. *In* Perceptions of
         Justice. Issues in Indigenous and Community Empowerment, K.M. Hazlehurst, ed.,
         pp. 245–274. Sydney: Avebury.
Smelser, N.J.
  1964   Towards a Theory of Modernisation. *In* Social Change, A. Etzioni and E.
         Etzioni, eds. New York: Basic Books.
Smith, D.M.
  1977   Human Geography: A Welfare Approach. London: Arnold.
Smith, Valene L., ed.
  1977   Hosts and Guests: The Anthropology of Tourism. Philadelphia: University of
         Pennsylvania.
  1989   Hosts and Guests: The Anthropology of Tourism (2nd edn). Philadelphia:
         University of Pennsylvania.
  2001   Hosts and Guests Re-visited: The Anthropology of Tourism. London: Elsevier
         Science.
Smith, Valene L., and Eadington, W., eds
  1992   Tourism Alternatives. Philadelphia: University of Pennsylvania Press.
Sofield, Florence A.
  1986   Solomon Islands National Study of the Child. Unpublished Report. Suva:
         UNICEF.
Sofield, Trevor H.B.
  1987   The Dynamics of South Pacific Regional Economic Cooperation. Presented at
         the Conference of the Regional Training Association of South Pacific Broadcasting
         Corporations, Honiara, Solomon Islands, October 1987.

1990a   The Politics of Tourism in the South Pacific. Presented at the Australian Political Science Association, Annual Conference, University of Tasmania, Hobart, September 1990.

1990b   The Impact of Tourism Development on Traditional Socio-cultural Values in the South Pacific: Conflict, Coexistence and Symbiosis. Proceedings of the International Congress on Marine and Coastal Tourism, East West Center, Honolulu, Hawaii, pp. 27–56. Honolulu: University of Hawaii.

1991a   Sustainable Ethnic Tourism in the South Pacific: Some Principles. Journal of Tourism Studies 2(1): 56–72.

1991b   Tourism for Development in the South Pacific. A Report Prepared for the Australian International Development Assistance Bureau, Vols 1 and 2, 440 pp. Townsville: James Cook University.

1991c   Legislative Impediments to Local Community Involvement in Tourism Development in Solomon Islands. A Report prepared for the Solomon Islands Government. Townsville: James Cook University.

1992   Indigenous Tourism Development. Annals of Tourism Research 20(4): 729–750.

1993   Ecotourism as an Appropriate Form of Development for Small Island States. Proceedings of the Fourth South Pacific Regional Conference on Nature Conservation and Protected Areas of the South Pacific, pp. 148–163. Apia: SPREP.

1994   Regional Tourism Development in the South Pacific. Annals of Tourism Research 21(1): 207–213.

1995   Tourism Planning and Development in Asia. Annals of Tourism Research 22(1): 215–217.

1996   Anuha Island Resort, Solomon Islands: A Case Study of Failure. *In* Tourism and Indigenous Peoples, Richard W. Butler and Tom Hinch, eds, pp. 176–202. London: International Thomson Business Press.

1997   Tourism as Sustainable Development for Indigenous Communities: A Study of the Concept of Empowerment. Ph.D. dissertation in Tropical Environment Science and Geography. Townsville: James Cook University.

1998   Sustainable Tourism in Islands and Small States. Annals of Tourism Research 25(1): 250–254.

1999a   Towards a "Touristic" Theory of Interstitiality: Globalization, Culture and Tourism. Conference on "Interconnected Worlds: Southeast Asian Tourism in the 21st Century", National University of Singapore, Singapore, September 1999.

1999b   China and its Touristic Imaging: The Anthropology of Cultural Tourism. International Conference on "Anthropology, Chinese Society and Tourism", Yunnan University and Chinese University of Hong Kong, Kunming, Yunnan, China, September 1999.

2000   Rethinking and Reconceptualizing Social and Cultural Issues of South East Asian Tourism. *In* Tourism in South and South East Asia: Issues and Cases, C. Michael Hall and Stephen Page, eds. London: Butterworth-Heinemann.

2001   Sustainability and World Heritage Cultural Sites: Pilgrimage Tourism to Sacred Power Places in the Kathmandu Valley, Nepal. In Hosts and Guests Re-visited: The Anthropology of Tourism, Valene L. Smith, ed. London: Elsevier Science.

2002   Pro Poor Tourism in the South Pacific. A Scoping Study for AusAID. Brisbane: Cooperative Research Centre for Sustainable Tourism.

Sofield, Trevor H.B., and Birtles, R. Alastair
1996   Indigenous Peoples Cultural Opportunity Spectrum for Tourism: IPCOST. *In* Tourism and Indigenous Peoples, Richard W. Butler and Tom Hinch, eds, pp. 396–434. London: International Thomson Business Press.
Sofield, Trevor, H.B., DeLacy, T., Bauer, J., Moore, S., and Daugherty, S.
2002 Pro Poor Tourism: A Scoping Study. 62pp. For AusAID, Department of Foreign Affairs & Trade, Canberra.
Sofield, Trevor H.B., and Donaghy, R.
1991   Cyclones, Floods and Tourism. Paper presented at the Australian Disaster Preparedness Conference, Townsville, October 1991.
Sofield, Trevor H.B., and Li, Fung Mei Sarah
1998   China: Tourism Development and Cultural Policies. Annals of Tourism Research 25(2): 362–392.
Solomon Islands Government
1978   The Constitution of Solomon Islands. Honiara: Government Printer.
1980   The Environmental Health Act 1980. Honiara: Government Printer.
1982   Town and Country Planning Act 1982. Honiara: Government Printer.
1984a   The Lands and Titles Act (and Amendments) 1984. Honiara: Government Printer.
1984b   Land and Investments in the Solomon Islands. Honiara: Government Printer.
1984c   Foreign Investment Regulations 1984. Honiara: Government Printer.
1986a   Third National Development Plan, 1986–1990. Honiara: Government Printer.
1986b   National Building Code. Honiara: Government Printer.
1987   Population Census, 1976–1986. Preliminary Report. Honiara: Government Printer.
1989a   Forestry Policy Statement. Honiara: Government Printer.
1989b   National Tourism Policy. Honiara: Government Printer.
Solomon Islands Ministry of Tourism and Aviation and the Tourism Council of the South Pacific
1990   Solomon Islands Tourism Development Plan 1991–2000. Suva: TCSP.
South Pacific Bureau for Economic Cooperation
1974   Agreement Establishing the South Pacific Bureau for Economic Cooperation Suva: SPEC.
1977   Tourism. Suva: SPEC
1988–2000   Annual Report. Suva: SPEC.
1996   Regional Trade Digest. Suva: SPEC.
South Pacific Forum
1971–1998 Final Communique [of annual Heads of Government Meetings]. Suva: SPEC.
South Pacific Tourism
1997–2000   First to Fourth Quarters.
Stake, R.E.
1995   The Art of Case Study Research. London: Sage Publications.
Steinbauer, F.
1979   Melanesian Cargo Cults. Translated by Max Wohl. Brisbane: University of Queensland Press.
Stymeist, David
1996   Transformation of the Vilavilairevo in Tourism. Annals of Tourism Research 32(1): 1–18.

Sudweeks, Fay, and Ess, Charles, eds
  2000   Cultural Attitudes towards Technology and Communication. Proceedings of the Second International Conference on Cultural Attitudes towards Technology and Communication, Perth, Australia, 12–15 July 2000. Perth: Murdoch University.
Sutton, F.X.
  1959   Representations and the Nature of Political Systems. Comparative Studies in Society and History 2(1): 1–10.
Swain, Margaret Byrne
  1989   Developing Ethnic Tourism in Yunnan, China: Shilin Sani. Tourism Recreation Research 14 (1): 33–39.
  1990a   Kuan-yin Pilgrimage. Review Essay. Annals of Tourism Research 19: 161–167.
  1990b   Commoditizing Ethnicity in Southwest China. Cultural Survival Quarterly 14(1): 26–29.
Sydney Morning Herald
  1996   "Ok Tedi Dispute Settled out of Court", 15 June, p. 2.
Sykes, J.B.
  1987   The Australian Concise Oxford English Dictionary (7th edn). Melbourne: Oxford University Press.
Syme, F.
  1980   Thoughts on the Consequences of Tourism. *In* Pacific Tourism as Islanders See It, Institute of Pacific Studies, pp. 57–58. Suva: University of the South Pacific.
Tannenbaum, A.S.
  1981   Control in Organizations. New York: McGraw-Hill.
Thomas, A.
  1992   Non-governmental Organizations and the Limits to Empowerment. *In* Development Policy and Public Action. M. Wuyts, M. Mackintosh and T. Hewitt, eds, pp. 61–74. Oxford: Oxford University Press.
Tisdell, C., Aislabie, C.J., and Stanton, P.J., eds
  1988   Economics of Tourism: Case Study and Analysis. Newcastle: University of Newcastle, Australia.
Tisdell, C., and McKee, David
  1988   Tourism as an Industry for the Economic Expansion of Archipelagos and Small Island States. *In* Economics of Tourism: Case Study and Analysis, C. Tisdell, C.J. Aislabie and P.J. Stanton, eds, pp. 181–204. Newcastle, Australia: University of Newcastle.
Tonga Government
  1984–1990 Annual Budget. Nuku'alofa: Ministry of Finance, Tonga Government.
Tonkinson, Robert
  1982   Kastom in Melanesia: Mankind 13(4): 302–315.
Tourism Council of the South Pacific (TCSP)
  1987a   Conceptual Design and Development of a Locally Owned Village Hotel/ Guest House Complex, Western Samoa. Suva: TCSP.
  1987b   Tourism Marketing Strategy and Promotion. Suva: TCSP.
  1988a   Nature Legislation and Nature Conservation as a Part of Tourism Development in the Island Pacific. Suva: TCSP.
  1988b   Tourist Guiding Training Course, Nuku'alofa, Tonga, June 1988. Suva: TCSP.
  1988c   First Meeting of South Pacific Ministers of Tourism, Nadi, 5 August 1988. Memorandum of Association. Suva: TCSP.

1989   Corporate Plan. Suva: TCSP.
1990a   Record of the Second Ministerial Meeting of Tourism Ministers, Suva, 27 June. Suva: TCSP.
1990b   Guidelines for the Integration of Tourism Development and Environmental Protection in the South Pacific. Suva: TCSP.
1991   Visitors Survey of Solomon Islands 1990. Suva: TCSP.
1991–1998   TCSP Tourism Topics. Bi-monthly Newsletter of the Tourism Council of the South Pacific. Suva: TCSP.
1996   Corporate Plan 1996. Suva: TCSP
Toye, J.F.J.
1987   Dilemmas of Development: Reflections on the Counter-revolution in Development Theory and Policy. Oxford: Blackwell.
Travis, Cheryl Brown
1988   Women and Health Psychology. Hillsdale: L. Erlbaum Associates.
Tuck, Richard, ed.
1991   Leviathan/Thomas Hobbes. Cambridge: Cambridge University Press.
Tucker, Halcrow and Associates
1985   Regional Civil Aviation Survey of the South Pacific. Final Report. Suva: SPEC.
Turnbull, C.
1982   Bali's New Gods. Natural History 1: 26–32.
Turner, F.J.
1961   Frontier and Section. Selected Essays of Frederick Jackson Turner. Introduction and Notes by Ray Allen Billington. Englewood Cliffs: Prentice-Hall.
Tuvalu Government
1987   Tuvalu. National Development Plan IV, 1987–1991. Funafuti: Government of Tuvalu Press.
1992   Tuvalu. National Development Plan V, 1992–1997. Funafuti: Government of Tuvalu Press.
UNDAT
1978   Report on Land Research Project in Solomon Islands. Suva: UNDAT.
UNESCO
1982   World Heritage Convention. Paris: UNESCO.
United Nations (UN)
1975   Seventh Special Session of the United Nations General Assembly on the New International Economic Order (NIEO). New York: United Nations.
1985   General Assembly Declaration and Program of Action on the Establishment of a New International Economic Order (NIEO), 7th Special Session of UNGA, September 1975. New York.
1987   United Nations General Assembly Resolution 46/128 of 17 December 1991 on the International Year for the Indigenous Peoples of the World, 1993. New York.
1992   Report of the United Nations Technical Meeting on the International Year for the World's Indigenous Peoples, 9–11 March 1992. New York.
United Nations Development Program (UNDP)
1950–1993   Annual Report. New York: United Nations.
1993   Human Development Report. Oxford: Oxford University Press.
United Nations Development Program/World Tourism Organization (UNDP/WTO)
1985   Economic Impact of International Tourism on the National Economy of Vanuatu. RAS/86/134. Madrid: WTO.

1986a   Manpower and Training for the Tourism Sector. Solomon Islands. UNDP/ WTO RAS/83/002. Madrid: WTO.
1986b   Manpower and Training for the Tourism Sector. Vanuatu. UNDP/WTO RAS/83/002. Madrid: WTO.
1988   Small Scale Indigenous Tourism Business Development in Solomon Islands. UNDP/WTO RAS/86/134. Madrid: WTO.
United Nations Economic Commission for Asia and the Far East (UNECAFE)
1955–1995 Annual Report. Bangkok: UNECAFE.
Urry, John
1991   The Tourist Gaze: Leisure and Travel in Contemporary Societies. London: Sage Publications.
van den Berghe, P.L., ed.
1965   Africa: Social Problems of Change and Conflict. New York: John Wiley.
van den Berghe, P.L.
1982   The Ethnic Phenomenon. New York: Elsevier.
1994   The Quest for the Other. Seattle and London: University of Washington.
van Haarsel, J.
1988   Tourism: An Exploration. Rapid City: National Publishers of the Black Hills.
van Niekerk, N.
1994   Desarollo Rural en Los Andes. Leiden Development Studies No. 13. Leiden: Institute of Cultural and Social Studies.
Vanuatu Government
1980   Constitution of the Republic of Vanuatu Act. Port Vila: Government Printer.
Varley, R.C.G.
1978   Tourism in Fiji: Some Economic and Social Problems. Cardiff: University of Wales Press.
Varma, Baidya Nath
1980   The Sociology and Politics of Development: A Theoretical Study. London: Routledge and Kegan Paul.
Verhagen, K.
1987   Self-help Promotion: A Challenge to the NGO Community. Dordrecht: Foris Publications.
Wall, Geoffrey
1993   Towards a Tourism Typology. *In* Tourism and Sustainable Development: Monitoring, Planning, Managing, J.G. Nelson, R.W. Butler and G. Wall, eds, Ontario: University of Waterloo, Department of Geography Publications Series.
Wallerstein, I.
1974   The Rise and Future Demise of the World Capitalist System: Concepts for Comparative Analysis. Comparative Studies in Societies and History 16(4): 21–36.
Wallerstein, N., and Bernstein, E.
1988   Empowerment Education: Freire's Ideas Adapted to Health Education. Health Education Quarterly 15(4): 379–394.
Wanhill, Stephen
1987   UK — Politics and Tourism. Tourism Management, 8(1): 54–58.
Ward, B., D'Anjou, L., and Runnals, J.D., eds
1971   The Widening Gap: Development in the 1970s. New York, London: Columbia University Press.
Ward, R.G.
1965   Land Use and Population in Fiji. London: Hutchinson.

1982   Dilemmas in South Pacific Agriculture. South Pacific Journal of Natural Science 3: 9–30.

Watts, R.
1990   Democratisation of Health Care: Challenge for Nursing. Advances in Nursing Science 12(2): 37–46.

Weber, M.
1930   The Protestant Ethic and the Spirit of Capitalism. New York: Charles Scribner.
1976   The Agrarian Sociology of Ancient Civilizations. New York: NLB.
1978   The Theory of Social and Economic Organisation. New York: The Free Press (original 1946, reprinted 1978).

Weiner, M.
1969   Review of L. and S. Rudolph: The Modernity of Tradition. Economic Development and Cultural Change 17(4): 657–661.

Weiner, M., and Huntington, S.P.
1987   Understanding Political Development. Boston: Little, Brown.

Western Samoa Government
1964   Taking of Land Act. Apia: Government Printer.
1965   Alienation of Customary Land Act. Apia: Government Printer.
1982   Socio-Economic Situation, Development Strategy and Assistance Needs. Apia: Department of Economic Development.

Wheeler, C., and Chinn, P.
1989   Peace and Power: A Handbook for Feminist Process (2nd edn). New York: National League for Nursing.

Williams, T.
1858   Fiji and the Fijians: The Islands and Their Inhabitants. London [reprinted by the Fiji National Museum, c. 1992].

Williams, A.M., and Shaw, G., eds
1988   Tourism and Economic Development: Western European Experience. London: Belhaven Press.

Wilson, D.
1981   Comment. Current Anthropology 22(5): 477.
1993   Time and Tides in the Anthropology of Tourism. *In* Tourism in South-East Asia, M. Hitchcock, V.T. King and M.J.G. Parnwell, eds, pp. 32–47. London: Routledge.

Wolfers, Ted
1983   Centralisation and Decentralisation Until Independence. *In* Solomon Islands — Politics and Government, Peter Larmour and S. Tarua, eds, pp. 146–163. Suva: University of the South Pacific.

Wood, Robert E.
1980   International Tourism and Cultural Change in Southeast Asia. Economic Development and Cultural Change 28(3): 561–581.
1993   Tourism, Culture and the Sociology of Development. *In* Tourism in South-East Asia, M. Hitchcock, V.T. King and M.J.G. Parnwell, eds, pp. 48–70. London: Routledge.

Woodley, Alison
1993   Tourism and Sustainable Development: The Community Perspective. *In* Tourism and Sustainable Development: Monitoring, Planning, Managing, J.G. Nelson, R.W. Butler and G. Wall, eds. Ontario: University of Waterloo, Department of Geography Publications Series.

Woolard, D.S.
1977   An Ecological Approach Applied to Solomon Island Housing. *In* Living in Town: Problems and Priorities in Urban Planning in the South Pacific. John Harre and Claudia Knapman, eds, pp. 115–124. Suva: USP.
World Bank
1974   World Bank Report. Washington: World Bank
1991   Towards Higher Growth in Pacific Island Economies: Lessons from the 1980s. Vol 2. Country Surveys. Washington: World Bank.
2001   World Development Report 2000/2001. Washington: World Bank.
World Commission on Environment and Development (WCED)
1987   Our Common Future. Oxford: Oxford University Press.
World Tourism Organization
2000 *Annual Report 2000*. Madrid: WTO.
World Travel and Tourism Council, World Tourism Organisation and Earth Council
1995   Agenda 21 for the Travel and Tourism Industry: Towards Environmentally Sustainable Development. Madrid: WTO.
World Tourism Organization (WTO)
1994   Tourism Planning. Madrid: WTO.
Worsley, Peter
1984   The Three Worlds: Culture and World Development. Chicago: University of Chicago Press.
Yamagishi, Toshio
1987   An Exchange Theoretical Approach to Network Positions. *In* Social Exchange Theory. K.S. Cook, ed., pp. 149–169. Newbury Park: Sage Publications.
Zaal, F.
1991   "Politieke ruimte en ecologische beperking: Niet gouvernementele organisaties in Burkina Faso". *In* NGO Landenstudie: Afrika: Burkina Faso/Zimbabwe, Impactstudie Medefinancieringsprogramma, z.p., pp. 5–28.
Zimmerman, L.J.
1965   Poor Lands, Rich Lands: The Widening Gap. New York: Random House.

Author Index

Subject Index